Linguistic Structure and Change

Linguistic Structure and Change

An Explanation from Language Processing

THOMAS BERG

CLARENDON PRESS · OXFORD
1998

Oxford University Press, Great Clarendon Street, Oxford OX2 6DP
Oxford New York
Athens Auckland Bangkok Bombay
Calcutta Cape Town Dar es Salaam Delhi
Florence Hong Kong Istanbul Karachi
Kuala Lumpur Madras Madrid Melbourne
Mexico City Nairobi Paris Singapore
Taipei Tokyo Toronto Warsaw
and associated companies in
Berlin Ibadan

Oxford is a trade mark of Oxford University Press

Published in the United States
by Oxford University Press Inc., New York

© Thomas Berg 1998

All rights reserved. No part of this publication may be reproduced, stored in a retrieval system, or transmitted, in any form or by any means, without the prior permission in writing of Oxford University Press. Within the UK, exceptions are allowed in respect of any fair dealing for the purpose of research or private study, or criticism or review, as permitted under the Copyright, Designs and Patents Act, 1988, or in the case of reprographic reproduction in accordance with the terms of the licences issued by the Copyright Licensing Agency. Enquiries concerning reproduction outside these terms and in other countries should be sent to the Rights Department, Oxford University Press, at the address above

British Library Cataloguing in Publication Data
Data available

Library of Congress Cataloging in Publication Data
Linguistic structure and change : an explanation from
language processing / Thomas Berg.
Includes bibliographical references.
1. Psycholinguistics. 2. Linguistic change. 3. Explanation
(Linguistics) I. Title.
P37.B47 1997   401'.9—dc21   97-40409
ISBN 0-19-823672-7

10 9 8 7 6 5 4 3 2 1

Typeset by Alliance Phototypesetters, Pondicherry
Printed in Great Britain on acid-free paper by
Biddles Ltd., Guildford and King's Lynn

For Winfried Boeder
who gave a new quality and direction to my life

Preface

This work represents the outcome of a position for postdoctorate study which I was lucky enough to obtain at the University of Oldenburg. I am grateful to the Faculty of Language and Literature for creating an atmosphere in which it was a pleasure to work. In particular, my counsellor Winfried Boeder has given me the requisite intellectual freedom while at the same time gently pushing me to broaden my horizon. I have greatly benefited from the many discussions in which he brought home to me the overall importance of the cross-linguistic and historical perspective. Without his knowledge and expertise in these areas, I in all probability would not have striven as hard for the symbiosis of synchrony and diachrony. The cross-linguistic perspective led me to rely on a number of native speakers. Hans Beelen compiled the list of noun/verb pairs in Dutch. Roelien van der Molen and Arie Sturm patiently answered my questions to help me understand what was wrong with my analysis. Hassan Abd-El-Jawad provided data and translations from Arabic. A special word of thanks is reserved for Heinz Grotzfeld, without whom the predictions concerning Arabic verse may have remained untested. He used a bout of illness to my advantage and helped me tremendously in my analysis of Arabic rhymes. Also, I wish to express my appreciation to Joe Stemberger whose work has been a continuing source of inspiration for me. On the more technical side, I was fortunate enough to find in Klaus Ritter a librarian who in times of austerity managed to fulfil almost all of my requests. Marcel Bingley furnished invaluable quantitative information by tapping the CELEX database for me during my stay at the Max Planck Institute for Psycholinguistics. Nigel Isle has undertaken the heroic effort of ploughing through the whole manuscript to smooth my non-native English. I will not forget this period of ideal cooperation. My daughter Stefanie, Andreas Kraft and Stefan Otte helped me with the printouts. Last but not least, Reinhard Wolf has accomplished the miracle of converting me not into a computer addict but into someone who is beginning to let go of his misgivings about these devil's playthings. The written version has greatly benefited from the detailed and thoughtful reports of Winfried Boeder, Ernst Burgschmidt, Pim Levelt and an anonymous Oxford University Press reviewer. All of the above-mentioned deserve more gratitude than I can express in words.

Contents

List of Abbreviations		xii
1.	On the 'Art' of Explanation	1
	1.1. The State of the Art in Generative Linguistics	1
	1.2. Explanation as an Epistemological Problem	8
	1.3. Is There Anything to Explain?	11
2.	Explanation from a Macrolinguistic Perspective	18
	2.1. The Neurological Approach	19
	2.2. The Phonetic Approach	23
	2.3. The Psychological Approach	27
	2.4. The Semiotic Approach	37
	2.5. The Functional-Communicative Approach	40
	2.6. The Pragmatic Approach	42
	2.7. The Sociocultural Approach	45
	2.8. The Historical Approach	49
	2.9. The System-Internal Approach	51
	2.10. Conclusion	53
3.	Method	56
	3.1. Prediction Instead of Post Hoc Explanation	56
	3.2. The Explanans: Psycholinguistic Patterns	58
	3.3. The Explanandum: Linguistic Patterns	63
	3.4. Relating Psycholinguistics to Linguistics	65
4.	Language Structure	68
	4.1. The Representational Status of Phonemes	69
	4.2. The Structure of Onsets and Codas	73
	4.3. The Structure of Syllable Contacts	79
	4.4. Word Onset Structure in German and Spanish	83
	4.5. Subsyllabic Suprasegmental Constituents	85
	4.6. Constraints on the Repetition of Identical Elements	88
	4.7. The Status of the Syllable	98
	4.8. The Role of Lexical Stress	102
	4.9. Stress and Its Effect on Consonants and Vowels	106
	4.10. Stress and Syllable Structure in English/German and Spanish	110
	4.11. Assimilation	113
	4.12. The Position of Phonological and Morphological Processes in Words	118

	4.13.	Morphophonology	120
	4.14.	Iconicity	123
	4.15.	The Morphophonology of Vowel Length	135
	4.16.	The Differential Ease of Morphological Processes: Substitution vs. addition	140
	4.17.	The Varying Strength of Linguistic Constraints	145
	4.18.	The Order of Inflectional and Derivational Suffixes	148
	4.19.	Blending	151
	4.20.	Linear Distance Effects	157
	4.21.	Adjective/Noun Order in Noun Phrases	161
5.	Language Change		165
	5.1.	Spontaneous Errors and Sound Change: A Macroscopic View	165
	5.2.	Spontaneous Errors and Sound Change: A Microscopic View	169
	5.3.	Phonological Similarity in Sound Change: I	185
	5.4.	Phonological Similarity in Sound Change: II	191
	5.5.	Dimensional Preferences in Consonant Change	194
	5.6.	Dimensional Preferences in Vowel Change	198
	5.7.	The Differential Susceptibility of Consonants and Vowels to Change	201
	5.8.	Repair Strategies in Sound Change	204
	5.9.	The Special Nature of /sC/ Clusters	206
	5.10.	Palatalization	211
	5.11.	The Differential Vulnerability of Word Beginnings and Ends	213
	5.12.	The Differential Strength of Reduction Processes in English and Spanish	216
	5.13.	The Differential Susceptibility of Open- and Closed-Class Items to Phonological Change	220
	5.14.	Paradigmatic Pressure Towards Pattern Symmetry	224
	5.15.	Resolving Phonological Problems at the Lexical Level	230
	5.16.	Verb Inflection	233
	5.17.	Local Frequency Effects	241
	5.18.	Global Frequency Effects	250
	5.19.	The Differential Stability of Word Class and Grammatical Gender	254
6.	Poetic Language		259
	6.1.	Imperfect Rhymes in German	259
	6.2.	The Onset of Rhymes in English and French	264
	6.3.	Rhymes in Arabic Verse	274
7.	Discussion		278
	7.1.	Overall Results	278
	7.2.	The Theoretical Significance of the Recalcitrant Data	279

8.	A Psycholinguistic Model of Language Structure and Change	282
	8.1. How Processing Biases Penetrate Language	282
	8.2. Three Ways of Conceiving the Explanatory Role of Processing	288
	8.3. Further Aspects of the Theory	291
	8.4. The Suffixing Preference Revisited	293
	8.5. Causality in Language Change	297
	8.6. The Psycholinguistic Basis of Poetry	298
9.	Implications for Psycholinguistic Theory	300
10.	The Overall Perspective: Reductionist or Non-Reductionist?	302
References		314
Index		333

List of Abbreviations

AE	American English
AS	Anglo Saxon
Av.	Avestian
D	Dutch
E	English
F	French
Gal.	Gallic
G	German
Germ.	Germanic
Goth.	Gothic
Gr.	Greek
Hom. Gr.	Homeric Greek
IG	Indo-Germanic
It.	Italian
Lat.	Latin
Latv.	Latvian
Lith.	Lithuanian
ME	Middle English
MHG	Middle High German
Mod. E	Modern English
Mod. G	Modern German
OE	Old English
OHel.	Old Helian
OHG	Old High German
OI	Old Indian
ON	Old Norse
OSax.	Old Saxon
Po.	Portuguese
PGerm.	Proto Germanic
PIE	Proto Indo-European
Sp.	Spanish
WSax.	West Saxon

The essence of language is human activity—activity on the part of one individual to make himself understood by another, and activity on the part of that other to understand what was in the mind of the first. These two individuals, the producer and the recipient of language, or as we may more conveniently call them, the speaker and the listener, and their relations to one another, should never be lost sight of if we want to understand the nature of language...

                        Otto Jespersen, *The Philosophy of Grammar*

1

On the 'Art' of Explanation

1.1. The State of the Art in Generative Linguistics

This work largely grew out of a dissatisfaction with the way the term 'explanation' has been used in linguistics. The standard practice of scientific inquiry is the four-step procedure of identification, description, explanation and prediction. A particular phenomenon is first identified, then described, and then explained within a theoretical model which serves to derive predictions about other, hitherto unexplained phenomena. Scientific progress involves the formulation, testing, and reformulation of theoretical accounts. In generative linguistics, which may be regarded as one of the most, if not the most influential school of thought,[1] the distinction between description and explanation is not generally respected. While generative linguists do not shy away from the term 'explanation', they often use it either as a mere paraphrase of description or in a rather superficial sense. Let us take an example from a recent textbook on phonology. In a discussion of onset and coda structures in various languages, Goldsmith (1990) states that a greater number of phonological contrasts are usually accommodated in onset than in coda positions. For instance, many languages allow a contrast between voiced and voiceless consonants in prevocalic though not in postvocalic loci. Goldsmith accounts for this asymmetry by introducing the concept of 'licensing'. He asserts that onset and coda segments are licensed by different 'licensing agencies', the former by a primary licenser (the syllable) and the latter by a secondary licenser (the coda itself). The greater restrictions on codas are 'explained' by their being less freely licensed. This is either a (tautological) restatement of the basic observation or the invocation of hard-to-justify assumptions whose ad hoc nature severely curtails their explanatory value.

Two aspects of Goldsmith's procedure are characteristic of linguistic research in general—the appeal to generalizations and to formalisms. Much linguistic work, past and present, is inspired by the desire to uncover 'linguistically significant generalizations'. This is undoubtedly a first step towards an explanation, although such statements tend to be rather more descriptive than explanatory in kind. However,

---

[1] Some scholars (e.g. Beaugrande 1996) equate generative linguistics with 'mainstream linguistics'. While this position tallies reasonably well with my own perception of the field, the label is less than felicitous because it is quite subjective and depends upon what one considers qualitatively and quantitatively important. Additionally, because it is a prestige term, it tends (rightly or wrongly) to perpetuate the hegemony of those to which this label is applied.

what is and what is not to be regarded as linguistically significant has remained extremely vague. The only available explication is that linguistic significance correlates with generality. The wider the scope of a given generalization, the higher its linguistic significance. This guideline is barely sufficient because there is a trade-off between the complexity of a generalization and its generality. The wider the coverage, the higher the number of special conditions that have to be incorporated in order to cope with exceptions. The difficulty is that it is not clear up to which level of complexity and from which degree of coverage a generalization can be claimed to be linguistically significant. As a logical consequence, a given generalization cannot be linguistically significant *per se*; it can only acquire significance in relation to a particular linguistic theory (Pullum 1975). In any event, it does not count as an explanation in any strong sense of the word.

In practice, linguistically significant generalizations are stated in terms of rules. To take a simple example, long vowels are shortened in syllables with final clusters (cf. *clean–cleanse*). Standardly, such generalizations are expressed not in prose but in formalizations such as (1).

(1) $\begin{bmatrix} V \\ +\text{long} \end{bmatrix} \rightarrow \begin{bmatrix} V \\ -\text{long} \end{bmatrix} / \_CC$

Recourse to formalism is predicated upon the conviction that language is a formal, quasi-mathematical object which can be examined as such. Clearly, formalisms have many advantages. Above all, they may achieve a higher degree of explicitness than can be attained by ordinary language. However, as Givón (1979: 5–6) put it: 'There is one thing ... that a formal model can never do: It cannot *explain* a single thing. Nor can it explain itself. Either of these two will amount to a tautology' (his emphasis) (for a similar view, see e.g. Chen 1972; Lass 1976; Ohala 1990)[2]. A formalistic approach involves the translation of a certain content from one language into another. Such a translation may lead to clarification, which may pave the way for an explanation, but it surely does not constitute an explanation by itself.

This recognition is counter to the prevailing thinking in linguistics. The following quotation is fairly typical: 'But if we assume, as in the theory of autosegmental phonology, that tonal features are *formally* separate from the elements which bear them ... then we can *explain* the partial independence of tonal features and the segments which bear them' (Odden 1986: 353; emphasis mine). It is clear from this quote that the author, in perfect agreement with many other linguists (see in particular the opening paragraph in Hayes 1982: 227), equates the move from informal to formal notation with the move from description to explanation.

None the less, there is no denying that the formalistic approach has been conducive to the discovery of far-reaching principles which are claimed to mark the essence of language. Two of these formal principles will be briefly discussed. Both

---

[2] It is notable that even Newmeyer (1994: 76) shares this view, as he is so strongly committed to overcoming the dichotomy between formal-descriptive and functional-explanatory approaches to language.

are taken from phonology, but a similar argument could be made on the basis of syntactic principles. The first is the Obligatory Contour Principle (OCP) and the second the constraint on crossing association lines. Both presuppose a non-linear model of phonological organization which consists, minimally, of a melodic and a skeleton tier. The former accommodates individual segments, the latter codes them in terms of their consonantalness or vocalicness (at least in one version of the theory). These two representational levels are connected via association lines which link the units at the melodic and skeleton tiers in one-to-one or one-to-many fashion. A sample representation is shown in (2) for the word *peach*.

(2) skeleton tier C V V C

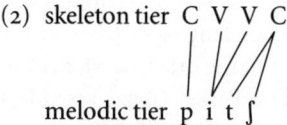

melodic tier p i t ʃ

The two principles to be reviewed impose constraints on what constitutes a possible formal representation, in other words, they define the conditions of well-formedness. The OCP prohibits the adjacency of two identical elements at the melodic tier (McCarthy 1986). In the Italian language, which has contrastive consonant length (i.e. single and double consonants), the representation of *notte* 'night' in (3) would be illicit. The well-formed solution is given in (4).

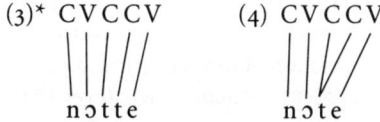

The other principle refers to the way the links between the skeleton and the melodic tiers are effected. It flatly forbids the crossing of association lines (Goldsmith 1979). Let us take an example from syllabification. It is quite possible in this formalism for one phoneme to 'belong' to two different syllables at the same time (cf. (5)). However, this is impossible for two adjacent segments, as shown in (6). The sample words are *mutter* and *muster*, respectively.

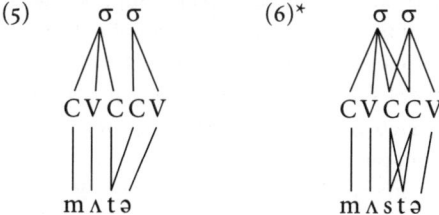

Representation (5) is well-formed in exactly the same manner as (4). The fact that the coronal stop is linked to two slots from different syllables formally expresses its ambisyllabic status. The ambisyllabicity of both /s/ and /t/ in (6) is ruled out on formal grounds because it involves a violation of the no-crossing constraint. Note in passing that the association of both /s/ and /t/ in *muster* with two different syllables is not as absurd as it might seem at first sight. A standard criterion for determining syllable membership is segmental distribution. On this score, the sequence /st/ may well be ambisyllabic because it is found in initial and final positions alike (e.g. *steam* and *beast*).

Both the OCP and the no-crossing constraint are widely recognized as very general and basic principles of phonological organization. They are typically regarded as irreducible in that they cannot be derived from other more fundamental principles (but see Sagey, 1988 for a contrary view regarding the no-crossing constraint). Perlmutter (1992) argues that the no-crossing constraint is even of a supramodal nature in that it holds not only for speech but also for sign language. Whether the same is true of the OCP has not yet been investigated. On the other hand, neither principle is assumed to be inviolable. Odden (1986) and Parker (1992) provide a number of counterexamples to the OCP, thus attesting to its limited, language-specific character. In a similar vein, McCarthy and Prince (1986) allow association lines to cross in exceptional circumstances, e.g. to account for reduplication. Bagemihl (1989) construes play languages in which the order of phonological units is reversed as instances of crossed association lines. The important point here is that these principles are not treated as sacrosanct in the linguistic literature: there is nothing that would make it impossible for them to be flouted.

The no-crossing constraint is considered explanatory as it purports to explain why ambisyllabicity is restricted to single segments. The no-crossing constraint provides not only an explanation but also a prediction about empirical patterns insofar as it rules out the ambisyllabicity of segment sequences, whatever their nature and whatever the language under examination.

Granting that there is a fair amount of support, both empirical and theory-internal, for the OCP and the no-crossing constraint, one might be content with the explanatory level reached and close the investigation at this point. However, the very nature of these principles should not be overlooked. They specify constraints on geometric configurations drawn on a piece of paper. One wonders what the possible status of these diagrams is and also exactly what they represent. To make them truly explanatory, one would therefore like to be able to interpret them. But the crucial question is: in terms of what? The discussion of this central issue will be deferred until enough is known about the conceptual frame within which the formal principles can be profitably interpreted. Suffice to note for the moment that as long as the linguistic principles remain uninterpreted, their status is mainly notational and implicationally their explanatory value unclear.

These formal principles lead up to what many take to be the pinnacle of explanation in linguistics. This line of reasoning originates with Chomsky, who introduced a distinction among three levels at which a linguistic description may be considered adequate—observational, descriptive and explanatory adequacy (e.g. Chomsky 1965; 1986). Observational adequacy refers to the correct description of the linguistic data. A given claim is descriptively adequate if it furnishes the correct description of the linguistic competence of the ideal speaker/hearer. The deepest level is that of explanatory adequacy, which is met when an analysis correctly describes one component of Universal Grammar. The highest explanatory aim in linguistics, then, is to deduce the primary linguistic data from general principles of Universal Grammar and the setting of parameters during language acquisition. The logic is basically as follows. If knowledge of language—for example whether certain sentences are admissible or inadmissible—cannot be ascribed to experience, it must be innate.

Chomsky's approach to explanation may be characterized as a *pseudobiological* one. It has a biological ring to it in that reference is made to the genetic endowment which the child brings to the task of language acquisition. However, Chomsky is not seriously concerned with biology as a natural science. His concepts are entirely abstract and unfold their meaning only within the theory of Universal Grammar. This view of explanation is highly problematical. While it is undisputed that children do not begin the language acquisition process as *tabulae rasae*, it is far from certain that their genetic predispositions are accurately described by what Chomsky means by Universal Grammar. This notion is largely untestable and has remained entirely speculative, with little empirical evidence emerging in its favour. Explanation in this conception thus means appealing to a theoretical construct of unclear validity.

There is also a methodological problem. By invoking Universal Grammar as the ultimate locus of linguistic explanation, Chomsky assigns the nature of language to a sphere where nothing can be examined and, by implication, where nothing can be explained (Winston 1982). In other words, language as an object of scientific investigation is made inaccessible. The appeal to Universal Grammar is a 'convenient though unjustified termination point for enquiry' (Hall 1992: 7). As a concomitant, alternative approaches are automatically discredited.

The conclusion that follows from this critique is that Chomsky's terminology is deceptive. What is claimed to be an explanation is, by all standards of scientific analysis, not an explanation at all. It is neither a theory of language nor a theory of language acquisition. It is at best a description, and one which is based upon uncertain premises (for further criticisms of the explanatory value of Chomsky's philosophy, see e.g. Prideaux 1971; Derwing 1973; Cook 1974; Clark and Haviland 1974; Linell 1976; Itkonen 1978; 1996; Hammarström 1978; Givón 1979, Winston 1982; Julià 1983; Clark and Malt 1984; Hawkins 1988; Botha 1989; Seidenberg 1994).

In conclusion, it seems fair to say that the generative linguists' attempts at grappling with the problem of explanation have been rather modest.[3] It is quite telling that the notion of explanation is rarely discussed *as a methodological problem*—a point which ties in with the fact that methodological issues are much less often discussed in linguistics than in other sciences such as psychology.[4] Customarily, such questions are only taken up within the context of a critical appraisal of the

[3] It is significant in this respect how often the word 'stipulation' is used in the relevant literature. It is evident that claims which are ultimately based upon stipulation cannot serve as explanations.
[4] Rare exceptions are Enkvist (1979), Perry (1980), and Coulmas (1981).

Chomskyan paradigm. Why is it, then, that many linguists are satisfied with descriptions or work with a rather idiosyncratic conception of explanation? I believe that much more is involved here than a limited awareness of methodological problems. My suspicion is that generative linguists are plagued with a deep-rooted fear of being forced by other scientific disciplines to relinquish their prerogative for making 'significant' statements about language. This fear makes them shy away from commonly accepted modes of explanation and develop their own in place.

To see this, it has to be acknowledged at the outset that language is a multi-faceted phenomenon: it is a neurological, physical, sociological, psychological reality among others. Hence, the neurologists, physicists, sociologists, psychologists and others may legitimately feel entitled to have something significant to say about language. Now, if this multi-faceted phenomenon that we call language is usurped by a host of non-linguists, what legitimation is left for the linguist? Differently put, what is truly linguistic about language which can *not* be claimed by any of the other disciplines? The generative linguists' reactions to these nagging questions have been to define their object of study in very narrow terms and subscribe to the autonomy assumption. In brief, this assumption holds that language can be meaningfully studied as an autonomous object, i.e. independently of its psychological, cultural, etc. foundations.[5] This definition was tailored to give a number of linguists their *raison d'être*, and helped to dissipate the worries about being swamped by researchers from other fields. Viewed in this light, it may be understandable why so many linguists swallowed the autonomy hypothesis so readily.

On the other hand, many must have, deep down, remained unconvinced by the autonomy assumption, sensing that it cuts away a great part of what really constitutes language. I maintain that this compunction created a susceptibility on the part of the linguists which would make them welcome non-linguistic influences *on condition that* these influences would not undermine the autonomy assumption and, by implication, their self-legitimation. One such influence had exactly the requisite features: Chomsky's (1972) subsumption of linguistics under (what he calls) cognitive psychology or even more radically, his equation of linguistics with psychology (Chomsky 1988), or most radically, his subsumption of linguistics under biology (Chomsky 1992). In the atmosphere just described, the field was all too ready to accept this doctrine because it quenched their remorse as to the autonomy hypothesis while allowing them to carry on their work as before. What is more, linguists were led to believe that they were on the right track by explicitly being told that what

---

[5] This conception of autonomy differs in subtle ways from that discussed by Newmeyer (1991), who stresses the existence of a genuinely linguistic system. According to him, a system is autonomous if its components cannot be reduced to concepts which are external to this system. This kind of autonomy is not at all unreasonable. For instance, certain linguistic phenomena may best be described in syntactic terms. However, the reality of a syntactic component does not imply that it is impervious to external influences. A linguistic component may be autonomous in being irreducible to other components but at the same time be non-autonomous in being open to other (sub)systems. A similar position is adopted by Givón (1995), who, as a committed functionalist, unhesitatingly acknowledges the existence of genuinely linguistic categories. In short, Newmeyer seems to attack a straw man.

they had been doing all along was not only psychologically meaningful but specifically cognitive psychology. The paradox of defining one's identity while respecting the conflicting desires of autonomy and non-autonomy appeared to be resolved.

It is my contention that many linguists have allowed themselves to be led astray. The paradox has not *and cannot* be resolved. The conflict between autonomy and non-autonomy is in this case principally irreconcilable. A psychologist's definition of cognitive psychology is completely different from that of a linguist. This is most evident in the vastly disparate methodological approaches that linguists and psychologists take, and it is equally evident in the different definitions of empiricalness.

As long as the conceptions diverge so radically, they can be easily identified and kept apart. The ground is more treacherous, however, when commonalities are suggested which are more apparent than real. A particularly delicate case is the choice of terminology. No area is better suited to illustrate the infelicitous construal of linguistics than cognitive psychology. As a consequence of this reinterpretation, a great many psychological terms began to invade the field of linguistics; but since they were incorporated in a new frame of reference, their meanings underwent a surreptitious change while their forms remained the same. Let us briefly examine a few pertinent examples.

A term of prime importance in generative linguistics is 'derivation'. It is common wisdom that the surface representation of a word is the outcome of a number of derivational steps through which an element runs. At each derivational stage, the linguistic unit may change its representation. The derivational stages are organized in a particular order so that some rules are said to apply late and others early.[6] On a commonsense reading, the adjectives *early* and *late* introduce a temporal dimension. That is, the use of these adjectives suggests to the unprejudiced reader that these processes take place in real time. But is this really the way linguists understand these terms? Do they conceive of derivation as a psychologically real process? The answer is emphatically 'no'. As a competence rather than a performance notion, derivation forms part of a theoretical framework in which issues of timing are irrelevant. The adjectives *early* and *late* cannot therefore be meant in their literal sense. Rather, they have to be understood metaphorically. But what would the metaphorical meaning of these words be once the time dimension is stripped out? More to the point, what kind of explanation may be forthcoming from these adjectives when the temporal dimension is abstracted away? Let us take an example from historical linguistics. Within the generative paradigm, Kiparsky (1968) and others argued that rules may undergo reordering during language change. As a matter of fact, language change does not take place in a vacuum but in the minds of language users whose productive and perceptual activities unfold in real time. It is not clear to me how a

---

[6] This is not to deny that there is a growing concern about rules and derivations in linguistics (see in particular the papers edited by Goldsmith, 1993). As a result, the emphasis has shifted from rules to constraints in recent works (e.g. Bird 1995). However, it seems fair to say that rules and derivations are still central notions which are entertained by the majority of generative linguists (cf. Kenstowicz 1994).

change which crucially relies upon the concept of time can be adequately captured within an inherently timeless framework. Therefore, I am inclined to conclude that the explanatory value of the metaphorical use of *early* and *late* is questionable, and that the whole notion of derivation as emcompassing a series of successive stages has little credibility.

The liberal use of metaphor is a general characteristic of linguistic argumentation. A rather blatant but by no means untypical example can be found in McCarthy (1979). In discussing problems of stress assignment, he states that 'the tendency to stress heavy syllables explains why a rule might *seek* the rightmost heavy syllable. If this tendency is thwarted by the absence of a heavy syllable, the rule defaults to the last syllable it *sees*' (McCarthy 1979: 447; emphasis mine). Of course, rules can neither 'seek' nor 'see'. However, much more than an infelicitous use of words is here at stake. The metaphorical use insinuates that rules can do everything linguists want them to do. This reification is problematical because it remains unclear what rules can, and perhaps cannot, do and where they get their power from.

That central concepts in generative linguistics are dangerously misleading can be seen not only from terms such as 'derivation' and 'rule' but also from 'representation' and 'process' among others. Despite the formal identity with words that unfold a (relatively) clear meaning in a psychological framework, these terms are not meant to be interpreted psychologically. Rather, they are given a non-psychological, linguistic interpretation which is very difficult to pinpoint because of its highly metaphorical nature. It may therefore be concluded that the linguistic terminology and the thinking that it reflects is *pseudopsychological*.

Why is this such a problem? The half-hearted allegiance with psychology has been conducive to a system of thought which is erected upon an esoteric vocabulary of unclear significance. All explanations that are put forward are meaningful only within this frame of reference, and cannot be more explicit than the frame of reference itself. Thus, my dissatisfaction with the linguists' use of 'explanation' ultimately derives from the pseudo-psychological framework within which generative linguists choose to work. A pseudo-vocabulary can only yield pseudo-explanations. This framework is insufficiently constrained and lacks explicitness partly because it is not intended as a psychological model. As a linguistic model, it can only provide explanations to the extent that language is cut off from all its vital dimensions referred to above. Whether this then can still be regarded as an explanation depends upon one's conception of what counts as an explanation. The following section will therefore provide a few general remarks on explanation in scientific theory, especially as some of these insights have already been presupposed in the preceding analysis.

1.2. Explanation as an Epistemological Problem

Like everything else, the term 'explanation' has a subjective quality (Hospers 1946). What is and what is not an explanation is a subjective decision. It depends upon the kind of question being asked, and the kind of question being asked depends upon one's personal interest, standards, capabilities, experience, knowledge and expectations. The most important of these factors is 'interest'. To the extent that two qualitatively different explanations may satisfy different interests equally well, neither can be regarded as objectively superior. Related to this, there is no clear demarcation line between description and explanation (Dretzke 1974). What counts as an explanation for one person may be little more than a description for another.

Despite this subjectivity, philosophers of science have identified several components that an explanatory theory should incorporate (see in particular Braithwaite 1968; Hempel 1965; Popper 1959; 1963; Rescher 1970; Stegmüller 1983, Thagard 1989). At a relatively shallow level, a given phenomenon is said to be explained when it can be shown to follow from, and consequently be subsumed under, a more or less general rule or principle (Hempel 1965). 'Linguistically significant generalizations' as discussed in the preceding section provide an example of this kind. However, it is not sufficient to express the relation between *clean* and *cleanse* in terms of a rule. We also have to ask why long vowels are generally shortened before consonant clusters (and also take the exceptions to this rule into account). This leads us to a deeper level of explanation.

A distinction that is regularly made is that between causal and teleological explanations. It corresponds to the difference between cause and effect. Causal explanations provide answers of the 'because' type, teleological explanations answers of the 'in order that' type (Braithwaite 1968). The main difference between these two types of explanation is the temporal perspective. Causal explanations refer to past (or timeless) events while teleological explanations refer to future events. Resuming the above example, a causal explanation of the vowel-shortening rule might be (rightly or wrongly) that speakers encountered difficulties in pronouncing rimes consisting of a long vowel and a consonant cluster. A teleological explanation might be that the rule has applied in order that the degree of articulatory difficulty is lessened. On this interpretation, a change is a goal-directed activity. There is a logical problem associated with teleological explanations. How can a present state or event be explained with reference to something that lies ahead in the future, i.e. is not part of the present world? Viewed from a different perspective, how can the future impinge on the present? Braithwaite's solution to this paradox is to claim that the future is in fact part of our present world. It is coded as intentions in the minds of human beings—intentions in the widest sense of the word, conscious as well as unconscious.

A crucial property of explanation is the infinity of the causal chain (Rescher 1970). There is no point at which the ultimate explanation has been reached (unless the ultimate explanation is taken to be a divine entity). To the question of why the vowel-shortening rule applied, we may answer that it accommodates speakers' needs. We may go on to ask: why is this change to the benefit of the speaker? And the answer might be: because speakers are lazy. The next answer would explain laziness by referring to the claim that the expenditure of energy is regulated by the returns of an action. This answer in turn leads to the question of why there is such an interaction which precipitates a further question, and so on. This tantalizing state of affairs implies that *all* explanations are necessarily partial, and that it is out of the question to ask for a final or ultimate explanation.

A further important feature of explanation is one that has been most forcefully articulated by Popper (1959). A scientific theory deserves its name only to the extent that it is principally falsifiable. For instance, the explanation according to which the vowel-shortening rule is put down to ease of articulation may be wrong. The genuine reason might of course lie elsewhere. The problem with unfalsifiable claims is that they cannot be shown to be superior or inferior to other unfalsifiable claims. They are therefore uninformative, if not useless, from a strictly scientific standpoint. Note that the Chomskyan type of explanation referred to above falls short of fulfilling this requirement in that it is not clear on what type of evidence, theoretical or empirical, his theory could be disproven. Imagine for instance that a biologist came up with the proof that human genes cannot code putatively innate properties such as structure-dependence. Given that the claim of structure-dependence is not framed in a genuinely biological conception (see above), it is largely immune to biological arguments.

As regards the relation between explanans and explanandum, it has to be pointed out that almost all phenomena are multiply determined. Monocausal states and events are extremely uncommon. This has a methodological consequence that is not always recognized in linguistics. A given hypothesis is often claimed to be vindicated when it is compatible with a certain range of empirical observations. However, this is not by itself an argument against the correctness of any other hypothesis (unless the hypotheses are logically contradictory). For example, the claim that the vowel difference in *clean* and *cleanse* evidences the principle of articulatory ease cannot principally be countered by recourse to the principle of perceptual contrast. On this latter account, the consonantal difference between the two lexical items is felt to be insufficient in maintaining the contrast between them. As a consequence, the contrast is enhanced by creating an additional difference in the vowel domain. In this way, the listener's task of keeping the two words apart is facilitated. Unless further arguments are adduced, there is no way of pitting the explanatory principles of articulatory ease and perceptual contrast against each other.

Actually, the problem goes deeper than this. To take a different example, Berg (1995a) argued that the voicing of final fricatives in Early Modern English (e.g. *is* → [ɪz]) is a local shortening process in high-frequency words. As epitomized by Zipf's principle of least effort, high frequency leads to a reduction of the formal means of expression. As voiced fricatives are substantially shorter than their voiceless cognates, voicing is one way of achieving this aim. However, coda consonants are not in general independent of the vowel that precedes them, particularly in terms of length. It is well known that voiced consonants lengthen preceding vowels. The diphthong is much longer in *ride* than in *right*. On the basis of this effect, one might develop the following counterargument. Voicing cannot be a shortening process because the concomitant change in vowel quantity will neutralize the shortening brought about by voicing. Is this a refutation of the shortening account? It is not because, although shortening and lengthening look contradictory on the face of it, they may very well coexist, especially as they refer to different portions of the word. There is no doubt that language is subject to conflicting tendencies which may even cancel each other out. As long as these tendencies are not mutually exclusive on logical grounds, recourse to one of them is not automatically an argument against the other.

What, then, is the core of 'explanation'? The definition upon which this work is based is adopted from Popper (1963). An explanatory theory should meet the following requirement (among others): 'The new theory should proceed from some *simple, new, and powerful, unifying idea* about some connection or relation ... between hitherto unconnected things ... or facts ... or new "theoretical entities" ' (Popper 1963: 241; his emphasis). Setting aside methodological issues for a moment, explaining means establishing a 'connection between hitherto unconnected things'. This connection may a priori be likely or unlikely, strong or weak, direct or indirect. The word 'unconnected' requires comment. The locus of the 'unconnection' is in the internal world, i.e. the mind of the researcher. The lack of connection is tantamount to a lack of knowledge. The 'things' in the external world must be of an intermediate level of connectivity. On the one hand, there must be some kind of connection between them, otherwise the scientist would hunt for a chimera. On the other hand, the 'things' must not be so strongly connected that they lose their independence and that the danger of artifactuality arises. In the *clean–cleanse* example, a link is established between the linguistic structure and the phonetic principle of articulatory ease. Phonetics and linguistics may be regarded as two areas which are to a certain extent independent but not completely unrelated. It is therefore appropriate to seek links between them.

The main challenge presented by this definition of explanation is the establishment of the connection. Popper proposes that this feat can be accomplished by developing an 'idea' about this connection, even though he remains rather inexplicit on that score. The idea in the *clean–cleanse* case is that the phonetic principle may be incorporated into the linguistic structure because it provides a permanent answer to the desire of saving articulatory energy. How the connection is established is a methodological problem of considerable import. It may ultimately depend upon the connection that is explored and consequently have more than one solution.

Any endeavour in the field of explanation presupposes an affirmative answer to the following question: does the external world contain the connections we are keen to explore? In other words:

1.3. Is There Anything to Explain?

Naturally, the issue of explanation in language can be meaningfully studied only if language is principally amenable to explanation. Whether this is so depends upon the level of explanation that is targeted and upon one's conception of language. At first glance, the question might provoke astonishment. Why should language not be amenable to explanation in the same way as other objects of scientific study such as human diseases, metals, or radioactivity? Most laymen and physicians would agree that although the cause, cure, and prevention of many diseases are not completely understood, we know at least something about the intricate functioning of biological organisms. This is because the human body is subject to certain physical, chemical (and other) principles which are open to scientific investigation. Is language any different from diseases? Imagine language is like a fashion. Fashions are highly variable along the place and time dimension. By virtue of their seemingly arbitrary nature, they are largely unpredictable and therefore largely unexplainable. There is no basis for predicting whether women (or men) will wear mini- or maxi-skirts in the year 2525 because fashions are not governed by anything like the principles that govern the occurrence of diseases.

The equation of language and fashion is at the heart of Lass's (1980) devastating critique of explanation in linguistics. His major claim is that the concept of explanation is not principally applicable to language change. Because all synchronic states derive from diachronic developments, we must broaden his critique to the effect that language in general, its structure, use, function, and development, is inexplicable. Lass's view is firmly grounded in a particular conception of language and a particular conception of explanation. He considers language to be chiefly, if not entirely, a cultural artifact. He likens language to a play, i.e. a system of arbitrary rules which is non-utilitarian and free from external constraints. On the assumption that language represents a separate world, it is indeed difficult to 'establish the connection', i.e. to explain it. Moreover, Lass (like Weinberg 1987) accepts only one type of explanation, called the deductive-nomological schema. The basic logic is that a given phenomenon is explained when it can be shown to follow *necessarily* from certain antecedent conditions and a set of general principles or laws. A deductive-nomological explanation thus is capable of predicting the occurrence of a phenomenon with absolute reliability (given the antecedent conditions and the laws). All other explanations, which are probabilistic in nature, are regarded by Lass as non-explanatory.

Within this definitional framework, Lass's conclusions are largely unassailable. However, his central thesis is considerably weakened once his background assumptions are subjected to scrutiny. In actual fact, he advocates a very narrow and even fallacious conception of language and explanation. Beginning with the latter, he maintains that the only venerable type of explanation is the deductive-nomological one. But, as Ohala (1987) rightly pointed out, such a type of explanation does not exist, neither in linguistics nor in any of the so-called hard sciences. It belongs in the realm of purely formal sciences such as mathematics and logic.[7] Thus, linguistics is

---

[7] Stegmüller (1983) claims that deductive-nomological explanations do exist, although he concedes that they constitute borderline cases. They presuppose that all antecedent conditions and laws are completely known. Because this is not generally, if ever, the case, this type of explanation loses much, if not all, of its practical significance.

not worse off than any other scientific discipline. What Lass actually does is to argue that it is impossible to reach a nonexistent goal.

Note that the problem is not the exceedingly high standards of explanation that Lass demands. Underlying his appeal to deductive-nomological explanations is a world-view which is most probably wrong. Deductive-nomological accounts are possible only in a deterministic world. However, our world is a probabilistic one. This is a necessary consequence of the issue of multi-causation which was treated in the preceding section. Once we are confronted with a multiplicity of (competing) causes and the possibility of interaction among these, we cannot help ending up with probabilistic outcomes. This is particularly true of language, which has to satisfy many different, even conflicting needs at the same time.

This brings us to Lass's conception of language. Language is clearly more than a cultural phenomenon. It is also a psychological phenomenon, a product of the human mind which functions according to certain principles which are amenable to investigation. Another set of principles derives from the fact that language is articulated and therefore subject to anatomical constraints. But even if language were reducible to a cultural phenomenon, it does not follow that it must defy all kinds of explanation. Even cultural values may have a rational basis. Why should it be impossible to explain why Muslims do not eat pork or why people have a meal during a celebration? There might be more arbitrariness involved in these habits than in non-cultural matters, but this remains to be demonstrated.

An essential aspect of Lass's thesis is his view of function. Explanations often are based upon functional arguments. Given that 'explanation' does not exist in Lass's framework, he is forced to attack the notion of function and to show that language change is non-functional. How does he substantiate this claim? He examines the following three functional explanations which have standardly been proposed in the linguistics literature: preservation of contrast, minimization of allomorphy, and avoidance of homophony. These explanations are very similar in that they all boil down to one general principle—the one-to-one relationship between form and meaning. Lass argues that it has not been convincingly established that language change moves in the direction of improving the one-to-one relationship, i.e. that it functions to repair one-to-many or many-to-one relationships. His argument is based upon the claim that functional explanations are weak because they are only compatible with the empirical observations. Alternative explanations are not considered, and therefore the functional explanation is not actually demonstrated to be required. On top of that, because of their entirely post hoc character, functional explanations in historical linguistics have no predictive value.

There is some truth in what Lass says, but again, he is asking more than an 'explanation' can possibly explain. All explanations are weak to the extent that it is virtually impossible to rule out *all* competing accounts. We must be similarly modest with respect to predictability. We cannot predict the occurrence of a certain development with a great deal of confidence. What we may be able to do, however, is to predict that one development is more likely to take place than another. Further, the existence of dysfunctional changes cannot automatically be taken as an argument against functional explanations. What dysfunctional changes simply show is that there are other principles which may contravene the ideal form/function relationship. Of course, it is of primary importance to identify these principles. In addition, the significance of these exceptions remains to be worked out from the statistical perspective. How many exceptions prove and how many disprove a given claim? Taken at face value, one might consider a hypothetical score of 5–5 to be unfavourable to a given principle. Lass appears to adhere to such a statistically naïve view. However, unless the baseline probability (the 'null hypothesis') has been estimated, raw numbers are next to useless. Even when a principle is supported by only a minority of cases (less than 50 per cent), there is no reason to proclaim its nonexistence.

This brings us to a more general point. What renders it easy for Lass to be so dismissive of functional explanations and explanation more generally is the scarcity of the empirical data and the unavailability of spoken documents over a sufficiently long stretch of time. In view of the heterogeneity of language, the slow pace of change, and the multitude of intervening factors, it is hardly surprising that all explanations must be tentative, preliminary, and on a less than firm footing.

However, despite this unfortunate state of affairs, we have every reason to assume that the form/function relationship furnishes *one* plausible functional explanation of language. From the synchronic viewpoint, there is little doubt that the one-to-one correspondence between form and function is a design principle of language. The majority of morphemes and words have only one form and only one basic function or meaning. Homophony and homography are not central aspects of language. There are good grounds for believing that synonymy does not exist at all. Suffice it to mention that true synonyms could never be kept apart by speakers, and would consequently always be outputted as blends. In language change, synonymy appears to be an unstable phenomenon. Either one member of the pair is lost or the two words diverge semantically. Children set out on the task of language acquisition armed with an intuitive notion of contrast. They implicitly assume that one form corresponds to one meaning and vice versa (Clark 1993).

Allomorphy is one principle which is opposed to the ideal form/function relationship in that it establishes a one-to-many relationship between function and form. However, it has the advantage of allowing ubiquitous rule application irrespective of phonological context. Allomorphy thus is facilitated by the principle that linguistic functions should always be formally realized. It can be seen, then, that an agglomeration of design principles has to be reckoned with. These principles may vie with one another and keep one another 'in check', thereby ineluctably leading to exceptions to any one principle. The existence of these exceptions should not therefore be taken, as Lass takes it, as counterevidence to functionalism in general.

Let us examine two individual cases to show that Lass's arguments are also not compelling at the microscopic level. The first is functional load. It derives from one particular aspect of the phoneme, its contrastive function. Two sound units are commonly assigned phonemic status if they serve to distinguish two lexical items. Phonemes may differ in their functional importance. Some may serve to keep many words apart (high functional load), others only a few (low functional load). The concept of functional load embodies a clear prediction for language change. If language change is functional, oppositions between phonemes of low functional load should be more liable to erosion that those of high functional load. Drawing upon King's (1967) diachronic analysis, Lass finds that there are about as many changes that support the prediction as there are changes that refute it, and concludes from this that functional load plays no role in language change.

This conclusion is open to criticism because it is based upon the implicit assumption that chance levels hover around 50 per cent. Since Lass does not make an attempt to compute chance, his interpretation is purely speculative. But even if his conclusion was correct, Lass's claim does not necessarily follow through. This is because it is based upon a widely accepted, albeit problematical conception of the phoneme. According to standard practice, (second-order) semantic information is used to define a phonemic unit. A moment's reflection makes it clear that this is a distinctly odd procedure. It would be more natural to define an element on the basis of criteria which are germane to the level at which this element is located. That is, a phoneme should be defined in formal terms. Its main function is not to establish contrast at the lexical but at the phonological level. In addition to these general problems, Berg (1993) argues that a phoneme that primarily serves a meaning-distinguishing function is not a viable concept from the psycholinguistic vantage-point. It is almost impossible to implement, as it would imply the potential reorganization of the entire lexicon whenever a word or a sound is added to or lost from the system. This in turn necessitates a device which may search through the whole lexicon for minimal pairs—a procedure which a linguist certainly is capable of using but which assumes a homunculus-like quality when applied to the mind.

Consonant with this analysis, Berg (1993) finds little evidence for the influence of functional load on the course of language acquisition and breakdown. Even though this result meshes nicely with Lass's contention, one should be wary about drawing the same conclusion. The psycholinguistic model in which Berg integrates the phoneme is highly interactive, such that influences from one level may make themselves felt at an adjacent one. This interactivity allows for the possibility that the representation at one level may be shaped by representations at another. However, these influences are relatively minor and cannot serve to make the distinctive function a defining trait of the phoneme. Nevertheless, these minor influences are real and may therefore have weak effects in both synchrony and diachrony. This would account for King's findings within a theory that assigns at least some importance to functional effects.

The point of the preceding discussion is that Lass's critique is levelled at one particular view of function, and that this view is highly problematic for independent reasons. When this view is abandoned, his critique falls by the wayside. A revised conception of the phoneme survives his attack unscathed and allows us to continue to entertain functionalist notions.

Lass's second line of attack centres around the issue of variation. Most usually, sound change is not implemented instantaneously. It may take quite a long time and may be accompanied by periods in which some words have changed while others have not, and by periods of fluctuation where one and the same word admits to both the old and the new pronunciation at virtually the same time. Lass considers that the gradualness of sound change is incompatible with functionalist approaches because under any sensible interpretation of function it must be a constant, and as such it cannot be held responsible for variation. This argument is far from convincing. First of all, I can see no reason why a given function cannot vary in strength. But let us assume the correctness of the constancy hypothesis for the sake of the argument. What Lass calls function may be more appropriately named the driving force by means of which linguistic change is actuated. This driving force cannot be examined independently of other forces, most notably the conservative force which strives to maintain the status quo. How effective the driving force is obviously depends upon the (variable) strength of the conservative force(s). One candidate for such a conservative force is lexical frequency. A reasonable assumption from the psycholinguistic point of view would be that high-frequency words are more resistant to change than low-frequency words because high frequency renders lexical access more reliable. The consequence of this retarding effect is that not all words will succumb to the change simultaneously and the innovation will diffuse gradually through the lexicon. Clearly, many other factors are involved in this process. The resultant variation is in no way incongruent with the idea of a functionalist motivation of sound change. It is a natural spin-off of complex interactions in a multicausal system.

Finally, Lass takes up the aforementioned difficulty associated with teleological explanations. He claims that such explanations are out of the question because language users cannot anticipate the (beneficial or harmful) effects of something that has not actually happened: 'we must credit speakers with the ability to compute the potential effects of sound change in advance, and shunt (potentially) offending items into the requisite minor rule ("If I let /y/ unround, 'shut' will come out as *shit*; better retract to /u/"). But this is surely absurd' (Lass 1980: 79). I fail to see what is so absurd about this reasoning. It might *sound* absurd because of Lass's tendentious wording, which suggests that language use is a conscious process and that speakers can intentionally manipulate language change (cf. especially Lass's concocted self-report about a naïve speaker's thoughts). On top of that, it might be countered that the naïve speaker's self-report is not utterly unrealistic. After all, a taboo word is at stake here and taboo words will be consciously avoided if deemed necessary. It is a commonplace experience to catch oneself on the verge of uttering a word which may be considered inappropriate in a particular social situation. The culprit may be, but need not be, a taboo word which is only a special case of situationally inappropriate language. We therefore conclude that teleological explanations are not principally inapplicable to diachronic issues. A more general solution to the problem of teleology will be proposed below.

Lass's important work has been treated at some length because a plea for explanation in linguistics calls for a reply to his forceful criticisms. Nevertheless, I could not do justice to his whole book. In the present context, it suffices to make the point that his pessimism is, at least in great part, unwarranted (see also Itkonen 1981; Harris 1982). I have taken pains to argue that explanation in linguistics is not impossible provided we do not expect too much of it (see Toon 1987) and are happy with more pragmatic modes of explanation. Let it be conceded to Lass that language has an arbitrary component. All the same, the question of why language is the way it is and changes the way it does cannot be considered on a par with the question of why this year's skirt length is different from last year's. This is not all there is to language.

It may be speculated that Lass's pessimism is partly nourished by the fact that he has worked within the circle of autonomous linguists and that, as argued above, real explanations have hardly been forthcoming from this paradigm. The alternative is to adopt a wider perspective on language because it increases the opportunity of creating links. This certainly is a more productive research strategy than Lass's philosophy which at best serves to sharpen our awareness of our limited intellectual capabilities and our utterly insufficient database in historical linguistics and at worst discourages students of language from trying to come to grips with their object of investigation. In this spirit, the next section will consider some types of explanation that have been emerging from a broader conception of language.

2

Explanation from a Macrolinguistic Perspective

Most of the studies that will be reviewed below share a conviction that is more often tacitly assumed than overtly stated. This view is made explicit by Menn and Obler (1982: 3), who reason that the 'explanation of linguistic phenomena must ultimately lie *outside* linguistics' (emphasis mine). Similar opinions have been voiced by Bybee and Moder (1983), Hall (1992), Comrie (1993), and others. The fundamental insight implicit in this view is that nothing is self-explanatory. We cannot understand plants unless we acknowledge their ecological functions such as providing nutrition to animals and giving rise to photosynthesis, that is, unless we establish a link between trees and the sun for instance. What are the links that should be set up in the case of language? Ohala (1983) sees three and only three linkages which we may conveniently abbreviate as 'the three m's'—mind, matter, and manners. The first refers to the abstract psychological dimension, the second to the concrete dimension including anatomy and the neurosciences, and the third to the social and cultural dimension. This tripartite distinction is a very useful point of departure, even though it might be rather too coarse-grained. For example, neurophysiological processes need not impose the same constraints on language as anatomical traits. It is expedient therefore to look at a maximum of approaches individually so as to be in a better position to assess the relative contribution of each. In view of a certain overlap that exists between these approaches, it will not be possible to keep all of their effects neatly apart.

The overall aim of this chapter is to evaluate the explanatory potential of several approaches by selecting representative cases from the relevant literature and gauging the depth of insight that they provide as well as their scope and limitations. This review is not primarily intended as a state-of-the-art report on the role of explanation in linguistic research. Its major function is to provide a basis from which it is possible to pinpoint the weaknesses of previous approaches and develop a novel one. The areas that will be covered are (in the order of presentation): the neurological, the phonetic, the psychological, the semiotic, the functional-communicative, the pragmatic, the socio-cultural, the historical and the system-internal approaches. The possible interactions among these approaches, whether they complement or conflict with one another, will be largely ignored. The synergetic account (Köhler and Altmann 1986) will not be given a separate treatment.

Similarly, no individual section will be devoted to the genetic approach. This is because I do not believe that it has much to contribute to our understanding of *particular* linguistic structures and *particular* historical developments. Genetics certainly plays a role but it is of a fairly general nature. At the most general level, we owe to genetics our language faculty, i.e. the genes code our predisposition to acquire (and use) language. Evidence for this claim comes from genetically transmitted language deficits such as discussed in Gopnik (1990), Gopnik et al. (1996), and Vargha-Khadem and Passingham (1990). Slightly less general is the hypothesis that the sensitive period for language acquisition as well as the slight superiority of girls to boys in acquiring language are genetically determined (see Hurford 1991 for an interesting discussion). While genetic coding is a reasonable possibility at this level of generality, the genes are less likely to code more specific information such as individual linguistic constraints.[1] We may therefore expect explanations from the genetic approach only for fairly general phenomena, not for the specific linguistic aspects around which this work is centred.

2.1. The Neurological Approach

The basic assumption of the neurological approach is that the workings of the neurological system impose constraints upon the form of language. Although it would be difficult to argue that this is not so, very little work has been forthcoming in which this connection is explicitly sought. This dearth can obviously be put down to the great conceptual distance between linguistics and neurology. In view of the widely divergent paradigms and terminologies, there is hardly any way of interpreting neurological results in linguistic terms. The following remark of Whitaker is as valid today as it was at the time it was made: 'given the present state of knowledge it would be hard to propose how membrane permeability relates to negation' (Whitaker 1971: 12). It is almost certain that there is no such specific relationship, but it is equally certain that there is a close relationship between language and the brain on a more general level. The real challenge, then, is to make the general link more specific. Three such attempts of varying degrees of persuasiveness have been singled out for closer analysis.

The first study investigates the phonological structure of words, in particular the recurrence of phonemes within words. The null hypothesis states that the probability of phoneme repetition is solely a function of the frequency of occurrence of a phoneme, the number of phonemes in the language and phonotactic constraints. This last factor is virtually negligible in CV languages. In a hypothetical CV language with ten consonants of equal frequency, the chance rate of phoneme repetition (e.g. a word of the structure C_xVC_xV) would be 10 per cent. MacKay (1970a) investigated the incidence of phoneme repetition in Hawaiian and Croatian, two unrelated languages with widely different phonological structures. He focused

---

[1] One such constraint will be examined in detail in Chapter 10.

upon the degree of separation between the identical phonemes in a word. In the above example, the degree of separation is 1 because the identical consonants are separated by a vowel. According to MacKay's calculations, the average chance rate of phoneme repetition is 7 per cent in Hawaiian and 3 per cent in Croatian. The author discovered an interaction between the probability of phoneme repetition and the degree of separation. In both languages, the likelihood of phoneme repetition was significantly *below* chance when no phoneme intervened between the critical segments but significantly *above* chance when three phonemes intervened. Despite large structural differences between Hawaiian and Croatian, this pattern was remarkably similar in the two languages.

MacKay's account of these findings is of particular interest in the present connection. He relates the likelihood of phoneme repetition to general principles of neural excitation which underlie all kinds of neural action. After a neuron has fired, it undergoes a period of self-inhibition which lasts about 200 ms. During this recovery phase it is unavailable, i.e. unable to fire. Subsequently, the neuron reaches a second peak of activity which is, however, smaller than the first ('post-inhibitory rebound').

MacKay's central move is to link the temporal characteristics of neural excitation to the linear structure of phonemes in a word. A phoneme cannot be repeated at very short intervals because the neurons responsible are not yet ready to fire again and therefore cannot support its immediate repetition. In contrast, the probability of phoneme repetition is enhanced at longer intervals because the neurons that support its production are especially likely to fire again. Thus, principles of neural action are purported to account for phonological structure.

The logic of MacKay's argument is clear. The form of language has to be in line with what is neurologically feasible. What is neurologically infeasible or at least more difficult is likely to be eliminated or not to happen in the first place. It is plausible that a neurological bias in favour of the occurrence of a given unit will over time be reflected in the structure of the language. The question of exactly how the incorporation of this bias takes place is not explicitly addressed by the author. There are many other open questions. MacKay does not undertake to measure the duration of the interval between repeated phonemes. According to his hypothesis, the second occurrence of C_x in C_xVCVC_x must take place 200 ms. after the first. Given the fact that segments have a phonetic duration in the order of 50–100 ms., the match between speaking time and neural recovery time is quite good. Note, however, that there may be a weakness in the procedure adopted. MacKay seems to have confounded the graphemic and the phonemic level, which unfortunately do not always display a one-to-one correspondence. For example, he talks about the repeated occurrence of /s/ in German *ausstehen* where in fact there is only one. Related to this, it is unclear how he dealt with gemination. Finally, his claims are of a universal nature since the mechanisms of neural excitation are not assumed to vary from language to language. Whether the patterns of phoneme repetition discovered by MacKay are of a universal nature remains to be established. It is clear that only a few counterexamples would suffice to invalidate his account. These uncertainties notwithstanding, MacKay's paper represents an outstanding attempt at relating linguistic structure to neural mechanisms.

The second example comes from the lexico-semantic area, more specifically the structure of the colour vocabulary. Like MacKay's work, it makes claims about universality, but has a much wider data base. Berlin and Kay (1969) examined the colour terminology in approximately 100 languages and found an intriguing stratification in the lexicon. If a given language has only two colour terms, these always correspond roughly to *black* and *white*. If a given language has six colour terms, these are always the equivalents of English *black, white, red, yellow, green*, and *blue*. Thus some colour terms are more basic than others, in the sense that the less basic terms presuppose the existence of the more basic ones. Berlin and Kay established that all languages make do with a limited set of eleven basic colour terms. Also, they extended their synchronic analysis to the diachronic domain, and interpreted the aforementioned stratification in terms of a temporal order in which the colour categories make their appearance. The more basic colour terms always enter a language before the less basic ones. If this were not so, they reasoned, languages with a deviant distribution of colour terms should be found (but in fact have not been).

Kay and McDaniel (1978) proposed a neurophysiological explanation which focuses upon the way colour information is processed at the retina and beyond. It is worth bearing in mind that on the physical level colours form a continuum. The wavelength of visible light ranges from 400 to 700 nm. Hence the categorical nature of colours is not inherent in the physical signal but imposed upon the signal by a particular hard-wired structure of the nervous system. Without going into too much detail, it should be noted that the input is pre-processed at the retinal level and passed on 'in bundles' to more central areas. There, the signal is processed by opponent response cells. These cells are called 'opponent' because they simultaneously promote the perception of one colour and inhibit the perception of another. Four types of opponent response cell have been identified by neurophysiologists—(+red, –green), (–red, +green), (+yellow, –blue) and (–yellow, +blue).[2] For instance, when the last mentioned cell type is stimulated by light of a wavelength corresponding to the focal colour 'blue' (475 nm), the properties of this cell type block the simultaneous perception of 'yellow'. Note that the simultaneous perception of different colours is not generally inhibited. Beyond these four cell types, there is no such inhibition. 'Yellow' can be readily perceived along with 'red'. In fact, this creates a mixture called 'orange'. Leaving 'black' and 'white' aside, all other colour sensations are brought about by varying response strengths of the four cell types in question.

The existence of this cell structure places a strong constraint on the emergence of colour terms in natural language. Because 'red' and 'green' lead to neurally

---

[2] Why the cells in charge of the four basic hues are organized in this way and not in any other is another example of the open-endedness of explanation.

incompatible responses, they cannot be acquired at the same time. In other words, properties of the nervous system enforce a temporal order on the emergence of colour terms. In this way, it is not only explained why 'green' and 'yellow' cannot enter a language at the same time but also why composite colours such as 'orange' and 'purple' appear later than their constituent colours 'red' × 'yellow' and 'red' × 'blue', respectively. However, this theory cannot explain the emergence of 'red' prior to 'green' and the emergence of 'yellow' prior to 'blue'.

Colour perception implicates the three dimensions of hue, brightness, and saturation. Only the first dimension has been touched upon here, and it is plain that more neurological theory is needed to provide a full account of the stratification of colour terminology. However, the link between neurology and linguistics is sufficiently clear. In this area the structure of a subsection of the lexicon, both synchronically and diachronically, can be shown to be determined by the structure of information processing in the brain.

The final example is remotely related to the preceding in that it purports to explain one aspect of phoneme acquisition in childhood. On the assumption that there is a connection between segment acquisition and the structure of segment inventories in adults, this example has implications for the phonological systems of the world's languages. Salus and Salus (1974) endeavour to account for the hypothesis that strident consonants (e.g. /s,f,ʃ/) are mastered at a later stage than non-strident ones (e.g. /θ,ð/). Their argument centres around the claim that strident consonants have a higher frequency range than non-strident ones and that young children are unable to perceive high-frequency signals. Because of this perceptual deficit, the acquisition of these phonological units is delayed. The authors explain the basis of the perceptual deficit in terms of immature (unmyelinated) nerve fibres which are incapable of transmitting high-frequency information. The development of the requisite (myelinated) nerve fibres is not complete until the age of 3 or 4.

On the whole, Salus and Salus's neurophysiological account of the developmental order does not appear to be viable. The perceptual deficit hypothesis remains totally unproven unless it is actually demonstrated that children at the critical age fail to discriminate minimal pairs like *sun* and *fun*, for example. It is a commonplace experience that children are quite capable of perceiving a contrast without being able to produce it properly. What is more, the empirical observation on which Salus and Salus base their argument is inaccurate. It is simply not true that the dental fricatives are acquired before the other fricative types and the affricates. In the large-scale study by Ingram et al. (1980), it was found for English children that /f/ was the first fricative to be acquired, followed by /ʃ/ and the affricates, with /s, z, v, θ/ appearing last.[3] By the same token, /θ/ and /ð/ are among the least frequent sounds among the languages of the world (Maddieson 1984).

Thus, the empirical problem that Salus and Salus chose to address does not seem to exist. It is well known that there is a general production difficulty with fricatives,

---

[3] The voiced dental fricative was not tested by Ingram et al. If anything, it is acquired later than its voiceless cognate because voiceless segments are generally mastered earlier than voiced ones.

but there is no indication that the order of acquisition within the group of fricatives is determined by stridency. Frequency seems to be a better predictor. For example, /s/ has the highest frequency and is among the earliest fricative acquisitions in Stoel-Gammon's (1985) data, and figures prominently among the languages of the world. It is probable that production problems coupled with frequency effects are responsible for the order of acquisition found in fricatives.

The neurological approach owes much of its attraction to its universal nature. Taking for granted that all human beings are equipped with the same neurological apparatus, all explanations of this sort are perforce valid for all languages. The assumed order of acquisition that Salus and Salus exclusively base upon the study of English children must indeed be language-independent. This is what makes these explanations wide open to disconfirmation, which is a laudable feature as argued above.

To conclude, the neurological approach generates strong hypotheses about language structure which are of wide generality because they reach into the deep recesses of the human brain. An unfortunate consequence of this is that the link between these deep recesses and language is notoriously fragile and difficult to establish. A further problem is that it is as yet unclear how much linguistic territory can be covered by neurological accounts.

2.2. The Phonetic Approach

Phonetics may a priori be expected to place strong constraints on the form of language insofar as language must be transformed into speech to be transmitted from the speaker to the listener. In this process, speech must pass the 'articulatory and auditory bottleneck' (see Lindblom, 1983 for the production side). That is, only that which is producible and perceptible can play a linguistic role. Any appeal to perceptual and productive principles therefore has the potential to yield explanations for language structure and change. An obvious example is the existence of phonotactic constraints which can be reduced in part, though not completely, to constraints on pronounceability. The perceptual side furnishes an explanation for the fact that adjacent sounds tend not to be too similar. As a paradigm case, one may cite the cross-linguistic rarity of /wu/ and /ji/ sequences (Maddieson and Precoda 1992). This rarity in all likelihood follows from the auditory similarity of the constituent sounds: /j/ and /i/ do not form the perceptual contrast that is required to interpret them as a *sequence* of sounds. Setting extreme cases aside, produceability and perceptibility impose gradual rather than absolute constraints. They favour the evolution of less difficult over more difficult sounds and sound sequences. The prevalence of consonant/vowel alternations may be understood in these terms. These are all instances which invite the conclusion that language is shaped by speech.

While it would be surprising if this were not so, the link between phonetics and phonology is not always regarded as self-evident in linguistics. Actually, quite a few linguists regard issues of phonetic implementation as largely irrelevant to phonological theorizing. The tension between the autonomy and non-autonomy of linguistics is nowhere as acutely felt as in the relationship between phonetics and phonology. This is for the simple reason that, of all the abstract levels of linguistic analysis, phonology is most directly connected with the materialization of language. The autonomous phonologists feel justified in their rejection of phonetics not only because of the general reservations about non-autonomy discussed above but also because the incompleteness of phonetic explanations is taken as an argument for regarding them as largely or entirely irrelevant (e.g. Dinnsen 1980; Lass 1980; Anderson 1981). This move is neither justified nor justifiable. An explanation cannot be refuted by arguing that it does not provide a complete account (see above). For example, the fact that the first element was lost in initial <wr> clusters in the history of English may have phonetic reasons (i.e. lack of perceptual contrast between the semi-vowel and the rhotic) alongside other, more systemic ones. By no means can these reasons be said to be mutually exclusive. In what follows, the role of the speaker, that of the listener and their interaction will be highlighted. Moreover, a striking example of the impact of rhythm on higher levels of organization will be provided.

John Ohala has been foremost among the phoneticians who endeavour to explain phonemic patterns by recourse to the phonetic materialization of language. One of the numerous examples may suffice to make the point that articulatory constraints shape phonological systems and their elements. Cross-linguistically, there is a well-known asymmetry to the effect that voiced obstruents are less frequent than their voiceless counterparts. The former generally presuppose the existence of the latter. As regards linguistic function, whenever neutralization of the voice opposition occurs, it is in the direction of the more common obstruent.

Ohala (1983) argues that this phonological asymmetry stems from aerodynamic constraints on the production of sounds. Voicing requires a critical difference between the subglottal and the supraglottal air pressure. For the vocal cords to vibrate, the subglottal pressure must be higher than the supraglottal one. In the case of stops, this difference in air pressure cannot be maintained for long because the closure in the oral cavity leads to a rapid increase in supraglottal pressure which in turn eventually quenches voicing. The instantiation of voicing is even more difficult in the case of fricatives. To create turbulence (i.e. frication noise) in the oral cavity, high supraglottal pressure is needed. However, as noted, the exact opposite is needed for the generation of voicing. There is thus a certain articulation-based incompatibility between voicing and frication. The claim is, then, that phonetic difficulty entails phonological asymmetry.

The active role of the listener in decoding a message has been highlighted by Ohala (1981), who argues that sound change may be explained by changing strategies which the listener employs in reconstructing utterances. Ohala discusses vowel fronting before coronal consonants, e.g. /u/ → /y/ /_ /t/. Taken in isolation, [u] has a low F1 and F2 while [t] has a low F1 and a high F2. When [u] and [t] are coarticulated, the F2 of the [t] 'spreads' to [u]. Given that the second formant represents backness, the [u] in [ut] takes on a more fronted quality, thus approximating to [y]. Now, the critical point is that listeners know about this speaker-induced variation and manage to neutralize it. That is, when a fronted vowel is heard in a coronal context, it is reconstructed as a back vowel by dint of an allophonic defronting rule. However, it may happen that this rule fails to apply because its structural conditions are not met. For instance, the coronal stop may be unreleased and hence difficult to hear. Since the listener cannot put the 'blame' for the variation on the [t], s/he has no way of identifying the speaker-induced variation as variation. As a consequence, the listener will interpret the front vowel in surface-true fashion, i.e. as [y], and will, as a speaker, end up producing a [y]. In so doing, the listener/speaker has completed a sound change.

It is convenient to talk about the listener and the speaker as if they were two different persons. In actual fact, however, the speaker and the listener reside in the same person. This truism raises the possibility that it is more profitable to look for interactions between perceptual and productive constraints than to study these constraints in isolation. This is the path taken by Lindblom, MacNeilage and Studdert-Kennedy (1984), who addressed the issue of how the universal phonetic signal space would be structured in the presence of articulatory, acoustic, and auditory constraints. The phonetic events were CV syllables which were defined by a trajectory from a point in the consonant space to a point in the vowel space. The constraints on which the computation of these points was based included ease of articulation and perceptual contrast. Computer simulations were run to determine the 'expensiveness' of syllables. It was found that the 'cheapest' syllables, i.e. those in which the consonant and the vowel create 'sufficient perceptual contrast at acceptable articulatory cost' (Lindblom et al. 1984: 193), are 'invented' most frequently. The preference for certain sound sequences can thus be understood as a compromise between the listener's and the speaker's needs. The one side keeps the other (as it were) from running wild. For example, the simultaneous generation of [ɖa], [d̪a], and [da] is avoided because these syllables are too similar in auditory terms.

Thus far, the discussion has been limited to aspects of segmental structure. That principles of phonetic implementation may also encroach upon the suprasegmental territory is apparent from a study by Kelly and Bock (1988). The empirical problem they addressed themselves to was the correlation between word class and stress in English. Nouns tend to be initially stressed whereas verbs show a certain predilection for final-syllable stress. This is most evident in noun–verb pairs from the same morphosemantic family, such as *to abstráct–the ábstract* and *to rebél–the rébel*. This difference is systematic in that no corresponding noun–verb pairs exist in which the verb is initially and the noun finally stressed. However, this difference is far from compulsory, in that it does not rule out word pairs in which the noun and the verb bear the same stress pattern, e.g. *to revíew–the revíew* and *to térrace–the térrace*.

Why should this stress difference exist? Kelly and Bock argue persuasively that it is linked to different rhythmic contexts in which nouns and verbs typically occur in English. Consider the following typical contexts for disyllabic nouns (6) and verbs

(7) with the place for the noun and the verb left blank. The stress pattern of the context appears in superscript (´ = stressed; ˘ = unstressed).

(6) Thĕ _____ léft thĕ búildiňg.
(7) Thĕ bóss _____ thĕ búildiňg.

In (6), the placeholder for the noun is preceded by an unstressed syllable (i.e. the definite article) and followed by a stressed syllable (i.e. the verb). It is the other way around in (7), where the placeholder for the verb is preceded by a stressed syllable (i.e. the noun) and followed by an unstressed one (i.e. the definite article).

What effect might this difference have upon the stress pattern of the two word classes? To answer this question, the authors appeal to a highly natural principle of rhythmic activity, indeed its most basic manifestation—the simple alternation of strong and weak beats. The effect of this principle can be directly seen in the above examples. In (6), the unstressed article favours a noun beginning with a stressed syllable while the stressed verb favours a noun ending in an unstressed syllable. The net result is a trochaic noun. By contrast, the stressed noun in (7) favours a verb beginning with an unstressed syllable while the unstressed article favours a verb ending in a stressed syllable. The net result is an iambic verb.

To summarize, Kelly and Bock argue that the principle of rhythmic alternation and the differing rhythmic contexts exert different kinds of pressure upon the two word classes and that, over time, nouns and verbs yield to this pressure. In a more general vein, their claim is that the structure of language can be understood as an adaptation to (non-linguistic) constraints on phonetic realization.[4]

In a nutshell, the studies reviewed make it clear that language is shaped by speech.[5] The way language is phonetically implemented has repercussions on its permanent form. It is not surprising to find that the levels of linguistic description which are closer to the material aspects of language are more susceptible to phonetic influences. However, as is evident from the Kelly and Bock study, the impact of phonetics reaches more deeply into the structure of language. The phonetic approach provides explanations where linguists have to resort to stipulation (as in the noun/verb difference discussed above). On the whole, these explanations are so compelling that the extreme view of a phonology which denies all links to phonetics appears untenable. On the other hand, phonology, let alone other levels further up the linguistic hierarchy, cannot be reduced to phonetics (Dressler 1984). The phonological component of a language is fed by many other factors (see e.g. Dressler and Moosmüller's (1991) socio-psycholinguistic framework). There is thus no reason to construe, as has often been done (e.g. Dinnsen 1980; Anderson 1981), the non-reducibility of phonology to phonetics as an argument for autonomous phonology.

[4] It is perhaps no coincidence—and fits in the general picture sketched in previous sections—that neither Bock nor Kelly is a linguist.
[5] Of course, only a small fraction of pertinent work could be reviewed here. A great deal of phonetic research is directly relevant to phonology (e.g. Stevens, 1972; 1989; Stevens and Keyser 1989).

2.3. The Psychological Approach

To convey a message, the speaker encodes ideas into a linguistic-phonetic form which acts as input to the articulatory mechanism. The listener in turn decodes the acoustic signal in an attempt to reconstruct what the speaker intended to say. Speaking and listening are eminently psychological activities, in that they presuppose internal structures and representations which the language user must generate and manipulate. Since these representations are in, not outside, the minds of the language users, they are most adequately captured in psychological, i.e. information-processing terms. The significance of the psychological approach centres around the relationship between the processor (i.e. the mental machinery underlying the use of language) and the information to be processed (i.e. the mental representation of language). The promise of the psychological approach thus resides in the possibility that the processor constrains the information to be processed. If such is the case, psycholinguistics may show itself capable of explaining the form of language. In its most extreme form, this conjecture must be almost trivially true. The nature of the processor imposes upper limits on the form of language in that only that which is processible can evidently be part of the speaker's and listener's activities and thus constitute language. To what extent the processor shapes the structure of language *within* these limits is an open question.

Processing explanations of language are not unpopular in linguistics. They have been advanced for a variety of phenomena covering all levels of linguistic description. One of the better-known attempts to relate linguistic facts to psycholinguistic mechanisms deals with asymmetries in morphological structure and goes by the name of 'the suffixing preference' (Cutler et al. 1985; Hawkins and Cutler 1988; Hawkins and Gilligan 1988; Hall 1988; Hawkins 1988). This phenomenon will be treated at some length, as it illuminates the logic and the pitfalls of this approach very well.

For any kind of morphological information, a choice has to be made whether it is to be carried by a prefix or a suffix, at least in those languages in which both possibilities are principally allowed. Although there is no aprioristic reason to expect a direct link between the kind of information to be coded and the question of leftward vs. rightward extension of the stem, it has transpired that suffixes are more likely to code morphological functions than prefixes in the languages of the world, hence the term 'suffixing preference'. An extreme case is grammatical case, which always appears as a suffix on nouns. By contrast, not a single category is exclusively prefixed. The only category which exhibits a bias towards prefixing is person (direct object) on nouns. More frequently, however, one encounters statistical tendencies to the effect that categories like definiteness and valence on verbs, for example, occur significantly more often as suffixes than as prefixes. Consonant with this skewing, more languages are exclusively suffixing than exclusively prefixing. Among the OV languages, not a single instance is found of a language which has only prefixes. VO languages, however, divide almost evenly between exclusively prefixing and exclusively suffixing. In general, then, stems precede rather than follow affixes.

Cutler et al.'s (1985) account of the suffixing preference boils down to the claim that stem + suffix structures are easier to process than prefix + stem structures. This ensues from a fixed temporal order of processing among stems and affixes. The former are processed prior to the latter, irrespective of their actual order in the spoken word. Stem + suffix structures comply with this order: what comes first is processed first. In contrast to this, prefix + stem structures are at odds with the natural processing order in that what comes first is processed last. While this does not represent an insuperable problem, it is a mismatch between linguistic structure and psycholinguistic processing which is generally avoided in a continuous effort to improve processing efficiency.

How do Cutler et al. defend their hypothesis about the processing order? They relegate affixes to syntactic processing but stems to lexical processing, and claim that lexical processing always takes place before syntactic processing. Furthermore, they base themselves upon the prefix-stripping hypothesis of Taft and Forster (1975), according to which prefixed words are not stored holistically in the lexicon. Rather, they are decomposed into a prefix and the stem. As a result, lexical access cannot proceed via the full form but only via the stem. In other words, the code of a prefixed word can only be cracked by means of the stem. Cutler et al. argue that the priority of the stem favours its placement in initial sites because processing is particularly efficient in these positions, and it is clearly beneficial to have the most important part in a place which is advantaged from the processing perspective. This psycholinguistic argument dovetails with the linguistic asymmetry between stems and affixes. Stems are logically prior to affixes in that stems may exist without affixes while the reverse is by definition impossible. Related to this, the meaning of a stem can be derived independently of an affix, whereas an affix unfolds its function largely in conjunction with a particular stem.

In evaluating this account, it should be noted that Cutler et al. chose the perspective of language comprehension, and it is not certain that they would have arrived at the same theoretical results had they focused upon language production. In Cutler et al.'s view, speakers have to generate the stem of a morphologically complex word before the prefix. If this is so, it would have to be assumed that speakers employ a reversal strategy prior to articulation whereby what has been activated early is outputted late and what has been activated late is outputted early. It is unclear whether such a reversal strategy is viable and whether Cutler et al. would want to vouch for its reality.

The critical aspect of Cutler et al.'s processing model is its seriality. The claim that the processing of the prefix is delayed until the stem has been heard is not only counterintuitive but also incompatible with a wide range of data. Colé et al. (1989) argue that only suffixed words are accessed analytically (i.e. via their stems) whereas prefixed words are accessed holistically. In other terms, prefix-stripping is not a regular procedure used during lexical access. This hypothesis is fully congruent with the natural order of occurrence. Processing begins on whatever morphological unit comes first. This is precisely the conclusion which Marslen-Wilson and Tyler (1980) arrived at in a series of word-recognition experiments. Processing begins immediately upon hearing the initial portions of a word.

Further problems of the Cutler et al. account are noted by Hall (1988; 1992) and Bybee (1988). These are of some relevance in that they pinpoint the general difficulties which explanations of this kind face. While being sympathetic to Cutler et al.'s general line of argument, Hall emphasizes the insufficiency of their account. He submits that it qualifies as an explanation only when the link between the processing principle and the linguistic structure has been firmly established. In particular, it has to be determined exactly how the processing principles mould language to take the shape it does. The problem basically is that there are, as always, alternative explanations and one would need to know why the processing account is superior to others. Some of these alternatives have been spelled out by Bybee (1988). Starting from the assumption that affixes arise historically from free morphemes, she notes the possibility that postposed material may fuse more readily with the 'stem' than preposed material, thus leading to a preference for suffixation. If this ease-of-fusion hypothesis is correct, there would be no need whatsoever for recourse to Cutler et al.'s processing principles in an account of the suffixing preference. Bybee joins Hall in stressing that only if the historical development of the linguistic patterns can be shown to be under the influence of the assumed processing principles can the psycholinguistic account be regarded as viable.

So what is the current status of Cutler et al.'s processing explanation? It seems likely that the psycholinguistic model to which the authors refer is inadequate. A more adequate conception would allow for more parallelness of processing such as is found in McClelland and Elman's (1986) model of speech perception. If Cutler et al. had resorted to their interactive activation model, they would not have been able to explain the *strong* asymmetry between prefixing and suffixing. However, even the McClelland and Elman model would predict a suffixing preference, albeit a weaker one, because it also incorporates serial processing, though to a lesser extent than the model Cutler et al. chose to work with. Unfortunately, it is currently impossible to quantify in precise terms how weak the suffixing preference must be to be compatible with the interactive activation model. Given that the suffixing preference is quite strong cross-linguistically, all that can be said with some certainty is the following. The serial processing model appears to make the correct predictions about language structure but is inadequate on psycholinguistic grounds. In contrast, the parallel interactive framework is psycholinguistically sound but does not seem to be able to predict the great strength of the suffixing preference. It is probable therefore that further factors are involved in the generation of the suffixing preference, factors which might relate to asymmetries in the behaviour of prefixes and suffixes in general (see section 8.4 for further discussion).

In addition to the choice of the correct psycholinguistic model, Cutler et al.'s work raises another fundamental problem. It is very hard to ascertain how much of the suffixing preference (viewed as a multicausal phenomenon) is to be attributed to psycholinguistic influences and how much to others. Proving that the suffixing preference is brought about by processing ease is almost impossible. And yet it seems likely that processing ease is a relevant factor (of unknown strength) because human beings generally maximize efficiency of behaviour while minimizing the requisite effort.

The psychological approach has been applied to a number of other morphological domains, of which three will be reviewed in the following. Menn and MacWhinney (1984) discuss a pervasive cross-linguistic trend in languages to avoid the immediate repetition of phonologically identical morphemes. (At the same time, the existence of reduplication shows that the repetition of identical morphemes is not completely disallowed.) This prohibition restricts the generality of rule application. When the output of a morphological rule is identical to the part of the stem to which it is attached, the rule generally fails to apply, or, in Stemberger's (1981) words, it applies vacuously. Moreover, when two affixes have the same form, they are merged into one, i.e. one morpheme takes on both functions. An example of the former kind comes from German. The word [laɪnen] may represent a noun *Leinen* ('linen') as well as an adjective *leinen* ('made of linen') because the end of the stem (*-en*) prevents the attachment of the adjective-forming suffix *-en*. The adjective *leinen-en* does not exist.

An example of the latter kind is the simultaneous application of the plural rule and the possessive marker in English. Both have the same allomorphy and the same phonetic realization. In [gɜːlz], the alveolar fricative may express plurality (*girls*) or possession (*girl's*). When possession has to be encoded on a plural noun, the two functions merge in one form. The form *girls's* [gɜːlzɪz] is prohibited. Note that there is no conflict with irregular plurals: *women's (clothes)* is impeccable.

In their account of the repeated morph constraint, Menn and MacWhinney abandon the notion of the addition of morphological material through rule application in favour of template matching. That is, morphological categories are matched onto canonical surface forms. So when a given surface form looks as if it has already undergone the morphological transformation, it is left untouched. Menn and MacWhinney postulate an affix-checking process whereby stems are inspected for their ends; if they satisfy a given criterion, they are exempted from a change. In a more psycholinguistically inspired vein, the authors argue that the activation of a given rule is blocked when its output is already present. So when a speaker intends to produce the past tense of *to hit*, the stem-final /t/ satisfies the past-tense rule and thus prevents it from applying.

The next example highlights an interaction between language type and the incidence of homonymy. Carstairs and Stemberger (1988) report that inflectional homonymy is found more frequently in flectional than in agglutinative languages. Inflectional homonymy refers to the formal identity of two different members of a morphological paradigm. In Latin, the genitive and the dative singular of nouns belonging to the *-a* declension are phonologically identical: *mensae* 'table'. In agglutinative languages, such ambiguity is not generally found. One form fulfils only one function. For example, the Turkish form *evleri* 'the houses (accusative)', which can be neatly decomposed into the stem *ev* 'house', *ler* 'plural' and *i* 'accusative', is functionally unambiguous.

Why should Turkish avoid inflectional homonymy while Latin allows it? Carstairs and Stemberger's explanation turns on the notion of processing ease. Homonymy in inflectional paradigms incurs no processing cost whereas homonymy in agglutinative paradigms leads to immense processing complexity. In flectional languages, homonymy is tolerated because the association of one form with two functions is offset by the elimination of one member of the paradigm. If there were no homonymy between *mensae* (genitive) and *mensae* (dative), a new form would be needed which did not exist before in the paradigm. A characteristic trait of flectional languages is that all compound affixes (i.e. those coding more than one function) are different (unless this tendency is counteracted by homonymy), so an already existing form does not do. By contrast, agglutinative languages are far less receptive to homonymy. The introduction of homonymy would not lead to a reduction in the number of affixes because the very same affixes recur in other paradigms in which they would be kept. Consider again the Turkish example *ev-ler-i* (plural accusative). If it was homonymous with *ev-ler-e* (plural dative), either the *e* or the *i* suffix might be dropped. One of two things might happen at this point. If one of these suffixes was dropped across paradigms, the system would end up with global rather than local homonymy, because *i* and *e* are similarly used to distinguish case in the singular paradigm, namely *ev-i* (singular accusative) vs. *ev-e* (singular dative). Clearly, global homonymy would put a great strain both on processing and on communication because the function of any individual form is hardly recoverable. As an alternative to global homonymy, the opposition between *i* and *e* might be neutralized in the plural but retained in the singular paradigm. Carstairs and Stemberger show by means of a computer simulation that this solution is unworkable, because the relevant form/function connections cannot be established or can only be established by considerably increasing the processing machinery. In short, homonymy in agglutinative languages is either impossible or extremely difficult to process.

The final example from the morphological domain is about another asymmetry between prefixes and suffixes. English has a good number of category-changing suffixes (e.g. *(to) run → (the) runner*) but only a handful of category-changing prefixes (e.g. *(the) friend → (to) befriend*). The few category-changing prefixes that do occur can attach only to morphologically simple words (e.g. *friend*), while the category-preserving prefixes are free to also attach to morphologically complex words (e.g. *de-activ-ate* and *de-moral-ize*). Hammond (1993) accounts for this difference by invoking the notion of processing difficulty with morphologically complex words. To begin with, suffixing is clearly preferred to prefixing (cf. the suffixing preference discussed above). Secondly, category-changing affixing is more 'costly' than category-preserving affixing. Thirdly, it is easier to attach an affix to an underived than to a derived stem. These three principles taken together explain the observed patterns in English. Hammond rejects a linguistic explanation in terms of an inherent restriction on the grammar, such as would be provided by Finite State Grammar, which cannot deal with the fact that category-changing prefixes do occur in English, though at a lower rate than category-changing suffixes and category-preserving prefixes. He compares the morphological issue at hand to centre-embedding in syntax, which is also understood as a 'performance constraint'. The problem common to both areas is the processing of non-local dependencies. In morphology there is a dependency between the suffixes and the prefixes, while the dependency in syntax is between the noun and the non-adjacent verb. These non-local dependencies are hard to process and therefore eschewed. Although the psycholinguistic details are not very clearly spelled out, it may be concluded that a processing account not only is less ad hoc but also predicts the quantitative and qualitative patterns more accurately than the linguistic account.

The second part of this section is devoted to syntactic issues, in particular word order and relative clauses. Various researchers have sought to explain syntactic phenomena within a theory of processing. This is remarkable insofar as syntax is typically regarded as a highly abstract system which is very remote from issues of communication.[6] The psycholinguistic investigation of syntax thus assumes a particular significance. If it can be shown that syntax is under the influence of processing constraints, it can no longer be treated as an autonomous system: the last fortress of autonomous linguistics would fall.

A good starting-point for the analysis of syntactic phenomena is the word order of freezes, i.e. sequences of independent words whose order is not changeable without destroying their holistic meaning. Freezes are less complex than non-frozen constructions because their word order is fixed and therefore their syntactic creativity reduced. Freezes thus provide an opportunity of studying syntactic effects in their 'frozen' form.

Cooper and Ross (1975) presented a very thorough analysis of freezes. They classified space reference in freezes according to three semantic relations: vertical (*up* vs. *down*), horizontal (*left* vs. *right*) and vertical vs. horizontal. An example of each is given below.

(8) rise and fall. *fall and rise.
(9) left–right motion. ?right–left motion.
(10) ordinate and abscissa. *abscissa and ordinate.

These cases attest to the (largely) irreversible nature of the word order in the expressions, although not all reversals are equally unacceptable (compare (9) and (10)). As illustrated by these examples, there is a natural order in these conjuncts: *up* precedes *down*, *left* more naturally precedes *right* than vice versa, and *vertical* precedes *horizontal*. Cooper and Ross relate the order in freezes to principles of information-

[6] This explains why syntax is considered by many to be the area where the autonomy of language can be studied in its purest form.

processing. Their general claim is that certain elements are placed earlier because they are more available in visual perception and performance. *Up* comes before *down* because the former concept is processed faster than the latter. The authors refer to a reaction time study in which subjects judged more quickly when a given word was above than when it was below a given object. That the left–right direction is more natural than the reverse is probably related to the right-handedness and the dominance of the left hemisphere in the majority of people, even though it is less than clear exactly how this link should be conceptualized. The vertical dimension also enjoys a processing advantage as compared to the horizontal dimension. This privilege is discernible in visual illusions where subjects tend to trust the vertical dimension more than the horizontal one. For instance, a vertical line is perceived as longer than a horizontal line although both are equally long. In short, the temporal priority of linguistic elements in freezes is seen as a consequence of their priority in processing.

Fenc-Oczlon (1989) uncovered another index of processing priority, to wit lexical frequency. The more frequent part in freezes generally occurs before the less frequent one. She finds that frequency is an excellent predictor of word order in her corpus, and argues that frequency is a strong determinant of 'cognitive cost' (for a very similar claim, see Sobkowiak 1993).

The impact of processing characteristics is not, however, confined to freezes. It extends to more creative language as well. Kelly et al. (1986) investigated the effects of prototypicality on sentence structure. As confirmed by a number of psychological studies, prototypical categories are more accessible than non-prototypical ones. It is thus possible to hypothesize that more prototypical items tend to precede rather than follow less prototypical items because what is more readily available should outdo what is less readily available, especially under temporal constraints. Given that the choice of the subject has repercussions for syntactic structure, it may be expected that sentence structure varies with the availability of lexical items. This is precisely what Kelly et al. found. Syntactic structures were favoured which allowed subjects to begin the sentence with a prototypical category. This result is important in that it shows that the principle of lexical accessibility makes itself felt not only in freezes but also in speaking situations where speakers are free to choose among a number of alternative grammatical structures. This interaction between the accessibility of lexical items and grammatical structures attests to the susceptibility of syntax to processing ease at the lexical level.

An early attempt to study the effects of processing constraints on syntax is the work of Bever and Langendoen (1971; 1972). They advanced a 'performance' explanation for the observation that subject relative pronouns are obligatory nowadays, whereas they used to be omitted in former stages of the language. Contrast (11) and (12).

(11) He sente after a cherl was in the toun. (from Chaucer's *Canterbury Tales*)
     'He sent after a fellow who was in the town.'
(12) *The man wants to see the boss is waiting downstairs.

No. (11) attests to the acceptability of subject pronoun deletion in relative clauses in Middle English. This is no longer possible today, compare (12). Bever and Langendoen's explanation turns on constraints upon sentence perception. In the absence of a relative pronoun, it is unclear whether the following verb (*was* in (11)) is part of the main clause or the relative clause. The authors claim that there is a perceptual rule by which speakers analyse an NP + following V as belonging to the same S node (cf. *The man wants to see the boss* in (12)). The application of this perceptual rule entails a misanalysis of the sentence, a situation which is avoided by the introduction of a relative clause marker. The danger of misanalysis did not arise in Old English because its nouns and verbs were highly inflected. This morphological information allowed for a relatively free word order and the unambiguous association of a verb with its corresponding noun: in other words, the inflections made a relative pronoun unnecessary. When the inflections were lost in Middle English times, listeners were at a loss to associate the verb with the correct noun. A new disambiguating mechanism was called for and the placement of the relative pronoun became mandatory.

A related processing principle has been invoked to account for the positioning of *that*-clauses in English. Grosu and Thompson (1977) find that these NP clauses are most acceptable in final, less acceptable in initial and least acceptable in medial positions:

(13) I am surprised that Siegfried was so much in love with Brünnhilde.
(14) ?That Siegfried was so much in love with Brünnhilde is strange.
(15) *I regard that Siegfried was so much in love with Brünnhilde as strange.

In (13) the main clause precedes the NP clause, while the reverse is true of (14). In (15) the NP clause is located within the main clause. Grosu and Thompson argue that the difference in acceptability of NP clauses stems from differences in processing ease. NP clauses which are internal to main clauses are most difficult to process because the matrix clause is interrupted. Consequently, the beginning of the matrix clause has to be held in suspense until the end of the sentence. This imposes a strain on short-term memory. Memory constraints are also at issue in sentences such as (14). That these are more acceptable than sentences such as (15) ensues from the fact that the main clause is not interrupted by the NP clause. The integrity of the main clause facilitates its processing. No processing problems are encountered in (13). Neither is there any interruption, nor is the natural order between the independent and the dependent clause reversed.

Grosu and Thompson's argument leads to the interesting conclusion that processing difficulty exerts an influence on judgements of grammaticality and, by implication, is in part responsible for the syntactic rules that exist in a given language. The rules that enter a language are those which respect the biases introduced by the processing system. Inversely, rules that tax the processor are avoided.

The most comprehensive analysis of psycholinguistic influences on syntax to date has been conducted by Hawkins (1990; 1994) who developed a processing account of a wide variety of word order patterns. Like others before him, he relies exclusively upon perceptual principles. His fundamental claim is that words are ordered within sentences in such a way, given the sequential nature of speech, as to allow the parser to do its job most efficiently (i.e. rapidly and reliably). A central task of the parser is to identify immediate constituents, i.e. to attach sister nodes to a common parent node. The difficulty of this task varies with word order. Compare (16a) and (16b).

(16) a. I introduced some friends that John had brought to the party to Mary.
 b. I introduced to Mary some friends that John had brought to the party.

The VP of (16) contains three Immediate Constituents—the verb, the PP, and the NP. To recognize this is easy in (16b) because this decision can be made rather early in the sentence. In contrast, (16a) is difficult to parse because this decision is considerably delayed by the heavy NP. By a relatively simple technique, Hawkins is able to quantify the varying degrees of processing difficulty. He divides the number of Immediate Constituents (IC) by the number of words that are needed for parent node construction. Consider again the NP with its three ICs in (16). In (16b), only four words are needed (*introduced, to, Mary,* and *some*). The determiner *some* is assumed to suffice for the identification of the NP. Thus, the IC-to-word ratio is 3 : 4 = 75 per cent. In (16a), however, eleven words are needed to recognize the same three constituents (all words from V to P), giving a ratio of 3 : 11 = 27 per cent.

Hawkins refines this method by computing the IC-to-word ratio at every new word slot and averaging the results across the entire sentence. For example, *Mary* has a ratio of 27 per cent in (16a) as it is in the third IC and the eleventh word in the VP. By contrast, *Mary* has a ratio of 67 per cent in (16b) as it is in the second IC and the third word in the VP. The aggregate ratio is 47 per cent for (16a) but 86 per cent for (16b). This difference is taken as an indicator of the processing difficulty of (16a) and the processing ease of (16b).

Hawkins gives an impressive demonstration of the predictive potential of this approach. The VP *went to that film* allows four theoretically possible word orders, given that branching is binary, that the PP is embedded in the VP, and that the order of DET and N is fixed. The four possibilities are listed below, along with their averaged IC-to-word ratio and the percentages of languages that are of this word order type. As can be seen from Table 1, the predictions for the calculation of the IC-to-word ratio are borne out by the frequency of the individual word order types. The less favourable the IC-to-word ratio, the less likely it is that a language is of this word-order type. There is strong evidence, then, that word order is adapted to perceptual processing needs.

The final example to be discussed is similar in spirit to Hawkins (1990; 1994). Dryer (1992) investigated word order correlations in a huge, balanced sample of 625 languages. His starting-point was the order of verb and object, and he examined possible correlations between this order and the order of other pairs of elements such as verb and negation as well as noun and genitive. He showed, for instance,

TABLE 1. *Predicted and actual frequencies of occurrence of four word-order types (Hawkins 1990)*

Word order type	Averaged IC-to-word ratio (%)	Languages fitting this type (%)
1. verb-initialness with preposition	100	77
2. verb-initialness with postposition	79	23
3. verb-finalness with postposition	100	93
4. verb-finalness with preposition	58	7

contrary to earlier claims, that there is no correlation between OV–VO and the adjective–noun order. As a positive example, VO languages tend to prefer verb–adverb order, while the opposite order is predominantly found with OV languages. On the basis of his data, Dryer rejects the consistent head-ordering principle whereby, at all descriptive levels, heads either precede or follow their dependents. Instead he espouses the Branching Direction Theory, according to which languages tend towards either right- or left-branching. This theory incorporates the distinction between lexical and phrasal categories. The linear ordering between these category types is assumed to be consistent across levels. Thus, given that V is a lexical and O a phrasal category (NP), a given pair of elements consisting of a lexical and a phrasal category will exhibit the same order, i.e. the lexical category will tend to precede the phrasal category in VO languages. The opposite holds for OV languages. Resuming one of the above examples, because the genitive is a phrasal and the noun a lexical category, VO languages favour the noun–genitive order.

According to Dryer (1992), the Branching Direction Theory is rooted in the nature of perceptual processing. He argues that it is easier to process languages which are consistently right- or left-branching than languages which exhibit a mixture of both. Unfortunately, Dryer remains inexplicit about the psycholinguistic model that he assumes and in particular about how the notion of processing ease can be defined within such a framework. He only notes that a mixture of left- and right-branching leads to centre-embedding, which is known to be very difficult to process. He also notes that his Branching Direction Theory is compatible with Hawkins's (1990) claims, both theoretical and empirical, and that Hawkins's psycholinguistic explanation may therefore be applicable to his data as well.

In this section, psycholinguistic approaches to language structure have been extensively though not exhaustively reviewed. Many other works have not been mentioned, partly for reasons of space and partly because they do not add anything radically new to the conceptualization of the link between language and processing. Among the studies that could not be given detailed consideration are Stein (1988), Culicover (1984), Antinucci et al. (1979), Rohdenburg (1996), Zabrocki (1986), Frazier and Rayner (1988), and Lightfoot (1981). This incomplete list, along with the aforementioned works, strongly suggests that the explanation of language structure in psycholinguistic terms is a productive approach. Moreover, it is applicable to all levels of linguistic analysis without any restriction. While the focus of this section has been on morphology and syntax, other areas are amenable to the same reasoning.

2.4. The Semiotic Approach

Language is a system of signs and as such subject to general semiotic principles. Semiotics may provide one of the links between linguistic and non-linguistic facts and in this way contribute to the explanation of the form of language. The semiotic approach is not widely used in linguistic research, but it is at the core of what may loosely be called the Austrian School of Natural Linguists, with Wolfgang Dressler as the leading figure. Viewing language from the perspective of communication and cognition, Dressler (1985a) takes semiotics, in particular Peirce's theory of signs, to be the appropriate metatheory of linguistics. Natural Linguistics thus has an extralinguistic foundation. The functions and properties of signs in general are assumed to explain the nature of linguistic signs. This approach has been applied to several branches of linguistics. My focus will be on morphology, an area in which Natural Linguists have been particularly active.

The first principle to be discussed is semiotic transparency, whereby the signans and the signatum enter a relationship which is maximally direct, i.e. minimally distorted by intervening variables. This principle predicts that morphological relationships should obey the transparency constraint. The more transparent a morphological relationship is, the more often it should occur in the languages of the world. Consider the nominalization of verbs in English (Dressler 1985a). The most transparent relationship is one in which the nominal suffix is attached to the verb without any modification of the former or the latter, e.g. *to punish* → *the punishment*. Less transparent cases involve modifications of the verb, the suffix or even both, e.g. *to deride* → *the derision*. Least transparent relationships are those subsumed under the term *suppletion*, e.g. *to die* → *the death*. The prediction of Natural Morphology is generally borne out. Even though large-scale quantitative analyses are at a premium, there is little doubt that more transparent relationships are preferred to less transparent ones.

Naturally, the relationship between signs may be gauged not only at the formal but also at the meaning level. By analogy with morphotactic transparency, morphosemantic transparency also has to be reckoned with. The general prediction is that the more transparent a word pair is from the semantic point of view, the more favoured it is cross-linguistically. In a study of comparison, Dressler (1986) showed this principle to hold. Generally, the meaning of the positive is fully preserved in comparatives and superlatives, as in *big* → *bigger*. Semantic opacity is rare in English comparison and occurs only mildly, as in *old* → *elder*. Note the attendant formal change in this example.

The second principle refers to the optimal size of the signans (Dressler 1988). The optimal signans is of word size because it is at this level that meaning and sound most effectively meet (Bybee 1991). The word fulfils two criteria at the same time. It is small enough in that it cannot be divided into smaller units without destroying the nature of the sign and it is large enough to be self-sufficient, i.e. it functions as an independent unit. The morphologically simple word thus belongs to the class of primary signs. Phrases and stems are regarded as secondary signs, the latter because they do not stand on their own and the former because they are composed of more basic signs.

The distinction between primary and secondary signs entails the following prediction: morphological rules should apply more frequently to words than to stems or phrases. This prediction may also be formulated as an implicational law. If a language possesses stem- or phrase-based rules, it must also have word-based rules, though the reverse does not hold. Dressler does not fail to point out that the strength of the word-based preference varies with the morphological type of the language in question (i.e. agglutinating, inflecting, etc.). Restricting ourselves to English, it is immediately apparent that the prediction from semiotics is correct. Inflection, derivation, and compounding are all prototypically based upon words, e.g. *fly* → *(he) flies*, *derive* → *derivation*, *book* → *bookshop*. Morphological rules applying to units other than words also exist but are decidedly uncommon. Above the word level, we find morphological complexes such as the following (in decreasing order of naturalness): *painstaking, unget-at-able* and *I feel particularly sit-around-and-do-nothing-ish today*.

What is the status of the principle of semiotic transparency and the primacy of the word? Are these irreducible concepts or interpretable in, for example, psycholinguistic terms? A morphotactically transparent word is clearly advantageous to the speaker because fewer rules have to be applied on-line in the generation of *investment* (on the basis of *to invest*) than in morphotactically less transparent forms such as *invention* (from *to invent*). The same holds true of the listener. Fewer rules are needed to recover *to invest* from *investment* than *to invent* from *invention*. Such processing arguments are advanced by Natural Morphologists themselves (e.g. Dressler 1985a).[7] The very same logic applies to morphosemantic transparency. The processing load for morphosemantically transparent items is lower than that for morphosemantically opaque ones. To comprehend the latter, the listener may have to resolve a conflict between the rule-based and the idiosyncratic meaning of a morphologically complex word. One example from Dressler (1986) is the comparative of German *alt* 'old', *älter*, which in addition to the ordinary meaning 'older than' can also mean 'between young and old'. Therefore, language users are likely to prefer transparent signs.

The primacy of the word also has a psycholinguistic basis. In comprehension, it acts as the locus at which top-down constraints (e.g. expectations about word structure) and bottom-up information (the acoustic signal) most naturally interact (Marslen-Wilson and Welsh 1978). In production, it is the semantically relevant unit that is most easily manipulable as a whole (as shown, for example, by the frequency of word errors in spontaneous slips of the tongue). The word is maximally handy in

---

[7] The validity of these arguments rests upon the assumption that nouns like *invention*, for example, are actually derived from their corresponding verbs.

that it represents a compromise between the two opponent forces of ease of manipulation, which leads to smaller size, and ease of perception, which leads to greater size. Taking a clue from Rosch (1978), the word may be identified as a basic category not only at the semantic but also at the formal level. It is in this sense the prototypical sound/meaning mediator.

A case can thus be made for interpreting central concepts of Natural Morphology (or Natural Linguistics more generally) in psycholinguistic terms.[8] Indeed, the link with psycholinguistics is not only my construal but is explicitly sought by the proponents of this approach. This occurs on two fronts. Firstly, Natural Morphology is mentalistic in the sense that the basic constructs it rests upon are assumed to be psychologically real (Dressler 1986). It seems, however, that the psychological reality of the Natural Linguistic constructs is in no small measure taken for granted rather than explicitly defended on the basis of psycholinguistic argumentation. For example, the question of the ontological status of (phonological, morphological, and morphophonological) rules is begged. Nevertheless, as argued above, there is a good deal of commensurability between psycholinguistic and Natural Linguistic notions. In a nutshell, naturalist approaches are not psychologically implausible.

Secondly, the data base upon which Natural Morphology draws includes psycholinguistic evidence such as is provided by children, 'normal' adults, and aphasics. It is worthwhile to stress, however, that the naturalist's database is not restricted to this source of information: more traditional domains such as synchronic alternations and diachronic developments are also taken into account. No stand appears to be taken on how to deal with conflicting sources of evidence, i.e. whether one source is in any sense more valuable or significant than another.

It should be emphasized that Natural Morphology does more than base itself upon a semiotic metatheory. According to Dressler (1988), it embraces the following three components: a subtheory of universal naturalness based upon a semiotic metatheory, a subtheory of language typology, and a subtheory of language-specific system adequacy. The first subtheory may indeed be congruent with psycholinguistic principles. Whether this is also the case for the second and the third can only be established when these theories have been worked out in sufficient detail.

This leaves us with the question of how the relationship between Natural Linguistics and psycholinguistics should be defined for the moment. It is unlikely that Natural Linguists would want their approach to be reduced to psycholinguistics, but Dressler (1990) points out that there is such a large overlap between Natural Linguistics and Cognitive Linguistics that the former can be included 'under the umbrella' of the latter. Although this statement underscores the affinity of naturalist and cognitive approaches, it is not clear that a complete assimilation of Natural Linguistics to psycholinguistics is warranted. Dressler (1985a: 325) states: 'Natural

---

[8] Only two such concepts have been discussed here, but the same can be said of others such as the figure/ground principle and the notion of prototype which also play a major part in naturalist research, e.g. Natural Textlinguistics. Since these principles in fact originated within psychology, it would be futile to transfer them into a psychological framework.

Morphology has neither a sociolinguistic nor a psycholinguistic theory of its own … but consistently refers to such theories.' Putting aside the problem that Dressler is rather inexplicit about which sociolinguistic and psycholinguistic theories he has in mind, this quotation views Natural Linguistics and psycholinguistics as conceptually separate domains. Indeed, given their divergent methodology and research aims, it seems preferable to keep the two disciplines apart.

In conclusion, the semiotic approach as endorsed by Natural Morphologists has some explanatory value in that it seeks an extralinguistic basis for linguistic phenomena. While this approach is quite successful in its predictions, its independence is seriously undermined by the fact that most, if not all, of the semiotic notions are also rooted in psychology. It is thus not certain that it is necessary to resort to (this kind of) semiotics. Dressler's publication of 1990 may be construed as an attempt to conflate naturalist and cognitive philosophies, but it remains to be seen whether this subsuming strategy does justice to all aspects of Natural Linguistics and the convictions of all Natural Linguists.

2.5. The Functional-Communicative Approach

The functional and the commmunicative approach to explanation in linguistics will be combined in this section because all functional explanations make a direct appeal to language as a means of communication. Functions that lie outside the communicative context are not taken into consideration. The basic assumption underlying the functional-communicative approach is that language can be explained with reference to the needs of the speaker and the listener. Since speaking and listening are psychological processes, the affinity with the psycholinguistic approach is immediately apparent. Similarly, there is some affinity with the semiotic approach which is given the attribute 'functional' by Natural Linguists. However, the functional-communicative approach should not be conflated with the psycholinguistic or the semiotic one. It is not certain that everything that is functional from the communicative perspective must also be preferred from the psycholinguistic or semiotic point of view.

A typical functional explanation has the following structure. In order to account for a particular property of language, it has to be shown that this property is to the advantage of the speaker and/or the listener. Unfortunately, it is not always easy to determine what counts as an advantage and how an advantage can be weighed against a disadvantage, because the criteria for evaluation are neither agreed upon nor all known. In short, a cost–benefit analysis is required. While these considerations do not weaken the power of functionalist accounts *per se*, they draw attention to the fact that it is relatively easy to come up with such accounts but much more difficult to follow them through.

Vachek (1961) may serve to illustrate this point. He argues that English preserved the opposition between voiced and voiceless obstruents in word-final positions for functional reasons. The starting-point of his line of reasoning is the fact that it is 'costly' to maintain this phonological opposition because voicing is very hard to realize on obstruents in final sites (see section 2.2 above). Hence, there must be a counteracting force which prevents the abolition of this distinction. This force is the function that this opposition fulfils. Voicing is used to code word class. Verbs end in a voiced obstruent while their corresponding nouns end in the voiceless counterpart, e.g. *to relieve–the relief*. The articulatory cost thus is offset by its morphological function.

If Vachek's explanation is valid, the inverse should also hold. If the voiced–voiceless opposition serves no morphological function, it should be lost in postvocalic positions. This does not seem to be true cross-linguistically. French is a case in point. It has not neutralized the voicing opposition but does not exploit it for morphological purposes (with the exception of a very small number of words in which it codes gender, e.g. *neuf* (masc.) vs. *neuve* (fem.) 'new'). Furthermore, the number of English word pairs in which a syntactic-category difference is signalled by a voicing difference is quite small in the light of the vast majority of noun–verb pairs which are formally identical (e.g. *the smack–to smack*). It may be inferred from this imbalance that if the functional explanation has anything to contribute, its significance should not be overrated.[9] This is not to say, however, that this approach is of no value.

A more forceful argument can be derived from the analysis of grammatical categories. Consider the case of gender in the grammatical and lexical systems. The personal-pronoun system of English makes a gender distinction in the third person singular (*he–she*) but neither in the second (*you*) nor in the first (*I*). Hawkins (1988) notes that there is an implicational hierarchy in the coding of gender in the known pronoun systems. All languages that make a gender distinction in the second person also make one in the third. Also, every language that makes a gender distinction in the first also makes one in the second and third person (Greenberg 1963). Hawkins's explanation is a functional-pragmatic one. The typical communicative situation consists of a speaker and a listener who are spatially and temporally contiguous. There is thus no need to distinguish verbally between a male and a female addressee. This would only be necessary when three interlocutors are present (and useful only when the two addressees are not of the same sex). A masculine and a feminine *you* are therefore helpful only under special circumstances. However, a masculine and a feminine *I* are helpful under no circumstances whatsoever, as the identity of the speaker is always clear from other sources such as visual ones ('the one who is moving his or her lips'). In stark contrast, a gender distinction is most useful in the third person. More commonly than not, the speaker and the listener talk about people who do not take part in the interaction. These people have to be unequivocally identified, and one way of doing so is by means of gender.

---

[9] In all fairness, it should be mentioned that Vachek (1961) does not view the opposition of voicing in isolation. In fact, the extent to which a given contrast is maintained in his view depends upon the degree to which an increase in synonymy can be tolerated by the individual language. Specifically, he argues that due to its analytic morphology, English is less free to give up this opposition than other languages with a lower level of synonymy.

Gender coding in the English lexicon is relatively unusual. We find it in generic terms (e.g. *man–woman*), kinship terms (e.g. *aunt–uncle*), and domesticated animals (e.g. *boar–sow*) for example. A functional explanation is handy in these cases. From the anthropocentric perspective, gender coding is simply more important in domesticated than in wild animals. Who cares about the sex of a leopard or an ant? But the sex of a bovine animal is essential not only to farmers.

Functionalist accounts have also been put forward to explain language change. Basically, the following logic is applied. The starting-point is the assumption that the linguistic system has to satisfy a number of sometimes antagonistic constraints simultaneously. There is a constant tug of war among these competing principles, and it is this dynamics which keeps the system endlessly in motion. At one point in time one force gains strength in comparison with another, while the reverse may happen at another point in time. It is developments like these that are captured by the hypothesis of local optimization (Ronneberger-Sibold 1980). One functional principle is elevated to a more important status in comparison with another. A pertinent example is the development of the plural marker on nouns. Here, the two economical principles of shortness and generality can be shown to redefine their status. In Middle English, plurality was realized as -*es* on most nouns irrespective of the nature of the stem-final consonant. Thus, the rule was applicable throughout but required the addition of a full syllable. This latter condition is at variance with Zipf's law, in that frequency correlates with shortness. Because the plural morpheme is very often used, it came under pressure of being shortened (in agreement with more general trends in the language). The reduction of the suffix vowel, however, brought about a limitation of the generality of the plural marker. Instead of one highly regular plural allomorph, several allomorphs had to be created which stood in complementary distribution and which were of limited applicability. Hence, the principle of generality was demoted and the principle of conciseness promoted.

To conclude, functional explanations are confronted with the following problems. First, as in the development of plural allomorphy in English, they provide no explanation for why the shift in importance of one principle relative to another initially occurred. Secondly and most importantly, what is functionally advantageous can only be determined if the assumed advantages are weighed against all possible disadvantages. Finally, functional principles cannot be established once and for all. What is locally optimal may differ from language to language and from epoch to epoch (see Wurzel's (1984) notion of system adequacy).

2.6. The Pragmatic Approach

It is notoriously difficult to draw a clear line between pragmatic and functional-communicative approaches. It appears justified, though, to devote a separate section to this approach because its emphasis is somewhat different from, and more specific than, the others. The basic assumption is that the use to which language is put has repercussions on its form. The way language is used depends upon the intention of the speaker and the context in which the communicative act is performed. This context is variable and may thus require varying strategies to cope with the contingencies of the situation.

Speakers' reliance on the extralinguistic context is quite heavy. The main reasons for this reliance appear to be that it allows speakers to save effort, to be more flexible, and, somewhat surprisingly, to be more precise. A paradigm example is the set of deictic terms which owe their existence to the mere fact that language is customarily realized in spatial and temporal contiguity of the interlocutors. The expression *over there* is certainly simpler than the phrase *the chimney of the house at 10 High Street*. The latter formulation may even be communicatively less efficient than the former because the listener cannot always be expected to know which house is No. 10. By definition, a deictic term can only be understood when listeners have availed themselves of the requisite non-linguistic clues such as the gaze or the pointing of the speaker. Most usually, this information is readily available because speakers take the listeners' perspective into account.

How profound the impact of context on language is can be gauged from a comparison of linguistic patterns in various speaking situations. When the situation is changed, the language changes simultaneously. Consider three typical communicative situations: (a) producer and perceiver are spatially and temporally contiguous; (b) producer and perceiver are temporally but not spatially contiguous; (c) producer and perceiver are neither spatially nor temporally contiguous. Prototypically, these types correspond to the three activities of face-to-face conversation, telephoning, and writing, respectively. As may be expected, the use of deictic terms differs vastly from one activity to another. Spatial-deictic expressions occur less frequently in telephone conversations than in face-to-face interactions. Similarly, the extent of spatial and temporal deixis is lower in written than in spoken language. However, it is not the case that deictic terms are completely absent from non-contiguous communication. Spatial deictics are found in telephone conversations despite the difference in location between speaker and listener. They are possible to the extent that the speaker can expect the listener to infer what is meant. For example, the meaning of *here* is recoverable even for a listener who is not present.

The situation is more complex is writing. When deictics occur, they of necessity have a different function because the non-contiguous reader cannot interpret them in the same way as the contiguous listener. The reader has to reconstruct the situation of the writer or narrator on the basis of the information provided, whereas the listener is free in the choice of extralinguistic information s/he brings to bear on the interpretation of deictic terms. Writers deliberately play upon the information deficit of the reader by using deictics, not to be more precise (like speakers) but to be more vague. For example, the cataphoric use of pronouns may create tension in that the reader is left in the dark about the identity of the referent. Such stylistic means presuppose a communicative context in which the recipient is 'inferior' to the producer and therefore has to accept the rules laid down by the latter. The principles of this oblique communication stand and fall with the context in which it is embedded.

The general point of the preceding remarks is that language cannot be studied and understood independently of the context in which it is put to use. There is no language system *per se* in general nor a deictic subsystem *per se* in particular. There is spoken language and written language (with a great number of intermediate shades) which are partially independent of each other. This includes a deictic subsystem in the written and one in the oral language, with partly divergent structure and function. An explanatory approach to language thus cannot afford to ignore the pragmatic perspective.

The effects of pragmatic principles extend not only to the lexicon but also to syntax. Fox and Thompson (1990) undertook an analysis of relative clauses in English, and argued that their grammatical properties are not only syntactically but also pragmatically conditioned. They examined the distribution of the syntactic roles of the head NP and the NP in the relative clause which refers to the Head in the main clause, and found that with non-human referents, subject heads tend to pattern with object-relatives while object heads are more balanced in their co-occurrence with Object and Subject relatives. Examples (17) and (18) are taken from Fox and Thompson (1990).

(17) Probably the only thing you'll see is like the table.
(18) if you give them the dimensions you want.

Case (17) evidences the predominant pattern: subject NP (*the only thing*) + object-relative (*you'll see* ___ $_{OBJ}$). Number (18) exemplifies the less common situation in which the grammatical role of the Head NP (*the dimensions*) is identical to that of the coreferent in the relative clause (*you want* ___ $_{OBJ}$).

In an attempt to explain this patterning, Fox and Thompson argue that the relative clauses fulfil different functions when the head NP is object or subject. In case of a subject head NP, the relative clause serves to ground the NP which is insufficiently grounded at the beginning of an utterance where subjects typically occur in English. This grounding is achieved by establishing a connection between the NP and the given discourse referent. In (17), for example, the hearer is directly addressed. The situation is quite different for object head NPs. These do not have to be grounded because, given the rules of English word order, the subject and the verb have already been uttered and provide the necessary information for grounding. Thus there is no need for relative clauses to do this job and they are free to exercise other functions, the commonest of which is that of characterization. Characterizing relative clauses, in turn, do not go together naturally with object-relatives. They prefer subject-relatives because characterizations are typically intransitive predicates which furnish information about the behaviour and appearance of their subjects (e.g. *flies airplanes*).

The essence of this account is captured by the notion of information flow between the participants of a conversation. Speakers make syntactic choices which are not (only) determined by the syntactic rules of the language but also guided by their desire to incorporate the listener's perspective. This discourse strategy not only facilitates comprehension but also makes listeners see the relevance of the message. As Fox and Thompson show, speakers are quite sensitive to the listeners' needs. They ground an NP only once and only when there is a need to do so.

Many other syntactic phenomena are amenable to an explanation at the discourse level. Two of them are word order and dislocation. The overarching principle is that speakers intend to create certain effects by deviating from so-called default patterns. These deviations extend the basic repertoire of rules and thus create a tension in the syntactic system. Rules which used to have a pragmatic function may develop into syntactic rules. This may be taken as evidence for the claim that an area as abstract as syntax is open to pragmatic influences and that, implicationally, pragmatics provides one valuable account of linguistic structure.

2.7. The Sociocultural Approach

There is no question that language is a sociocultural reality. It emanates from and regulates the interactions among members of a social group. The social embeddedness of language makes the sociocultural approach a prima facie candidate for explanation. The functions of organizing social relationships and of serving the needs of speakers as social beings are likely to make an impact upon the form of language. It will be shown below that non-linguistic influences permeate the whole linguistic system. Only a few examples can be selected from the vast array of relevant material.

Let us begin with a brief look at address systems. More often than not, languages code the intimacy between speaker and listener in their personal pronoun systems. A formal distinction is made between an intimate *you* and a non-intimate *you*, e.g. *du–Sie* in German and *tu–usted* in Spanish. Because English has no such distinction it has to resort to other means, in particular names and titles. Varying degrees of intimacy are expressed when somebody is addressed as *Bill, Mr Clinton*, or *Mr President*. The existence of these linguistic differences is readily explained in social-psychological terms. Human beings are filled with anti-egalitarian desires. They do not want to treat everybody alike, nor do they want to be treated alike by everybody. They prefer to express, maintain, or create closeness or distance *vis-à-vis* their interlocutors through the use of appropriate address terms. Thus the way speakers organize their social relationships may qualify as an explanation of language structure and use.

The anti-egalitarian force is to some degree part of the cultural heritage. This may be inferred from the fact that languages differ widely in the extent to which the intimacy dimension is incorporated. Japanese and Korean, for example, have fairly elaborate address systems. On the view that language is a reflection of extralinguistic reality, it may be claimed that social inequality is one aspect that has to be taken into account in the explanation of language structure.

A very close bond between cultural norms and language is assumed by what might be labelled 'ideological linguistics', such as marxist or feminist approaches. A particularly clear example of the latter kind has been submitted by Hellinger (1990), who is concerned with the historical development of the morphological marking of gender in the German language. She draws a distinction between symmetrical and asymmetrical coding, the former being represented by two different suffixes for the masculine and the feminine form and the latter by a feminine form which is created by attaching a suffix to the (affixless) masculine form. Hellinger asserts that, during the Old High German period, a shift from a basically symmetrical to an asymmetrical coding of gender occurred. Her explanation is of particular relevance in the present connection. She claims that society underwent Christianization, in the course of which women lost their former rights and independence. The inferior status to which women were allegedly relegated was conducive to a restructuring of the morphological system. The male-dependent status of women in society was paralleled by masculine-dependent morphological marking in language.

We are not concerned here with the veracity of this account (but see Berg, 1992d). What matters more in the present context is the extremely close link that is established between language and society. To be more precise, dominance relationships between social groups (males and females) are presumed to mould the structure of the language, i.e. to entail dominance relationships in one of the 'innermost' layers of language, viz. the morphological system.

Another example of the assumed susceptibility of morphology to extralinguistic influences is provided by Braunmüller (1984). He develops the notable hypothesis that there is a causal link between morphological opacity and the isolation of a linguistic community. The less the contact of a given community with the rest of the world, the greater the likelihood that its morphology is complex. As support for his claim, Braunmüller refers to Icelandic, Faroese, and North Frisian, all of which are 'linguistic islands' with a rich and complex morphological structure. By contrast, 'geographically larger' languages such as Dutch, English, and Danish have a less complex morphology because their speakers have constantly entertained exchanges with other nations. The underlying logic of Braunmüller's conjecture is that successful communication with other communities presupposes a language that is not too difficult for foreigners to learn. Differently put, it is its function as a means of communication *between* (not within) linguistic communities which ensures that a language does not become immensely complicated. No matter whether Braunmüller's claim is right or wrong, it is outstanding in the directness of the link that is assumed to hold between morphological patterns and the geopolitical situation of a particular speech community. It is certainly rewarding to seek such links, but to establish them requires very thorough investigation.

Even phonology has been claimed to be sensitive to social parameters. Trudgill (1974) reports that in Gros Ventre, an Amerindian language, men use palatalized dental stops in positions where women produce palatalized velar stops. For example, *bread* is /djatsa/ in male speech but /kjatsa/ in female speech. Women and men can therefore be said to possess (partially) different phonemic systems. The sex of the speaker determines (in part) the phonological system.

Of course, the link to the sex of the speaker qualifies only as a first step towards an explanation. The next step involves recourse to the history of the language. A plausible diachronic explanation for the sex-based difference is that at some time in the past women and men had the same phonemic system and that a change from /kj/ to /dj/ took place, a change which was carried through by men though not by women. The latter thus use an 'archaic' sound. This account naturally precipitates the question of how it was possible for the sound change to respect the 'sex boundary' so neatly. We are thus led back to the social dimension of the problem. The sensitivity of the change to the sex variable may be taken as an indication of a strict segregation of the two sexes in Gros Ventre society. Another point that calls for an explanation is why women appear to be more conservative in their speech than men. This phenomenon has to do with social stereotypes and differing conceptions of prestige between the two sexes (see e.g. Trudgill, 1972 and below).

A further aspect of the anti-egalitarian drive in human beings is their struggle for prestige. Speaking a certain linguistic variant may be regarded as desirable because this variant is spoken by certain people who are associated with social values such as affluence and power. What is and what is not regarded as prestigious—both linguistically and extralinguistically—is highly variable and difficult to predict. One factor that appears to play a role in this game is frequency. The desire to be different from others implies behaving in the way of a *minority* group. If one behaved like the majority group, one would hardly be recognized as different. It is therefore necessary to pick out and cultivate a characteristic trait that is not often found. These traits then become markers of a specific group of people.

An example from language is the deliberate, though not necessarily conscious, use of a particular phoneme that has fallen or is about to fall into disuse. Such a case has been documented by Henton (1990), who examined the pronunciation of /ʌ/ in three English dialects (Received Pronunciation, Northern British English, and West Coast American English). In the course of her study, she discovered an interesting paradox. On the one hand, this vowel is highly unstable. Its pronunciation is subject to enormous variation, covering almost completely the lower part of the quadrilateral. Acoustic analyses indicated that /ʌ/ has a low auditory distinctiveness in that it is very similar to neighbouring vowels such as /ə/ and /ɑ/. In particular, /ʌ/ is remarkably close to schwa in terms of its F1 value. These factors would suggest that /ʌ/ will sooner or later disappear from the English phoneme system (and explain its cross-linguistic rarity). On the other hand, this vowel is still alive in RP and regularly used by female speakers of the northern variety of British English. Henton interprets these results in sociolinguistic terms. She argues that /ʌ/ is a prestige-carrier because it functions as one of the distinguishing features of the prestigious RP. In agreement with many other studies, she goes on to claim that women tend more towards the standard language than men. How culture- and region-specific sociolinguistic attitudes are can be seen from the finding that /ʌ/ does not seem to be a prestige factor in the US. This explains why /ʌ/ is more susceptible to merging with vowels such as schwa in West Coast American English.

What is so noteworthy about this outcome is that sociolinguistic influences may be antithetical to phonetic principles, i.e. they may induce phonetically 'unnatural' developments or prevent phonetically 'natural' ones from taking place (see Kroch 1978). Prestige factors thus introduce a seemingly arbitrary element into the game, but nevertheless qualify as genuine explanations. The adherence to certain sociolinguistic norms turns out to be one major determinant of language structure. In the present instance, the adherence to different norms explains the (partially) different phoneme systems of male and female speakers of Northern British English.[10]

The domain where the influence of the outside world is most easily perceived is the lexicon. The lexical level is the primary locus at which non-linguistic concepts and linguistic forms make contact (see section 2.4). Which concepts are relevant depends upon the values in a society and the environment in which its members live. The more relevant a concept is to a given community, the more likely it is to be lexicalized (Bybee 1985). Obviously, a religious people will have a more elaborate terminology for religious matters than a heathen or atheistic community. While this may sound trivial, it is not at all trivial to gauge the impact of the outside world upon the lexicon. In any case, the general approach is that the structure of the lexicon can be explained by the structure of the outside world as perceived and construed by human beings in social settings.

An area where the sociolinguistic approach unfolds its explanatory potential most forcefully is historical linguistics. The claim that a social change may entail a linguistic change can be nicely illustrated by another look at address terms. Brown and Gilman (1960) traced the semantic evolution of intimate and non-intimate *you* in Indo-European languages. Their study revealed an interesting change in the meaning and use of these address terms. Well into the nineteenth century, the choice of the appropriate form was determined by the power relationship between the speaker and the listener. When the speaker perceived the listener as more powerful than him- or herself, the non-intimate form was used. The same form was used, for example, by children addressing their parents. However, when the listener was perceived as less powerful, the intimate form was chosen, for example the customer in a restaurant on addressing the waiter. This system gradually changed in the last century. The power semantic gave way to a solidarity semantic: that is to say, the intimate form was preferred when the speaker wished to express a solidarity relationship to the listener. Accordingly, the use of the intimate form spread within the family or at work.

Brown and Gilman attribute this development to cultural and structural changes in western European society. The power semantic was abandoned because it reflected social values such as power as birthright which had been called into question

---

[10] The reason why women and men tend to gravitate towards different norms would involve another course of study.

(cf. the French Revolution). A new set of values emerged in which equality and reciprocity came to play a major part. Additionally, social mobility increased, with the result that relationships had to be negotiated on the spot.[11] This change of social values is considered instrumental in bringing about the change in language. Therefore, the sociolinguistic approach has an explanatory quality.

The sociocultural approach is a very pervasive factor whose importance can hardly be overestimated. It affects not only the lexicon but all other levels of linguistic analysis where its influence may at first glance seem less obvious. Phonological as well as morphological patterns may function as social markers. This link between linguistic and social features proves critical in elucidating the causes of language change. The interaction among members of a society, the interaction of members from different linguistic communities (dialect or language mixture), status change, and changes in the value system all create a dynamics which precludes the possibility of language coming to a standstill. Social change thus provides a powerful explanation for language change.

2.8. The Historical Approach

To understand the present presupposes understanding how it evolved from the past, so it is said. Indeed, the past is a precondition for the present in that any development that has led to the present had its starting-point in the past. The banality of these remarks disappears once it is realized that a development cannot be viewed independently of the state on which it operates, i.e. which it changes. A certain development may probably only take place if a number of antecedent conditions are met. When these properties are lacking, the development will in all probability not take place. Similarly, the nature of the antecedent conditions may determine the direction that a certain development takes. Consequently, the effect of one and the same force need not be identical when applied to different historical states. The resolution of a conflict between antagonistic forces may vary in accordance with the biases introduced by language-particular constellations. Given this, the point of departure of a change is of utmost importance in understanding the development that led to a subsequent (e.g. present) state.

On the other hand, reference to a previous state can only be a very incomplete explanation. Strictly speaking, it says nothing about the causes of a development. It can only contribute to explaining the course a development has followed. This puts the explanatory potential of the historical approach in a more modest light than is usually found in the literature. A noteworthy example is Givón (1971), who defends the view that yesterday's syntax is today's morphology, i.e. morphological patterns derive diachronically from syntactic ones. The dynamics of syntax thus explains the genesis of morphology. In particular, Givón maintains that the order of affixal

---

[11] Eventually, this change of values might even lead to the elimination of the distinction between intimate and non-intimate pronouns, a development spearheaded by English.

morphology is a historical reflex of the order of syntactic elements. In various languages, verbs developed into affixes. If the formerly independent verb preceded its complement, Givón argues, it will appear as a prefix. If, by contrast, it followed its complement at the syntactic stage, it will appear as a suffix at the morphological stage. Succinctly put, constituent order is preserved during the change.

An example may serve to illustrate this claim. English may place negation affixes before and after the stem. Typically, they appear as prefixes such as *in-* and *un-* before adjectives and verbs (e.g. *infelicitous, to undo*). However, one also finds the negative suffix *-less* after nouns (e.g. *careless*). Givón explains the disparate positioning of the negation marker with reference to the different positioning of the corresponding free-standing elements at an earlier stage. The suffix *-less* derives from a verb (*to lose*), and refers back to Proto-Germanic times, when the verb appeared after its complement in the VP. On the other hand, the negative prefixes are the historical remnants of free-standing negation particles which used to precede the verb.

Givón (1971: 394, 397) asserts that his claims not only explain the rise of morphology but also 'fully' explain the order of morphemes. However, neither claim can be upheld in its strong form. In the first instance, the rise of morphology is not explained at all by Givón's model. His paper identifies some constraints on linguistic change but does not address its underlying motivation. It transpires, then, that the mere recourse to historical states does not qualify as an explanation.

In the second instance, it is not true that the morphological order is 'fully' explained by earlier syntactic order. However plausible it may sound, it is a potential explanation at best. It would be natural to expect that a given change respects the rules of the language to a maximum degree (except of course for the one that undergoes the change). Changes cannot be expected to be 'chaotic' because the linguistic system continues to fulfil its communicative function even during the period of change. The appeal to communicative needs brings us closer to an explanation. The preservation of constituent order may be accounted for on the assumption that changes are of a local kind and do not involve more than is necessary so as to avoid communication breakdown. This account has to be buttressed by two other theories—a linguistic as well as a psycholinguistic theory about the independence of elements and relations (to come to grips with the fact that the morphological or syntactic status of a unit may change independently of a particular ordering relation). Additionally, a processing account is needed to explicate why cross-level harmony in the ordering of constituents is favoured. Last but not least, a crucial aspect of Givón's theory is a diachronic change of constituent order at the same level. A comprehensive account would therefore also have to explicate under which conditions a change of constituent order may or may not take place.

The inherent limitation of historical accounts can also be seen in the following example, which is explicitly offered as an explanation. Bybee (1988) addresses the cross-linguistic observation that the future tense is rarely used to signal pure future sense but often develops modal meanings such as desire and obligation. The reason why futurity and modality are both carried by one grammatical marker is, according to Bybee, a diachronic one. She argues that the future-tense markers of Modern English originate from lexical material that carried such meanings as desire and obligation. The loss of the lexical status of these items did not entail the loss of their original meaning. However, it paved the way for the development of future time reference. The disappearance of some semantic features loosened the co-occurrence restrictions and led to a more general meaning, that of futurity. As the older meanings were not dispensed with, futurity did not emerge in a 'pure' form; rather, it is a new function overlaid by older functions. This diachronic development is claimed to be universally valid.

Bybee's account is valuable in that it shows how diachronic developments serve to elucidate synchronic states. In the case at hand, the synchronic state is explained by the hypothesis that futurity is a relatively recent dimension which fails to suppress the older meanings. However, like all historical accounts, this one leaves unaddressed (among others) the following important questions: Why should futurity be a relatively late achievement of human languages? Why does the futurity sense fail to eliminate the modality senses? Will this elimination happen some time in the future? If not, why is this principally impossible? Is this account really valid for all languages? Moreover, alternative accounts, in particular a cognitive one, have to be considered. It is not unreasonable to assume that languages do not keep modality and futurity apart just because speakers cannot do so. On this hypothesis, human beings are unable to conceptualize futurity without their personal involvement, which may take the form of desire, intention and the like. If humans have no other way of coming to grips with the elusive concept of futurity, it is no surprise that languages do not code futurity independent of modality.

In conclusion, the assessment of the import of the historical approach appears somewhat ambivalent. On the one hand, it is a yardstick for all accounts of synchronic phenomena. These accounts stand and fall on the criterion of whether the diachronic development is compatible with them. On the other hand, reference to a historical development is insufficient as an explanation of a given fact. It should always be asked why a certain development follows one path rather than another and why it took place at all. These questions lead from history to sociology, psychology, and other areas. Hence, it is only in conjunction with these fields that the historical approach deploys its explanatory power.

2.9. The System-Internal Approach

Given that language is standardly construed as a system of (sub)systems, the possibility arises of explaining one subsystem in terms of another. In this section, attention will be focused upon the two most basic subsystems of language, form and meaning. The question thus is: can aspects of form be explained by aspects of meaning and vice versa? It has repeatedly been claimed that form can be explained in terms of meaning. Whether meaning can be explained by form is a most controversial issue that goes by the name of the Sapir–Whorf hypothesis. In this section we will limit ourselves to discussing the influence of meaning on form.

The general conjecture holds that aspects of form, whether they are of the phonological, morphological, or syntactic kind, are a more or less direct reflection of aspects of meaning. Let us briefly look at some lines of evidence in support of this claim. The first highlights one of the most general form/meaning relationships one might imagine: one meaning unit should generate one and only one formal unit. The unitary concept BIRD should be rendered by a unitary formal unit, here the morpheme *bird*. This principle is at its clearest in contrasts like *blackboard* vs. *black board*, which code one or two concepts, respectively. The pervasiveness of this principle is particularly apparent from the exceptional status of discontinuous elements which express one meaning unit by means of two independent formal units which may be intercalated. The phrasal verbs in English are a case in point (e.g. *Can you put us up for the night?*).

Interesting implications of this rather trivial-sounding one form/one meaning principle have been sounded out by Haiman (1983). He defends the claim that the linguistic distance between two expressions reflects their conceptual distance. Linguistic distance is measured by the depth of the cleft between two units. Depth 1 would involve a morpheme boundary, depth 2 a word boundary, and depth 3 an intervening word. Conceptual distance is roughly a function of the semantic similarity between the two units. An example from English may suffice, although stronger support for Haiman's claim comes from morphologically richer languages. The verb *to kill* has a depth 0 and *to cause to die* a depth 2 level. Haiman argues that this difference in formal distance matches the semantic distance between the two expressions. The single morpheme *to kill* codes a unitary concept in which cause and result are inextricably welded. By contrast, this is not so in *to cause to die*, where cause and result may be separated in place as well as time. The implications are slightly different in (19) and (20).

(19) The prisoner killed the guardian.
(20) The prisoner caused the guardian to die.

The notion of conceptual distance has been made more explicit by Bybee (1985). She introduces the concept of 'relevance', by which she refers to the extent to which the semantics of one unit is affected or modified by the semantics of another unit. Bybee argues that the degree of relevance is an index of the probability of lexicalization. The more relevant two meaning units are to each other, the more likely they are to be coded as one form unit. Take the contrast between *to walk with an injured leg* and *to walk with an injured arm*. The first expression is lexicalized (*to limp*) while the second is not. Bybee's explanation would be that the injured leg is highly relevant to the manner of motion in that it directly affects, if not interferes with, the act of walking. The injured arm, however, is completely irrelevant in upright gait. This conceptual distance prevents the two ideas from merging into one formal unit.

The impact of semantics makes itself felt not only at the lexical but also at the morphosyntactic level (see also Hawkins 1988). As Keenan (1979) observed, there are pervasive form/meaning dependency relationships in natural languages. Take the example of adjectives which may agree with nouns (e.g. in terms of number and gender) but not vice versa. In Dutch, the suffix -*e* is required on adjectives that modify non-neuter nouns (e.g. *groene stoel* 'green chair') but does not appear on adjectives that modify neuter nouns (e.g. *groen bed* 'green bed'). Keenan's account of this asymmetry is based upon the asymmetrical relationship in the semantics of the noun and the adjective. The meaning of the noun is relatively constant, i.e. independent of the adjective by which it is accompanied. However, the meaning of the adjective is rather variable, i.e. dependent upon the particular noun it accompanies. A road is a road irrespective of whether it is dusty, flat, or winding. In contrast, *flat* takes on different meanings when it is associated with *tyres*, *voices*, or *roads*. Thus, semantic dominance is mirrored by morphosyntactic dominance.

The above examples show that the pairing of sound and meaning is not wholly arbitrary. Rather, it embodies iconic aspects. Can iconicity, then, be taken as an explanatory principle of language form? It is true that iconicity establishes a link between two conceptually separate components (i.e. form and meaning) and hence meets one criterion of what counts as an explanation. In addition, this approach enjoys some aprioristic plausibility, because it makes intuitive sense that the translation from meaning into form should be 'content-preserving' to some degree. However, while the quest for iconicity is a valuable strategy, it is not a self-sufficient concept. Iconicity is the product of certain constraints on the translation from meaning to sound in language production (and secondarily from sound to meaning in language comprehension). This translation is a psychological process and can therefore be adequately captured only in a psycholinguistic framework. That is to say, iconicity unfolds its full explanatory power when viewed against a psycholinguistic background. Unfortunately, a psycholinguistic theory of iconicity is not in the offing (but see section 4.14). To the extent that such a theory is lacking, it will be difficult actually to predict at which point iconicity ends and arbitrariness takes over.

The system-internal approach, as highlighted by the principle of iconicity, goes some way towards explanation. However, it cannot stand on its own if a deeper level of explanation is sought. This amounts to the claim that the system-internal approach is only a first step in the right direction. To reach a fuller understanding, it has to be transcended by interpreting the linguistic construct (here iconicity) in non-linguistic (i.e. psycholinguistic) terms.

2.10. Conclusion

The first issue to be addressed is the relationship among the approaches discussed above. If all approaches covered different territory, they could be said to stand in a complementary relationship. There would then be no point in pitting one against another. However, the preceding discussion suggests a certain overlap in empirical coverage. Two different kinds of competition were found. The individual accounts may provide alternative explanations for the same phenomenon. This rather common state of affairs can be illustrated by the problem of repeated use of identical linguistic units. While MacKay (1970a) favoured a neurological explanation, Menn and MacWhinney (1984) favoured a psychological one. The two accounts are by no means mutually exclusive: it could well be that one is correct and the other incorrect, but it is also possible that they are equally valid. For example, the one might reinforce the other.

The second kind of competition is less often remarked upon but certainly no less important than the first. One account may be antithetical to another. Both affect the same phenomenon though with opposite effects. Which outcome prevails depends upon the relative strength of the rival approaches. A relevant example from the above review is the fate of /ʌ/. Its development is concurrently determined by phonetic and social factors. As noted before, /ʌ/ is a phonetically unstable sound. This instability is counteracted by its status as a prestige marker which invigorates it (at least in certain walks of life). This is a case of phonetic unnaturalness being overridden by social factors.

To conclude, the relationship among the various approaches is characterized by *both* complementariness and competition. In spite of an enormous disparity among the approaches and despite their basic irreducibility, there are empirical phenomena at which even diverse approaches may 'meet'. These meeting points allow us to examine the strength of individual effects and their intricate interaction.

However, before the issue of interaction can be seriously addressed, it is imperative to know as much as possible about the overall contribution of each single approach. Obviously, the importance of all approaches cannot be assessed here. It is therefore not possible to avoid imposing restrictions upon the analysis. For several reasons, it was decided to focus upon the psycholinguistic approach. First, it is comprehensive in the sense that it potentially bears upon all levels of linguistic analysis. For instance, syntax may be as amenable to it as phonology. Secondly, the psycholinguistic approach is basic in the sense that it shares territory with other non-psycholinguistic approaches. As noted, much of what the semiotic approach claims is also covered by the psycholinguistic one. Thirdly, the psycholinguistic approach has a certain a priori plausibility because speaking and listening, as psychological activities, are so fundamental to language that productive and perceptual processes are likely to exert an influence upon the information to be processed.

How can an individual approach be isolated and its impact best be assessed? As shown in the preceding sections, most previous work (with the notable exception of Hawkins 1994) has been dominated by the following methodological principle: first uncover a linguistic pattern and then find an explanation for it. Although standard practice, this post hoc procedure suffers from a serious deficiency. There are an enormous number of areas from which it may be possible to develop candidate explanations. The researcher is free to choose whichever area suits the linguistic data best, in the hope that some kind of match between data and theory can be effected. The problem with this strategy is that the selection of the area from which the explanation is taken is an unprincipled one. The link between explanans and explanandum must remain tenuous. What one would like to know is whether one particular approach can do better than account for individual cases for which alternative explanations are almost always conceivable. This calls for a more systematic analysis of the relevance of a given approach than can be afforded by the standard methodology.

This kind of eclecticism is found not only in the selection of a particular discipline but also within the discipline itself. When the help of psycholinguistics is sought, recourse is taken not to comprehensive theories but to individual processing principles. The problem is that, like any other branch of science, psycholinguistics is a heterogeneous and multifaceted discipline. Psycholinguistic theories may be informed by data from various subject groups with various levels of competence engaging in various tasks from various domains. A given processing principle need not be germane to all facets of psycholinguistics alike. So whenever reference is made to individual processing principles, it should be established that the one principle invoked is not contradicted by another.

The dangers of eclecticism can be partly avoided by moving from individual processing principles to more comprehensive theories in which these processing principles form a coherent set. The crux is that there are a number of competing psycholinguistic models on offer, and it is not a foregone conclusion which one is most adequate. Obviously, the selection of the 'best' model is critical. Let us imagine a situation in which a given linguistic pattern is 'explained' by a processing account which itself rests upon shaky foundations (cf. Cutler et al.'s (1985) account of the suffixing preference). The immediate consequence would of course be that the processing principle invoked cannot be claimed to provide an explanation of the phenomenon in question. A further consequence would be that it is not justifiable to argue that psycholinguistics in general is not a viable candidate for the explanation of linguistic data. The strength of the impact of psycholinguistics upon linguistics can be reliably gauged only if the psycholinguistically most adequate model is selected. Needless to say, there is no agreement in the literature over which model is the best.

The following chapter on methodology will deal with each of these problems in turn. Section 3.1 lays out the general procedure that will be adopted; section 3.2 introduces the processing model underlying the present work; section 3.3 motivates the choice of psycholinguistic data that are most likely to have a bearing upon language structure.

3

Method

3.1. Prediction Instead of Post Hoc Explanation

As argued in the preceding chapter, the link between the explanans and the explanandum is weakened by the fact that students of language are free to take their explanation from any area that appears suitable to them. The connection between language and the extralinguistic world would be more compelling if this freedom were curtailed by restricting the pool of possible explanations to a single area, viz. psycholinguistics. This restriction should make it possible to gauge more precisely the contribution that language processing can make to the explanation of linguistic structure. While this procedure by no means negates the importance of other disciplines, it focuses upon only one in an attempt to ascertain how far this one takes us. Implicationally, interactions among various disciplines have to be ignored.

A second modification concerns the direction of analysis. Whereas previous investigations moved from linguistic patterns to extralinguistic explanations, the present study moves from extralinguistic (i.e. processing) patterns to language structure. This reversal of direction is reflected in a change of terminology. Linguistic facts are no longer explained post hoc but predicted. The basic assumption is that it is possible to derive predictions about language structure from processing principles. If these predictions are borne out, a particular linguistic structure may be said to be explainable in terms of these processing principles. Importantly, this explanation is different in kind from the conventional one. The explanation-by-prediction is not post hoc.

Three reasons have motivated this innovation, two objective and one subjective. Beginning with the latter, the direction from psycholinguistics to linguistics matches my personal background. My original research interest was in psycholinguistics. With time, it shifted to (or rather broadened to include) the more structural aspects of language. To give a rather drastic example, when I examined psycholinguistic data from Arabic, I discovered that the processing model had implications for the structure of poetic rhymes. I am not ashamed to confess that I did not have the slightest idea of Arabic verse when I formulated the relevant predictions (see section 6.3 for the outcome of this strand of research).

The second reason has already been hinted at above. The explanation-by-prediction is more restrictive in that it reduces the risk that a given account fits a given linguistic pattern by chance. The probability of finding an explanation for a certain phenomenon *somewhere* is not too low, given the wide range of theoretically possible approaches. This freedom certainly involves some degree of fortuitousness. By contrast, the methodological principle adhered to here allows immediate falsification because a prediction cannot eschew its data.[1] It must either be correct or incorrect. Given a null hypothesis, it is possible to get at least some idea of the explanatory potential of one account or rather one set of accounts.

A further advantage of the explanation-by-prediction method is that it invites new analyses of linguistic data. By their post hoc nature, conventional explanations do not add to the stock of empirical data (although they may lead to novel predictions). In contrast, predictions may call for tests that have never been carried out before. They therefore have a value beyond the overall aim of establishing a connection between language structure and language processing. They sharpen the analyst's expectations and may yield new empirical results.

It should be noted that the issue of prediction does not hinge on the novelty of the analysis. An independently derived prediction remains a prediction irrespective of whether the critical test has already been performed. This term thus is not necessarily directed to *future* work. In fact, this slightly more liberal use of the term 'prediction' is common practice. As one example for many others, reference may be made to Liljencrants and Lindblom's (1972) theory of perceptual contrast according to which the vowels should be dispersed in the vowel space so as to be maximally distinct from one another. This phonetic principle leads to clear predictions of the kind: if a language possesses a certain number of vowels, these should include /A, B, and C/. For instance, if a language has three vowels, the theory of perceptual contrast predicts that these are /i, a, u/. Liljencrants and Lindblom tested these predictions against previously published typologies of vowel systems (and found their predictions supported). Their use of the term 'prediction' is justified because the phonetic theory has been devised *independently* of the linguistic data to which it is applied. The same holds good for the present project. The psycholinguistic theory is based upon psycholinguistic evidence, and is consequently conceptually separate from the linguistic patterns for which it is used to generate predictions.

Note, however, that processing models are informed by processing data which may or may not be influenced by the particular structure of a language. It is appropriate therefore to distinguish between two types of prediction. The first type is based upon psycholinguistic data which are truly independent of the domain to which the prediction is applied. A paradigm case is diachronic linguistics. Predictions regarding the historical development of a language cannot be artifactual because they are derived from synchronic data, i.e. from the behaviour of speakers of the language as it is spoken today. By all rules of common sense, these speakers do not walk around with knowledge of Old English or Old High German. The developments that have taken place in a language cannot be assumed to shape the way subjects behave in natural or experimental speaking and listening situations.

---
[1] However, an explanation can eschew the data. If a particular explanation which ought to fit does not work, it is tempting to ignore it and resort to another one.

The second type of prediction cannot claim to be based upon data which are completely independent from those that are to be examined. The data types are clearly different, psycholinguistic in the first case and linguistic in the second. However, the possibility cannot be ruled out that the behavioural data are the way they are because the language is the way it is. Whether or not this is the case is not normally known beforehand, so the relative dependence or independence between the psycholinguistic and the linguistic data has to be established in every single case. When this problem arises, it will be dealt with individually in each analysis as necessary. If an independence can be reasonably established, there will be no problem. But even if a dependence appears possible or likely, the major aim of demonstrating the connection between language structure and language processing is not in jeopardy, as the dependence is itself an argument in favour of this connection.

If this mutual dependence exists, it is futile to look for a starting-point at which processing was uninfluenced by the information to be processed (or vice versa). In view of this state of affairs, the only solution is to tap into the system at some point and see whether an influence of one component upon the other can be demonstrated. For reasons given above, the most promising research strategy seems to be to move from psycholinguistics to linguistics rather than the other way round.

Note that at this point it is an open question whether there is an interaction between language processing and language structure. If a significant influence of one component on the other is found, the interactional hypothesis is indirectly supported. On the other hand, a meagre influence would be more compatible with the non-interactional view. Against this background, an attempt will be made to gauge the impact of processing principles upon language structure.

3.2. The Explanans: Psycholinguistic Patterns

3.2.1. *The psycholinguistic model*

The procedure that will be applied throughout this work is to derive predictions from psycholinguistic evidence and test them against linguistic data. The psycholinguistic evidence may be theoretical as well as empirical. Ideally, theoretical and empirical arguments go together and reinforce each other, but clearly not all pieces of psycholinguistic evidence are equally well supported from the theoretical and the empirical side. What pieces of psycholinguistic evidence have been selected for the present study? The main criterion for inclusion was whether the psycholinguistic evidence allows the formulation of predictions as to linguistic structure in a relatively direct way. The bulk of this evidence is empirical because empirical data are generally more robust than theoretical claims, which tend to change over time. Many though certainly not all of these lines of empirical evidence have been taken as support for one theoretical framework known as the interactive activation model (Stemberger 1985b; Dell 1986; MacKay 1987). The other lines which have not been interpreted within this framework are at least not incompatible with it.

In the following, the interactive activation model will be described in broad outline. More detailed aspects will be mentioned as appropriate for the individual analyses. Since the primary objective of this work is not a psycholinguistic one, no attempt will be made to defend this processing model against its competitors. Let it simply be said that this model has been selected because it furnishes (in my opinion) a more powerful, explicit, and fine-grained account of a wide range of psycholinguistic data than any other model at present available.

Interactive activation models form part of a larger class of so-called local connectionist approaches. One fundamental insight of connectionism is that a single network can function as a representational as well as processing system. It thus represents a hypothesis not only about the organization and storage of linguistic knowledge but also about how this knowledge is put to use. The network consists of only two primitives—nodes and connections. In local connectionist models, each node represents a linguistic unit such as a phoneme or an idiom. These nodes may be of varying kinds. Nodes of the same kind are organized in one layer. We may therefore distinguish a phoneme and a feature layer, for example. The layers themselves are hierarchically arranged, with the phoneme layer being superordinate to the feature layer. This arrangement reflects the hierarchical organization of language. The individual nodes are linked via connections. For instance, the word node for *beat* connects to the phoneme node /b/. In this way, the part/whole relation which is so characteristic of language is expressed. A node may be conceived of as a junction of connections. For example, the lexical link from *beat* and the featural link from [bilabial] converge on the /b/ node. Each linguistic unit is represented only once. That is, there is only one node for /b/, which subserves all words in the lexicon that contain it. Links may be either excitatory or inhibitory. Links between units at the same layer are always of the latter kind (e.g. /b/ inhibits /p/), while links between units from different layers are always of the former kind (e.g. *beat* excites /b/). The connections between network nodes are of variable strength, depending upon such factors as frequency. For example, the connections from a frequent word to its constituents at the phoneme layer are stronger than those from an infrequent word to its phonemes.

Processing is instantiated by 'energy' that is spread through the network along the hard-wired connections. In speaking, the energy originates within the conceptual system, whereas in listening it is the acoustic signal which causes the network to 'vibrate'. Depending upon the pathways along which the energy travels, the information may be excitatory or inhibitory in nature. The former case is called activation, the latter inhibition. The effect of passing activation from node A to node B is that the availability of node B is enhanced. Inversely, inhibitory information reaching node B entails a reduction of its availability. The amount of information that is spread through the system depends upon two main factors, the initial activation and the linkage strength. Each node represents the beginning and end of many connections. Its activation value is therefore multiply influenced, in that it is determined by the summation of all the positive and negative information that accumulates on the node at any given point in time.

The information that arrives at a given node is immediately passed on to all its neighbours. Some models assume a minimum activation value that a node has to attain in order to be able to forward activation. In any case, a node need not reach its activational maximum before it can pass on information. The net effect of this principle is a basically parallel information flow. Because the spread of activation from one level to another occurs faster than the build-up of activation on a node, every node may be simultaneously influenced by many different sources. For example, a higher node not only activates a lower node but is also activated by it. That is, both top-down and bottom-up information contribute to a processing decision. From the perspective of production, the former is called *feedforward*, the latter *feedback*. Feedback always produces weaker effects than feedforward. Parallelness and feedback go hand in hand because on-line feedback is one of the ways in which parallelness is instantiated.

Speech is a sequential activity. The basically parallel information flow thus has to be turned into a predominantly serial one. Serialization is the province of syntax. The problem of serial order arises at various levels. Hence we need a syntax for words, a syntax for morphemes, and a syntax for phonemes. The notion of syntax in psycholinguistics is thus broader than in linguistics. It includes not only the so-called creative aspects (i.e. word order) but also the so-called non-creative aspects (i.e. the fixed order of phonemes in a word) of language. The serial-ordering mechanism is separate but not independent from the information to be serialized. For example, the syntax of words and the lexicon interact, in that the word choice affects the selection of the appropriate sentence structure and vice versa. Sequentialization is effected by inspecting the activation pattern at a given level at a certain point in time and selecting the node which is most highly activated. This process is repeated at regular intervals. For the production of the word *tip*, for instance, three selection procedures, one for each phoneme, would be needed. At t_1, the alveolar stop is selected, the vowel at t_2, and the bilabial at t_3. The activation pattern thus changes with every new phoneme to be outputted.

To a certain extent, perception is the reverse of production. The acoustic signal reaching the listener is inherently sequential. The listener's task is to transform the sequential percept into a parallel representation, with the final result that a certain set of conceptual nodes is activated. To this end, the dynamic system has to settle in a stable state. This means that all relevant nodes are activated and all irrelevant ones inhibited. The system has stabilized when the activation pattern at t_{n-1} is identical to that at t_n. Comprehension is based upon such a constellation of active nodes.

The final stage in production is the conversion of the activation pattern in the mental network into action. Nodes are commonly assumed to have an upper threshold. Only when this activation threshold is exceeded is a unit available for selection. However, selection is not tantamount to action. Therefore, it is necessary to posit a further, neuromotor stage at which production is instantiated. Generally, connectionist models have little to say about this interface because their focus is upon the abstract psychological rather than upon the concrete motor processes.

Connectionist networks also have a learning component, i.e. they are subject to modification over time. Knowledge is coded in the strengths or weights of the linkages among nodes. We know that the word *boy* begins with a /b/ because there is a strong permanent connection between the two nodes. These linkages may change their weights, and indeed this is the way learning in childhood is standardly conceptualized in these models. There are two basic learning procedures—supervised and unsupervised learning—but the details need not concern us here. What matters more is that the system is principally malleable enough not only to move from a less perfect into a more perfect state in children but also to move from one 'perfect' state into another equally perfect state in adults (though the latter change has not yet received a great deal of attention in the relevant literature).

It should be stressed that connectionist models are psychological in that they draw exclusively upon evidence from learning, production, and perception. Despite the fact that they are inspired by neurological theory, their primary objective is not to capture a neurological reality. Thus, the terms 'activation' and 'inhibition' are here used as abstract, metaphorical concepts. Whether and how they translate into neurophysiological mechanisms is an important question but irrelevant to the present argument.

As noted above, no attempt will be made to compare rival models of language processing. However, to the extent that the predictions from the connectionist model are borne out by the structure of language, this type of model receives additional support and may thus be argued to be superior to its competitors.

3.2.2. *The psycholinguistic evidence*

The empirical data upon which psycholinguistic models rely are varied in nature. It is therefore incumbent on me to examine which data types are most germane to the issue of language structure. At first glance one might be led to believe that all data are equally useful, but this is not so. The permanent form of language is unlikely to be shaped to the same extent by all types of language user or by all modalities in which language may be realized. Let us begin with the former.

The subjects in psycholinguistic investigations fall into three main categories— children, adults, and aphasics. Although all of them have contributed extensively to psycholinguistic theory, their relevance to understanding the structure of language varies considerably. I submit that the source of information that is most likely to make a significant impact upon linguistic structure is adult language processing. The evidence from aphasics may be neglected not only because of the language they speak but also because of their inferior social status. Disordered language is by definition regarded as deficient (and in need of therapy) and does not therefore act as a model that others might wish to emulate. If the linguistic deficit is taken to reflect a cognitive deficit, the chances of an influence are even less. And these chances are nil if the disorder is so severe that the patients are cut off from 'normal' communicative activities.

The case of child language is more difficult to assess. Quite a few authors (e.g. Paul 1880; Baron 1977; Stampe 1969) hold the view that children are instrumental in bringing about language change. The rationale is that problems arise in the transmission of linguistic knowledge from one generation to the next. Young learners may refuse to accept an established form and may replace it by one which is more congenial to them. If their innovation finds its way into the adult language, it may in turn replace the established form and effect a linguistic change. A classic example is the regularization of past tenses. As is well known, children tend to overgeneralize the regular past-tense ending and apply it to irregular verbs (e.g. *he goed*). A parallel development is found in language history. The ratio of regular to irregular verbs has shifted towards the former over time (see section 5.16). Is it possible to argue on the basis of this similarity that the historical change was caused by children? The answer is probably no. Children can cause a change only if the adults approve of it. Whether they approve or disapprove depends upon how congenial the change is to them. Hence, there is reason to believe that children's biases can only take effect if adults share the same biases. In this case, however, it is questionable whether the children are the causal agents of the change any more so than the adults.[2] Given that both these populations may be responsible for linguistic change, it is desirable to know whether both contribute equally to the change or whether one of them is more decisive than the other.

In fact, Bybee and Slobin (1982b) tried to tease out the influences of the two populations upon language change. They elicited morphological errors from children of various age levels as well as from adults, and compared these errors with the historical record. They found that the adult data matched the diachronic development more closely than did the child data. The young children's errors were best characterized as being shaped by universal constraints upon high-level and low-level processing, whereas the older children's and the adults' innovations were more clearly the manifestation of language-particular influences. Since language change is most usually language-particular change, the tendencies in the elder groups of subjects are more relevant to diachronic developments than are those in young children. Our focus will therefore be upon the behaviour of healthy adults.

As regards the visual and aural modes, the latter will be given priority in this study. This decision is based upon the time-honoured tradition of viewing oral language as primary and written language as derived. This is true both ontogenetically and phylogenetically. Children acquire oral language before written language, and so did *homo loquens*. Written language is a means of representing the fleeting oral word in more permanent fashion. Language change takes place in the spoken

---

[2] A very similar argument holds at the phonological level. The parallels between child language and diachronic change at this level are too high in number and too specific in kind to be attributable to chance. However, this does not justify the postulation of a causal link. As argued by Clumeck (1979) and Greenlee and Ohala (1980), these parallels are to be expected given that adults and children share the same phonetic apparatus. Note that there are also plenty of phonological differences between child language and diachronic change (e.g. Drachman 1978; Vihman 1980).

medium and sooner or later enters the written medium. The other way around appears only as a remote possibility. Therefore, it is justified to consider the processing of oral language a more reliable predictor of language structure and change than the written language.[3] This is almost certainly true of the pre-Caxtonian time, when the written language was accessible to only a very select group of people. Nowadays, the situation has to be reassessed. With virtually everybody being exposed to written language and with the written modality as a principal means of standardizing the language, it would be preposterous to exclude the written modality as a relevant factor in language change. Also, it cannot be ruled out that the written language may make an impact upon the processing of oral language. However, since the acquisition of written language usually takes place well after the oral language has been mastered, a dramatic reorganization of the processor appears unlikely. It may be concluded, then, that oral-language processing is a more probable source of information for understanding language structure and change than written-language processing; but this is not to deny that the latter may play a more minor role.

There is no sense in which production is primary and perception secondary or vice versa. Both are essential ingredients of the communication process. This is most evident in language change, which is impossible to conceive without either the speaker or the listener. An innovation has to be made by a speaker and 'accepted' by a listener. As long as perceptual and productive principles concur, there is no need to argue the primacy of one or the other. Similarly, when the productive system introduces a bias while the perceptual system remains neutral (or vice versa), there is nothing to worry about. However, in case of a conflict between these principles a decision is called for. It is unlikely that this decision can be taken once and for all; there are different kinds of conflict, with varying strengths of the competing forces. It might be thought that the speaker and the listener are equally important. On the one hand, perception might be held to outweigh production because the hearer has to confirm the change introduced by the speaker. When the former 'vetoes' the latter's innovation, no change will ever take place. On the other hand, the speaker is the one who materializes an innovation, so the production system may be assumed to be 'closer' to the change. So, whenever possible, both have to be considered in conjunction. Unfortunately, few areas of psycholinguistic research have progressed to a stage where it is possible directly to contrast the impact of the productive and the perceptual system upon a particular issue. Hence, one is often limited to exploring the implications of only one side while ignoring the other in the hope that no contradictory evidence will one day be brought to the fore.

3.3. The Explanandum: Linguistic Patterns

In the preceding sections, the psycholinguistic side has been dealt with. It is now time to take a closer look at the explanandum—linguistic patterns. The question

---

[3] However, this is not to say that the linguistic features of oral and written texts are identical. In fact, they are not equivalent (Biber 1988), but this does not undercut the above analysis.

that immediately arises at this point is: which aspects of language can and should be explained by processing principles? Three interrelated aspects spring to mind—language use, language structure, and language change. 'Language use' is meant here to refer to all linguistic (not psycholinguistic) phenomena arising from the process of converting abstract knowledge into concrete linguistic patterns, such as the appropriate choice of words in specific speaking situations and the care with which words are pronounced. This variation in language use is clearly an area for which psycholinguistics can make relevant predictions. However, this aspect will be largely (though not completely) neglected in the following, because the relationship between language use and processing mechanisms may be viewed as suspiciously close. Both components are process-oriented and manifest themselves in concrete communicative acts. It might therefore be held that an influence of processing upon the use of language is close to artifactual. Hence, language use is not the ideal area in which to convince the sceptic of the virtues of the psycholinguistic approach.

Undoubtedly, a more challenging area of investigation is language structure. It provides quite a strong testing ground for psycholinguistic principles because process and structure are less closely linked than process and use. Processing principles are dynamic, language structure is static. The former represent procedural knowledge, the latter declarative knowledge. The clear conceptual separation between the structure of the information to be processed and the processing apparatus itself is indicative of a certain distance between them. There is the real possibility that the information to be processed is mainly shaped by factors other than the processor itself. Any effect of the processor on the form of language is thus not self-evident. My focus will accordingly be on language structure as a domain which is relatively remote from language processing.

The structure of language at any given point in time does not come out of the blue. It is the momentary stage in a historical development. Thus, diachronic change engenders synchronic structure. Any synchronic state can only be the way it is because of a particular development that has led up to it. If processing principles are of any value, they must therefore be applicable to language change and language structure alike. The processing principles do not really distinguish between diachrony and synchrony. However, for practical reasons some data may lend themselves better to static (i.e. synchronic) than to dynamic (i.e. diachronic) predictions (and vice versa). My second focus will therefore be on language change. If psycholinguistic principles have something significant to say about diachronic developments, they also gain in plausibility as a potential account of synchronic structure.

In addition to the two foci just mentioned, a third area will be explored which at first sight appears unrelated to the preceding ones and barely within the purview of general linguistics. This area is the one of poetry and its formal aspects, in particular rhyme patterns. It would seem reasonable to expect poetic language to respect certain conventions which have developed historically from the usage of individual authorities, a usage that began as more or less idiosyncratic but was standardized over time. Poetic traditions are ordinarily regarded as a cultural rather than a psychological phenomenon. What counts as poetry varies dramatically from culture to culture, and may appear quite capricious to the outside observer. The principles of poetry therefore seem extremely far from the principles of processing. Thus, psycholinguistic predictions regarding poetic form possibly provide the strongest test case: if poetry can be shown to be influenced by processing constraints, the credibility of the psycholinguistic approach is further strengthened.

This work has both a language-universal and a language-particular orientation. Processing principles have a universal flavour, and it is held by some (e.g. Cutler et al. 1992) that the aim of psycholinguistics is to uncover the universal principles underlying language processing. However, the extent to which different languages are subserved by exactly the same processing machinery is not at all clear. In any case, the search for processing universals requires the psycholinguistic analysis of hundreds of languages (much as is done in the search for linguistic universals), but the day on which psycholinguists have such a wide array of data at their disposal is a long way ahead. Very few languages have so far been subjected to psycholinguistic experimentation and these few are for the most part from the Indo-European family. There is as yet no rational basis for speaking of processing universals.

Since English has been more thoroughly investigated from the processing angle than any other language, it is expedient to concentrate upon this language as the testing ground for the psycholinguistic predictions. However, the main objective of this study precludes an exclusive focus on English. The plausibility of the hypothesized link between language processing and language structure would be appreciably enhanced if the predictions were tested against other languages as well. This can and will be done in two ways. In the first instance, where relevant psycholinguistic research into languages other than English has been conducted, it will be taken into account. This may shed light upon aspects which do not occur, or have not been examined, in English. In the second instance, the perspective of contrastive (psycho)linguistics will be adopted. It is of particular interest to look at domains for which processing considerations lead to divergent predictions for individual languages. This procedure stresses the language-dependence of processing mechanisms. Both strategies significantly extend the area of inquiry, and in this way allow a clearer assessment of the explanatory power of the psycholinguistic approach.

3.4. Relating Psycholinguistics to Linguistics

The overall objective of this study is to establish a relationship between psycholinguistic processing and linguistic patterns and in so doing to explain the latter in terms of the former. The basic procedure is to derive predictions from the psycholinguistic data (and theory) and test these against linguistic patterns. Obviously, if a prediction is disconfirmed, there is no reason to assume that the process can account for the final product; if, however, a prediction is confirmed, psycholinguistics qualifies as *one* candidate for the explanation of language. It should be noted that we are not justified in making any stronger claims on the basis of individual tests.

Owing to the multicausal nature of linguistic phenomena, it is always possible with a little imagination to think up alternative accounts. All that can be safely said is that a psycholinguistic explanation is available. To prove that the psycholinguistic explanation is the correct one, it would be necessary to show that all other potential accounts are inadequate. This is undoubtedly a futile undertaking for two reasons. The number of potential accounts is virtually unlimited, and it cannot be known when the limit is reached. Further, it is extremely difficult to establish that a particular link does *not* exist. A failure to find a link may reflect the inadequacy of the method employed, and cannot simply be taken to mean that the link is absent. Trying out all possible methods is unrealistic because, again, the number of methods is infinite.

There is only one way out of this unfortunate state of affairs. This method is known as the *cumulative-evidence argument*. The basic idea is that, as the theoretical value of any individual test is perforce limited, the number of tests has to be fairly high to reach reliable conclusions. If the psycholinguistic approach can be shown to make the correct predictions for a wide spectrum of data, it gains in credibility not only on a general level but also at the level of each individual analysis. A correct prediction for one particular data set is no more than suggestive of the explanatory potential of processing principles; but correct predictions for a wide range of materials may warrant the claim that processing should be taken seriously as an explanation of linguistic patterns. Only such an approach can establish a link between psycholinguistics and linguistics. For it is clearly possible to find alternative accounts for individual analyses, but it is much more difficult to provide alternative accounts for *all* analyses performed, and it is most difficult to find a single coherent approach that may replace the psycholinguistic one.

The design of this study takes this problem into account. On the one hand, a high number of tests is necessary to avoid the risk of accidental matches. Clearly, the larger the number of tests with a positive outcome, the greater the confidence that can be placed in the link between processing and linguistic structure. In the logic of the cumulative-evidence method, there cannot be evidentiary overkill. On the other hand, the analyses themselves have to be detailed enough to be convincing. I have tried to steer a middle course between depth and breadth. Of course, the individual analyses differ in depth, depending upon such factors as availability of data and the possibility of collecting new data within a not too protracted period of time.

Making psycholinguistic predictions concerning linguistic patterns is not always without its problems. It is relatively straightforward in the case of language structure, where the linguistic and the psycholinguistic data are contemporaneous. The processing mechanisms from which the predictions are derived are at work at the same time as the linguistic structures that are targeted. Specifically, the current language is investigated from the perspective of current processing strategies. However, this is not so in the case of language change, where psycholinguistic principles of this decade or so are used to predict (or rather retrodict) developments, which took place, let us say, a millennium ago. What is the relevance, one may well ask, of today's psycholinguistics to yesterday's language? It is clearly conceivable that the processing principles have changed over time, and that it is therefore impossible to derive adequate predictions from them. To what extent and at what speed processing principles may change is not known, although it is highly likely that they need not change automatically as the language changes. This is because there is no one-to-one correspondence between linguistic forms and psycholinguistic principles. Processing mechanisms should rather be viewed as a superstructure which subserves whole sets of linguistic phenomena. Therefore, a local change may take place without any repercussion on the processing level. An almost trivial example is the addition of a new word to a language, which certainly does not necessitate the rise of a new processing principle. We may therefore tentatively conclude that the processing apparatus, both at the coarse- and fine-grained level, is less subject to change than the information to be processed.

Be that as it may, when a psycholinguistic prediction is not supported by the historical data, the possibility cannot be ruled out that the negative result is simply the consequence of a prediction which may be successfully applied to present-day data but is inapplicable to past developments, which took place under the aegis of different processing principles. As argued above, this does not appear very probable. However, when a psycholinguistic prediction is borne out by the diachronic evidence, no difficulty arises. A positive result would suggest that the processing principles have not profoundly changed, and that the psycholinguistic machinery of today is capable of making relevant statements about historical developments.

Essentially the same comments apply to poetic language. The poetic conventions have their origins in the more or less distant past. Hence there was plenty of opportunity for the processor to change. If the processing predictions nevertheless turn out to be correct, the psycholinguistic approach will be all the stronger for it.

4

Language Structure

The main body of this monograph is organized as follows. The first part is about language structure (Chapter 4), the second about language change (Chapter 5), and the third about poetic language (Chapter 6). Qualitatively and quantitatively, the first and second parts are much more important than the third. Its main function is to illustrate the diversity of domains for which relevant hypotheses may be developed. The logic of the argument is quite similar across the individual sections. A review of psycholinguistic evidence serves as the background against which pertinent predictions as to language structure are derived. These predictions are subsequently put to the test and evaluated. This procedure will be adopted irrespective of whether the linguistic data are taken from the relevant literature or presented for the first time. The logic of the argumentation is reflected in the somewhat unconventional structure of the individual sections: psycholinguistic evidence → predictions as to language structure → test and evaluation. My major objective is to assess the value of the processing approach, not the value of more linguistically oriented approaches. This precludes an exhaustive review of the linguistic literature on each topic. Alternative accounts are only considered when they are immediately relevant to the issue at hand, in particular when they can be directly contrasted with the approach advocated here. Unless stated otherwise, the hypotheses advanced below should not be taken automatically to invalidate other claims made in the literature. Rather, they should be construed as additive in two respects. Because of the multiple causation of linguistic phenomena, one explanation does not rule out another, as mentioned. The approach taken here may also provide a deeper understanding of well-known linguistic phenomena by showing how the empirical data follow naturally from a particular conception of language, and how the extant theoretical claims may benefit from being placed in a wider perspective.

The division of this monograph into a synchronic part and a diachronic part is mainly for expository reasons, although this distinction is not clear-cut. Actually, there is some degree of parallelness in the topics that are treated in the diachronic and synchronic sections. The treatment of certain basic issues did not always justify separate synchronic and diachronic sections, as in the case of the first section, to which we now turn.

4.1. The Representational Status of Phonemes

We will begin with the well-known but still ill-understood phenomenon of homonymy, whose existence has baffled linguists for a long time. The problem is that it has been found difficult to reserve this phenomenon a natural place in a framework which views language as a highly efficient means of communication. From a functional point of view, homonymy should not occur, or should at least be extremely rare, because it represents a potential or real threat to successful communication. Linguists have therefore tended to discredit it as exceptional and accidental. In the following, it will be shown that the psycholinguistic approach presents homonymy in a different light.

Our starting-point is the phoneme, which is considered a linguistically significant unit by virtue of the function it performs in the language system. Its main role is to establish a formal contrast between two meaning elements. The defining characteristic of phonemes may be termed their 'second-order semantic content'. This trait is critical. When two sound units do not distinguish meaning elements, they cannot have phonemic status and hence must be assigned to a different representational level.

While this logic is common ground in structuralist linguistics,[1] it does not carry over easily into the domain of language processing. Berg (1993) explored the psycholinguistic implications of the notion of second-order semantics and concluded that this notion is unrepresentable. Generally speaking, properties of linguistic units are easy to represent. They are simply 'tagged' onto their carrier elements and in this way become part of a unit's long-term memory representation. This association process works fine in such cases as gender on nouns and word class on lexical items. By contrast, the meaning-distinguishing property of phonemes cannot be represented in any straightforward manner. Recall how this function is standardly ascertained. Whether a sound is or is not a phoneme is determined by finding a partner for it with whom it can establish lexical contrast. How does this search for a partner proceed? For linguists, this is in principle an easy though time-consuming task. They take a dictionary of the language and systematically replace each sound of each entry with each other sound to check whether this procedure creates a different word. However, it is unrealistic to expect ordinary speakers to do likewise. Whenever they acquire a new word, they would have to compare it to all other extant entries with a view to finding minimal pairs and eventually to changing the phonological representation of well-established items (from an allophonic to a phonemic one). Neither children nor adults can be reasonably expected to perform such a laborious analysis, which is additionally also of doubtful processing value.

The consequence of all this is that phonemes as the distinctive units envisioned by linguists cannot form a psycholinguistically meaningful level of representation. Distinctiveness cannot be represented as a static feature on each phonemic

---

[1] The schools which reject the concept of the phoneme obviously also dismiss its distinctive function.

constituent of a word. However, this is not to say that distinctiveness plays no role at all from the processing perspective. To negate distinctiveness implies abolishing the distinction between phonetics and phonology, which is rather implausible from the psycholinguistic point of view. Berg (1993) suggests that distinctiveness functions as a design feature of the entire mental network and therefore is more of a global than local nature. One criterion for adjusting the links in the network is the role they take in the bottom-up access of linguistic units. The more important a lower-level node is for the access of a higher-level unit, the stronger the connection. For example, the links between the feature [voice] and the sonorants are weaker than those between [voice] and the obstruents because voice is critical in the latter but largely irrelevant in the former (see Berg 1991b). In this way, the phonemic level makes an impact upon the feature level by acting upon the links that connect the two levels, and by indirectly acting upon the representations that are built up at the superordinate level. Note that such a bottom-up influence is only possible in a parallel processing system.

There is an effect of lexical contrast but it is of an indirect, rather unspecific nature. When, let us say, many words are distinguished by /p/ vs. /b/, strong links between the features and the phoneme levels are created. Linkages can only be influenced by masses of words. Individual items (e.g. a single minimal pair) are almost without effect. The linguistic methodology of ignoring quantity—one minimal pair suffices to establish phonemic status—stands in sharp contrast to the quantity-sensitive coding of distinctiveness in the mental network. To mark off the linguistic from the psycholinguistic approach, Berg reserved the term 'segment' for the smallest sequentializable unit which is basically free from second-order semantic content.

This reasoning, which is exclusively based upon psycholinguistic arguments, makes interesting predictions for language structure and change. When sound units are segments rather than phonemes, the aspect of distinctiveness cannot be a decisive factor. We may therefore expect to find violations of the one-to-one relationship between form and meaning on not too small a scale. Unfortunately, it is difficult to derive precise quantitative predictions as to the incidence of such violations. All we can say is that they should not be exceptional. Counteracting effects of communicative efficiency may be present but should generally be weak. They may be stronger, though, when an endangered contrast is relevant in a great number of items.

The general impression is that it is not fair to assign homophony, homography[2], and homonymy (and polysemy) an exceptional status in natural languages. To gain a more precise idea of how widespread these departures from the one-to-one correspondence between form and meaning are, a sample analysis of the extent of homonymy in the English lexicon has been performed. I have chosen *Collins English Learner's Dictionary* (1974), which is neither too small to contain a severely

---

[2] The inclusion of homography presupposes that graphemes are redefined in the same way as phonemes, i.e. as units establishing formal but no second-order semantic contrast.

frequency-biased sample of the English language nor too large to include entries which are too specialist or obsolete. This dictionary distinguishes between homonymy and polysemy by giving the former separate entries and the latter separate subentries. The analysis was confined to all main entries beginning with the letter <g>. Derived words, such as *government* from *to govern*, were discarded. Also ignored were the past tense/past particle forms of irregular verbs, and orthographic variants of the same word. Since meaning can be more naturally associated with lexical than with grammatical words, it was decided to restrict the investigation to the three major word classes of nouns, verbs, and adjectives.

With homonyms counted individually, the <g> chapter contains 420 entries. Of these, 31 are homonyms, accounting for 7.4 per cent of the entire set. Thus every 13.5th word is homonymous with another. This is a remarkable percentage which argues against the view of homonymy as an exceptional mishap. It may be inferred from this finding that homonymy is not very successfully avoided. This is what one would expect if the phoneme is redefined as a unit whose major function is not to distinguish meaning. Despite the vagueness with which the above prediction had to be formulated, it can be argued that the expectation derived from the processing perspective is fulfilled.[3]

The psycholinguistic conception of the phoneme has ramifications not only for the lexical but also for the postlexical level. On the traditional view of the phoneme, assimilation processes should stay within the confines of the phoneme, i.e. involve elements at the allophonic level. If they crossed phoneme boundaries, the critical function of the phoneme would be undermined. The realization of a phoneme, as revealed through assimilation, should be as shown in (21) but not as in (22).

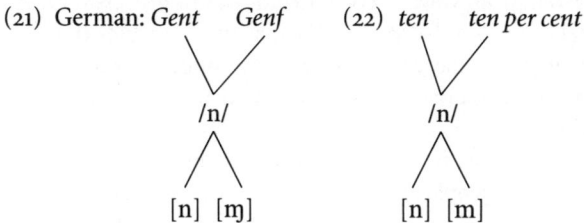

(21) German: *Gent   Genf*   (22) *ten   ten per cent*

In (21), the phoneme /n/ is shown to have the two allophones [n] and [ɱ]. The latter is the result of an assimilation of the place-of-articulation feature of the following obstruent. As the [ɱ] does not have phonemic status, the assimilation does not endanger the communicative process. In (22), by contrast, the distinction between

---

[3] Because the boundary between homonymy and polysemy is a fuzzy one, it might be of interest to report the incidence of polysemy. Of the 420 words subjected to scrutiny, 150 are polysemous and 270 monosemous. Ignoring the difference between items with two to ten different meanings, polysemy occurs in 35.7% of the words. There is some indication that this percentage still grossly underrates the importance of polysemy. Mańczak (1980) has shown that there is a correlation between frequency and polysemy. The more frequent a lexical item is, the higher is the number of meanings that it develops (Zipf's Third Law). Even if the mechanisms underlying homonymy and polysemy are different, it is obvious that the occurrence of neither phenomenon is massively counteracted.

two different phonemic categories is blurred. When *ten per cent* is rendered as [tempɜːsent], the /m/ encroaches upon the territory of the /n/ by 'usurping' its major allophone. Under the traditional view, such processes should be avoided by all means.

The psycholinguistic approach takes a different view. It predicts that assimilatory processes should not be constrained by the phonological status of the output. Because the segment is not defined as a semantic contrast-inducing device, phoneme boundaries may be easily crossed. As a matter of fact, this can be regularly observed in assimilations. Whether or not an assimilation takes place depends upon a variety of factors such as the formality of the speaking situation and the nature of the segments involved, but it does not appear to depend upon whether the resultant allophone belongs to the same or a different phonemic category. This result is entirely congruent with the psycholinguistic prediction.

Further evidence in favour of this conclusion comes from diachrony. From the functional perspective, the loss of a phonemic contrast is as unexpected as the occurrence of homonymy. However, such losses are not uncommon in the history of languages. When a given phoneme /X/ merges with the phoneme /Y/ which is already part of the phonological inventory, the contrast between /X/ and /Y/ is eliminated. These cases are not infrequent, probably because it is easier for a sound to develop into an existing sound (for which a motor programme is already available) than into a completely new sound (for which a motor programme has yet to be set up). A well-known case of merger is the development from /z/ to /r/ in Proto-Germanic, e.g. PGerm. *aiz* → OE *ar* 'ore'. In this way, homonymy was created between the OE words ar_1 'metal' and ar_2 'messenger'. In Middle English times, unrounding can be observed in front vowels. The outcome of this process is identical to the already extant set of unrounded vowels. We may thus conclude that it is principally possible for languages to change in countercommunicative ways. This is quite what one would expect if distinctiveness is not the hard and fast criterion for phonemic change to respect.

However, it has also been predicted that sound change may be impeded when a large number of oppositions are jeopardized. This condition is ideally fulfilled when a phonological opposition carries a morphological function. In that case the number of oppositions is virtually unlimited, especially when inflectional affixes are at stake, since these generally have very few restrictions on their attachment to stems. Indeed, many examples have been reported in which a so-called regular sound change stops short when the segment to be affected acts as a morphological marker. Chen and Wang (1975) note a tendency in Latin to lose stops in word-final positions including /t/. However, the coronal consonant was retained when it coded 3rd person singular information on verbs. In the history of English, the word-final voiced stops following nasals underwent deletion, as in *climb* and *bang*. Notably, the voiced alveolar stop was immune to this development. The /d/ was almost certainly preserved because its disappearance would have made it impossible to code the past tense on all verbs ending in a nasal. Substantial corroboration for this view comes from the fact that the second member of a final consonant cluster may be dropped in casual speech by English speakers (see Kiparsky, 1972 and references cited therein). This happens even in past tense forms like *kept* → *kep'*, though less often in regular forms like *passed* → *pass'*. The reason in all probability is that the /t/ in *passed* is alone in signalling past tense whereas it is aided by the vowel in *kept*. This renders the /t/ indispensable in *passed* but dispensable in *kept*. On the other hand, morphological marking is no guarantee for preservation. Case syncretism in Middle English is an example. The general weakening and eventual disappearance of word endings could not be stopped by their morphological relevance. It is worthwhile to point out, however, that case on nouns is semantically less important than tense on verbs.

It may be concluded that the psycholinguistic account makes the correct predictions for language structure and change. It provides a natural explanation for an apparently unnatural phenomenon. How can language allow for the existence of countercommunicative phenomena which may even occur on a relatively large scale? The answer suggested by the above analysis is that formal and semantic types of information are represented on distinct levels, and that there is a gap between them which can only be bridged to a certain extent. Because there is no room for the direct representation of second-order semantic information at the phonological level, phonemes are (to a certain extent) blind to, and develop independently of, semantic information. This relative independence is at the core of the non-prevention, i.e. occurrence, of one-to-many relationships between form and meaning. At the same time, the parallel information flow ensures a two-way communication among the various levels of representation. Developments at one level always take into account (again, to a limited degree) the possible consequences this development would entail on a neighbouring level. Thus, parallel processing and level-specific coding strike a balance between the independence and the interaction of psycholinguistic as well as linguistic levels of representation.

4.2. The Structure of Onsets and Codas

It has transpired from many studies that the constituents of the syllable are not processed alike. For instance, the beginning of a word is a more effective cue to its retrieval than the end (Nooteboom 1981). Disruptions to the retrieval process are most efficiently overcome by providing the (word) onset, as can be seen in amnesic aphasics. Similarly, in intermediate stages of lexical access speakers can often specify the onset of the word on the tip of their tongue without being able to retrieve its full form. Further, the phonological encoding of words by normals is facilitated by knowledge of the onset but not by knowledge of the coda (Meyer 1991). Onsets are significantly more often involved in speech errors than codas:

(23)   *a bee wit* for *a wee bit*
(24)   *I have a stick neff* for *a stiff neck* (both from Shattuck-Hufnagel 1987)

The exchanges in (23) and (24) implicate an onset and a coda respectively. In the psycholinguistics literature, the increased error rate in onset position is standardly associated with an increased level of activation. To be specific, it is assumed that more activation accumulates on onset than on coda positions. This idea makes good sense, in that onsets have to be produced before codas and smooth delivery will be facilitated by an enhanced availability of what comes first.

In order to derive predictions from the processing difference between onsets and codas, a few words about phonological encoding are called for. It is taken for granted that the production of words requires the assignment of segments to structural positions. Both slots and fillers have to be generated during the production process. Which elements at the slot and the filler level are selected and associated with each other depends upon the pattern of activation prevalent in the processing network. The more strongly a given position is activated, the better its chances of attracting candidate fillers. On this logic, it is to be expected that onsets are more successful than codas in binding consonants to them. In particular, the maximum number of onset consonants should exceed the maximum number of coda consonants. One may also predict that the number of different consonant (cluster) types in onset positions should be greater than that in coda positions. Since the propensity to onset slips is best documented for English (Shattuck-Hufnagel 1987), these predictions will be tested against English syllable structure.

The first decision that needs to be made concerns the inclusion of inflectional forms. It was decided to restrict the analysis to uninflected forms because our focus is upon phonology in its pure form, not upon the secondary effects that morphology makes on phonological structure. The inclusion of inflected forms would doubtlessly have shifted the onset/coda ratio towards the latter as all inflections are postposed in English.

Let us begin with the maximum number of consonants that may occupy onsets and codas. Do onsets host a greater number of consonants than codas? Contrary to expectation, onsets are not privileged in this respect. Codas can accommodate the same number of consonants as onsets (from 0 to 3). If there is an asymmetry, it is to the advantage of the coda. In inflected forms, word onsets may have a maximum of three consonants whereas word offsets can include up to four (e.g. *preempts*). The first prediction is thus belied by the empirical facts.

It may well be that a simple count of the number of possible consonants reflects too narrow a view of linguistic reality. The absolute numbers are perhaps uninterpretable without taking the possible cluster types into account. If only one or two CCC cluster types existed, the asymmetry in favour of the coda would really be of very limited significance. It is necessary therefore to examine whether the asymmetry still holds when cluster types are subjected to analysis. Dewey (1923) and Roberts (1965) present lists of initial and final singleton consonants and consonant clusters in American English. Roberts' appendices XVII and XXI are summarized in Table 2, from which it is plain that the number of different consonant/cluster types is greater in coda than in onset positions. Apparently, codas are in a better position to accommodate clusters than onsets. Interestingly, this tendency is the more pronounced the 'heavier' the clusters are. At the level of single consonants, onsets and codas appear equally suited to accommodate segments. There is an equal number of possible fillers for onset and coda positions. This symmetry is due to the fact that almost all consonants are inherently neutral with respect to syllable position. Only two segments have a defective distribution: /ŋ/ does not occur initially and /h/ does not occur finally. One level of complexity upwards, this balance is disturbed. There are twice as many biconsonantal coda than onset clusters. With triconsonantal clusters, the ratio soars to 6–8 : 1 in favour of the coda. The general pattern thus is that the asymmetry between onset and coda cluster types increases with the number of consonants. This result flies in the face of the research hypothesis.

Before an attempt is made to interpret these findings, the analysis will be carried one step further by probing into the frequency of the consonant/cluster types in English. Even if the number of different consonant/cluster types in coda positions exceeds that in onset positions, it is still conceivable that onsets lodge the more common and codas the less common consonant clusters. Evidently the two factors —the number of different clusters and their frequency—are not entirely dissociable from each other, but a certain independence is at least theoretically possible, even if it may not appear likely. Given this relative independence, it would be more natural to expect the more frequent clusters in final sites. However, should these occur predominantly in onset sites, we would have come across quite a surprising pattern.

In light of the pivotal role of the following analysis, a thorough attempt was made at obtaining exact frequency information. This information was drawn from the *Collins Cobuild Dictionary of British English*, which is available in computerized form at the Centre for Lexical Information (CELEX) in Nijmegen. All bisyllabic words were selected not only because they form the most frequent category (Roberts 1965) but also because they allow for a balanced representation of stressed

TABLE 2. *Type frequency of onset and coda clusters (after Roberts 1965)*

Type	Onset	Coda
C	23	23 (−1)
CC	31	67 (−17)
CCC	5	49 (−18)
TOTAL	59	139 (−36)

Note: The numbers in brackets indicate the subset of coda consonants coda clusters beginning with /r/. Since the rhotic is not pronounced in postvocalic positions in British English (RP), these numbers have to be deducted from the count of the American English consonant types.

and unstressed syllables. Possible effects of stress would therefore appear to be minimized. Regularly inflected word forms were not taken into account. Homophonous forms were counted only once. The results of the computer-based analysis are given in Table 3.

Surprisingly enough, the trend displayed in Table 3 is exactly reversed compared to that of Table 2. It is plain from Table 3 that onsets attract the more frequent and codas the less frequent consonant clusters. This pattern is especially striking as the opposite would be expected on the basis of the number of possible consonants/clusters in onset and coda positions. The elevated number imparts to codas an advantage which they are unable to preserve in the token frequency count. Thus codas appear to take a wider variety of infrequent consonant clusters, whereas onsets draw upon a more restricted set of frequently occurring clusters. Again in contradistinction to Table 2, the onset/coda asymmetry increases as the number of consonants per position increases. Already at the one-consonant level, there are more words containing filled onsets than filled codas. This difference increases significantly from the singleton consonant to the biconsonantal cluster level. The increment from the CC to the CCC is even steeper. The onset/coda ratio doubles as we move from the biconsonantal to the triconsonantal clusters. All in all, Table 3 invites the conclusion that the more frequent and the heavier a consonant cluster is, the more likely it is to turn up in onset rather than in coda positions. This result is in perfect keeping with the research hypothesis.

In the foregoing, a count has been made of the number of words in which a given consonant or cluster appears. These words have, of course, a frequency of their own which will be investigated next. It is possible that word frequency correlates with consonant/cluster frequency in that the more common a cluster is in a particular position, the more common is the word in which it occurs. However, in view of the discrepancies between Tables 2 and 3 it would not be altogether surprising if the patterns were again reversed. In the former case, our confidence would be strengthened in taking the results of Table 3 seriously. In the latter case, however, Table 3 would have to be regarded as exceptional, and it may then be problematical to attach a great deal of theoretical significance to it. To calculate the token frequency, recourse was made to the information pool that served as input for the compilation of the *Collins Cobuild Dictionary*. This pool comprised approximately 18 million words, taken

TABLE 3. *Token frequency of onset and coda consonants/clusters in disyllabic words*

Type	Onset	Coda	Onset/coda
C	16,042	11,370	1.4
CC	3,914	1,650	2.4
CCC	314	66	4.8
TOTAL	20,270	13,086	1.5 (Average)

from written as well as spoken sources. The information contained in Table 4 is based upon exactly the same linguistic material that has been used for Table 3. That is to say, Table 4 gives the frequency of the words whose onset and coda structures were subjected to quantitative analysis in Table 3.

Interestingly, Table 4 by and large replicates the discoveries of Table 3. Words with filled onsets have a higher lexical frequency than words with filled codas. When all cluster types are taken together, the onset/coda ratio amounts to 1.5 : 1 in both tables. There is thus a certain affinity between onset clusters and more frequent words on the one hand and between coda clusters and less frequent words on the other. It is remarkable that the trend evident in Table 2 is reversed, which is strong indication that quite a powerful force must be here at work. Note that, unlike the patterns in Table 3, a simple correlation between cluster weight and the onset/coda ratio does not seem to hold. It is true that there is an increment from C to CC, but the ratio goes down as we move from CC to CCC structures. The reason for this unexpected decrement is not known.

In the preceding, four analyses have been conducted in an attempt to test the prediction that English onsets should be structurally more complex than codas. There is no denying that the results are mixed. Two analyses lend support to the research hypothesis whereas the other two fail to do so. This ambiguity in the data points to a more specific relationship between processing principles and language structure than has hitherto been assumed. It may be that not all aspects of language structure are equally likely to be shaped by the way linguistic information is processed. Let us recall the structure of the argument. Speech error data have been interpreted in terms of differential activational strategies in onset and coda positions. Higher levels of activation increase the binding power of structural positions and consequently the likelihood of attracting consonants.

Where do the differential activational strategies come from? It is probable that they arise in the lexicon at large, i.e. that they are of a global nature. If this is correct, processing principles are more likely to make themselves felt at a global, not at a local, level. Hence, quantitative effects throughout the lexicon should be more sensitive to processing biases. On the other hand, individual cases should not have the power to influence global processing principles. We therefore expect on this post hoc analysis that the information on phonological token frequency should be

TABLE 4. *Frequency of occurrence of disyllabic words as a function of their onset and coda structure*

Type	Onset	Coda	Onset/coda
C	4,762,400	3,179,974	1.5
CC	835,604	478,025	1.7
CCC	51,200	41,544	1.2
TOTAL	5,649,204	3,699,543	1.5 (Average)

most favourable to the research hypothesis. This is exactly what was found. The recalcitrance of the data from the first two analyses can now be explained as following from their local nature, which makes them resist processing influences rather successfully. Take the extreme example of one or two monomorphemic words ending in a four-member consonant cluster. According to the logic of the first analysis, this would mean that codas are heavier than onsets because they can accommodate one consonant more. However, these two words do not have the slightest chance of altering global activation patterns in the lexicon. It may be argued, then, that the research hypothesis holds in areas where it is most likely to have an effect but does not hold in areas where it is less likely to do so.

By way of conclusion, a relatively involved picture emerges. There is no unambiguous support for the contention that the processing principle invoked here entails a greater complexity of onsets as compared to codas. The problem is that the prediction derived from the psycholinguistic principle does not specify what exactly is meant by linguistic complexity. It has been argued that processing principles are most likely to be shaped by global information. Individual cases are unlikely to make an impact. This is why linguistic complexity should not be understood here in the traditional sense. It does not refer to the maximum number of consonants or cluster types but rather to the frequency with which consonants and clusters occur in certain loci. As soon as structural complexity is conceived of in these terms, the research hypothesis is borne out by the empirical data. It thus seems that the processing difference between onsets and codas makes an impact upon linguistic structure.

The preceding investigation was exclusively directed to English because the processing principle that was predicted to determine phonological structure was established for English. Even if there is no justification for assigning it a universal status, it might be worth the effort to inquire into the generality of the onset dominance. What gives the processing principle at hand a certain universal flavour is the argument that the psycholinguistic system does well to give priority to the beginning, as the onset has to be produced prior to the coda. Since this is universally true, it might be predicted that, cross-linguistically, onset structures should be more complex than coda structures. In the absence of phonological frequency information on other languages, I had to resort to simple counts of cluster types and content myself with examining whether onsets accommodate a higher number of different clusters than codas across the world's languages. The answer appears to be yes. In Greenberg's (1965) sample of 104 languages, there are 90 onset cluster types but only 62 coda cluster types. It is notable that this difference contrasts sharply with what has been found for English. The language that has been investigated here thus seems to be unusual in terms of the number of consonant cluster types per position. This test suggests that processing principles make an impact not only upon the structure of a particular language but also upon the structure of languages in general.

4.3. The Structure of Syllable Contacts

The most common pattern of concatenating phonological units is the simple alternation of consonants and vowels. The CV structure is the only syllable type that is found in every language and the first to be acquired by children. Any extension of this most basic syllable type ineluctably creates an adjacency of two consonants or two vowels. The latter situation (hiatus) is less tolerated by natural languages than the former. My attention will be placed upon the structure of adjacent consonants, in particular upon adjacent consonants which are separated by a syllable boundary. These cases are called 'syllable contacts' by Vennemann (1988). Syllable contacts are special in that they may be assumed to be free from phonotactic constraints which are usually defined within, not between, syllables. There is another related reason which argues for the liberalness of syllable contacts. Because the consonants are by definition non-constituents, their combinatorial possibilities cannot be a matter of constituency.

What high-level constraints may be assumed to be operative in syllable contacts? To answer this question, it is necessary to be clear about the central functions of the language-production mechanism. One of its major tasks is to line up a string of elements in the correct serial order. It is a reasonable assumption that users of this system strive for maximum efficacy, i.e. that they are intent upon minimizing the danger of interference. Interference is in large measure caused by similarity. The more similar two units are, the more likely the processor is to get confused over them. This explains why the CV structure is the most preferred in the languages of the world. Prototypical consonants and vowels are maximally distinct, so that there is no mistaking which element to select next. However, when two consonants abut on each other, the potential for confusion arises because the two elements to be serialized are identical in terms of their consonanthood. This danger is particularly acute in view of the fact that adjacent elements are already 'similar' by virtue of their adjacency. That is, because the one segment has to be outputted directly after the other, the activation level of the second is relatively high while the first is being produced.

Given the inherent danger of confusing adjacent elements of the same major class (i.e. consonants), there is a strong need on the part of the processor to keep them maximally distinct. How can the phonological similarity of consonants be assessed? The standard method is to align the consonants on a scale of consonanthood which goes by the name of sonority or strength in the phonological literature. The idea is simply to compare the various consonants to vowels with a view to determining which consonants have more vocalic properties than others. This allows one to derive a measure of phonological distance between the consonants themselves. For example, because vowels are generally voiced, voiced consonants are more vowel-like than voiceless ones. By this principle, all consonants or consonant classes can be arranged as follows.

(25) (increasing) degree of consonanthood: glides—rhotic—lateral—nasals—voiced fricatives—voiceless fricatives, voiced stops—voiceless stops

This scale serves the purpose of evaluating the distance between consonant types. The further two types are apart on the scale, the less similar they are.

On the basis of the production principle outlined above, we may now formulate the following prediction. Syllable contacts should predominantly involve consonants from the opposite end of the sonority scale. Inversely, syllable contacts recruited from the same consonant class should be strongly discouraged. Note that this prediction is of a universal nature, given the logic of the argument. Each psycholinguistic system may be expected to avoid processing conflicts irrespective of the particular information to be processed. Note also that the psycholinguistic prediction is inherently neutral with respect to the order of the consonants involved. A more consonant-like consonant may be followed by a less consonant-like consonant, as well as vice versa. This is not to say that possible asymmetries are incompatible with the above prediction or underivable from other psycholinguistic principles. The point is simply that the processor's desire to keep adjacent consonants maximally distinct is not apt to account for serial-order effects in syllable contacts.

The psycholinguistic prediction will be tested against syllable contacts in English. A search through the CELEX data base yields seventy-nine two-member syllable contacts in disyllabic words such as /zb/ in *lesbian* and /mb/ in *member*. Three-member clusters such as /mbr/ in *membrane* are treated like two-member clusters, i.e. the rhotic is ignored because it belongs to the same syllabic constituent as the /b/ and does not establish a direct contact with /m/. Table 5 presents the frequency information on all syllable contacts in English disyllabic words. Both type and token frequencies are provided. As far as was deemed useful, the consonants were grouped into classes.

As can be gathered from Table 5, there are very strong asymmetries in the syllable contact patterns. By far the most preferred structure is the nasal + stop sequence. Nasal + fricative combinations are second most frequent and fricative + stop combinations third most frequent. There is also a strong asymmetry of linear order. With the exception of nasal + liquid sequences, decreasing-sonority clusters are much more common than those of the increasing-sonority type. The absence of a clear preference in the case of nasal + liquid sequences might be linked to their closeness on the sonority scale. However, the problem of linear order will not be elaborated upon because it is not within the scope of the psycholinguistic prediction. Roughly speaking, the token frequencies translate reasonably well into type frequencies, so there is no need to give them a separate treatment.

Table 6 conveniently summarizes the results of Table 5 according to the difference in sonority between the constituents of the syllable contacts. The sonority scale is reduced to its essentials and takes the following form: stops, fricatives, nasals, liquids. The similarity between the constituents is measured in terms of their distance on the scale. For example, two stops have the distance 0, whereas a stop and a liquid have the distance 3. The general trend that emerges in Table 6 is the one predicted by the processing considerations. The less the distance between the two

TABLE 5. *Type and token frequency of syllable contacts in English disyllabic words*

Decreasing sonority	Type	Token	Increasing sonority	Type	Token	Sonority plateau	Type	Token
liquid–nasal	5	173	nasal–liquid	6	10,430	stop–stop	22	3,067
liquid–fricative	14	17,009	fricative–liquid	7	445	fricative–fricative	1	29
liquid–stop	21	15,672	stop–liquid	9	134	nasal–nasal	0	0
nasal–fricative	69	7,596	fricative–nasal	6	201	liquid–liquid	1	10
nasal–stop	240	43,126	stop–nasal	17	1,478			
fricative–stop	20	6,742	stop–fricative	35	4,228			
TOTAL	369	90,318		81	16,916		24	4,006

consonants which make up the syllable contact, the less often they occur in the language. Adjacent consonants from the same sonority category are strongly disfavoured. As can be seen from Table 5, fricative + fricative, nasal + nasal, and liquid + liquid sequences are almost completely absent. The adjacency of liquids is severely constrained by the fact that the rhotic does not occur in syllable-final position in British English. Only stop + stop structures are encountered with moderate frequency. It is likely that the high frequency of stops in general language usage is mainly responsible for this effect.

The 'distance 0' clusters listed in Table 5 all involve non-identical consonants. Theoretically, it is also possible to envision syllable contacts made up of identical consonants such as /m.m/ and /t.t/. These sequences are even more strongly prohibited than sequences of non-identical elements. When structures like /m.m/ and /t.t/, for example, arise through historical change, they are eliminated through degemination. Obviously, when a single consonant remains, the serial-order problem has completely disappeared (even if this consonant is ambisyllabic).

As expected, 'distance 2' clusters are significantly more frequent than 'distance 1' clusters, which in turn are significantly more common than 'distance 0' clusters. Yet the 'distance 3' cases pose a problem. Although they were expected to occur most often, the raw data show them to be quite rare.[4] They are about as (in)frequent as the 'distance 0' clusters (in terms of their type, not token frequency). Upon closer inspection, however, several explanations of the low frequency of 'distance 3' clusters come to mind. Chief among them is the fact that the structure of the language does not provide an equal opportunity of occurrence for all cluster types. 'Distance 3' clusters are disadvantaged in quite a few respects. As mentioned, the absence of /r/ in coda position in Received Pronunciation eliminates the possibility of /r.C/ contacts. Thus only one element, the lateral, is left with which 'distance 3' clusters can be formed. This one segment is, of course, of lower frequency than the fricatives and stops taken as a group. Moreover, the probability of /C.l/ and /C.r/ contacts is

TABLE 6. *Type and token frequency of syllable contacts as a function of the sonority distance of their constituents*

Distance	Type frequency	Token frequency
0	24	3,106
1	141	29,370
2	278	62,058
3	30	15,806

[4] It is interesting to note though, that liquid-stop (as well as liquid-fricative) sequences have astonishingly high token frequencies (see Table 5). This might be taken as an indirect indication of their preferred status as syllable contacts.

severely reduced by the fact that these sequences form ideal tautosyllabic clusters as in *patron*, and consequently resist their positioning around syllable boundaries. Finally, the baseline probabilities of the four types of syllable contact are not the same. There are four pairings of 'distance o' (stop—stop, fricative—fricative etc.), three pairings of 'distance 1', two pairings of 'distance 2', and only one pairing of 'distance 3' (i.e. liquid—stop) clusters. All these factors, especially the preference of stop + liquid combinations for tautosyllabicity, are jointly responsible for the rarity of 'distance 3' clusters.

This section may be summarized as follows. It has been shown that the consonants of syllable contacts in English obey the principle of phonological dissimilarity. The less similar they are, the more preferred they are. Because syllable contacts by definition involve an onset and a coda, the present result has implications for onsets and codas in general. No matter whether these are heterosyllabic or tautosyllabic, they should be maximally distinct. However, this trend towards dissimilarity is tempered by another principle which governs the assignment of consonants to identical or different syllables. Some of the clusters which make ideal syllable contacts from the perspective of phonological dissimilarity are also ideal syllable constituents. Because the forces which lead to tautosyllabicity are stronger than those leading to heterosyllabicity in this case, clusters like /tr/ are not available as syllable contacts. The principle of phonological dissimilarity has been argued to be grounded in the language users' desire to keep the elements to be serialized maximally distinct so as to minimize the risk of confusion, i.e. of error. The structure of the language thus is claimed to be responsive to the requirements of the sequencing system.

4.4. Word Onset Structure in German and Spanish

As shown in section 4.2, onsets and codas are asymmetrically processed. This asymmetry is even more pronounced in word onsets than in syllable onsets. Actually, word onsets are most frequently affected in slips of the tongue, with percentages climbing up to 80 per cent. This result holds good of English, German, Dutch, and Swedish (see Berg, 1987 for a review). Interestingly, the onset dominance fails to arise in Spanish, where the consonantal beginnings of words are *less* often involved in errors than would be expected by chance (Berg 1991a). It is therefore appropriate to speak of a word onset stability in Spanish[5] but of a word onset vulnerability in the Germanic languages, as far as phonological processing is concerned. Four examples, two from German and two from Spanish, are given below.

(26) G: *Ich muß mich spächtig muten* for *mächtig sputen*
              [ʃpɛçtɪç muːtən   mɛçtɪç ʃpuːtən]
       'I must hurry up'

---

[5] Note that the word onset stability in Spanish does not generalize to a syllable-onset stability. In fact, it is paired with a syllable onset vulnerability much as is found in the Germanic languages.

(27) G: *Du kannst dich ja ohne Wascher wassen* for *Wasser waschen*
   [vaʃɛr vasən   vasɛr vaʃən]
   'Why don't you wash yourself without water?'
(28) Sp.: *en la pejor mareja* for *mejor pareja*
   [pexor marexa mexor parexa]
   '(Let's take) the best couple'
(29) Sp.: *con sabor a jabón– a jamón*
   [sabor xabon xamon]
   'with ham flavour'

While examples (26) and (28) involve word onsets, the errors in (27) and (29) take place in non-word-initial position, with ambisyllabic segments being affected in (27) and syllable-initial consonants in (29). The first example documents an exchange of two word onsets of which one is a consonant cluster.

It might be held that there is more opportunity for German than for Spanish word onsets (relative to syllable onsets) to be involved in malfunctions. In particular, the ratio of word onsets to syllable onsets might be higher in German than in Spanish. However, this is not the case. The syllable onset/word onset ratio is equal in the two languages (Berg 1991a).

The psycholinguistic interpretation of this cross-linguistic difference is straightforward in a spreading-activation model. More activation is sent to German than to Spanish word onset consonants. This heightened availability allows word onsets to intrude upon other word onsets more frequently in German than in Spanish. As argued in section 4.2, segments have to be associated with structural positions and this association process is under the control of activational patterns. The more activation accumulates on the word onset, the more activation is passed on to the candidate segments and, by implication, the stronger the competition among them.

Given that more activation accrues on German word onsets, they can be claimed to be in a better position to attract consonants than Spanish word onsets. Thus the expectation for language structure would be that the Spanish word onsets should be 'lighter' than the German ones. This prediction divides in two parts. For one thing, a higher number of clusters should be found in German than in Spanish and for another, vowel-initial words should be more common in Spanish than in German.

To test these predictions, recourse was made to two quantitative analyses, a Spanish one from Lloyd and Schnitzer (1967) and a German one from Berg (1988a). The Spanish count is a dictionary study while the German one considers open-class words only. As closed-class items are vanishingly rare in terms of type frequency compared to open-class words, this difference appears to be negligible. The German data set is much smaller than the Spanish one. The results of the frequency analysis are tabulated in Table 7. The empirical data are as predicted. German is more propitious to consonant clustering than Spanish. Biconsonantal clusters are more than twice as frequent in the former than in the latter language. Triconsonantal clusters, while rare in German, are completely missing from Spanish. At the same time,

Spanish outweighs German in the rate of vowel-initial words. There are 10 per cent more words of this kind in Spanish than in German. Thus, in full agreement with the predictions, Spanish can be shown to be more hostile towards heavy word onsets than German.

The phonological weight of word onsets is a general principle which accounts for the relative rarity of clusters as well as the relative commonness of vowel-initialness in Spanish (and conversely in German) and illuminates how these two structural aspects are related. The less activation the onset position can spread the more likely it is to be empty. Similarly, the more activation the onset slot has at its disposal the greater its likelihood of attracting more than one consonant. Differences in activation levels are therefore argued to be linked to differences in linguistic structure.

TABLE 7. *Word onset structure in Spanish and German*

Language	V-initial (%)	C-initial (%)	CC-initial (%)	CCC-initial (%)
German	19.9	63.5	15.8	0.7
Spanish	30.1	63.1	6.8	0.0

4.5. Subsyllabic Suprasegmental Constituents

In a hierarchical conception of language, it is undisputed that syllables are superordinated to segments. What is less certain is whether any intermediate constituents between these two levels have to be recognized. If so, the organization of the syllable would be referred to as hierarchical; if not, it would be called flat. While there is only one type of flat structure, the hierarchical structure knows several variants. Let us examine the simple example of a CVC syllable, which could be easily extended to more complex consonantal clusters in initial and final sites. The absence of any consonants in onset or coda positions is more difficult to deal with from the theoretical vantage-point, and will be ignored in what follows. Logically, the CVC syllable allows for two hierarchical representations: the vowel ties more closely either to the preceding or to the following consonant. The first possibility is ordinarily called left-branching, the second right-branching. The graphic representation is given in (30–2).

(30) flat structure

(31) left-branching hierarchical structure

(32) right-branching hierarchical structure

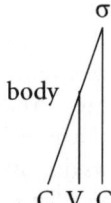

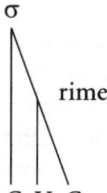

Choosing among these three alternatives is an empirical issue which is based upon the differing predictions that they entail. The flat-structure hypothesis predicts that the two consonants exhibit symmetrical behaviour because they are symmetrically represented. By contrast, according to the hierarchical-structure hypothesis, an asymmetry predictably arises between the initial and the final consonant. In a left-branching structure, the initial consonant forms a unit with the following vowel. This intermediate unit is named the 'body'. In a right-branching structure, the vowel forms a unit with the final consonant. This intermediate unit is called the *rime*. The body node predicts that the initial consonant and the vowel tend to act together. The rime node, in turn, predicts that the vowel and the final consonant form a unit to which rules may refer.

Many lines of empirical evidence may be brought to bear upon the organization of segments within the syllable. These include poetic rhymes, speech errors, language games, stuttering, and low-level phonetic as well as high-level phonological rules. Since they all converge on the same result, we will content ourselves with discussing one data type, spontaneous errors.

In the course of a malfunction, a phonological unit may be shifted from its original location to a different one. Most usually this element corresponds to a single phoneme, but larger units may also be implicated. With respect to phoneme combinations, the three models (30–2) make differing predictions. The flat-structure hypothesis predicts that CV units should be as frequently shifted around as VC units. The left-branching hierarchical structure hypothesis predicts that CV units should be more frequently involved in errors than VC units. The opposite prediction is made by the right-branching hierarchical model of syllable structure. For purposes of illustration, a CV and a VC slip follow.

(33) *He said 'Have you studied a lot?' and I sot– and I said 'No, not very much'*
(34) *the cutting widge of his et* for *the cutting edge of his wit* (both from Shattuck-Hufnagel 1983)

Error (33) exemplifies the substitution of /ed/ by /at/, i.e. one VC unit ousts another. In (34), a CV sequence is moved as a unit. The phoneme combination /wɪ/ from *wit* is shifted to the beginning of the target word *edge* to yield *widge*. All available speech error collections disclose the same pattern for English. VC slips clearly outnumber CV slips (e.g. Shattuck-Hufnagel 1983). The empirical materials thus unambiguously favour the right-branching hierarchical model of the syllable. In this view, the error in (33) documents the movement of a phonological constituent, the rime. Number (34), in contrast, involves a non-constituent and has to be regarded as a chance outcome of the production mechanism.[6]

What implications does the assumed existence of a rime node in language processing have for language structure? The obvious answer is that the rime should be a relevant unit in the analysis of the phonotactics of a language. More specifically, stronger phonotactic constraints should exist within the rime than within the body,[7] as the rime binds its constituent phonemes more closely together than the body does. Because of the greater restrictions on the phonological structure of rimes, the number of rime types should be smaller than the number of body types.

This prediction will be tested against English data. It is clearly of the language-particular kind because the rime node is not a phonological universal (see section 4.6). The probe will be restricted to monosyllabic words. In this way, all complications introduced by the fuzziness of syllable boundaries are avoided. As in previous analyses, the computerized lexicon of English compiled at CELEX is used. The CELEX database lists a total of 12,354 monosyllabics. Because each syllable has a body as well as a rime (even if it consists of the vocalic part only), the number of body and rime tokens must be identical. The number of body and rime *types* (including those with 'zero consonants') may, however, be different. The computer-assisted search through the 12,354 monosyllabics yields 519 rime types and 759 body types. As predicted, the number of different bodies is higher than that of different rimes. This disparity is statistically significant ($\chi^2(1) = 22.7$, $p < 0.001$). This result lends support to the claim that the deployment of a rime node during processing entails more severe phonotactic restrictions in the rime than in the body domain. A concomitant result is that the token/type ratio for rimes is 1.46 times greater than that for bodies (23.8 vs. 16.3). That is to say, each rime type occurs on average approximately one and a half times more often than each body type. Rimes may thus be said to carry less information than bodies.

This brings us to the issue of independence between the psycholinguistic and the linguistic patterns. Could it be that speech errors tend to treat VC sequences as a unit *because* rimes have a relatively high token/type ratio? This possibility is not at all remote. One might argue that the processing system capitalizes upon the elevated

---

[6] The linguistic interpretation of psycholinguistic data cannot help but being rather crude in many cases. The reason is that behavioural data are almost always of a statistical nature whereas linguistic descriptions tend to be all-or-none. In the above example, the choice is strictly binary: either a given segment combination is or is not a phonological constituent. It is generally difficult to represent any kind of intermediateness within the conceptual framework of theoretical linguistics. It may be that the processing vocabulary knows only constituents and non-constituents. But it may also be that there exist degrees of constituency for the expression of which a more malleable framework would be called for.

[7] The use of this term is purely descriptive. It is intended to refer to a consonant–vowel sequence and does not imply a psychologically real unit.

redundancy of VC sequences by developing a production strategy which allows the two constituents of a rime to be activated in tandem. This is tantamount to the introduction of a psycholinguistic rime node. The processing system would thus be responsive to transitional probabilities on the phonological level.

What reduces the plausibility of this account is that it leaves completely unexplained why the structure of bodies and rimes is at all asymmetrical. I consider it more likely that right-branching has been introduced for other psycholinguistic reasons, in particular because it incurs less processing cost. In this view, the phonotactic structure of rimes and bodies derives from decisions which have been made in the processing system on independent grounds.

To conclude, the psycholinguistic prediction is clearly backed up by the empirical data. The vowel and the following consonant are processed differently from the vowel and the preceding consonant. This psycholinguistic asymmetry is paralleled by a phonotactic asymmetry to the effect that VC structures exhibit lower variability and higher token frequency than CV structures. There is thus a correspondence between psycholinguistic processing and linguistic structure.

4.6. Constraints on the Repetition of Identical Elements

To what extent languages allow the repetition of identical phonemes within the same morpheme is a theme which was introduced in section 2.1. MacKay (1970a) showed that in Hawaiian and Serbo-Croatian, the probability of a phoneme being followed by an identical phoneme is below chance immediately afterwards but above chance somewhat later within the utterance. MacKay had recourse to constraints on the firing potential of neurons. The claim that psycholinguistic reasons have to be considered in addition to these neurological factors will be elaborated in this section.

Our point of departure is the assumption that processing problems are avoided as much as possible and that identical segments in close succession constitute such a problem (Stemberger and MacWhinney 1986b). To understand why the repetition of identical elements may cause trouble, it is again necessary to go into the problem of serial order. The production of language involves converting an abstract 'timeless' representation into a sequence of units which are ordered in time. As Lashley (1951) argued, order is not inherent in a word because the same phonemes may combine in different ways to yield different words in English. The unordered set of the phonemes /p/, /t/, and /æ/ may give rise to *pat, apt,* and *tap* out of a total of six theoretically possible combinations. Thus a mechanism has to be postulated which activates the constituents of an utterance in a certain order. How does this serialization mechanism operate? It seems clear that some sort of coding must be implicated. A variety of coding procedures have been proposed. What is common to all is that each element needs to be 'individualized' so as to make it distinct from all others. For example, a prevocalic consonant may be distinguished from a postvocalic one by putting different tags on them. The former may be labelled 'onset', the latter 'coda', thus specifying the position a given element occupies within a higher-level unit. A general rule stating that onsets are produced before codas will then ensure the correct ordering. This principle suffices to distinguish singleton consonants within a syllable but not two prevocalic consonants from different syllables from each other. Hence, further labels are called for, such as 'onset of first syllable' and 'onset of second syllable'. These requirements obviously extend at least up to the sentence level. The phrase level contains information relevant to the serialization of words, and so does the syllable level with respect to the serialization of phonemes. Since language is hierarchically organized, the serialization mechanism is also assumed to operate in hierarchic fashion.

What is the evidence for position-sensitive coding? It has been noted that labelling is a means of making two elements more dissimilar. Two unlabelled consonants are evidently more similar to each other than two disparately labelled ones. Slips of the tongue are an excellent index of the degree of similarity between linguistic elements. The greater the similarity, the more likely two elements are to be confused in an error. When two units are unwilling to interact, we are entitled to claim that their representations are too dissimilar to bring them into contact. One such dissimilatory relationship is illustrated by the case of prevocalic and postvocalic consonants. These are very reluctant to interact in tongue slips. In more than 90 per cent of cases, prevocalic consonants interact with other prevocalic consonants. A typical speech error is presented in (35), an untypical one in (36).

(35) *canpakes* for *pancakes*
(36) *shiff* for *fish* (both from Fromkin 1973)

No. (35) is a typical slip in which two elements from like syllable positions interact. The onset /k/ and the onset /p/ exchange places. The opportunity for an interaction between segments from different loci was given but not taken. No. (36) is a rare instance of an intrasyllabic error which of necessity involves consonants from non-identical sites. The onset takes the position of the coda and vice versa. The conclusion that can be drawn from this pattern is that prevocalic (postvocalic) consonants must be related to other prevocalic (postvocalic) consonants in a way that they are not to postvocalic (prevocalic) ones. A close relationship is expressed by identical tags, a remote relationship by disparate tags. As mentioned, these tags serve the purpose of rendering each element of an utterance unique, thereby minimizing the danger of confusion. Clearly, then, position-specific coding is an aid in the serialization process.

In view of its obvious use, it comes as no surprise that the constraint on the interaction of consonants from like syllable positions has been found to operate in (almost) every language that has thus far been examined. However, there is one notable exception: it does not generally hold in Arabic (Berg and Abd-El-Jawad 1996). In this language, the interaction of consonants from unlike syllable positions is far less discouraged than in English or German. Consider the following two examples. The transliteration of these and all other examples from Arabic is largely phonemic.

(37) *yabað* for *yaðab*
     'attracted, pulled'
(38) *fidli* for *fildi*
     'raincoat'

Case (37) is similar to (36) in that it documents the interaction of an onset and a coda consonant from the same syllable. It differs from (36), however, in that it occurs in a disyllabic word where the possibility of a between-syllable error exists. In (38), two adjacent consonants from different syllables swap places. Note that the reversal takes place across the syllable boundary.

By analogy with what has been claimed for the English data, the largely unconstrained interaction between prevocalic and postvocalic consonants inclines us to the conclusion that they have the same representational status. That is, they cannot be labelled as 'onset' and 'coda' consonants. The simplest solution is to refrain from labelling them at all. They are 'just' consonants.[8]

Even if the distinction between onsets and codas proves to be inapplicable to Arabic, it is still possible for segments to be marked for the syllable they are associated with. Take (38) as an example. The phonemes /f/ and /l/ might be indiscriminately coded as 'first-syllable consonants'. If this were the case, the interaction between elements from different syllables should be discouraged. This is not so, however. Prevocalic and postvocalic consonants interact freely, irrespective of whether they are separated by a syllable boundary. Hence, coding by syllable membership is not supported by the empirical data. The only representation appropriate for Arabic appears to be the unlabelled linear one depicted in (39). In contrast, the Germanic languages require a hierarchical structure augmented by node labelling, as in (40). The details of this structure are irrelevant and will not be defended here. We will look at monosyllabic (a) as well as polysyllabic (b) words, the latter of which are more typical of Arabic. For better comparison, the same skeleton (and later on the same melody) will be assumed for both languages. The symbol *W* stands for 'word'.

(39) Arabic   a.   σ   b.   W

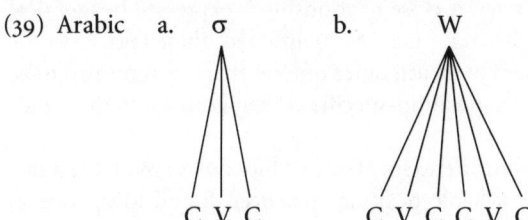

        C V C   C V C C V C

---

[8] This discussion is somewhat simplified compared to Berg and Abd-El-Jawad (1996). In particular, the time dimension is left out of account here.

(40) English

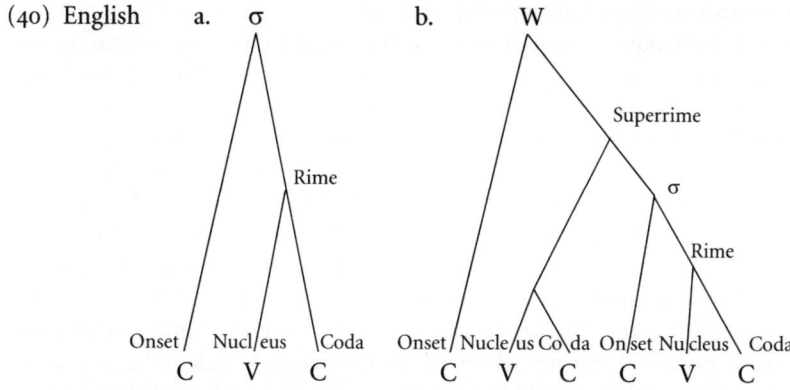

How does the serialization mechanism work in the two languages? Given the disparate representations in (39) and (40), it must operate linearly in Arabic but hierarchically in English. That is to say, when an English (monosyllabic) word is readied for production, it is recoded as onset and rime. The onset as the leftmost node is activated first and the rime node next. The nucleus and coda nodes can only be activated through the intermediary of the rime. The procedure is much simpler in Arabic, where a scanning from left to right is the only option available. That is, the first segment is activated first, then the second, and so on. How strongly a segment is activated depends upon how far it is from the current position. No intermediate nodes influence the activation levels.

At first glance, the Arabic solution seems simpler and the English one unnecessarily complicated. It may thus be suspected that there is a processing advantage to the more complex alternative and a processing disadvantage to the simpler alternative. This is in fact the case. The English model makes sure that each consonant is uniquely identified. So when the phonemes of a word are serialized, it is (relatively) easy for the sequentialization mechanism to keep track of which segment it has just reached. For example, when the sequencer has reached the /m/ in *litmus*, it is clear that it occupies the onset of the second syllable because it is represented as an onset which is dominated by a superrime node (see (40b)). This is what makes it different from all other phonemes of the word. What about a word like *canteen* in which one phoneme appears twice? As a matter of fact there is no problem at all, because the two /n/s are kept distinct by the same coding principles as apply to any two non-identical segments. Specifically, the first /n/ is a coda which is dominated by a rime node which in turn is dominated by a superrime node, whereas the second /n/ is dominated by a rime node which in turn is dominated by a syllable node. A similar difference in dominance relationships applies to monosyllabic words such as *kick*.

Now let us look at the situation in Arabic. Even with a left-to-right scanning mechanism, there is no problem with generating the order of constituents in words in which each segment type occurs only once. This is for the simple reason that the melodic level alone suffices to ensure the distinctness of the segments. The suprasegmental coding of distinctness is not necessary. Thus the scanner does not run the risk of getting confused. However, if one segment type occurs twice, the distinctness requirement at the melody level is not met. Because the suprasegmental representation is the same for all consonants of a word (39), identical consonants cannot be kept apart. Let us take the phoneme sequence /ʃiʃ/ and assume for the sake of the argument that it is a real form in Arabic. How does the sequencing mechanism deal with this sequence? Under normal circumstances, the first segment is outputted before the second, the second before the third, etc. So after the generation of the first /ʃ/, the sequencer must take charge of the vowel. But how does the sequencer know that the /i/ is to be uttered next rather than the beginning of the following word? Because all segments are represented only once in the mental network (see section 3.2.1), the just-selected /ʃ/ may either be the first or the second. No matter how this problem might be solved, it is clear that there is a problem and one that is likely to confuse the sequencing mechanism.

There is an obvious way out. Taking it as given that the suprasegmental level cannot help out of this difficulty, the only possibility is to prevent the problem from arising in the first place. This means that the repetition of identical segments within a morpheme must be avoided. It is therefore predicted that Arabic morphemes do not contain identical segments. Since Arabic roots are usually made up of three consonants, two theoretical possibilities have to be reckoned with. The identical segments might be either contiguous ($C_xC_xC_y$ and $C_xC_yC_y$) or non-contiguous ($C_xC_yC_x$) on the consonantal tier. Both possibilities are ruled out by prediction because they create confusion as to the position that is currently being processed.

One might argue, however, that the first possibility is more troublesome than the second because the linear distance between the identical segments is smaller and thus the likelihood of confusion greater. The logic behind this psycholinguistic argument is that by the time the sequencer has arrived at the final segment in the sequence $C_xC_yC_x$, it has already 'forgotten' about having produced the same consonant before. We would therefore predict that $C_xC_xC_y$ and $C_xC_yC_y$ structures are more consistently banned than $C_xC_yC_x$ structures. What is not banned, however, is gemination. In autosegmental theory, geminates are represented as one element at the melodic tier being linked to two positions in the skeleton. This phonological representation has been found to be phonetically realistic (Lahiri and Hankamer 1988). There is thus no repetition problem.

As regards English (and other Germanic languages), no prohibition of the kind predicted for Arabic is expected. Tokens of the same segment type may recur freely within a morpheme. This prediction is clearly supported by the data. Even within monosyllabic words, English allows the repetition of identical consonants. Quite a few words exist in which onset and coda are identical, e.g. *cock, gag, pop, Bob, tit, deed, cease, nun, mime, loll,* and *roar* (AE). Even in more complex syllables, identical consonants are principally possible, e.g. *state* and *flail*.[9] What is hardly any problem

[9] It should be noted, though, that more severe restrictions on the occurrence of identical elements hold in relative syllable positions (i.e. post-initial and pre-final) than in absolute positions (i.e. initial and

at the level of monosyllabic words is evidently even less of a problem in multisyllabic words. Thus the psycholinguistic prediction for English is clearly correct.

Let us now return to Arabic. Before embarking upon the analysis proper, it should be pointed out that a large part of the Arabic lexicon consists of discontinuous morphemes. Words are created on the basis of consonantal roots which are enriched by vocalic transfixes. The roots most usually consist of three consonants, but bi- and quadriconsonantal roots also occur. The well-known Arabic verb k-t-b 'to write' may serve as an illustration. Inflection and derivation occur by intercalation of vowel patterns such as *kitaabii* 'my book' and *maktab* 'office'. The root consonants are normally separated by a vocalic segment, as in the first example, but they may also be contiguous by dint of vowel deletion rules as in the second example. The consonants and vowels of Arabic words are underlyingly represented on separate tiers, reflecting the functional unity of the consonants and that of the vowels as well as the functional independence between the two major segment classes. During the derivation, the two tiers are conflated to yield the linear surface form of Arabic words. The nature and order of the root consonants is customarily preserved from underlying to surface representation.

The examination of the phonemic structure of Arabic words brings forth intriguing results. The classic study on this topic is that of Greenberg (1950), who investigated the combinatorial possibilities in 3775 triconsonantal roots. The analysis of the consonants will be carried out pairwise, thus C_1–C_2, C_1–C_3, and C_2–C_3. We will consider each part in turn. Among the 3775 root morphemes, there is not a single one in which C_1 and C_2 are identical. Moreover, there is a strong constraint on the repetition of *similar* segments. Homorganic consonants such as g-k-C_3 and b-m-C_3 are also absent. This provides quite striking support for the research hypothesis.

As for the relationship between C_1 and C_3, Greenberg's table 2 lists twenty cases in which $C_1 = C_3$. One of these is q-l-q 'to be disturbed'. To appreciate this figure fully, it is imperative to estimate chance. According to Greenberg (and the dictionaries he relies upon), there are 28 consonantal phonemes. Each phoneme paired with each other and itself yields 784 possibilities, i.e. cells in a two-dimensional matrix. Given a data base of 3775 roots, each cell should contain 3775/784 = 4.8 entries on an average (ignoring frequency effects). As noted, the 28 cells in which two identical segments are paired contain only 20 items altogether (0.7 items per cell on an average).

---

final). Words of the type $C_xC_yVC_yC_z$ are lacking in English. Also, words of the type $C_xC_yVC_y$ are rare. As Davis (1984) points out, C_y cannot be a nasal in sC_yVC_y. This constraint holds irrespective of whether these segments are separated by a syllable boundary. Davis (1989) notes the existence of some repetition constraints operating at the featural rather than segmental level. In all probability, these cooccurrence restrictions have to do with a heightened difficulty of accessing relative as compared to absolute syllable positions (Stemberger and Treiman 1986). This difficulty testifies that segment repetition in English is rather a problem, much as would be expected on the basis of MacKay's (1970a) findings. However, this problem is only of medium severity: it can make an impact only in conjunction with other problems. When there is no problem of position-specific access, the melody level licenses the recurrence of identical segments.

This is significantly different from chance ($\chi^2(1) = 60.6$, $p < 0.001$). We may conclude that an identity between C_1 and C_3 is strongly discouraged, though not completely banned, in Arabic root morphemes. The constraint on phoneme repetition can thus be argued to be in operation, although it is not quite as powerful as in the relationship between C_1 and C_2.

This result is fully compatible with the psycholinguistic prediction. Because the identical segments are separated by a different consonant, their interfering effect upon each other is mitigated and a minor amount of consonant identity is allowed. Basically, though, the repetition constraint *is* obeyed, going by the high percentage (99.5 per cent) of confirming cases. Additional evidence for the operation of this principle comes from the fact that homorganic consonants do not generally occupy C_1 and C_3 positions. As in the case of segments, the restriction on feature repetition is less severe with C_1 and C_3 than with C_1 and C_2.

Finally, the relationship between C_2 and C_3 will be subjected to scrutiny. Quite unexpectedly, table 3 in Greenberg (1950) lists 340 root morphemes with $C_2 = C_3$. These make up almost 10 per cent of the entire database. In view of a total of 28 different consonantal phonemes, the average number of lexical entries per cell is 12.1. This is considerably *more* than would be expected on a chance distribution: $\chi^2(1) = 49.3$, $p < 0.001$. It can therefore be established that consonant repetition is not discouraged in positions C_2 and C_3. Quite to the contrary, the repetition of identical material is strongly encouraged. There is thus no way around the conclusion that the repetition constraint on identical segments does not hold in positions C_2 and C_3. It is worthy of mention, however, that a repetition constraint on similar segments *is* generally respected. Homorganic consonants are largely excluded in the loci under consideration. So while *ʃ-k-k* is a possible and indeed extant morpheme (meaning 'to split'), *ʃ-k-g* is not.

There is no question that the C_2–C_3 patterns are flatly counter to prediction. Theoretically, two ways of dealing with this discrepancy are discernible. The processing considerations either make false predictions or capture something that is missed by the foregoing analysis. In the former case the claim about the influence of processing on language would be undercut, while it might be salvaged in the latter. Let us look at the two possibilities in turn. There are at least two reasons which argue against an outright rejection of the psycholinguistic account. For one thing, it makes the correct predictions with respect to the C_1–C_2 and C_1–C_3 positions. For another, the processing account makes partly correct predictions with respect to C_2–C_3. The repetition constraint is not completely absent in that it makes an impact at the feature (though not at the segment) level. If the psycholinguistic account were dismissed lightly, one would be at a loss to explain why it works in the majority of cases.

There is thus good reason to take a deeper look at the empirical data. Our attention so far has been directed to surface patterns. Given that segmental identity is predicted not to occur, we might be well advised to look for it somewhere else, to wit in underlying representation. The expectation would then be that there exist significant differences between underlying and surface forms and that the psycholinguistic predictions pertain to the underlying level rather than to surface patterns. In other words, the surface forms are claimed to be 'distorted' and to conceal the 'true' nature of Arabic root morphemes. For this possibility to be more than a gimmick, the distinction between the underlying and the surface level has to be shown to be psychologically real, i.e. to be independently motivatable.

Fortunately, there are strong processing arguments in favour of disparate representations of Arabic words at the surface and underlying levels. As mentioned, surface forms are linear strings of discontinuous morphemes. There is psycholinguistic evidence to suggest that the linear continuity of segments is not preserved in underlying representation. That Arabic words are decomposed into roots and transfixes (at one level of representation), even though these are discontinuous, is suggested by several lines of external evidence including speech errors and language games. In both data types, roots may be 'picked out' even though they are discontinuous. Refer to the following slip of the tongue:

(41)   *il ḥasas il wattaar* for *il watar il ḥassaas*
       'to get to the heart of the issue'

Case (41) documents the reversal of two triconsonantal roots with the structure being left untouched. It would be preposterous to assume that three segmental malfunctions (in word-initial, medial, and final loci) took place simultaneously but independently in this tongue slip. An explanation in terms of a unitary modification of a linguistic unit is much more likely. This unit corresponds exactly to what linguists have identified as the root morpheme. Note that (41) occurred at one specific level of representation, and that it consequently does not necessarily argue against the possibility that Arabic words may be represented holistically at a different level. In fact, whole-word errors are also observed. It is apparent, then, that the same hierarchy of representational levels exists in English and Arabic. A morphemic representation coexists with a word representation even though the word structure of the two languages is so vastly different. We may therefore postulate a psychologically real underlying level representing unpronounceable material in Arabic.

In what way should the underlying representation differ from the surface representation? According to the psycholinguistic predictions formulated above, underlying representations should do without repeated segments. A surface stem such as *s-m-m* 'to poison' should be underlyingly represented as /s-m/. What superficially looks like a triconsonantal stem would 'in reality' be a biconsonantal stem. Such an underlying representation would eliminate the disagreement between the processing predictions and the empirical data. So the obvious question to ask is whether there is psycholinguistic evidence in support of non-repeated segments in underlying representation.

To answer this question, a relatively simple diagnostic test suggests itself. It only has to be ascertained whether stems with repeated segments behave like bi- or triconsonantal roots. Language games provide one source of evidence. In comparison with internal data, their advantage is that they attest to the productive application of rules because it is unlikely, though not impossible, that the transformed output is stored in long-term memory. McCarthy (1982) discusses an Arabic language game in which the consonants of the root morpheme may be freely permuted while everything else remains in its place. There are five (3!–1) possibilities of permutation in triconsonantal roots but only one (2!–1) in biconsonantal stems. If >*s-m-m*< is represented in surface-true fashion, it should behave like other triconsonantal roots; if, however, it is represented as /sm/ it should allow for only one productive output.

As it turns out, the latter alternative is the correct one. The form *sammam* 'he poisoned' can only be recoded as *massas*. Although five formally distinct output patterns cannot be generated from *s-m-m* stems on the triconsonantal account, some patterns can be generated which are impossible on the biconsonantal hypothesis. One critical piece of evidence is the form *mammas*, which is illicit in this language game. This is expected if *s-m-m* is treated as a biconsonantal root but incompatible with its analysis in terms of a triconsonantal root.

A second language game, reported on in McCarthy (1985), leads to a similar conclusion. It is used as a secret language and played by certain speakers of Amharic, an Ethiopian language with quadriconsonantal roots. Without going into details, this game involves the replacement of the vocalism, the preservation of the nature and order of the root consonants, and their reassociation with a different prosodic template. Three such templates, differing only in their medial consonantism, are used: a) CVCVC, b) CVCCVC, and c) CVCCCVC. For instance, *kifu* 'cruel' becomes *kayfəf*. The biconsonantal root is associated with the canonical pattern CVCVC and surfaces as a triconsonantal form. The crucial issue is by which criteria the decision among the three templates is made. One possibility that immediately comes to mind is that the number of consonants determines the choice of the appropriate skeleton. However, this is not so. The choice of the skeleton is determined by the number of *different* consonants in the base form. A triconsonantal root with two identical segments behaves like a biconsonantal root with non-identical segments. That is to say, repeated consonants count as one. A form like *wəddəd* 'love', for example, is transformed into *waydəd*. As can be seen, recourse is made to the same canonical CV pattern as in the *kifu* example above. Genuine triconsonantal roots such as *gabbəzə* 'to invite to' are expanded on the basis of the CVCCVC template and surface as *gaybuzəz*. We may infer that at the level at which base forms undergo transformations, repeated consonants are represented only once.

On the assumption that underlying representations of Arabic roots are type- rather than token-based, a duplication rule has to be posited for the generation of surface forms of *s-m-m*-type roots. Is there any evidence for the active use of such a rule? It might be held that the above language games constitute a case in point insofar as they attest to the repeated association of the same unit at the root tier with two different positions at the skeletal tier. This description is tantamount to a duplication process. However, the evidence from the language games is weakened by the possibility that the copying rule may be part of a machinery specifically designed for the generation of verbal play. Again, speech errors prove to be an invaluable source of information. What would be the prediction to be derived from the assumption that repeated consonants are underlyingly absent? Provided that malfunctions operate at the underlying level (i.e. before the copying rule applies), an error on the segment to be duplicated later should manifest itself at *two* different locations in the surface string. Take the example of the stem *s-m-m*, provisionally represented as /s-m/. If, for instance, the labial nasal is inadvertently replaced by a uvular stop and the surface string consists of a CVCVC template, it is to be expected that both the second and the third consonant positions will be occupied by /q/. The error form would then be *sVqVq*. Remarkably, in some slips the duplication rule can be seen to operate 'in nature'. Consider (42) and (43):

(42) *xaffu damiim* for *dammu xafiif*
    'He is full of charm'
(43) *sibb id daad* for *sidd il baab*
    'Close the door'

Number (42) illustrates the interaction between a superficially triconsonantal and a biconsonantal root. The triconsonantal morpheme *x-f-f* has identical segments in positions C_2 and C_3, the biconsonantal root *d-m* contains a geminate which functions like a singleton phoneme in slips of the tongue. The interesting aspect about (42) is how the two elements of the biconsonantal root are spread across the triconsonantal skeleton. Given that there are three slots and two fillers, two possibilities are conceivable. Either the number of slots must be decreased or the number of fillers increased. More specifically, a slot may be dropped or a filler duplicated. In the latter case we would have evidence for the on-line application of the copying rule. As is apparent from (42), the labial nasal appears twice in the error word *damiim*. The most obvious interpretation is that the nasal which is singly represented at the underlying level has been duplicated by dint of a phonological rule.

Unlike (42), (43) involves the transposition of segments rather than roots. In all probability, the final /d/ in *sidd* changed places with the final /b/ in *baab*. However, this is not all there is to it. What is intriguing about (43) is that the error word is not *baad* but *daad*. That is, the initial consonant has also been altered in compliance with the modification in final position. This subsidiary process is understandable only on the assumption that the target word, *baab*, is underlyingly a monoconsonantal root and that the error process affected this underlying consonant before the copying rule was applied. Thus a single error process may manifest itself at two different locations. It can be seen, then, that both (42) and (43), despite their seeming complexity, are amenable to a straightforward analysis once it is granted that Arabic possesses a psychologically real duplication rule which is actively deployed in language production.

Our conclusion is therefore that Arabic roots with identical consonants are represented in non-surface-true fashion at the underlying level. *Contra* Hudson (1986), identical adjacent segments are represented only once and, if necessary, are duplicated during the transition from the underlying to the superficial level. As has been suggested above, the reason for the prohibition against adjacent identical segments lies in the vulnerability of the serialization mechanism. When there are two identical segments next to each other, the sequencer is liable to make errors. In particular, after the production of the first token, it may not know whether to continue with the second token or with one of a different type. The constraint on segment repetition can now be construed as a *trouble-avoidance strategy*. Linguistic structures that are difficult to deal with are not generated in the first place. This is a further example of the linguistic structure adjusting itself to the constraints of the processor.

Summarizing, it can be established that, given appropriate background assumptions, all the predictions derived from the postulated workings of the production mechanism are borne out by the structure of the language. Unlike what can be observed in concatenative languages, Arabic puts a ban on the repetition of identical segments—a constraint which is very tight in the case of adjacent phonemes and somewhat looser in the case of non-adjacent units. Some data which at first sight appeared to be at odds with the psycholinguistic prediction turned out not to be recalcitrant on closer inspection. Arabic does evidence the repetition of identical segments in the second and third positions of triconsonantal roots,[10] but it could be shown that this is a surface phenomenon and that there is an underlying level at which identical segments are represented only once.

The hypothesis of an underlying structure and the absence of repeated segments in underlying representation are far from ad hoc procedures of 'getting the data right'. These two claims have been motivated on independent grounds and arguably reflect a psychological reality. That the psycholinguistic prediction applies to the underlying rather than the surface level is not surprising, given that it is based on speech error patterns and that slips of the tongue have been demonstrated to arise at the underlying level, that is, prior to the application of certain phonological rules (e.g. Berg 1989b; Postma and Noordanus 1996).

4.7. The Status of the Syllable

The syllable is one of the most interesting and elusive units of analysis, both in linguistics and in psycholinguistics. What makes this notion so extremely difficult to come to grips with is that it appears to play a role at a relatively low level but has both direct and indirect repercussions on higher levels of analysis. How this hybrid nature can be adequately modelled is an open question. In the following, the role of the syllable in the process of language production will be briefly discussed with a view to deriving predictions regarding linguistic structure and variation.

Perhaps the most astonishing aspect about the syllable is its immunity to malfunction. While almost all linguistic units (excepting the chunks above the word

---

[10] On the possible origin of $C_xC_yC_y$ roots, see Kuryłowicz (1972).

level) have been shown to be subject to error, syllables as wholes are not normally involved in (syntagmatic) error processes. With the possible exception of Japanese, this absence has been confirmed for all the languages investigated so far. The number of syllabic slips of the tongue (see (44)) is as infinitesimal as that of errors involving non-constituents as in (45). Syllabic errors may thus be suspected to occur at chance level.

(44) *How about Lou Alcindor?* for *Al Lucindor*
(45) *journicle article* for *journal article* (both from Shattuck-Hufnagel 1983)

Shattuck-Hufnagel (1983) classifies (44) as a whole-syllable slip in which the segment sequences /æl/ and /lu:/ exchange places. However, this interpretation is arguable, as *Al* as the short form of *Alister* is an independent word. This is not true of /lu:/ as the first syllable of *Lucindor*, although this phoneme sequence also constitutes a short form of a proper name as well as a separate word (*loo*). So at least one part of the exchange does not unequivocally involve a syllabic unit. Number (45) documents the substitution of [əl] by [ɪkl]. The erroneous sequence comprises the nucleus of one syllable, a syllable boundary, the onset, and the bearer of another syllable. These three phonemes do not form a phonological constituent and yet they act as a unit in this slip of the tongue. The rarity of such errors as (44–5) justifies regarding them as random aberrations of the language generation system.

In a psycholinguistic analysis of the role of the syllable, Berg (1992a) concludes that the linguistic information is not represented in terms of syllables at the stage of the production process at which errors come about, i.e. during high-level programming. Metaphorically speaking, syllables are not the gist of the psycholinguistic mill.

However, one exception to this pattern exists. Non-contextual losses of syllables as in (46) and (47) do occur above chance frequency.

(46) That's really thetic– pathetic (from Stemberger, unpublished)
(47) G: Ernst Dieter Lueg hat die erregende batte– Debatte im Bundestag miterlebt. [batə de:bátə]
 'Ernst Dieter Lueg [proper name] has witnessed the exciting debate in parliament'

Both tongue slips exemplify the loss of a syllable, [pə] in (46) and [de:] in (47). This error type is relatively often encountered. Berg (1992a) identifies three factors which facilitate its occurrence. Syllable omissions are most likely (a) in word-initial positions, (b) when the syllable is unstressed, and (c) when the syllable has a reduced vowel. All three criteria are fulfilled in (46), the first two in (47). While the first two constraints find unambiguous empirical support, the validity of the third could only be suggested rather than demonstrated on the basis of the German data. This uncertainty arises from the fact that, although omissions of schwa-based syllables abound, almost all of them can also be analysed as prefix losses and hence cannot be unequivocally assigned to the class of syllable slips.

The psycholinguistic evidence admits to the following predictions. Because syllables are absent from high-level processing, they should play no role in the phonological component of the language. Note that this claim makes explicit reference to syllables as wholes, not to syllabic constituents or syllable boundaries. From the diachronic angle, historical change should not involve the reordering or addition of syllables. By contrast, the loss of entire syllables is expressly licensed. Thus the psycholinguistic predictions apply to diachrony and synchrony alike. What qualifies (or does not qualify) as a diachronic process should also qualify (or not qualify) as a synchronic process.

Beginning with synchrony, there do not seem to be phonological or morphological rules in English and German which make reference to the syllable as a unit. Granted, syllables may function as anchor points for some suprasegmental features. For example, stress in German and English (Berg 1990a) and pharyngealization in Modern Aramaic (Hoberman 1988) are associated with syllables rather than smaller elements, but this cannot be taken as evidence for the *manipulation* of syllabic units. A good test case is the process of reduplication in which the addition of segmental material can be systematically studied. The prediction from psycholinguistic processing is that the reduplication of whole syllables should be a very rare event in natural languages.[11] This expectation is strikingly confirmed by Marantz's (1982) analysis of reduplicative processes across the world. His survey encompasses only one language which reduplicates segmental material on a syllabic basis. This is the Australian language Yidin^y in which pluralization may occur by reduplicating the first two syllables of the singular noun, as in *gindelba* 'lizard' → *gindelgindelba* 'lizards'. It should be pointed out that the reduplication of double syllables coexists with the absence of single syllables as reduplicating material.

Note, however, that the significance of this result is slightly weakened by the fact that reduplication need not involve phonological or morphological constituents. Even though the greater number of reduplicative processes implicate constituents such as morphemes and words, Marantz also discusses several examples which are not amenable to an analysis in terms of constituents, e.g. the onset/nucleus sequence in CVC syllables. However, Marantz has not demonstrated that the phoneme sequences involved in reduplicative processes are blind to constituency, i.e. that all sequences occur at chance frequency. This is very much to be doubted.

While expressing satisfaction with the formal achievements of his theory, Marantz (1982: 456) is puzzled by the almost complete absence of syllable-based reduplication and calls it a mystery. Although I do not wish to claim that this mystery has been fully elucidated here, I submit that part of the answer lies in the realm of high-level programming, where syllabic representations do not exist and implicationally syllables cannot be manipulated as units.[12]

---

[11] Evidently, this holds true only to the extent that the processing patterns observed for English, German and a couple of other languages are universally valid.

[12] This presupposes that the would-be syllable-error rule and the would-be reduplication rule apply at roughly the same representational stage.

Contrary to the substitution and addition of syllables, syllabic loss, known as aphaeresis, is not at all uncommon. In particular, the constraints under which it operates are exactly the ones predicted by the speech error data. The omissions occur in word-initial positions and affect unstressed syllables containing reduced vowels. Quite often, the syllable only consists of a vowel. In that case, ambiguity arises as to the nature of the unit being lost. Since these 'naked' syllables do not in any way behave differently from more complex syllables and since it is very rare that vowels are dropped (aphesis) and tautosyllabic consonants retained, there is reason to regard initial vowel deletions as special instances of syllable omissions. In other words, aphesis can be subsumed under aphaeresis for the most part.

The instability of initial syllables and vowels can be observed throughout the development of the English language. Because aphaeresis operates on initial unstressed syllables, it presupposes a rhythmic structure which is rather untypical of English words. It comes as no surprise, then, that this process was most prevalent at the time when French submerged the English language. For example, Old French *assembler* became Middle English *semblen* and *estranger* developed into *stranger*. In this way, the borrowings were made to better fit the English stress pattern. Aphaeresis in the history of the language is at the heart of what now appear to be synchronic alternations. Cases in point include *special–especial, spy–espionage, bashful–abashed*, and *with bated breath–to abate*. These pairs show that the original form is not obliterated. The historical process thus is an optional one (Alexander 1988). What used to be simple variants may, but need not, acquire lexical status and in this way enlarge the lexicon.

Indeed, aphaeresis occurs on a wide scale in the spoken language of today (and yesterday). As is apparent from Kypriotaki's (1973) work on American English, synchronic aphaeresis is subject to exactly the same constraints as its diachronic counterpart. The syllable to be deleted must be unstressed, word-initial, and contain either /ɪ/ or /ə/. Typical examples include *about* in *How 'bout that?* and *unless* in *I ain't going 'less you do*. Fisher and McDavid (1976) assert that syllable deletion is not restricted to allegro speech. Relaxed circumstances are all that is needed for aphaeresis to occur. According to Kypriotaki, unstressed syllable deletion does not occur across the board. It takes place more often in some lexical items but rarely or not at all in others. Although she does not make an attempt to determine what makes a particular item more deletion-prone than another, it is clear from her published data that frequency plays a major role. In accordance with the expectations set out in section 5.17, aphaeresis is a frequency-sensitive process. Because it reduces articulatory effort, it should affect the most common words first. In actual fact, all the words listed in Fisher and McDavid and most of Kypriotaki's examples are high-frequency items.

The tendency to drop initial unstressed syllables can also be observed in proper names. Due to their frequent use, they are liable to undergo shortening, sometimes in rather drastic ways. When the full name begins with a stressed syllable, it is almost invariably retained. But when its first syllable is unstressed, it may be deleted, as in

Liz for *Elizabeth, Shelley* for *Michelle*, and *Becky* for *Rebecca*. This phenomenon is not peculiar to English. German examples are *Tina* for *Bettina*, *Bine* for *Sabine*, and *Hans* for *Johannes*. The last case illustrates the transition from a non-lexicalized variant of *Johannes* to an independent lexicalized item which has severed its connection with the unreduced form. Whether or not this lexicalization process takes place is a matter of social acceptability or personal taste rather than a linguistic or psycholinguistic issue.

To conclude, the predictions derived from the analysis of language production data are clearly borne out by the synchronic and diachronic patterns. Because whole syllables are not manipulated by the language processor, they cannot be used in morphological processes such as reduplication. The only possibility for syllables to be manipulated is deletion, but only under the strict conditions imposed by the processing system. All these conditions are satisfied in both synchrony and diachrony. When one of these requirements is not met, the deletion process is less likely, or fails, to take place.

There is, however, one aspect of the loss of unstressed initial syllables which has not been predicted by the processing principles—its optional nature. While the process itself has been quite active (in the past and the present), it has generally produced alternatives to, rather than substitutions for, already existent words. The full and the clipped forms entered a relationship of complementary distribution. As suggested in the analysis of proper names, the question of whether a reduced form gains lexical status is unrelated to the mechanism underlying its generation. The issue is rather how well the shortened form manages to supplant the full form. It may be that this process is not so powerful (or takes a long time to complete) because shortened variants are stigmatized as instances of sloppy articulation and therefore do not oust more highly regarded forms very fast. Since the relationship between full and reduced forms is independent of the process which gives rise to syllable deletion, the validity of the psycholinguistic prediction is not vitiated by the preservation of the full-length words.

4.8. The Role of Lexical Stress

A central issue in language comprehension research is the analysis of the lexical access code, i.e. the prelexical representation (or set of representations) by which an item is located in the mental lexicon. A reasonable assumption to begin with would be that the speech signal is exploited to the maximum for this task. The richer the prelexical representation, the argument runs, the more reliably lexical entries may be accessed. On the other hand, it cannot be taken for granted that all conceivable pieces of information are represented at the prelexical stage. It may be that some of them cannot be computed or, if they could, would be of no use during lexical access. For example, the computation of a given piece of information might be possible only in conjunction with lexical information. In such a case it can evidently not serve as part of the prelexical access code. It is also possible that the computation does not take place because this information would not increase the probability of hitting the mark.

One potential access feature is word stress—at least in those languages where stress is not fixed and can therefore function distinctively. The role of word stress prior to lexical retrieval has been investigated in an ingenious set of experiments by Cutler (1986). She tested whether this piece of information functions to constrain lexical access in language comprehension in English. Her reasoning was as follows. Two words which differ only on where they receive lexical stress are represented in a similar fashion at the prelexical stage, if they produce identical effects during lexical access. To put it succinctly, they would be treated as homophones by the parser even though they are not—neither at the surface phonetic level nor as lexical entries. If, however, these two words produce distinct effects, these effects may be attributed to their structural difference which implicationally must be included in the prelexical representation. What is needed, therefore, is a set of stimulus pairs which are distinguished only by differential stress placement, i.e. stimuli with identical segmental make-up. Two such examples are *forebear* as the noun [fɔ́:bɛə] and *forbear* as the verb [fɔ:bɛ́ə] and *discount* as the noun [dískaʊnt] and the verb [dɪskáʊnt].

In determining whether [fɔ́:bɛə] and [fɔ:bɛ́ə] really are homophones, the critical task is one of finding the right 'litmus test'. Cutler chose as a diagnostic test Swinney's (1979) results on the processing of homophonous words. He demonstrated that during the earliest phases of lexical access, both readings of a homophonous word are activated regardless of the fact that only one of them is contextually appropriate. Capitalizing upon this effect, Cutler reasoned that if the two versions of, let us say, *forbear* behave like homophones, the processing of one should lead to the activation of both meanings. For instance, both versions should prime the noun *ancestor* as well as the verb *to be patient*. That is to say, in a lexical-decision task, subjects should respond more quickly to these stimuli than to semantically unrelated control words. Interestingly enough, Cutler was able to establish such a priming effect. Words which are related to one of the two meanings of the 'homophone' were closer to the recognition threshold, suggesting a heightened level of activation. According to this test, then, [fɔ́:bɛə] and [fɔ:bɛ́ə] behave in the same way as *him* and *hymn*. Cutler inferred from this finding that [fɔ́:bɛə] is homophonous with [fɔ:bɛ́ə] at the prelexical access stage.

The predictions that follow from this astonishing psycholinguistic result are fairly straightforward. Since language has to be comprehended by the listener, it can justly be expected to possess only those properties which the comprehension device can deal with. Properties to which the processor is blind are expectedly absent from language. This expectation is the strongest when the properties in question are the only criterion by which two given lexical items can be distinguished. In such a case, the processor would evidently be unable to address the desired entry in the lexicon *on the basis of this particular source of information*. Thus, two predictions may be formulated for English. Word pairs which differ on their stress pattern alone should be non-existent and examples such as *forbear* and *discount* which are distinguished also by word class should be extremely rare.

Both predictions are clearly borne out. Cutler (1986) found a total of eleven pairs of the *forbear* type. None of these word pairs was of the same syntactic category. Therefore it is quite possible that the processing mechanism singles out the intended lexical item from all others on the basis of word class rather than prosodic information. It can be claimed, then, that the total absence of word pairs whose only distinguishing feature is lexical stress and the rarity of pairs like [fɔ́ːbɛə] vs. [fɔːbɛ́ə] is due to the processor's inability to keep these word pairs distinct on the basis of their differing stress placement during the stages of lexical access.

Is the rarity or even lack of relevant word pairs the reason why the comprehension device has not felt the need to evolve a sensitivity to lexical stress? If so, the processor would not be unable but would simply not have learned to deal with this type of information. Cutler (1986) does not seem to allow for this possibility. She argues that the prelexical stage is principally incapable of computing the correct stress placement because this computation depends upon prior knowledge of the word boundary, a piece of information which cannot be presupposed at this level of analysis as it becomes definitively available only upon word recognition.

Since this explanation is of the universalist kind, it invites the prediction that word pairs whose sole distinguishing feature is lexical stress cannot occur, and that the number of pairs of the *forbear* type should be very low in the languages of the world. Differently put, word stress should function as a concomitant rather than as a major distinctive feature. This hypothesis will now be tested against Spanish and German data.

Spanish distinguishes three conjugational classes of regular verbs, those ending in *-ar*, *-er*, and *-ir*. The 1st person singular of the present tense is formed by adding the suffix *-o* to the verb stem in all groups, e.g. *am-ar* 'to love' → *am-o* 'I love' and *viv-ir* 'to live' → *viv-o* 'I live'. The 3rd person singular of the *Pretérito Indefinido*, which roughly corresponds to the Simple Past in English, also takes an *-o* in the case of the verbs ending in *-ar*. In violation of the general stress rules of Spanish, this *o* is the bearer of stress, e.g. *am-ar* 'to love' → *am-ó* 'he loved'. There is thus a stress contrast in *ámo* and *amó* without any concomitant segmental contrast.[13] One might be led to believe that the stress contrast in these pairs is not truly distinctive because there is a further criterion by which *ámo* and *amó* can be told apart, namely person. However, the personal pronoun as the carrier unit for the category *person* is not used in the unmarked case. Person information is encoded only in the suffix. This property of Spanish may lead to identical microcontexts for both forms, as in (48).

(48) a. *Amo la vida* 'I love to live'
 b. *Amó la vida* 'He loved to live'

---

[13] The vowels are pronounced more or less alike. Only their intensity, not their duration differs as a function of whether they are stressed or unstressed.

On the surface, then, the only distinguishing feature is stress. The contrast between *ámo* and *amó* is a systematic one in Spanish, in that it may potentially arise in a great number of cases.

Like Spanish, German exhibits a stress contrast in its verbal system, but it involves derivational rather than inflectional morphology. German makes heavy use of prefixation as a means of modifying the meaning of the base verb. During prefixation, main stress may either stay on the stem or shift to the prefix. This decision is rule-governed in that it depends upon the semantic transparency of the complex word. When the prefix retains its independent status semantically, it attracts stress. When, however, it is integrated in the stem and forms a semantic complex with it, the stem receives main stress. As an example, one might cite *untergraben* with the two pronunciations [úntɛr#graːbən] 'to dig under' and [úntɛr#gráːbən] 'to undermine'. As can be seen from the transcriptions, there is no segmental difference between the two versions of *untergraben*. The difference in stress placement correlates with a morphosyntactic one. The verbs with initial stress placement split the prefix from the stem in the finite forms while the verbs with non-initial stress do not. Thus the suprasegmental difference is accompanied by a syntactic one when these verbs are used in their finite forms. When they appear as non-finite forms, however, the possibility arises that two sentences are only distinguished by the placement of stress, witness the ambiguity in (49).

(49) Er will ihn *übersetzen*

With stress on the prefix, (49) may be translated as 'He wants to get him across'; with stress on the stem, the translation would be 'He wants to translate it'.

Theoretically the number of such doublets is relatively high, as the possibilities of combining stems and prefixes are considerable in German. Ortmann (1983) lists more than 100 such pairs and another 100 or so pairs consisting of words of different syntactic categories. However, many of these examples appear highly stilted. There is an objective basis for this intuition. In many cases, the frequency of the one word contrasts sharply with the (extreme) infrequency of the other. Because some items look more like potential than real words, the contrast is hardly felt as such. Still, there is no denying that lexical stress is the sole distinguishing feature in a fraction of the German lexicon.

Further evidence comes from individual monomorphemic pairs such as *Tenor* [teːnoːr], which means 'male singer with high voice' when the first syllable is stressed but 'general direction' when the stress falls on the second syllable. Another example is *August* [august], which is either a male first name or the name of a month, depending on stress placement. In addition to the identical grammatical category, these examples share the same gender (i.e. masculine). Stress is thus the only formal criterion by which these pairs can be distinguished.

The preceding analysis has made it quite clear that the strong claim that can be derived from Cutler's study is not warranted. Languages such as German and Spanish do possess word pairs which are formally distinguished by stress alone.

Implicationally, Cutler's explanation of the irrelevance of lexical stress during the prelexical access stage cannot be right. On her account, it would be impossible for Germans to understand the intended meaning of sentences like *Ich mag den August* beyond chance frequency. Listeners should interpret it randomly either as 'I like [the month of] August' or as 'I like August [proper name]'. However, there is absolutely no evidence that such utterances exceed listeners' decoding abilities. Hence it is not quite fair to say that the psycholinguistic model has failed adequately to predict the empirical patterns. The crux is rather that (one aspect of) the psycholinguistic model is flawed[14] and therefore cannot be expected to generate the correct predictions.

On the other hand, the predictions from Cutler's model are not totally off the mark. While both German and Spanish make use of lexical stress as a distinctive trait, they exhibit a certain reluctance to elevate it to a feature of primary importance. Most commonly, prosodic differences do not appear on their own but are accompanied by other formal differences such as segmental ones (cf. *to rebel* vs. *the rebel*). Contrasts such as *Ténor* vs. *Tenór* are exceedingly rare in German and completely missing in English. In morphologically complex words stress-based oppositions are theoretically possible on a larger scale, but in practice their status is clearly marginal in German. A weaker claim that can be formulated on the basis of Cutler's psycholinguistic findings is thus compatible with the linguistic data. The uncommonness of *forbear*-type words in English and *Tenor*-type words in German can now be argued to emanate from a *difficulty* the comprehension device has with the computation of word stress during lexical access.

4.9. Stress and Its Effect on Consonants and Vowels

Simplifying somewhat, syllables consist of consonants and vowels and can be stressed or unstressed. Stress is a feature that is standardly associated with the syllable[15] and may reach the segment level only through the intermediary of the syllable level. This section will begin with the question of whether stress affects consonants and vowels to the same degree.

A straightforward way of testing for an interaction between segment type and stress is to examine the impact of stress upon consonantal and vocalic speech errors. If it can be shown that vowel errors occur more frequently in stressed position than consonant errors (or vice versa), it can be argued that vowels are more sensitive

---

[14] Hence a revision of Cutler's theory is called for. Since the thrust of the present work is not psycholinguistic, this will not be attempted here. Suffice it to point out that Cutler's results are questionable from the psycholinguistic perspective as well. For example, one wonders how it is possible for the lexical representation to contain a piece of information which is not available at the prelexical level. Since the prelexical representation cannot feed the lexical one in this case, the lexicon must have got its information from somewhere else. However, this 'somewhere else' is a complete mystery.

[15] This claim makes good sense from the psycholinguistic viewpoint. The processing system treats stress unequivocally as a suprasegmental feature (Stemberger 1983). Segments and stress are largely, though not completely, independently computed.

to stress than consonants (or vice versa). The following four slips lead us into the problem.

(50) *from inflated pray– prices*
(51) *hesertation– hesitation or reservation* (both from Shattuck-Hufnagel 1986)
(52) *noman numeral* for *Roman numeral*
(53) *in the argon lexicot* for *argot lexicon* (both from Fromkin 1973)

In these slips, consonants and vowels undergo malfunctioning in stressed and unstressed loci. The error is stressed in (50) and (52) but unstressed in (51) and (53). It involves a vowel in (50) and (51) but a consonant in (52) and (53). Shattuck-Hufnagel (1986) investigated on the basis of her speech-error data whether the ratio of stressed/unstressed vowel errors differs from that of stressed/unstressed consonant errors. She reports that 79 per cent of the vowel errors in her corpus of naturally occurring slips of the tongue have both target and error in stressed positions. In contrast, in only 65 per cent of the consonant errors[16] does she find the same constellation. This difference is significant beyond the 0.005 level ($\chi^2(1) = 9.0$). It can be inferred from this that stress promotes the occurrence of vowel errors to a greater extent than that of consonant errors. That is, vowels are more sensitive to stress than consonants.

This finding was replicated and extended by Berg (1990a) for German. While Shattuck-Hufnagel (1986) limited her analysis to between-word slips, Berg focused in one part of his study on within-morpheme mistakes. The basic disparity between the two error categories is that only one constituent of the error process can receive primary stress. Differently put, an equality in stress values between source and target segment is impossible to achieve. Therefore, the source can shift either from an unstressed into a stressed position or vice versa. (A shift from an unstressed into another unstressed site is irrelevant to the research hypothesis.) Berg finds that consonants show no clear predilection for either the former or the latter possibility. Vowels, however, are almost three times more likely to be misplaced when they come from stressed than when they come from unstressed sources. This result may be interpreted to mean that stressed vowels have more power to oust target units than unstressed ones.

The psycholinguistic interpretation of these data is as follows (Berg 1990a). Stress is coded as a specific amount of activation that is passed on to a syllabic unit. Stressed syllables receive more activation than unstressed ones. This activation is handed down to the segment level in unequal fashion. Vowels take a greater share than consonants. This heightened activity makes vowels more ready for intrusion. Stressed vowels can therefore supplant other segments more easily than stressed consonants. Note that a simple structural explanation for the stronger spread of activation from a syllable to a vowel as compared to a consonant does not work. It is not the case that vowels are more frequent than consonants and are therefore at an

[16] Unlike the vocalic slips, the consonant errors have been obtained under experimental conditions (Shattuck-Hufnagel 1985).

advantage. Quite the opposite is true. The average consonant/vowel ratio per syllable is 60 : 40 per cent in English.

Given that vowels are more heavily influenced by stress than consonants, what impact may this difference have upon language structure? Quite simply, stressed and unstressed syllables should differ more with respect to their vocalic make-up than with respect to their consonantal make-up. Since consonants do not profit very much from the extra activation that is accorded to stressed syllables, little difference is to be expected between the set of stressed consonants and the set of unstressed consonants. However, in regard to vowels we should expect a wider array of vowels to occur in stressed than in unstressed syllables. Also, a higher number of different vowels should be frequently found in stressed than in unstressed syllables.

Denes (1963) published a segmental analysis of more than 10,000 stressed and almost 20,000 unstressed syllables in American English. Table 8 is based upon Denes's table v. Denes presents his data in such a way that all stressed consonants and vowels add up to 100 per cent. To make the stressed and unstressed subsets commensurable, the values in each of the four categories (i.e. stressed vowels, unstressed vowels, stressed consonants, unstressed consonants) have been multiplied so as to yield 100 per cent. For example, the lateral has a frequency of 6.4 per cent in stressed and a frequency of 5.9 per cent in unstressed syllables. The asymmetrical distribution of a sound across stressed and unstressed syllables is calculated by dividing the larger percentage by the smaller one. When a given segment distributes perfectly evenly across stressed and unstressed syllables, its value is, of course, 1.0. In the case of /l/, the distributional value is 6.4 : 5.9 per cent = 1.1.

Table 8, summarizing the distributional characteristics of all American English segments as a function of their affinity with stressed or unstressed syllables, presents a very clear picture. There is a huge difference in the impact of stress upon the vocalic and consonantal make-up of syllables. The consonants show very little sensitivity to syllable stress. Their frequency of occurrence is largely the same in stressed and unstressed syllables (mean value: 1.7). Certain distributional asymmetries are found with /ð/ and /dʒ/ (and a few other segments). In Denes's count, /ð/ occurs five times as often in unstressed as in stressed syllables. To understand this, it has to be noted that Denes included monosyllabic words in his analysis of stress. Although he is not explicit on this matter, he almost certainly assigned a [+ stress] value to open class words and a [− stress] value to closed class items. As all English words beginning in /ð/ belong to the closed class family, this consonant figures more prominently in the unstressed than in the stressed set.

It is not shown in Table 8 that /dʒ/ and the velar stops prefer stressed to unstressed syllables. One explanation for this skewing is that /g/ and /k/ are more difficult in articulatory terms than the other series of stops. As one piece of evidence, let it be noted that they figure among the late acquisitions in children (Dyson 1986). The same is true of /dʒ/, which is furthermore characterized by its extreme infrequency. It is not unlikely that these difficulties can be offset more easily by stressed than by

TABLE 8. *Distributional differences of consonants and vowels as a function of syllable stress (based upon Denes 1963)*

	Distributional value					
	Consonants			Vowels		
	1.0–1.9	2.0–2.9	≥3.0	1.0–1.9	2.0–2.9	≥3.0
No. of segments	18	4	2	6	2	12
	t	k	ð	aɪ	eɪ	e
	n	g	dʒ	iː	ɜː	ɪ
	s	p		uː		əʊ
	d	ŋ		ʊ		ʌ
	l			eə		a
	m			ʊə		ɒ
	r					ɔː
	w					ɑː
	f					aʊ
	z					ɪə
	b					ɔɪ
	h					ə
	v					
	j					
	θ					
	ʃ					
	tʃ					
	ʒ					

unstressed syllables. That /ŋ/ occurs almost three times as often in unstressed as in stressed syllables may be linked to its odd morphophonological distribution. It only occurs syllable-finally and tends to prefer word-final sites in running speech (mostly in the suffix *-ing*). Since this suffix is always unstressed, there is a strong bias for the velar nasal to show up in unstressed positions. To sum up, there is a pronounced symmetry in the distribution of consonants across stressed and unstressed syllables. The few exceptions to this pattern can be mostly put down to structural quirks of the English language.

In stark contrast, the majority of the vowels distribute very unevenly across stressed and unstressed syllables (mean value: 21.6). While only two occur more frequently in unstressed syllables, the remaining vowels prefer stressed syllables. As is well known, schwa is almost totally confined to unstressed syllables. The same trend, though much less extreme, is evident in /ɪ/. These two vowels account for almost two-thirds of the entire unstressed vowel set. It is clear, then, that the range of vowels is much more restricted in unstressed than in stressed syllables. The data in Table 8 temper the claim that there is an affinity between stressed syllables and long vowels (e.g. Vennemann 1988). Even the short vowels (excepting /ɪ/ and /ə/, of course) preferentially occur in stressed syllables, with some showing up four times as frequently in stressed as compared to unstressed syllables (e.g. /e/ and /ʌ/). As a subsidiary result, we may note that diphthongs and long monophthongs do not differ in their sensitivity to stress. Both sets have a mean distributional value of 3.1.

It may be concluded that stressed syllables exploit the full gamut of vowels whereas unstressed syllables draw exclusively upon a very limited subset of vowels. This is not to say that unstressed syllables are principally incapable of hosting certain vowels. It is just that the vast majority of vowels are discouraged to occur in unstressed syllables. Taking an arbitrary frequency level of 3 per cent, we find thirteen stressed vowels as against five unstressed vowels that exceed this threshold.

Summarizing, the research hypothesis is clearly corroborated by the linguistic data. Consonants remain largely unaffected by stress whereas the selection of vowels is contingent upon their appearing in stressed or unstressed syllables. This difference may be argued to follow from the psycholinguistic observation that vowels benefit more from the stress of a syllable than do consonants.

4.10. Stress and Syllable Structure in English/German and Spanish

It is an oft-made claim that there is an interaction between stress and syllable structure. A stressed syllable is widely believed to possess a more complex structure than an unstressed one. This is true of some languages though not of others, and it is this cross-linguistic variation that the present section sets out to explain.

In German and English, there is a strong tendency for phonological slips of the tongue to occur in stressed syllables. For English, Boomer and Laver (1968) note that the target and source of an error tend to be in metrically similar positions which are both stressed. When they are not metrically similar, either the target or the source segment tends to occupy the most salient locus in an utterance—the tonic syllable. Fromkin (1977) caters for relevant quantitative information. The examination of a subset of her data shows 82 per cent of the errors to take place in stressed syllables. Unfortunately, Fromkin indicates neither whether this subset is a representative cross-section of her corpus nor which error types were included in her analysis. These uncertainties notwithstanding, the preponderance of phonological errors in stressed syllables is beyond doubt.

A similar conclusion can be reached for German. In my speech error collection, the percentage of stressed slips ranges from 55 per cent to 80 per cent, depending upon the particular error category being investigated. Of the contextual segment slips in onset position, 55.7 per cent involve stressed syllables (Berg 1991a). This is clearly less than Fromkin reports for her English data, but it has to be acknowledged that these outcomes are difficult to compare given the non-identical data sets on which the percentages are based. In any event, what really counts is the demonstration that the numbers exceed chance. Since every word can have only one primary stress and German words have an average length of 2.59 syllables,[17] the probability of hitting upon a stressed syllable by chance is 100/2.59 = 38.6 per cent. This is significantly less than is actually observed ($p < 0.01$). Hence, stress attracts segmental slips of the tongue in German. The same can obviously be said of English, where the number of segment errors in stressed syllables is apparently higher but the length of words (as measured by the number of syllables) is not appreciably shorter.

In Spanish, however, the picture looks rather different. According to an analysis carried out in Berg (1991a), 60 per cent of all syllable- and word-initial monopositional slips involve unstressed syllables. In view of the fact that the words in which the errors (and sources) occur are on an average 2.5 syllables long, the actual patterns exactly match chance-level expectations. In other words, after eliminating the bias of linguistic structure, phonological speech errors can be shown to occur as often in stressed as in unstressed syllables. Stress thus is not a facilitatory effect in Spanish slips of the tongue. The modification of segments from stressed and unstressed syllables is illustrated in (54–7), with the first two extracted from an English and the last two from a Spanish data base.

(54) *A Tanadian from Toronto* for *Canadian*
(55) *the firing of– the hiring of the minority faculty* (both from Fromkin 1973)
(56) *Y entonces, la cada– la casa se queda*
 [káda kása kéda]
 'And then the house remains empty'
(57) *Hemos visto salpar– saltar a un hombre muy rápido* (both from del Viso et al. 1987) [salpár saltár rápido]
 'We saw a man jumping very rapidly'

While the English examples both involve word-initial consonants, the Spanish errors affect the (non-word-initial) syllable-initial position. The error locus is stressed in (55) and (57) but unstressed in (54) and (56). The stress value of the source element seems to be of secondary importance.

How should this difference between English/German and Spanish be interpreted in psycholinguistic terms? A basic assumption in speech-error research is that the intruding segment has accumulated more activation than the target segment and therefore is in a position to force its way out. The strength of a unit's activation is determined by a variety of influences, one of them being stress (see section 4.9). A reasonable claim is that stress in English and German propagates an extra amount of activation to a syllable's segments. The heightened activational state of a stressed syllable gives it more power, i.e. it can do things an unstressed syllable cannot do. For example, Treiman and Zukowski's (1990) syllabification experiments demonstrated that stressed syllables outdo unstressed syllables in their ability to attract 'floating' consonants. Let us contrast *campaign* and *trumpet*, which share the same medial

[17] Note that only those words entered the calculation which are susceptible of hosting segmental slips, i.e. open-class words. As the phonological structure of closed-class items is rather invulnerable to error, it would be inadequate to include these items in the calculation of word length.

cluster but are differently stressed. Treiman and Zukowski's subjects assigned the /m/ in *trumpet* more often to the first syllable that that in *campaign*. This finding is compatible with the view that stressed syllables are more successful in binding 'floating' consonants to them than are unstressed syllables. Since Spanish segments are indifferent to stress, it has to be assumed that stressed and unstressed syllables spread an equal amount of activation to their segmental constituents.

Predictions concerning language structure fall out naturally from this cross-linguistic processing difference. Because English affords an advantage to stressed syllables, their structure should be more complex than that of unstressed syllables. In contrast, the difference between stressed and unstressed syllables in Spanish should not engender any differences in syllable complexity. Their phonological make-up should be relatively constant.

Let us proceed to the empirical test and address the question of whether stress and syllable structure interact more strongly in English than in Spanish. Table 9 presents a rank ordering of the frequency of basic syllable types. The Spanish data come from Lloyd and Schnitzer's (1967) quantitative analysis of all the entries in the *Diccionario de la lengua española*, numbering over 70,000. The English data are adapted from Dauer (1983). The asterisked numbers are taken from CELEX. The table shows a pronounced difference between the Spanish and the English materials. Whereas the rank ordering of Spanish syllables is only marginally disrupted by stress, this feature determines the frequency of English syllable types to a far greater extent. In the Spanish list there is an almost complete symmetry, which is marred only by the syllable type V, which is more at home in unstressed than in stressed syllables. Apart from this special case, whether or not a syllable type is stressed does not affect its rank ordering. This outcome is of particular significance for the by far most frequent syllable types CV and CVC. Whether CV receives stress or not, it is always the most frequent syllable type. It is precisely on this point that the Spanish and the English data differ. In the English language, stress does determine which syllable type ranks highest. The more complex type CVC wins in stressed syllables while the less complex type CV is favoured in unstressed syllables. This result

TABLE 9. *Rank ordering of the occurrence of frequent syllable types in English and Spanish*

English			Spanish		
Type	Stressed	Unstressed	Type	Stressed	Unstressed
CVC	1	2	CV	1	1
CV	2	1	CVC	2	2
CVCC	3	6*	CCV	3	4
CCVC	4	5*	VC	4	5
VC	5*	3	V	5	3
V	6*	4	CCVC	6	6

accords well with the predicted interaction between stress and syllable complexity in English. More generally, the difference in the sensitivity of syllable types to stress between English and Spanish comes out as predicted.

4.11. Assimilation

4.11.1. *The direction of assimilation*

Speech is a sequential activity which happens in real time. At any particular moment, some stretches of an utterance have already been completely articulated while others have yet to be produced. Speakers are well advised to allocate their attentional resources more to the future than to the past because planned units have to be outputted while used elements are no longer needed. However, it would be unwise to forget immediately about the past because the past may have implications for the present. Speakers must keep track of what they have already said in order to be able to decide what they are going to say next. So, in response to the requirements of speech, speakers' primary focus will normally be upon upcoming events and their secondary focus upon past events.

There is solid evidence that the psycholinguistic system operates in keeping with this principle. In general terms, it can be said that imminent material is more highly activated than that which has been already executed. Hence, upcoming material should make a stronger impact on current events than already articulated stretches of speech. This asymmetry is clearly observed in slips of the tongue which display a predominance of anticipations (right-to-left influence) over perseverations (left-to-right influence).

(58) *Tathy can type* for *Kathy can type*
(59) *Jack's peck* for *Jack's pen* (both from Fromkin 1973)

Example (58) shows the intrusion of /t/ upon /k/. The intruding segment belongs to the word *type*, which is to come later in the utterance. The opposite situation holds in (59), where the intruding segment stems from the word *Jack*, which had already been articulated at the moment when the coda of the word *pen* was selected. The numerical imbalance between anticipations and perseverations recurs in all error corpora that have so far been examined irrespective of the language in which the malfunctions manifest themselves. This asymmetry holds across virtually all error types, with some minor exceptions which will be mentioned in section 5.2.3.

The standard interpretation of the preponderance of anticipatory errors is that upcoming units are closer to production threshold than used elements. Given this greater activational strength of not-yet-produced units relative to already-produced ones, it can be predicted that regressive assimilation will be more common than the progressive type. This claim follows from the greater activational strength of not-yet-produced units relative to already-produced ones. Because the psycholinguistic mechanism that is involved here is independent of the information to be worked upon, it can be further predicted that this asymmetry should hold universally. The following analysis focuses upon German and English for which the psycholinguistic asymmetry has been clearly established. Since it proves difficult to attack this issue from a quantitative viewpoint, a more qualitative approach will be taken.

Let us begin with German. Perhaps the best known type of assimilation involves nasals which are very facile at yielding to the place-of-articulation feature of their neighbours. Within the same syllable, nasals can be followed by obstruents in postvocalic positions and preceded by obstruents in prevocalic ones. The syllable coda accepts many obstruents after nasals, including velars. The syllable onset in German rarely accommodates obstruent + nasal structures. In fact, only velar stops (and marginally /p/) go with nasals. Thus, the only direct parallelism is the combination of nasals and stops. Words like *Knie* [kniː] 'knee', *Gnu* [gnuː] 'gnu', and *pneumatisch* [pnɔɪmaːtɪʃ] 'pneumatic' contrast with words like *Dank* [daŋk] 'thanks', *Sprung* [ʃpruŋk] 'jump', and *plump* [plump] 'rude'. As is apparent from the transcriptions, the nasal assimilates to the following stop though not to the preceding one, in line with the research hypothesis. This pattern is highly regular in that /-nk/ and /-np/ do not occur. It holds good of all postvocalic nasal/obstruent combinations with a few exceptions such as /-mt/ and /-nf/.[18]

Virtually the same situation recurs in the cross-syllable domain. Regressive assimilation operates unhesitatingly across the syllable boundary whereas the progressive type does not do so; cf. *trinken* [triŋ.kən] 'to drink' and *Lampe* [lam.pə] 'lamp' vs. *Akne* [ak.nə] 'pimples', *(sich) wappnen* [vap.nən] 'to arm', and *atmen* [aːt.mən] 'to breathe'. The phonotactics disallows /n.k/ and /m.p/ but no such restrictions hold in the reverse case.

At this point a caveat should be entered. The greater strength of regressive assimilation may not be a spin-off function of the predominance of anticipatory processing but may be connected with the unequal status of onsets and codas (see section 4.2). In the *trinken* and *Akne* examples above, it can be seen that the onset of the second syllable may influence the coda of the first while the coda of the first is incapable of acting upon the onset of the second syllable. It might therefore be suspected that the observed linguistic asymmetry is for reasons other than those under examination.

Note first of all that even if this criticism were valid, it would in no way undermine the assumed relationship between psycholinguistic processing and linguistic structure because the enhanced strength of the onset is a principle which is every bit as psycholinguistic in nature as the anticipatory dominance principle. In that case, we would be confronted with two processing principles which make exactly the same predictions and which may be jointly responsible for the assimilatory patterns. Is it possible to tease the two effects apart and show that the anticipatory-dominance principle may operate independently of the onset-dominance principle?

The within-syllable domain suggests that this question can be answered in the affirmative. Recall that assimilation takes place in complex codas (e.g. /ŋk/) but not

---

[18] Remarkably, /nf/ is often changed to [ɱf] in relaxed speech, see (21).

in complex onsets (e.g. /kn/). If the rightmost position was generally stronger than the leftmost position in consonant clusters, it would be possible to account for the assimilatory patterns without recourse to asymmetries in directionality. However, the empirical data speak against this view. Stemberger and Treiman (1986) argued that the first consonant in initial clusters is stronger than the second. Hence, initial clusters should evidence progressive assimilation. Since this is not the case, it appears justified to link the assimilation patterns to asymmetries in the pre-selection and post-selection phases of activating linguistic units.

This conclusion receives further support from segmental interactions in unclustered syllables. Let us take the two English syllables [næp] and [pæn]. Under the onset–dominance hypothesis, the vowel should be nasalized in [næp] though not in [pæn], whereas the opposite prediction is made by the anticipatory-dominance hypothesis. It is beyond doubt that the phonetic realization vindicates the latter claim. Nasalization may occur, and usually does, in [pæ̃n], but not in [næp]. We may thus conclude that the assimilatory patterns occur under regressive influence.

So far, assimilation has in the main been explored in terms of its effects upon the more permanent structure of lexical entries. However, assimilation makes itself felt even more strongly in casual speech, where the segmental make-up of words is altered so as to reduce the expenditure of articulatory energy. As a consequence of assimilation, individual segments become less distinct. The basic difference between this and the above assimilation type is their differing degrees of lexicalization. Assimilation is a lexical process in the one case but generated postlexically in the other. By implication, assimilation is compulsory at the higher level but optional at the lower one. Thus, a more superficial (phonetic) and a deeper (phonological) type of assimilation should be distinguished.

Since the regressive type of assimilation is stronger, it may be predicted to be the only one to be able to reach the deeper layer of linguistic structure. In contrast, it is to be expected that the shallower layer of linguistic use can also be reached by the progressive type of assimilation (in addition to the regressive type). This prediction is borne out by the data from English and German. Whereas the phonological type hardly knows progressive assimilation,[19] the phonetic one makes some limited use of it. According to Ramers (1990), it is confined to syllabic nasals in German (60). The same holds true of English (61). Thus, we find examples like the following:

---

[19] An apparent exception is the phonologically conditioned alternation between [x] and [ç] in German. The palatal fricative occurs *after* front vowels and the velar fricative *after* back vowels. This is clearly an instance of progressive assimilation but it is not exactly parallel to the regressive nasal assimilation discussed above. Whereas at least two of the nasals being assimilated (/n/, /m/) are separate phonemes, the phonological status of [x] and [ç] is somewhat blurred. As they do not contrast in monomorphemic words, they may be regarded as allophones of a common phoneme, which in fact would place this type of assimilation between the deep and the shallow type. It is not deep because allophones rather than phonemes are involved, and it is not shallow because it applies in a mandatory rather than optional fashion. Hence, at the deepest phonological level progressive assimilation may be claimed to be absent.

(60) a. Happen [hapən] → [hapn] → [hapm̩] 'a mouthful'
b. lenken [lɛŋkən] → [lɛŋkn] → [lɛŋkŋ̩] 'to steer'
(61) a. happen [hæpən] → [hæpn] → [hæpm̩]
b. bacon [beɪkən] → [beɪkn] → [beɪkŋ̩]

Nos. (60–1) illustrate that the syllabic nasal takes on the place-of-articulation feature of the preceding tautosyllabic consonant. When the schwa is not deleted, progressive assimilation does not take place, e.g. *[hæpəm]. It is thus restricted to contiguous segments. Regressive assimilation operates across morpheme (62) and word (63) boundaries. The first set is from German, the second from English.

(62) a. Anklage [an#klaːgə] → [aŋ#klaːgə] 'charge'
b. Hausschuh [haus#ʃuː] → [hauʃ#ʃuː] 'slipper'
(63) a. that person [ðæt pɜːsn] → [ðæp pɜːsn]
b. this shoe [ðɪs ʃuː] → [ðɪʃʃuː] (both from Roach 1989)

In all cases the assimilation is regressive in nature and crosses linguistic boundaries while the assimilated segment abuts upon the assimilating one. Further, many consonantal categories are involved, not just nasals. This shows that regressive assimilation is a fairly general process. The progressive type, however, is much less widespread. Pronunciations like [haus#suː] and [ðəttɜːsn], for instance, are very bizarre. This amplifies the conclusion, reached above, that regressive assimilation is more natural and of a larger scope than the progressive type.

Actually, the linguistic patterns are more complex than is suggested by the above analysis. It has been assumed in the foregoing that assimilations can arise at least at two levels, the phonological and the phonetic one. This is probably an oversimplification, in that there are many different speech rates and degrees of articulatory sloppiness which may promote the occurrence of assimilation. It is difficult therefore to compare the progressive and the regressive assimilation types (especially in quantitative terms) because any two tokens of these types may have arisen at different degrees of articulatory relaxation. Let us look at a striking example from German. Kohler (1974) notes the following seven (*sic!*) renditions of the word *Hemden* 'shirts' which are all taken from natural speech.

(64) Hemden [hɛmdən] → [hɛmbn], [hɛmpn], [hɛmbm], [hɛmpm]; [hɛmmm], [hɛmnn], [hɛmmn]

While the first four renditions involve a progressive assimilation of the place feature, the last three attest to a regressive assimilation of the feature [nasal]. The diversity of actually occurring forms is tantalizing and foreshadows the complexity of low-level articulatory processes. To better understand this diversity, it would be necessary to know the frequency of occurrence of these forms and the speech rate and speaking situations in which these forms are embedded. Unfortunately, Kohler does not furnish any information on these issues. It is to be suspected both that the seven pronunciations in (64) are not equally common and that they do not arise with the same degree of articulatory sloppiness. In particular, the token frequency of regressive assimilations is predicted to be higher than that of progressive assimilations. Also, the progressive type is predicted to occur at a faster speech rate and a lower degree of articulatory care than the regressive type.

In lieu of a conclusion, let us critically discuss one previous account from the linguistics literature. Lenerz (1985) proposes what he calls an 'intuitive' explanation for the preponderance of the regressive type of assimilation. He speculates that the direction of assimilatory influence is related to how distinctly speech sounds are executed. The more care is taken in articulating them, the stronger the regressive assimilation type becomes. Lenerz does not adduce any empirical evidence for the claim that sloppy articulation leads to progressive assimilation while careful articulation leads to regressive assimilation. This conjecture appears to me to be totally unsupported. The more natural assumption to make is that careful articulation leads to no assimilation at all! More generally, the problem with Lenerz's account seems to be his attempt at reducing assimilation to a low-level phenomenon, which it is not, at least not exclusively. An adequate understanding of assimilation requires that due consideration be given to the high-level aspects of this process. These provide one probable explanation for why the effects of regressive rather than progressive assimilation have been incorporated into the permanent phonological structure of words.

4.11.2. *The preference for certain types of assimilation*

Phonological slips of the tongue usually involve single segments which differ on only one feature. It thus is a straightforward task to determine the vulnerability of phonological dimensions. The following three errors exemplify modifications along the dimensions of place, manner and voice, respectively.

(65) *ripe it* or *type it* for *write it*
(66) *god to seen* for *gone to seed*
(67) *vactive verbs* for *factive verbs* (all from Fromkin 1973)

The effect of the malfunction is to make the elements more similar than they would have been in the intended utterance. Place of articulation is the dimension along which /p/ and /t/ are assimilated in (65), manner of articulation is implicated in (66) and voice in (67). Speech errors are very selective about the phonological dimensions they affect. Place of articulation is changed most often, manner less often, and voice least often. This pattern holds true of English as well as German. The reasons for this differential vulnerability are not yet well understood. It may be that the number of features that are subsumed under a phonological dimension plays a role. The fewer features it hosts, the more resistant to change they are.

The predictions that can be derived from the psycholinguistic data are obvious. We would expect assimilation of place to be most common, assimilation of manner less common, and assimilation of voice least common. The data from English appear to be in good accord with the psycholinguistic predictions. Roach (1989) notes that the domain of place assimilation is much less limited than that of the other types. For example, between-word assimilations of voice can only be regressive in nature whereas assimilations of place are not so constrained. Roach goes on to state that manner assimilates only in the most casual and rapid speech styles while assimilations of place require fewer facilitatory conditions. The following examples are taken from Roach (1989). He gives no example of voicing assimilation and states that a voiceless consonant never assimilates to a voiced one (across word boundaries).

(68) a. bright colour → [braɪkkʌlə]
    b. that thing → [ðæt̪θɪŋ]
(69) good night [gʊnnaɪt]

In (68a), the alveolar consonant assimilates to the velarity of the following obstruent and surfaces as a velar stop. In (68b), the alveolar stop adjusts to the dental nature of the following fricative and the dental allophone [t̪] is selected. In (69), the nasality feature is copied onto the oral stop which now appears as the alveolar nasal.

To conclude, the predictions regarding the preference for various assimilatory processes are largely correct. Place assimilations are clearly more natural than manner assimilations, i.e. they are less dependent upon facilitatory conditions. In line with the psycholinguistic expectation, voicing assimilations hardly occur across word boundaries. However, they do occur in contiguous obstruents where divergent voice specifications are avoided. I suggest that this pattern follows from constraints which are unrelated to the high-level processing arguments at issue here. Low-level constraints provide a likely explanation in that such sequences are very difficult to pronounce.

4.12. The Position of Phonological and Morphological Processes in Words

The central problem of lexical access during language comprehension is the matching of the acoustic signal onto a mental representation of word size. Given the existence of productive constraints, the acoustic signal reaches the listener's ears in roughly segment-by-segment order. Listeners now have two options at their disposal. They may begin their lexical search as soon as the first segment has been uttered or they may wait until all of the relevant information has been obtained. Experiments using the gating paradigm (e.g. Warren and Marslen-Wilson 1987) and priming experiments (e.g. Marslen-Wilson and Zwitserlood 1989) have demonstrated the sequential and immediate nature of lexical access. Listeners begin working on the acoustic input without delay. However, this does not mean that the access occurs in *strictly* left-to-right fashion. Through the deployment of top-down information during word recognition, a parallel effect is introduced. To be specific, the phonetic information that arrives activates segments (in sequence) which in turn activate word nodes. These candidates send their activation to all of their segmental constituents. This leads to a parallel activation at the segment level. Due to the integration of bottom-up and top-down information (Marslen-Wilson and Welsh 1978), lexical access combines serial and parallel processing strategies. Since bottom-up information is, at least in the initial stages, more important in guiding lexical access than top-down information, the sequential effect can be considered stronger than the parallel one.

It is quite typical for lexical items not to be invariant. Words may be modified by a multitude of phonological and morphological processes, thereby occurring in different 'guises'. It is unlikely that all these processes are lexicalized[20], i.e. that there are as many individual entries in the mental lexicon as there are surface forms. The extreme version of such a full-listing model fails because the number of surface forms is immense (Hankamer 1989) and because it does not capture the creative aspects of language. It is therefore preferable to postulate a base form from which individual variants can be derived through the application of phonological and morphological rules. In other words, it is assumed that these linguistic processes play an active role in language comprehension. Consequently, listeners must actively recover the underlying form.

Given that the identification of a lexical item may occur at any time during lexical access, it is reasonable to expect the following. The application of a linguistic rule should cause no comprehension problems after the identification of the lexical item. By contrast, before the recognition of the item, a linguistic rule should complicate the access procedure. As the likelihood of identification increases from left to right, the interferential nature of a linguistic rule should decrease from left to right.

This line of reasoning leads to a clear prediction regarding language structure. Taking for granted that listeners are intent upon minimizing the problems involved in matching the acoustic input onto an entry in the mental lexicon, linguistic rules should exhibit a skewing towards occurrence in the right-hand portions of words. More precisely, their probability should increase from left to right. Note that this prediction is of a universal nature because it is based upon language-independent processing arguments.

There are clear indications that this prediction is borne out by the linguistic facts. Linguistic processes cluster towards the ends of words. Commonest among them appears to be the addition of linguistic units of which morphology makes maximum use (witness the suffixing preference). The substitution of final consonants is also frequently observed, e.g. in word-final devoicing in many languages. The deletion of word-final consonants is often found in more casual speech styles as well as in certain sociolects (e.g. Black American English).

Word-internally, we have ablaut, umlaut, and vowel harmony in the vocalic domain. It is telling that these processes are already less general (both within a language and cross-linguistically) than the aforementioned ones. Umlaut, for instance, affects a smaller portion of the lexicon than the final devoicing of obstruents.

[20] Lexicalization may be a matter of degree and differ from one process to another.

Moreover, processes in the middle of words tend to be more lexicalized than those occurring in final portions. Take the example of ablaut in German. Its inconsistent, unpredictable nature is good evidence of its being lexicalized. Of course, all problems of access are avoided on that condition.

Interestingly, despite the difficulties they supposedly create, low- and high-level processes are not entirely banned from word-initial positions. In the phonetic domain, allophonic variation is certainly not unusual. The [k] in *kit* is clearly different from that in *cool*. However, this is a low-level process which taxes the listener's decoding capabilities less than the more challenging processes such as restoring missing segments or stripping suffixes. Indeed, it even enhances perceptibility as the particular variant of the [k] contains clues to the nature (frontness/backness) of the following vowel.

Consonant with the prediction, high-level phonological processes in word-initial sites are exceedingly rare in the languages of the world. One of the very few is consonant mutation in the Celtic languages. This is a morphophonological process whereby the word-initial consonant of the base form is transformed into a different segment in congruence with the morphosyntactic context. In Irish, for example, there are two types of mutation traditionally called lenition and eclipsis (Ó Siadhail 1989). To illustrate, the /p/ in the base form *punt* 'pound' undergoes lenition in *tri phunt* [tri:funt] '£3' and eclipsis in *seacht bpunt* [saxt bunt] '£7'. While the change from the base to the mutated consonant is consistent and describable as a (relatively) natural phonological process, the structural conditions under which it takes place are somewhat more difficult to state.

Whether morphophonological change in initial positions exists also in English and German is highly questionable. One of the few examples in German is the pair *Erde* [e:rdə] 'earth' vs. *irden* [ɪrdən] 'earthen'. An example from English is *expect* [ɪkspekt] vs. *expectation* [ekspekteɪʃn]. It should be noted that it is the vowel that alternates here. Since the prototypical syllable or word begins with a consonant, it may be argued that the initialness of these alternations is not genuine but a consequence of the accidental fact that these words begin with a vowel. In any event, it is highly likely that these morphophonological changes are lexicalized.

To conclude, the processing cost that is incurred by morphological and phonological rules in initial positions, predicts the rarity of such phenomena across languages, and this is in fact the case. More generally, the analysis has suggested that linguistic processes tend to be more common and less lexicalized as one moves from left to right in a word. This effect is readily understandable if it is seen as a consequence of basic principles of lexical access in language comprehension. The diachronic implications of these processing principles will be sounded out in section 5.11.

4.13. Morphophonology

This and the following section will be concerned with the most salient property of the psycholinguistic model from which the predictions about linguistic structure are generated. In fact the model owes its name to this property, i.e. its *parallel*-interactive nature. The possibility of interaction between adjacent (and indirectly, non-adjacent) processing levels is what sets this model apart from the modular approaches. The controversy of parallelness vs. serialness crystallizes in the temporal relationship between two adjacent levels which are hierarchically organized in a processing network. According to the strictly serialist position, processing on the higher level must be completed before processing at the lower level can begin. Put another way, there is no temporal overlap between the two levels. An important implication of this view is that higher levels can act upon lower levels though never vice versa. In contrast, the parallelist dogma holds that two processing levels are able to operate simultaneously even if they are hierarchically ordered. That is, processing at the lower level may begin before processing at the higher level is completed.

The focus of this section will be upon the relationship between morphology and phonology. Pertinent psycholinguistic evidence comes from 'accommodated' errors, i.e. slips in which the primary malfunction is accompanied by a repair process.

(70) *a kice ream cone* for *an ice cream cone* (from Fromkin 1973)

The primary error process in (70) is the leftward shift of the /k/ from *cream* to *ice*. This slip creates a follow-up problem in that the indefinite article had been selected for the correct form but now is inappropriate for the incorrect form. As this example shows, the allomorph is selected which is appropriate to the microcontext irrespective of whether this context contains an error. Note that this accommodation process is not compulsory. A failure is exemplified in (71).

(71) Fat impotes [tɪz]– imposes its own strain (from Stemberger 1983)

Here, the substitution of /z/ by /t/ does not entail the selection of the appropriate allomorph. The inappropriate syllabic allomorph remains in place. Stemberger and Lewis (1986) argue that the question of accommodation vs. non-accommodation sheds some light upon the temporal relationship of the error and the allomorph selection process. When the error occurs early, the chances are that the allomorph has not yet been selected. When, however, the error occurs late, the allomorph selection process has already been completed and can no longer be revised.

How does accommodation bear upon the issue of parallelness vs. seriality? A serial model would hold that allomorph selection occurs after phoneme selection has been completed. Undoubtedly, there is a certain oddity about this hypothesis because a higher level is assumed to operate subsequent to a lower level. This may be taken as a first indication that the serial model is flawed. Even worse, while the serial approach might be claimed to be able to deal with the regular cases of accommodation, it cannot account for accommodation failures. A theory that can explain both accommodations and accommodation failures has to postulate that the processing of morphological and phonological units occurs largely in parallel. This parallelness naturally leads to accommodation. Non-accommodation testifies to the limits of parallelness. Given the top-down orientation of language production, it is clear that there must be a point at which processing at the upper level can no longer be held in suspense. However, this point should occur fairly late in a parallel model and because of this, accommodation failures should be rare events. That this is the case argues strongly in favour of parallel processing at the morphological and phonological level.

Parallelism introduces a potential into the psycholinguistic machinery which may be exploited by the structure of the language. In particular, linguistic phenomena may arise which cannot be neatly located on any one level. It is important to stress that the interactive nature of processing furnishes an opportunity which languages may or may not take. No compulsion is at stake here. Rather, it seems more appropriate to regard interactivity as an option which may be resorted to when a conflict has to be resolved. In such a case, interactivity might pave the way for a more sophisticated solution than could be envisioned without it.

To illustrate, let us focus upon the interface of inflectional morphology and phonology and start out from a previous stage of the language. As mentioned in section 2.5, Middle English knew one main plural marker, -*es*, which attached indifferently to nouns. This morphological marking may therefore be regarded as a within-level process. With the erosion of the vowel of the suffix, the system was in a quandary. Two problems had to be dealt with if the vowel disappeared completely. For one thing, /-Cs/ clusters would be created, among them also voiced consonant + /s/ sequences which are very difficult to articulate. For another, the geminate cluster /ss/ would be created in those stems ending in a voiceless alveolar fricative. This would lead to a conflation of the stem and the suffix and as a consequence, plurality could not be identified by the hearer. Both problems would not affect the whole lexicon but a significant portion of it.

There was no easy way out. It might have been possible to allow no plural exponent on /-s/ stems, much as is found in the past tense of some /-t/ verbs in the modern language (e.g. *to put*). This solution is evidently unsatisfactory, and so the vowel of the suffix had to be preserved. The juxtaposition of voiced and voiceless obstruents called for a different solution. Because stems are in a sense stronger than affixes, the former could impose their voicing feature on the latter and in this way make the clusters easier to pronounce. However, this phonological process of assimilation had serious consequences for the morphology. The context-independent single-allomorph system had to yield to a context-sensitive multiple-allomorph system. The obvious advantage is that it allows for across-the-board marking of plurality, an advantage that is gained at the expense of a more complex allomorphy.

The critical question is this. How costly is the build-up of allomorphy? Given that the mutual exchange of information between the morphological and the phonological system is a design feature of the processing system, it can be argued that this complexification is largely cost-free. In any case, the morphological processing level is informed (to a certain extent) about what is going on at the phonological level, irrespective of whether a particular language produces or does not produce morphophonological variation. So when the need for morphophonology was felt in Middle English, nothing novel had to be invented in the minds of the speakers. The potential for a morphological repair strategy had always been there, so an interactive solution was not only elegant and efficient but also relatively cost-free for the processor.

This interpretation is amplified by the generality of morphophonological processes in Modern English. In addition to the plural morpheme, they can be found in other inflectional morphemes such as the possessive, the 3rd person singular present-tense marker and the past tense. Morphophonological processes are also found in derivation, though these are less systematic and less widespread.

It is noteworthy that this psycholinguistic account construes morphophonology as a fairly natural process, while reserving no particular processing level for it. Morphophonology derives its existence entirely from the interaction between the morphological and phonological levels. This view implies that we should not find morphophonological phenomena which cannot be reduced to either the phonological or the morphological level or both. In other terms, these phenomena must not have unique properties. This is exactly the conclusion Dressler (1985b) reaches through a linguistic analysis of morphophonological processes in a great many languages. He argues that there exists no independent morphophonological component in the grammar of languages.

It transpires, then, that the interactive option provides an excellent means of seeking unrestricted applicability of a linguistic process without relaxing the requirements of articulatory ease and perceptual salience. It is true that the solution entails the introduction of phonologically conditioned allomorphy, but these rules are all very natural and the psycholinguistic system is biased towards such a solution because the requisite processing mechanisms are in operation anyway. From the psycholinguistic angle it is impossible to predict that morphophonological variation must exist, but it can at least be stated that the processing system creates conditions which are favourable to the rise of morphophonological structures.

4.14. Iconicity

While the preceding section dealt with the effects of parallel processing at the phonological and morphological levels, this section probes possible interactions between the phonological and the lexical level. It would not be contentious to say that the evidence for phonological influences upon lexical decisions is overwhelming. Wherever one looks, feedback effects are discernible. Here is a cross-section of such effects. An important category of whole-word substitutions testify to a phonological resemblance between error and target word.

(72) *the native vowels* for *the native values* (from Fromkin 1973)

In (72), target and error word share the initial and final phonemes, the stress pattern as well as the number of syllables. They can thus be said to be phonologically related. As Dell and Reich (1981) point out, the existence of this error class is troublesome for serial models which have no way of accounting for the occurrence of form-based word substitutions. By contrast, a parallel system in which the word selection process is influenced not only from above (i.e. the semantics) but also from below (i.e. the phonology) has no difficulty at all in coming to grips with this error category.

This bottom-up effect is even more striking in a class of errors which have been termed non-plan-internal. Their defining characteristic is the intrusion of a word that is not directly related to the utterance being spoken. In environmental-contamination errors, an intended item may be ousted by a word whose availability is due to the speaker's visual processing at the time of speaking. Let us consider the following example.

(73) *She had a little bank– ha, a little badge with 'S' written on it* (from Harley 1990)

The utterance in (73) was spoken while the speaker was reading *Lloyds Bank* on a building. Thus the perceptual stimulus was strong enough to activate the word node for *bank* to such an extent that it could intrude upon *badge*. Owing to the extrinsic source of these errors, it is to be expected that they are less subject to formal similarity than plan-internal slips. As Harley (1990) showed, this is in fact the case. However, he also demonstrated that a minor effect of phonological facilitation could be observed in this error category.

The final class of tongue slips illuminates another facet of the interaction between the lexical and the phonological levels. So far, phonological similarity has been defined against the substituting and the substituted word. However, the impact of the phonology on lexical access is more general than that. Even the phonology of a word in the syntagmatic context may contribute to the occurrence of an error somewhere else, as exemplified in (74).

(74) G: *Das ist die richtige Physik– Musik für meine Frau*
 [fy:zi:k mu:zi:k fy:r]
 'That is the physics– the music my wife fancies'

The most likely interpretation of (74) is that of a whole-word substitution. Both target and error word are very similar in their segmental and suprasegmental structure. However, this is not all there is to it. It seems as if the intrusion of the word *Physik* has been triggered by the concurrently planned preposition *für* which shares the first two segments with *Physik*. On this account, the lexical selection process is not only open to phonological processing on current elements (i.e. those that are about to be selected) but also on non-current units (i.e. those that have already been outputted or are intended to be outputted later in the utterance). Non-current elements which are phonologically similar to the substituting word occur with above-chance frequency in my corpus of German slips of the tongue. It is therefore justified to speak of a triggering effect on a substitution error nearby. This is a further demonstration of the susceptibility of the lexical selection process to phonological influences.

Viewed together, the three error types (and various others not mentioned) attest to the ubiquity of bottom-up effects in language production. They have been reviewed in some detail because they allow us to argue that a compelling case for parallelism can be made.

Given this conclusion, we may now proceed to an examination of the possible impact of parallelism upon language structure. Phrased in its most general terms, the expectation would be that the psycholinguistic interaction between the lexical and phonological levels results in a particular form/meaning relationship. It is commonplace to divide the linguistic sign into its conceptual and formal side (the *signifié* and the *signifiant* in de Saussure's terminology). For our purposes, it is convenient to equate the lexical and the phonological processing levels with the *signifié* and the *signifiant*, respectively. De Saussure (1916/1978) claimed that the relationship between the *signifiant* and the *signifié* is an arbitrary one—in other words that there is no interaction between the two. It is precisely this claim that is challenged by parallelism. In fact, the opposite hypothesis is put forward. It is predicted that the psycholinguistic non-independence is mirrored by a non-independent relationship between the two sides of the linguistic sign. Such a non-independence is known as *iconicity* in linguistics (see section 2.9).

Of course, it is not claimed here that the relationship between the *signifiant* and the *signifié* is wholly exempt from arbitrariness. Rather, the bone of contention is the extent to which the linguistic sign is pervaded by iconicity. On the serialist view, iconicity has to be principally absent whereas the parallel approach predicts a certain degree of iconicity. The latter would always regard iconicity as an effect of secondary importance because it is assumed to stem from feedback which, as noted above, is principally subordinated to feedforward and can therefore have only relatively minor consequences on the structure of language.

Parallelism is a property of the language-processing system which is independent of the particular language being processed. Since it is a psycholinguistic universal, the predictions that may be derived from this property will have universal applicability. The empirical tests to be reported below will therefore be of a cross-linguistic nature.

What kind of structural effects can be expected to emanate from parallel processing? It is plausible to presume that certain properties at the one level are replicated at the other. The problem with this prediction is that the lexical and the phonological levels generate different representations and use different processing vocabularies which may not be commensurate. Fortunately enough, there is one concept that applies to both levels equally well, that of similarity. We may speak of formal similarity in much the same way as we refer to semantic similarity. The structural implication of parallel processing is that formal similarity should match semantic similarity. This prediction will be tested by comparing the semantic similarity of two items with their phonological similarity. Two kinds of similarity will be examined—similarity in terms of features and similarity in terms of integration. Let us begin with the former.

In a structuralist approach to language, the similarity between two given elements is defined by counting the number of shared features. Featural analyses have been applied to both *signifiants* and *signifiés*. Lexical meaning can be described in terms of semantic features and phonemes are composed of distinctive features. The specific prediction of the parallel model is thus that the higher the number of identical semantic features, the higher the number of identical phonological features should be. As semantic features can be identified less easily than formal ones, it is appropriate to select cases where there is little debate about which of two given word pairs should be considered more similar semantically. Of course, not all phonologists agree as to the proper set of distinctive features, but for most phoneme pairs the degree of similarity can be determined fairly uncontroversially.

We will examine two aspects of feature-based similarity. To begin with, it will be asked whether there is a correlation between semantic and phonological similarity. Once such a correlation has been established, it is possible to test the stronger hypothesis according to which a difference in phonological similarity corresponds to a difference in semantic similarity.

An obvious way to examine the first aspect is to take semantically related words and see whether they are also formally related. This is trivially true at the macroscopic level for members of morphosemantic sets such as *execute, executive,* and *execution*. However, it is not necessarily true at the distinctive-feature level, the lowest level at which phonological similarity can be determined. We will therefore address the issue of whether the non-identical corresponding segments of semantically related words are more similar to each other than can be expected by chance. In light of the processing principle sketched above, it is predicted that this will indeed be the case.

My focus will be upon word pairs such as *heat–hot* in which the semantic relatedness does not have to be questioned. The issue is whether the phonological relationship between /i:/ and /ɒ/ reflects the semantic similarity between the two words. The work of Moessner (1978), who analysed an important part of English morphophonology, will serve as the database for the ensuing investigation. Phonological similarity can be measured by a type or a token frequency count. A type frequency count lists all the segmental oppositions that can be found in morphosemantically related words. These oppositions will then be grouped according to the formal similarity of their constituents. This will allow one to calculate the number of elements in the high- and the low-similarity categories. As Moessner provides a complete listing of the words in which the morphophonological alternations occur, it is also possible to perform a token frequency count, which constitutes a more exact test. By this method, it is determined how often a particular segmental opposition is utilized by morphophonemic alternants. It is expected that only a low number of word pairs have critical segments which are dissimilar, while a high number of word pairs is expected to have critical segments which are similar. Given that English vowels and consonants can be specified on three relevant dimensions (voice, manner, and place in the case of consonants; length, height, and backness in the case of vowels), a minimal change is a one-feature switch and a maximal change a three-feature switch. Approximately, the null hypothesis will be in the order of a two-feature change. Table 10 presents the results for consonantal and vocalic alternations separately. The consonantal alternations differ in 1.59 features and the vocalic alternations in 1.69 features on an average. These results reveal a significant trend towards enhanced phonological similarity between morphophonologically alternating segments ($\chi^2(2) = 523.3$, $p < 0.0001$ for consonants; $\chi^2(2) = 265.4$, $p < 0.0001$ for vowels). It is clear from Table 10 that three-feature switches are far less common than one-feature switches.

However, Table 10 also indicates a higher number of two-feature switches than one-feature switches for both consonants and vowels, even though the opposite would be expected on the hypothesis under consideration. It is thus worth asking whether there might be something spurious about these findings. It will be recalled that similarity is defined in a non-sophisticated manner with reference to individual phonological dimensions rather than with reference to the structure of the segment system as a whole. Let us take the example of the /t/–/ʃ/ alternation in *alternate–alternation*. This segmental opposition is classified as a two-feature switch because /t/ differs from /ʃ/ in terms of manner as well as place of articulation. This procedure, however, misses one crucial point: it ignores the fact that there is no palato-alveolar stop in the English phonological system. This means that if a change on the place dimension (from alveolar to palato-alveolar) takes place, it cannot help but affect the manner dimension as well. Because the manner change is contingent upon the place change, the /t/–/ʃ/ alternation should not be viewed as two independent feature switches. If this alternation is reclassified as a one-feature switch, the picture in Table 10 changes dramatically (see below).

Vocalic alternations disclose another inadequacy of the standard method. Given the dimensions of height and backness, a one-feature switch of necessity involves either moving vertically or horizontally in the vowel space. Moving across cannot be counted as a one-feature switch in this conception, although the trajectory may be of the same length. It is not necessary to assume that moving diagonally in the quadrilateral is more complex than moving vertically or horizontally, as long as length is held constant. Moving diagonally is standardly referred to as (de)centralization. There are three such cases among the two-feature switches in Table 10:

TABLE 10. *Token frequency of morphological alternants as a function of the phonological difference between the critical segments (preliminary version)*

	One-feature change	Two-feature change	Three-feature change
Consonant	617	807	20
Vowel	204	430	7

/ɪ/–/ə/, /æ/–/ə/, and /ɒ/–/ə/. If these are counted as one feature switches, the pattern that emerges is quite different from Table 10. As shown in Table 11, one-feature changes outnumber two-feature changes which in turn outnumber three-feature changes. The difference between two alternating consonants is 1.12 features, that between alternating vowels 1.22 features on average. These values allow us to reject the null hypothesis. The pairs of consonants and vowels that are implicated in morphophonological alternations are clearly more similar than would be expected by chance. This accords well with the predictions outlined above. We may therefore conclude that formal similarity between alternating segments is an index of the semantic similarity between the words of which they are a part. This is one dimension of an iconic relationship between *signifiant* and *signifié*.

Now that a general correlation between the semantic and the phonological levels has been ascertained, it is fitting to explore more specifically whether a difference in semantic similarity between two sets of words is reflected in a difference in phonological similarity between them. One area which lends itself well to a comparison is ablaut, which figures prominently in various morphological relationships. Specifically, it is found in the tense system and in noun–verb alternations. A change of tense may be signalled by a vowel change as in *to light, lit, lit*. Also, a change of word class may be accompanied by a change of the tonic vowel, e.g. *to convene–the convention*.

As far as the semantics is concerned, there can be little doubt that the meaning of a verb is not normally changed when it is transformed from the present tense to a past-tense form. Exceptional cases aside, time is external to the actual meaning of a word. The verb *to run* describes an act of motion regardless of when this action takes place. The difference between a present-tense verb and its corresponding past-tense form in terms of their core meaning can therefore be regarded as minimal.

In contrast, the semantic consequences of a word-class change may be substantial. Note first of all that particular word classes prototypically code particular concepts (Hopper and Thompson 1984)—nouns tend to denote entities, verbs actions, and adjectives properties. Though indirect, the relationship between syntactic and semantic features captures important regularities on a probabilistic level. So when a verb like *to kick* is transformed into a noun, concomitant changes in the semantic domain are almost inevitable. The process of kicking turns into an event or even

TABLE 11. *Token frequency of morphological alternants as a function of the phonological difference between the critical segments (revised version)*

	One-feature change	Two-feature change	Three-feature change
Consonant	1,279	145	20
Vowel	510	124	7

into a result or function. Moreover, the semantic change induced by the word-class change is not always as predictable as in the *kick* example. There is nothing in the verb *to polish* that allows us to predict that the corresponding noun refers to a substance rather than to the act of polishing. The pair *to point–the point* is an extreme case in point, where noun and verb are hardly related semantically (at least on their most common readings). Also, it cannot be reliably predicted which of the several meanings of a verb will be inherited by the nominalized form. As a striking example, Butterworth (1983) discusses the nominalizations of *to induce*, which can take either the suffix *-ment* or the suffix *-ion*. He notes the following five meanings of the verb: 'to persuade', 'to cause', 'to produce current', 'to infer from cases', and 'to induct'. The first two meanings are covered by the noun *inducement* and the latter three by *induction*. Which sense is expressed by which noun does not seem to be rule-governed. It can be concluded, then, that a change of word class quite commonly induces a change in meaning.

Comparing the semantic relationship between members of a morphosemantic set and tense-differentiated verb forms, it can be seen that the latter are very close in meaning while the former are more distant. This analysis leads to the prediction that ablaut should create a greater formal difference in noun/verb pairs than in present/past-tense forms. This prediction will be examined by focusing upon the quantitative differences brought about by the vowel change. Hence, the length of the vowel is expected to remain untouched more often in present/past-tense forms than in noun/verb alternations. In German and Dutch there are a good number of noun/verb pairs which are characterized by a vowel shift. Two parallel examples from each language are given in (75–6).

(75) a. G: *sprechen—Sprache* [ʃprɛçən ʃpraːə] 'to speak'—'language'
 b. D: *spreken—spraak* [sprɛkən spraːk] 'to speak'—'language'
(76) a. G: *klingen—Klang* [kliŋgən klaŋk] 'to sound'—'sound'
 b. D: *klinken—klank* [kliŋkən klaŋk] 'to sound'—'sound'

In (75), the vowel shift is accompanied by a quantitative change. The short vowel of the verb is lengthened in the noun. In (76), however, the length of the vowel is kept constant. Only a qualitative change takes place. In the absence of complete lists, I have compiled a good number of relevant word pairs. These are not claimed to be exhaustive, but are sufficiently numerous to present a representative picture.

Unlike Dutch and German, English has very few noun/verb pairs which are formally distinguished by a vocalic segment (e.g. *to live–the life*). I could find only twelve pertinent cases. To perform a reliable analysis, it is necessary therefore to enlarge the data base and include both verb/adjective and noun/adjective pairs which are subject to the same semantic constraints as the noun/verb alternations discussed above. For instance, the adjective *inductive* does not carry all the meanings of the verb *to induce*. Again, the data are taken from Moessner (1978). The analysis is restricted to tonic vowels. By this procedure, the influence of stress on vowel length is eliminated. More importantly, this decision is motivated by the desire to make the two data sets comparable. Because the present/past-tense forms all involve alternations of the tonic vowel, the same criterion should be valid for the members of the morphosemantic families.

The so-called strong verbs figure in all three languages in question. Those irregular verbs which involve a change beyond the vowel change have also been included. Of the three base forms (infinitive, past, past participle), only the first two are considered, because if a quantitative change occurs, it occurs in these forms. The present/past tense alternants have been exhaustively investigated on the basis of the following works. The Dutch data are from Geerts et al. (1984), the English ones from Bloch (1947), and the German ones from the *Duden* (1973). One example from each language follows.

(77) E: *to weep–wept–wept*
(78) G: *reiten–ritt–geritten* 'to ride (on horseback)'
(79) D: *helpen–hielp–geholpen* 'to help'

All three examples involve a change in vowel length. In (77–8) the infinitive is long and the past tense form short, whereas the opposite is true of (79). Diphthongs as in (78) count as phonologically long segments. Table 12 provides information on how often a length change occurs in the two data sets from the three languages.

An inspection of the table discloses that vowel length varies more often among members of morphosemantic sets than among tense variants of ablaut verbs. Indeed, this difference reaches standard levels of statistical significance in all three languages: English: $\chi^2(1) = 43.1$, $p < 0.001$; German: $\chi^2(1) = 5.4$, $p < 0.025$; Dutch: $\chi^2(1) = 8.6$, $p < 0.005$. This is clear indication of the correctness of the research hypothesis. The relative reluctance of verb forms to change vowel length can now be understood as a reflection of the semantic similarity of present and past-tense forms. It is as if the strong semantic similarity between them keeps the tonic vowels from drifting too far apart. It is also noteworthy in Table 12 that the rate of vowel-length changes differs from language to language. This issue will be treated in the next section.

The second part of this section examines the degree to which an affix is integrated within the stem of a morphologically complex word. As pointed out above, the integration of an affix is another aspect which can be looked at from both the

TABLE 12. *Frequency of vowel length change in tense alternations of verbs and members of morphosemantic families*

	Vowel length in			
	Tense alternations of verbs		Members of morphosemantic sets	
	Unchanged	Changed	Unchanged	Changed
English	66	61	6	76
German	133	56	33	28
Dutch	174	38	34	20

semantic and the formal angles, thus providing a further test of the iconicity principle. According to the parallel processing model, the semantic integration of stems and affixes is expected to parallel the formal one. That is, the higher the integration at the semantic level, the higher it should be on the phonological level. The logic is the same as in the first part of this section and will not be repeated here. Integration at the semantic level implies that the meaning of a morphologically complex word is the result of an interaction between the meaning of the stem and that of the affix. Focusing upon inflectional and derivational morphemes, it is clear that the former interact less with the meaning of the stem than the latter. It may thus be predicted that derivational affixes are more tightly integrated with the stem than inflectional ones.

The combination of a stem and an affix can take a variety of forms. Apart from the simplest case of linear concatenation, as in *assess + -ment → assessment*, where no formal change at all is implicated, the stem may act on the form of the affix, the affix may act on the form of the stem, or both may interact. Material at the juncture of the stem and the affix may be deleted, added, or substituted. All these processes contribute to blurring the morpheme boundary. In addition, the stress pattern and the syllabification of the stem may differ from those of the complex word. Other modifications further away from the morpheme boundary are also attested.

The prediction that derivational affixes are more highly fused with their stems than inflectional ones will be tested against the morphological patterns of English. It should be noted initially that it is impossible to examine this prediction by simply counting the number of tokens undergoing some kind of fusion. By their very nature, inflectional morphemes have a wider application than derivational ones and accordingly produce a higher number of relevant cases. This procedure does not provide a just comparison of derivational and inflectional affixes because their differing opportunities of occurrence are not monitored. It is necessary, therefore, to focus upon the types of interaction that may arise during the concatenation of morphemes. The number of interactional types and their drasticness are appropriate criteria against which the research hypothesis may be evaluated.

In general, it is fair to say that inflectional suffixes are attached to stems either without any formal modification at all, as in *play + -ing → playing*, or with highly systematic modification. Four major types of modification can be identified. First, because the suffix begins with a vowel (and thus is of a syllabic nature), the string of phonemic units has to be resyllabified in accordance with a general tendency to fill the onset of a syllable. Hence, the stem-final consonant in *wait* and *hiss* is resyllabified in *waited*, *waiting*, and *hisses*. This process is widely held to be a low-level phenomenon; it represents the most shallow type of fusion one can imagine.

Secondly, inflectional affixes may readily adjust themselves to the stem they attach to. The most common allomorphic process in English is a change in voicing. Non-syllabic morphemes take on the voicing feature of the stem-final segment, e.g. *play* + PAST → [pleɪd] and *like* + PAST → [laɪkt]. Additionally, a neutral vowel is inserted when the stem-final consonant and the inflectional morpheme are phonologically too similar, as in *to fish* + 3rd pers. sg. pres. tense → *she fishes* and *to mould*

\+ PAST → *moulded*. These modifications are highly regular and still of a relatively shallow nature, even though they make a greater impact on the word form than resyllabification. For one thing, they leave the stem, which is the more important of the two morphemes, untouched. Only the form of the affix is affected. For another, these modifications are a response to phonotactic rules which in turn are a response to both articulatory and auditory constraints.

Third is the phenomenon of *linking-r* which arises in some dialects of British, though not in Standard American English. In the former case, final <r>s in the graphemic structure are not pronounced, e.g. *to bar* [bɑː] and *to tour* [tʊə]. However, when a vowel-initial suffix is added, the 'mute r' is pronounced: *to bar* + *-ing* → [bɑːrɪŋ]. This represents a somewhat stronger form of interaction between the stem and the affix in that a new consonant is apparently inserted before the suffix. The reason for this process is clear. It serves to lubricate the joining of two morphemes of which the first ends in, and the second begins with, a vowel. That is, a phonotactic situation is created (*hiatus*) which is universally disfavoured. One of the means of resolving this problem is to insert a consonant, which is what has taken place here. It must be added that the consonant-insertion rule is only one way of describing the relevant facts. On another interpretation, the infinitive is subject to a rule which deletes the final consonant. A third alternative is to assume that the stem has the two variants [bɑː] and [bɑːr] whose selection is determined by the material to follow. In any event, the degree of fusion between the stem and the suffix is still relatively low because the morpheme boundary remains clearly discernible. There is no question that the /r/ belongs to the stem rather than the suffix, as the same thing happens with other vowel-initial suffixes such as *-able* and *-er*.

The fourth type of modification is the most serious because it affects the stem rather than the affix. There is one area of English morphophonology where the suffix induces a change on the stem, viz. a subset of plural nouns. A small group of nouns (N = 19)[21] form their plural by voicing their stem-final fricative in addition to the regular suffixation process, e.g. *house* is pluralized as [haʊzɪz] rather than *[haʊsɪz]. What appears today as an irregular process is the remnant of a phonetically fairly natural rule ('intervocalic voicing') whose structural conditions have changed. It is plain that these plural nouns flout the principle of stem-form preservation, but it has to be acknowledged that these cases are exceedingly rare in view of the thousands of regular nouns. Significantly, only the plural morpheme impinges upon the shape of the stem. Other morphemes, which have exactly the same phonological form, are incapable of inducing such changes. Compare the effect of the plural and the possessive marker on the stem in *wife–wives* vs. *wife–wife's*.[22]

Summarizing so far, we may say that the combination of a stem and an inflectional suffix leaves the integrity of both parts largely intact. Changes on the stem are

---

[21] Some nouns vacillate between stem constancy and stem change, e.g. *scalf* + PLURAL → *scarfs* or *scarves*. These are not included in this number.

[22] Note parenthetically that there are some special cases of plural formation such as *child–children* and *woman–women*. These cases for the most part do not involve stem + suffix structures and thus are

almost completely absent. A subset of plural nouns qualifies as the only exception to this rule. Changes on the inflectional suffix occur regularly, but they are all conditioned by low-level rules whose function it is to make the form of the message suitable to pass the 'articulatory bottleneck' as well as to ensure that the inflectional marker is not absorbed by the stem and consequently unrecoverable for the listener. The changes that are necessary to satisfy these constraints are caused by a minimum number of very general principles which leave the morpheme boundary intact. Thus the stem and the inflectional suffix are fused to a relatively low degree.

Turning now to the derivational morphemes, the picture looks rather different. Although cases of non-interaction between stem and derivational affix are quite common, there are numerous types of interaction unknown to the inflectional domain. Some are exemplified below.

(80) divine–divinity
(81) opaque–opacity
(82) moral–morality
(83) remember–remembrance
(84) refute–refutation
(85) anticipate–anticipation
(86) decide–decision
(87) bomb–bombard
(88) haste–hasten
(89) pervade–pervasive
(90) please–pleasure
(91) depart–departure
(92) magic–magician
(93) petulant–petulance
(94) advise–advice
(95) review–review
(96) compare–comparable
(97) example–exemplify

This list, which is by no means exhaustive, makes it quite clear that the interaction between stems and derivational suffixes is much more involved than that between stems and inflectional suffixes. The three most frequently encountered processes in derivation are stress shift, vocalic changes, and consonantal changes in the final part of the stem. The placement of stress may be a function of the suffix, but many suffixes are not consistent in their influence, contrast (81) to (82). Vowels, whether tonic or atonic, often undergo quantitative and qualitative changes. The well-known trisyllabic laxing rule, illustrated in (80) and (86), captures many of these cases. Others, like (96) and (97), are more idiosyncratic. Consonant changes at the end of the stem can take three theoretically possible forms, all of which are attested. A consonant is added in (87) and deleted in (88). Much more frequently, the final consonant is changed: for example, spirantization occurs in (89) and affrication in (91). The voicing value tends to remain unaffected, as in (86), though not always (89). In many cases, the consonantal substitution can be phonetically motivated, at least from the diachronic point of view. The palatalization of fricatives and stops as in (90) and (92) may be viewed as an assimilation of the stem-final consonant to the following palatal vowel or glide. The palato-alveolar fricatives /ʃ/ and /ʒ/ developed from /sj/ and /zj/, respectively (Samuels 1972). Granted, these assimilations increase

not amenable to the same analysis as carried out above. Furthermore, they are limited in number and subject to different psycholinguistic constraints, especially frequency (see section 5.17). They will therefore not be given any further attention here.

the ease of articulation but they are in no way compulsory. So, from the phonotactic view-point, there would be nothing wrong with forms such as [dɪsɪd(j)ən] and [plɛzə] instead of [dɪsɪʒən] and [plɛʒə]. These stem changes cannot therefore be motivated synchronically.

Stem-determined variation in the suffix, as shown in (84) and (85), is the first step towards blurring the distinction between stem and suffix. This distinction is even less clear in (93). Should -*ant* be analysed as the adjectival suffix of *petulant*, notwithstanding the fact that *petul*- is a non-word? In (94), the distinction between stem and affix is fully inapplicable.

Apart from the phenomenon of zero derivation in (95), the form of the stem is altered in all of the above cases. As these changes occur at the juncture of stems and suffixes, these structures form fairly tightly integrated wholes. Although this does not hold good for all derivation, it applies to a significant portion of the lexicon.[23]

A comparison between inflected and derived words suggests quite strongly that stem + inflectional suffix combinations are much more loosely associated with each other than stem + derivational suffix structures. Derivational suffixes have the power to formally modify the stem, whereas inflectional suffixes do not. The looser semantic relationship between stems and inflectional suffixes is thus mirrored by a looser formal relationship between them. This match between the semantic and the phonological levels can be taken as further support for an iconic relationship between the *signifiant* and the *signifié*.

It is worthy of note that there is a mutual influence between stem and affix. Derivational and inflectional suffixes display an interesting contrast in that the former are relatively invariant and tend to act on the stem, whereas the latter have a high degree of allomorphy which is caused by the phonological properties of the stem. In a nutshell, derivational suffixes change stems and stems change inflectional suffixes. Clearly, the former change is more dramatic because the stem is most important for lexical access during comprehension and therefore has to exhibit formal constancy. Formal variability in inflectional suffixes is less of a problem because their paradigm is much more limited. That allomorphy exists at all in inflectional suffixes follows from the necessity of making them as widely applicable as possible.

This section has examined a major implication of parallel processing for language structure. It has been predicted that an iconic relationship should obtain between the *signifiant* and the *signifié* of the linguistic sign. This prediction has been tested by looking for parallels between the semantic and phonological levels. It was found that the phonological similarity between two words parallels their semantic similarity, and that the phonological interaction between a stem and an affix mirrors their semantic interaction. There is thus clear support for the research hypothesis.

---

[23] This is not to deny that speakers generally prefer morphologically complex words, in which the form of the stem is preserved, to those in which it undergoes a change following suffixation (Cutler 1980; 1981). The reason is simply that the former are easier to process than the latter, both for the speaker and the listener. It is all the more remarkable that so many derived words run counter to this natural tendency of stem-form preservation (see section 2.4).

4.15. The Morphophonology of Vowel Length

Distinctive vowel length is a nice example of how languages may differ, quite unexpectedly, in the processing of one and the same linguistic phenomenon. From a global perspective, vowel length is rather similar in German, English and Dutch. It may act distinctively, as evidenced in the pairs E *fool–full*, G *bitten–bieten* 'to ask'–'to offer', D *zoen–zon* 'son'–'sun', though the number of such minimal pairs is limited in the three languages. In addition, a change along the length dimension entails a qualitative change, with the short variants tending to involve more central articulations than the long ones. Basically, there are three ways of representing vowel length. A long vowel may be analysed as a sequence of two identical short monophthongs ('geminates') or the properties [long] and [short] may enjoy the same status as other distinctive features such as [nasal] or [bilabial]. Unlike the second, the third possibility treats vowel length as a non-inherent feature, i.e. as a piece of information which is not included in the segmental specification but coded on a separate level of representation. The latter two alternatives may be referred to as the subsegmental (featural) and suprasegmental (prosodic) analysis respectively.

The manner in which vowel length is dealt with by the processor can be straightforwardly assessed in slips of the tongue in which two vowels of differing length interact. As the integrity of segments is ordinarily preserved during the error process, vowel length would be expected to accompany the migrating segment on the segmental interpretation. Under the suprasegmental analysis, however, the dislocated unit would be free to leave its length specification behind. Both possibilities will be exemplified with one error from English (98), one from Dutch (99), and two from German (100–101).

(98) [minuːs-muːnisipl] (municipal) (from Stemberger 1984a)
(99) *artaalaarie granaten* for *artillerie granaten* (from Berg 1988b)
 [ʌːʌ: ʌːʌ: i u]
 'artillery grenades'
(100) Ich bin da nicht engagiert worden, um
 feman– feministische Brandreden zu halten
 [feːman feːmiːnɪstɪʃə brantreːdən]
 'I wasn't hired to deliver fervent speeches on behalf of feminism'
(101) Sie möchten nicht unbedingt Löhrer– Lehrer werden
 [mœçtən   løːrɛr   leːrɛr]
 'You don't really want to be a teacher, do you?'

While (98–100) document the simple substitution of a long by a short vowel (or vice versa), case (101) is more complex. Here, the short vowel [œ] entered a location which was originally destined for the long vowel [eː] and surfaced as its long congener [øː]. That is, the intruding segment took on the length specification of the vowel it replaced. The implication is that the malfunction was blind to the quantity of the moving segment. In this way, quantitative and qualitative features may be dissociated in the error process.

A look at the complete set of relevant errors in Stemberger's English database reveals that the integrity of the vowel is preserved in all of the forty-one cases where a split would have been possible. The same situation holds of Dutch. In the Dutch sample analysed by Berg (1988b), eighteen slips take the length feature with them, while only one leaves it behind. By contrast, my German collection contains eighty-one pertinent vowel errors of which sixty-five (80 per cent) evince a dissociation between length and the 'segmental core' and sixteen (20 per cent) follow the English/Dutch pattern (cf. Berg 1988b). German and English thus exhibit diametrically opposite trends: whereas length acts cohesively in English and Dutch, the vowels tend to break apart in German. It follows that vowel length in English and Dutch seems to be a segmental but German vowel length a suprasegmental feature.[24]

It is worthy of note that the three languages are not entirely symmetrical in their opposite trends. While the pattern is close to absolute in English and Dutch, the German data require a more quantitative formulation. There is an obvious reason for this asymmetry. Remaining intact can most usefully be viewed as the unmarked case. Breaking apart is a more difficult operation to carry out, since the integrity of a segment has to be destroyed and a new feature bundle has to be created. It is therefore expected that disintegrative slips have a lower baseline probability than unitary ones.

What predictions can be derived from the psycholinguistic data in terms of language structure? The German slips of the tongue demonstrate that vowel length is very reluctant to undergo alteration. The length value of any given vowel in a certain position tends to remain constant. English and Dutch vowel length, however, is more flexibly processed. Whenever necessary, a change from [long] to [short] or vice versa is effected. This processing difference between the three languages has clear implications for linguistic structure. In German, a change in vowel quantity should be less common than in English and Dutch. Of course, to predict that the percentages found in the speech-error data mirror exactly those encountered in the structure of language would not be realistic. Unquestionably, linguistic structure is determined by more than a single processing principle. We can only predict that, if processing plays a role, the rate of vowel-quantity change should be higher in English and Dutch than in German.

An ideal testing-ground for the above prediction is morphophonemic alternations, in particular the verbal ablaut system (see section 4.14), because the ablaut systems compare well across the three languages. A further advantage of investigating this area is that it guarantees maximum independence between the domain in which the prediction is formulated and the domain in which the prediction is put to the test. None of the German and Dutch speech errors whose behaviour allowed us to derive the processing principle at hand implicates morphophonemic alternations. All of them testify to the interaction of vowels from morphosemantically

---

[24] See Berg (1988c) for a fuller discussion of whether these terms adequately reflect the empirical picture.

unrelated words. As far as I can tell, the same holds true of the English database. The linguistic context of the errors thus cannot be held responsible for the patterns to be reported below.

Let us begin with some examples to illustrate the possibility of changing vs. preserving vowel length. For our purposes, it is sufficient to focus upon the infinitive, the past tense, and the past participle. From these base forms, the length of the vowel can be computed for all tenses and all conjugated forms.

(102) G: *frieren–fror–gefroren* 'to be cold'
(103) G: *bitten–bat–gebeten* 'to ask'
(104) E: *to seek–sought–sought*
(105) E: *to keep–kept–kept*
(106) D: *blazen–blies–geblazen* 'to blow'
(107) D: *gaan–ging–gegaan* 'to go'

In (102), (104), and (106), the length of the vowel is kept constant in the ablauted forms while the vowel is lengthened in (103) but shortened in (105) and (107). The English data are taken from Bloch's (1947) list of irregular verbs and augmented by a few cases such as *to lie* and *to chide* which he apparently overlooked. All verbs in which the vowel quality remains the same, as in *to cost* and *to learn*, are excluded. So was the auxiliary *to be*. The verbs which possess a strong as well as a weak variant were included (e.g. *to dream* and *to crow*). Verbs such as *to cleave* and *to stride* which know two different ablaut rules are counted twice. In case of a divergence of British and American usage, the former variant was chosen. All in all, 127 English verbs entered the analysis.

The German data are based upon the *Duden* (1973), the standard reference of the German language. The criteria applied in the selection of the English verbs by and large carry over to the German data. The auxiliary *sein* 'to be' was excluded but the verbs which are in transit from the strong to the weak class, i.e. those which have obsolescent past tense forms (e.g. *backen* 'to bake' and *fragen* 'to ask') were included. The total number of pertinent verbs is 189. The Dutch data are taken from Geerts et al. (1984). All of the verbs with vowel change were taken into account.

Table 13 summarizes the analysis of the German, English, and Dutch strong verbs in terms of their vocalic length. The eight columns correspond to the eight theoretical possibilities in which the constellation of long and short vowels manifests itself.

TABLE 13. *Frequency of vowel quantity change in ablaut verbs*

	sss	lll	sll	sls	ssl	lss	lsl	lls	sum
German	62	68	1	19	0	36	0	0	189
English	28	38	7	3	0	38	4	9	127
Dutch	53	121	5	9	0	3	21	0	212

Note: s = short; l = long.

The first position codes the infinitive, the second the past-tense form, and the third the past participle. 's' stands for 'short' and 'l' for 'long'. The sequence 'sss' thus means that the vowel is short in all three forms of the verb. Diphthongs are counted as long.

Let us begin with a comparison of English and German. Fifty-six German verbs involve a vowel-length change while 133 keep vowel length constant. In English, 66 verbs have either a long or a short vowel in all three base forms while vowel length is altered in 61 examples. Thus 70.4 per cent of the German but only 52.0 per cent of the English verbs display a stable vowel quantity. This difference goes in the predicted direction and is statistically significant ($\chi^2(1) = 11.1$, $p < 0.001$). The research hypothesis is therefore supported: vowel length in English is modified more often than in German.

However, the Dutch data are counter to expectation. Thirty-eight (17.9 per cent) verbs undergo a length change in their ablaut series, while as many as 174 (82.1 per cent) fail to do so. The percentages show that Dutch verbs are even less receptive to vowel-length change than the German ones, although they would have been expected to mirror the English pattern. There seems to be a very powerful force which prevents changes of vocalic length in Dutch. This part of the prediction is thus not borne out by the empirical materials.

Table 13 further discloses that if a change of vowel length occurs, it can almost always be observed between the present and the past tense forms. This pattern is exceptionless in German (56 : 0) and Dutch (38 : 0) and strongly predominant in English (52 : 9). Once vowel length is understood as a contrast-inducing device, this finding can be readily explained. The distinction between the second and the third base forms need not be strongly marked at the phonological level because the syntactic structures in which they occur are already different. The first and the second base forms, however, can occur in the same syntactic context: compare *they run a business* and *they ran a business*. To ensure correct communication, therefore, it is necessary more fully to exploit the length difference as a means of securing formal contrast. There is, then, support for the idea that the major cut is between the present and the non-present forms rather than within the non-present tenses.

Next, the cross-linguistic analysis of vowel length will be extended to morphophonemic alternations in word pairs from different syntactic categories. We may conveniently draw upon the data presented in Table 12. It is evident that vowel-length changes predominate in English but are less frequent in German (46 per cent). This difference between the two languages replicates the results obtained in the analysis of the ablaut verbs and cements the research hypothesis. Again, the Dutch data run counter to expectation. As in the case of the ablaut verbs, they are more strongly resistant to vowel-length change than the German pairs: only 37 per cent show such a change. It is likely that the factor that accounts for the stability of vowel length in the noun/verb pairs is identical to that which accounts for the stability of this feature in the ablaut series.

One objection remains to be dealt with. The empirical difference in the phonological structure of English and German might be due to the differing severity of phonotactic constraints in the two languages, that is, stronger constraints in German than in English. It is well known that short tonic vowels cannot occur in open syllables and that long vowels tend to be shortened in closed syllables (see Myers, 1985; 1987 for English). More generally, long vowels are the more strongly discouraged when the number of consonants following them is higher. If phonotactic constraints did not allow for the alternation between long and short vowels, an identity in vowel quantity would be artifactual and could not be used as evidence for or against a particular processing principle.

To meet this objection, all cases in which phonotactic constraints disallow the alternation of long and short vowels have to be eliminated. In both the German and English groups of ablaut verbs, there are 36 instances each which have to be discarded. Among the 36 German verbs only one exhibits a change in vowel quantity. The English set consists of 32 cases of identical vowel length and 4 cases of non-identical vowel length. Subtracting these illicit cases, we end up with 98 (64 per cent) German and 34 (37 per cent) English verbs with stable vowel length in all three base forms, but 55 (36 per cent) German and 57 (63 per cent) English verbs with variable vowel length. This difference between the two languages is statistically reliable ($\chi^2(1) = 15.9$, $p < 0.001$). In fact, the χ^2 value is even higher than in the larger database. The purification thus leads to a decrease in the number of quantity-preserving verbs. This is quite understandable, as phonotactic constraints by their very nature hold a given structure constant. If verbs in which phonotactic constraints are operative are excluded, it will preferably be those in which the length of the vowel remains unchanged. It can be concluded, then, that phonotactic constraints cannot explain the differential ease with which vowel length is altered in English and German strong verbs.

Could it be that taking phonotactic constraints into account eliminates the recalcitrance of the Dutch data? This possibility has to be considered because, as argued immediately above, monitoring for this factor might increase the number of length-changing cases, and such an increase would bring the data closer to the predicted pattern. Therefore the Dutch ablaut verbs have been divided into those in which phonotactic constraints would forbid a vowel of a different length and those in which a length change would not violate any phonotactic constraints. Only the latter group provides for a proper test of the susceptibility of vowel length to morphosemantic change. Of the 212 ablaut verbs, 58 do not allow a vowel change for phonotactic reasons. For example, in

(108)   *vlechten, vlocht, gevlochten* 'to plait'

the past-tense vowel /ɔ/ cannot be lengthened because a long vowel may not be followed by two tautosyllabic consonants. The remaining 154 verbs in which a length change would be phonotactically possible distribute as follows: 123 (79.9 per cent) belong to the 'sss' or 'lll' category while 31 (20.1 per cent) involve a length change from the infinitive to the past-tense form. Despite a minor change in the desired direction, this result does not differ significantly from the above analysis of the entire data set ($\chi^2 < 1$). It must be concluded that phonotactic constraints cannot be held responsible for the unexpected patterning of the Dutch materials.

Perhaps there is a radical way of salvaging the psycholinguistic account. It might be the case that length is not processed in Dutch in the same way as it is in English (and German). Specifically, the possibility has to be entertained that length is not independently manipulated as a high-level processing variable in Dutch. Instead, it might be subordinated to decisions about vowel quality and be programmed at a relatively low level of processing. In that case, the length variation in Dutch would be irrelevant to the psycholinguistic prediction—or, to look at it from the other side, the psycholinguistic prediction could not be falsified by evidence from Dutch. Indeed, this interpretation of Dutch vowel length may not be too far off the mark. Some students of Dutch phonology claimed that vowels are not specified for length. A radical view is voiced by Cohen et al. (1961: 16), who argue that quantitative differences of vowels play no role in the phonology of native words (though they do in some loanwords). Similarly, Hermkens (1969) considers vowel quantity to be a redundant feature. Others such as Moulton (1962) regard it as redundant for the high vowels but distinctive for the mid and low vowels. Van den Berg (1958), by contrast, draws a distinction between [short] and [non-short]. It transpires that the phonological status of vowel length is far from clear from the linguistic perspective. In the absence of pertinent evidence, the same can be said from the processing perspective. Hence it cannot be ruled out that vowel length is not independently controlled during high-level processing. If this view is correct, the empirical data cannot be used to refute the psycholinguistic approach taken here.

To summarize, an analysis of slips of the tongue has supported the prediction that morphophonemic alternations in English and Dutch should involve a vowel-length change less often than those in German. One part of the prediction was fulfilled: a change from a long vowel to its short counterpart (and vice versa) occurs more commonly in English than in German. This finding suggests that the specification of vowel quantity in the phonological make-up of words is controlled by psycholinguistic principles of information processing. However, the Dutch data do not exhibit the expected instability of vowel length: this feature turns out to be very reluctant to change. It is unclear whether this finding should be construed as falsifying the psycholinguistic approach. It is at least possible that length is not independently controlled at the processing level at which slips of the tongue arise. If this is the case, the psycholinguistic prediction would be inapplicable to the linguistic data under consideration.

4.16. The Differential Ease of Morphological Processes: Substitution vs. Addition

The premiss underlying this section is that morphological processes are psychologically real and may be applied on-line. Basically, there are two ways in which morphology may manifest itself—through substitution or through addition. In the latter case linguistic material is added to the base form, whereas in the former, part of the base form is replaced. There is a third logical possibility—subtraction. As this principle of coding morphological information is extremely rare, it will not receive further attention. Suffice to say that it is anti-iconic to code additional information (e.g. plurality) by obliterating formal means of expression.

Substitutions and additions may occur at any point in a word or morpheme. The topic of this section thus is not fully independent from the issue of positionality raised in section 4.12. We will therefore be able to draw upon the conclusion that the likelihood of morphological change increases as one moves from left to right in a word.

From the processing point of view, it makes a great difference whether a morphological process is instantiated by substitution or by addition. Simply enough, an addition involves the generation of material and its placement in a position which used to be 'empty'. In contrast, a substitution involves the generation of material and its placement in a position which is already filled. There is thus a conflict between the material to be replaced and the material to be produced in its stead. This conflict is apparent in the following slips of the tongue.

(109) *He had wind up making $200* for *He had wound up*
(110) *Some of these will wound up being orphans* for *wind up* (both from Stemberger 1985a)

The speakers who produced these utterances err on exactly the same verb (*to wind up*). In (109), the ablaut rule should have applied but did not, whereas in (110) it should not have applied but did. One explanation for (109) is that the base vowel was activated highly enough to resist its being supplanted by the ablaut vowel. The directionality of the substitution process is worth emphasizing. Base vowels are generally stronger than ablaut vowels. As a result, errors such as (109) outnumber those exemplified in (110). The reciprocity of the two slips is good evidence for the competition between the base and the derived vowel. This implies that to effect a segmental change involves not only the generation of the derived vowel but also the suppression of the base vowel. In other words, the application of a morphological substitution process is hindered by the element to be substituted. On this logic, it can be argued that morphological substitution processes are inherently more difficult to perform.

Such a hindrance is absent in addition processes because by definition there is nothing to suppress. Additions enjoy a second advantage. As noted by Stemberger (1991), the psycholinguistic system is subject to an addition bias which prejudices the system towards outputting more rather than less. Although Stemberger formulated this principle to account for phonological phenomena, there is every reason to expect it to hold at the morphological level as well.

From these processing considerations, predictions about the frequency of morphological processes may be derived. Because ablaut and umlaut involve by definition substitution processes and prefixing and suffixing addition processes, it may be predicted that affixation is a more favoured means of expression than internal vowel change. In view of the fact that recourse has been made to general processing principles, these predictions have a universal flavour.

The case of ablaut in the English verb system is clear evidence for the correctness of the research hypothesis. Ablaut verbs are classified as irregular because their number is much lower than that of non-ablauted ones. In view of the thousands of regular verbs, ablauted verbs have an estimated type frequency of less than 10 per cent (although their token frequency is certainly higher). Among the irregular verbs, however, verbs involving a vowel change constitute the largest group. After subtracting all suppletive and modal verbs as well as the fluctuating forms, there remain 170 irregular verbs in Bloch's (1947) list. Of these 123 (72.4 per cent) involve a vowel change, whereas the rest use other means such as final consonant change and no formal change whatsoever. These alternative means of coding the past tense make it easy to explain the preponderance of vowel changes. Obviously, no tense marking at all is orthogonal to the ideal one-to-one relationship between form and meaning. Final consonant changes, as in *to bend, bent, bent*, rely upon the voicing opposition, which is difficult to maintain in final positions for articulatory reasons. Ablaut thus qualifies as the best among all forms of word-internal morphological marking.

Umlaut in German should be similar to ablaut in English in its secondary status. Three predictions may be formulated. First, umlaut should be restricted in the type of morphological information that it codes. Secondly, umlaut is expected to be less frequent than other morphological markers; thirdly, it should tend to mark a morphological function in conjunction with other morphemes rather than on its own.

Beginning with the first prediction, umlaut on its own codes only a single type of morphological information (i.e. plurality) whereas prefixes and suffixes are far less constrained in this respect. The limited scope of umlaut becomes even clearer when one looks at the words in which umlaut is the sole morphological marker. Mugdan (1977) analysed a corpus of 828 nouns from the basic German vocabulary. Of these, 171 (20.7 per cent) undergo umlaut in the plural. The remaining 657 nouns fall into two groups—those that lack an umlautable vowel and those that are not umlauted, even though they contain an umlautable vowel. Of the 171 umlauted plural forms, 20 (11.7 per cent) rely exclusively upon umlaut as the coding device for plurality. The other 151 (88.3 per cent) draw upon a suffix in addition to umlaut. These data include all nouns irrespective of their gender. Thus, singular/plural pairs such as *der Vater–die Väter* 'the father'–'the fathers' may not even be seen as valid examples of plural marking by umlaut alone because the noun's article also codes plurality. If all such cases are eliminated, the number of pertinent examples is drastically reduced. In fact, only feminine nouns can be retained because the plural article is identical to the feminine singular article. Of the 171 umlauted plural nouns, only two are of feminine gender, *die Mutter* 'the mother' and *die Tochter* 'the daughter'. There is no doubt, then, that umlaut is not a primary plural marker in German: it serves only a subsidiary function, in that it is almost always accompanied by other means of expression. Because these means regularly occur on their own, umlaut is clearly secondary to them.

That umlaut is a fairly unproductive phenomenon can be gathered from the morphological integration of loan words into German. An index of productivity is the frequency with which the umlaut rule applies to plural formations in appropriate structural (e.g. phonological) conditions. Köpcke (1988) examined 182 nouns which have recently entered the German language. Since 33 of these have not settled on a single plural morpheme, the total number of plural assignments is 215. Of these, only 15 (7.0 per cent) use umlaut as the only marker of plurality. Following Köpcke (1988), this may be taken to mean that umlaut is a disfavoured option among the possible plural markers of German.

In the light of all the evidence *against* umlaut, one might wonder why it has not disappeared altogether. The diachronic perspective reveals that umlaut has even proved rather stable over time. One explanation for this somewhat unexpected finding is its high cue reliability (see also Wurzel 1984). The fact that umlaut applies to a single morphological domain not only attests to its weakness but, paradoxically, also explains its strength. Because umlaut alone codes no other inflectional information, listeners can take it as an umambiguous cue for plurality. Another reason for the diachronic stability of umlaut is that it figures prominently among the most frequent words which are fairly reluctant to change (see section 5.17). Finally, umlaut is a homogeneous process at the phonological level. It can be exhaustively described as a process of vowel fronting (Wiese 1996). This might further enhance its stability.

The psycholinguistic prediction also holds for word-final positions. Substitutions at the end of words (e.g. *to send, sent, sent*) are far less frequent than additions to the end of words (e.g. *to mend, mended, mended*). The same holds true of word-initial loci. Prefixing is much more frequent than consonant mutation. However, the processes operating in word-internal sites appear to run counter to prediction. If additions are generally more frequent than substitutions, infixing should be found more often than umlaut and ablaut. Although a large-scale cross-linguistic comparison does not seem to be available, infixing is very probably less prevalent than umlaut and ablaut. It certainly is an extremely uncommon phenomenon in the languages of the world (e.g. Moravcsik 1977; Marantz 1982; Broselow and McCarthy 1983-4). The standard explanation in linguistics of this rarity is that infixing destroys the unity of the morpheme and therefore leads to a considerably more complicated relationship between the *signifiant* and the *signifié*. Even though linguists do not generally conceive of this account in psycholinguistic terms, there is good reason to argue that the ultimate explanation is a psycholinguistic one. An infixed word is quite difficult to process for the speaker as well as the listener because the stem, which is stored in unitary fashion in the lexicon, has to be split up by the speaker and put together by the listener. While not impossible, this indubitably requires a substantial processing effort.

Umlaut and ablaut also break up the unity of a word, in that they induce an internal modification. However, this modification can be argued to be less radical once the multi-layered representation of linguistic units is taken into account. Umlaut is the shallowest type of modification conceivable, because it affects only the melodic level and leaves the suprasegmental structure intact. The length specification of the vowel which is umlauted is always preserved. Even in case of a length change, only the skeleton would be affected but not the levels further up the hierarchy. In contrast, infixing by its very nature entails a considerable restructuring at the suprasegmental level. No matter what structure is added, be it CV, VC, or something else, it leads to a severe reorganization of the subsyllabic/suprasegmental levels. In most cases a new syllable node has to be created. In essence, my claim is that infixing is less tolerable than umlaut and ablaut because it involves a modification at more and deeper levels of (psycho)linguistic representation.[25] On this account, the difference between infixation and umlaut/ablaut is a gradual one.

The preceding analysis sheds further light upon the issue of vowel quantity treated in section 4.15. It was shown there that modifications of vowel length are more common in English than in German. On the other hand, given the absence of umlaut, English resorts far less frequently to vowel change in general than German. It might be that these two interlingual differences are related. Since German makes widespread use of vowel modification, which incurs a certain processing cost, it is expedient to keep this cost to a minimum. Because changes in vowel quantity have repercussions on the CV tier, they are discouraged in this language. The changes that do occur tend to be restricted to the most shallow types. In English, however, morphologically conditioned changes of vowel quantity are less frequent and less productive. This increases the likelihood of their being lexicalized. In that case, the production of a derived form is less dependent upon the spontaneous application of a rule and the structural change has more freedom to ignore the minimal-distance requirement for easy production and easy recovery during comprehension.

Summarizing, there is good evidence that morphological processes are better implemented by the addition rather than the substitution of phonological material. Thus vowel changes such as ablaut and umlaut in English and German are of secondary importance as morphological marking devices—exactly as predicted by the processing arguments. However, additions are preferred to substitutions only when they occur at the margins of the base form. In the within-word domain, substitutions appear to predominate because they leave a greater number of representational levels unaffected and are therefore easier to process for the listener as well as the speaker. Thus the empirical data are entirely compatible with what may be expected on psycholinguistic grounds. The only result that was slightly surprising is the diachronic stability of umlaut in German. It may be that it owes its stability to other stabilizing features such as fequency; but it may also be that the stability of umlaut is a more ephemeral phenomenon, and that an analysis 500 years from now will yield results which are more in line with the research hypothesis.

[25] Note that no (or very little) modification of the base form is required for prefixing and suffixing.

4.17. The Varying Strength of Linguistic Constraints

Many linguistic constraints at different descriptive levels have been uncovered in the past few decades. The problem with these constraints is that most of them are not inviolable and no satisfactory answer has been found as to how these exceptions should be handled. In addition, it has proved difficult to accommodate the finding that the strength of one and the same constraint may not be constant. It is the principal claim of this section that the non-absolute, variable strength of these constraints is mediated by psycholinguistic principles. The focus will be upon the repetition constraint, discussed in section 4.6, and upon how it interacts with various linguistic boundaries.

To understand better the predictions that follow from the processing considerations, it is necessary to highlight three characteristics of the psycholinguistic model. The first is representational redundancy. In linguistics, it is commonplace to argue in either/or fashion. For example, a morphologically complex word may be either holistically or analytically represented. Many psycholinguists, however, are now considering seriously the idea of multiple representations (e.g. MacWhinney and Anderson 1986; Frauenfelder and Schreuder 1991). That is, a morphologically complex word may be *both* holistically and analytically represented. Indeed, the available evidence points to redundant coding in the mental lexicon. Butterworth (1983) came to the conclusion that complex words are likely to be listed in holistic fashion. He does not deny the existence of morphological processing principles, but argues convincingly that they alone cannot explain the bulk of the evidence. On the other hand, Schriefers et al. (1991) showed that processing is mainly non-compositional but that a holistic approach alone is insufficient to account for their results. Thus, two levels of representation are implicated in the storage of individual words.

This double representation can be well illustrated by slips of the tongue. Compare (111–12) with (113), all from German.

(111) Durch die Entblu– Durchblutung entspannt der Körper.
[ɛnt#blu: durç#blu:tuŋk ɛnt#ʃpant]
'Following more intensive blood circulation, your body relaxes'

(112) Es bringt mir viele Vorteilung– Vorteile, die Anpassung an die Umwelt da
[fo:r#taɪl#uŋk fo:r#tail#ə an#pas#uŋk]
'I find it advantageous to adjust myself to the environment'

(113) Er wird diesen Vorschlag– diese Ankündigung vor seinem Rücktritt verbinden
[fo:r#ʃla:k an#kyndi:g#uŋk]
mit dem Vorschlag
'Before he steps down, he is going to connect his announcement to the proposal...'

Cases (111–12) involve the morphological level. They document the anticipation of an affix, a prefix in (111) and a suffix in (112). Without a morphological decomposition of words, the moving units would have to be regarded as random strings of segments. Thus there is evidence for their analytic representation and a morphological processing level. Number (113) involves the lexical level. A morphologically complex word (*Vorschlag*) is dislocated as a unit. This suggests that the word was represented holistically at the moment the malfunction arose. The two error types occur frequently enough to justify the claim that both a lexical and a morphological processing stage exist.

The second issue is representational strength. Psycholinguistic representations need not be all or nothing. Like the distinctness of a picture on a screen, they may be of variable strength. At the lexical level, the distinctness of a representation is called its degree of lexicalization. Lexicalization depends upon a variety of factors, in particular upon the syntacticity of the affixed material. The more syntactic the nature of the affix, the lower the degree of lexicalization. Therefore, derived words are more highly lexicalized than inflected words.

The third issue is related to the second. The processing system treats prefixes and suffixes differently. Suffixes are processed in closer union with the stem than prefixes. This can be seen from the fact that prefix slips (111) occur much more frequently than suffix slips (112) (see section 8.4 for more details).

In the following, it will be enquired how the constraint on the repetition of identical material might interact with the psycholinguistic representation of lexical items. If complex words were exclusively represented in terms of the morphemes that make them up, the constraint should operate only within morphemes. That is, /αβ#αβ/ should be a perfectly natural sequence. Alternatively, if complex words were exclusively represented in holistic fashion, the constraint should hold within and across morpheme boundaries alike. As argued above, both characterizations of the processing system are inadequate. On the assumption of multiple representations, a different prediction emerges. The phonotactic constraint should be the stronger, the higher the degree of lexicalization. Recourse to various types of boundary allows us to make this prediction more specific. The constraint should be strongest at the phoneme boundary, weaker at the stem/derivational suffix boundary, still weaker at the derivational prefix/stem boundary, and weakest at the stem/inflectional suffix boundary. This hierarchy is a direct reflection of the degree of lexicalization. Two adjacent segments (within a word) are most likely to be lexicalized, whereas a combination of stem + inflectional affix is least likely to be lexicalized. Because of this difference, the different morphemes have more or less opportunity to act upon each other. As a consequence, the constraint may manifest itself more or less strongly. Notice that in this way gradualness is introduced into the picture. A constraint may be more or less powerful, and there is in principle nothing suspect about violating it.

The constraint on the repetition of identical segments within morphemes was discussed in section 2.1. The within-morpheme constraint is quite severe and interacts with a syllable-position constraint. In the between-morpheme case, the constraint on segment repetition is still in operation, albeit less strongly than in the within-morpheme case. In line with the psycholinguistic prediction, derivational suffixes follow this constraint more rigidly than inflectional ones. The ideal example to show this is phonological material that can serve an inflectional as well as a derivational function. If the respect for the repetition constraint varies with the function of particular segment sequences, it can be ascribed to their differing linguistic status. In fact, such an example can be found in Dressler (1977). The German morpheme *-en* can act both as a derivational and as an inflectional suffix. It marks denominal adjectives in the former case and the accusative in the latter case.

(114) *Gold* 'gold' + adjectival suffix *-en* → *golden* 'golden'
(115) *Roggen* 'rye' + adjectival suffix *-en* → **roggenen*
(116) *der graulodene Mantel* + accusative marker *-en* → *den graulodenen Mantel* 'the grey woollen coat'

A typical instance of suffixation is illustrated in (114): by adding *-en*, a noun is turned into an adjective. This process is blocked, not for semantic but for formal reasons in (115). As it happens, the end of the lexical morpheme *Roggen* is phonologically identical to the shape of the grammatical morpheme. The same can be said of (116), yet the suffix rule applies. As other factors are held constant, this disparity can be attributed to the involvement of different types of boundary. Inflected words are less lexicalized than derived ones. Therefore, the haplological constraint finds it easier to cross inflectional than derivational boundaries. A further example is German *-er*, which also performs a double function in morphology (i.e. agens and comparative morpheme) and behaves like *-en* above. There are no counterexamples where an inflectional rule is blocked while a derivational one applies.

The predicted difference between prefixes and suffixes also appears to hold, although a definitive assessment requires a much larger analysis than can be provided here. In general, prefixes are reluctant to attach to stems whose beginning is identical to their phonological form. However, they appear to be less reluctant than suffixes to attach to stems if a repetitive segment sequence is thereby created. The resistance to repetition can be seen in *un-intelligible*, which derives from Latin *in-intelligibilis*. The prefix *-in* has dissimilated to *-un* in view of the phonological beginning of the stem (Dressler 1977). However, the repetition of identical material is not too infrequent. Examples from German include *un-unterbrochen* 'un-interrupted', *ge-geben* 'given', and *er-erben* 'to inherit'.

The repetition constraint is strongest in inflectional suffixes. Two phonologically identical inflectional suffixes can never occur next to each other. In case of phonological identity between the suffix and the preceding material, the rule does not usually apply. One pertinent example is the adverbial suffix *-ly*, which does not attach to words such as *friendly* and *orderly*. However, not all *-lily* forms are banned to the same degree by the linguistic community (Bauer 1991). As pointed out in Menn and MacWhinney (1984), while most forms like *likelily* are rejected outright, others, such as *sillily* and *surlily*, sound less offensive to some speakers. Derivational suffixes are generally prohibited following stems whose end is formally identical to the grammatical morpheme. Cases like *cater-er* and *barter-er* are genuine violations of the repetition constraint only to the extent that the stem and the suffix are presumed to end in /r/ in underlying representation. At the surface level, there is no repetition of identical sequences (at least not in Standard British English).

In the absence of any comprehensive quantitative investigation, the conclusions can be no more than tentative. However, the available data are compatible with the claims that prefixes and stems respect the repetition constraint less strongly than stems and suffixes, and that derived words are more subject to this prohibition than inflected ones. These differences are argued to follow from differences in the strength of lexical representations. The more lexicalized a morphologically complex unit, the greater the opportunity for the repetition constraint to make the phonological form conform.

It should be noted finally that the preceding analysis extends the set of explanations that have been offered in the relevant literature. Both Dressler (1977) and Menn and MacWhinney (1984) favour a perceptual account. They claim that the decoding device has difficulty parsing repeated identical material to the left and the right of a morpheme boundary because it is hard for the listener to decide to which morpheme the phonological sequences belong. While not questioning this hypothesis, I submit that it is not the whole story. A comprehensive explanation has to take into account the productive constraints to which language is subject. These constraints correctly predict the linguistic patterns, and should therefore be viewed as serious candidates for an understanding of the repetition constraint and its non-absolute, variable nature.

4.18. The Order of Inflectional and Derivational Suffixes

This section will take up the best-known ordering principle in morphology and shed light upon how it is psycholinguistically mediated. Derivational suffixes tend towards the centre and inflectional suffixes to the periphery of words. Bybee's (1985) account of this ordering relationship is that a derivational morpheme is more relevant to the meaning of the stem than an inflectional one. Her explanation is basically iconic, in that the closeness in form is ascribed to a closeness in meaning. I argued in section 2.9 that, even though this type of approach is a valuable one, it is inherently limited because it leaves unexplained how and why this link between meaning and form is created the way it is. The major aim of the present section is to show how a look at processing may contribute to making the nature of this link more explicit, and in this way lead to a deeper understanding of the ordering relationship under debate.

A window on the processing system is provided by morphological slips of the tongue. The critical question is whether derivational and inflectional suffixes behave differently in their relation to the stem.

(117) *There's the apartment on the deposit up here* for *the deposit on the apartment*
(118) *Can I have a full nudal frontity?* for *frontal nudity*
(119) *I presume you could get light in poorer pictures* for *pictures in poorer light*
(120) *You just count wheels on a light* for *lights on a wheel* (all from Stemberger 1985b)

Derivational suffixes are at issue in (117–18), inflectional ones in (119–20). Examples (117) and (119) attest to the cohesive behaviour of the suffixes. In (117), the nominal suffix -*ment* is driven out of position along with its stem. The same happened to the plural morpheme in (119). By contrast, the cases in (118) and (120) exemplify the dissociation between the stem and its suffix. In (118), both the nominal ending -*ity* and the adjectival ending -*al* are separated from their respective stems and attached to different ones. Contrary to (119), the plural morpheme in (120) stays in its original location and is accordingly attached to its new stem.

A comparison between (119) and (120) indicates that the type of morpheme implicated does not uniquely determine whether or not the suffix is dissociated from its stem. The same morpheme stays put in (120) but accompanies the stem in (119). However, this does not mean that the morpheme type does not exert an influence upon the frequency with which a given suffix remains attached to its stem in the error process. Stemberger (1985a) examined the degree of togetherness as a function of morpheme type and found diametrically opposite results for inflectional and derivational morphemes. Out of 12 pertinent slips, the derivational suffix is left behind in 3 but misordered along with the stem in 9 cases. In sharp contrast, among a total of 100 errors, there are 90 in which the inflectional suffix remains immobile and 10 in which it accompanies the stem to its new location. This difference is highly significant: $\chi^2(1) = 32.9$, $p < 0.001$. There thus is strong evidence that stems and derivational suffixes are treated as more cohesive units by the language processor than stems and inflectional suffixes.

Note that the greater immovability of inflectional suffixes and the greater movability of derivational suffixes is not attributable to the fact that the former, and not the latter, occupy the word margin. In the slips of the tongue upon which the statistics are based, inflectional suffixes stand as close to the stem as derivational ones because they are embedded in words consisting of a stem and only one suffix (see (117–20)).

The psycholinguistic interpretation of the differing 'stickiness' of derivational and inflectional morphemes draws upon the principles underlying the selection of linguistic elements. When does an error occur at the lexical, when at the morphological level? In other words, when does a word act in unitary fashion and when does it fall apart? Berg (1989c) argued that the degree of cohesiveness of two units depends upon the similarity of two items in terms of their activation values. The more similar these values, the more cohesive the units. Because selection is conditional upon maximum activation, cohesiveness may be construed more precisely as a function of the activation value of the second unit at the moment of the selection of the first. If both are activated to a similarly high degree, they are selected in unison; if, however, the activation value of the second unit is relatively low when it comes to selecting the first, only the latter will be selected. Applying this principle to morphology, inflectional suffixes can be argued to split easily from their stems because they are not sufficiently activated during stem selection. By contrast, derivational suffixes are so highly activated when the stem is prepared for output that the selection mechanism looks upon the two morphemes as one unit. Hence, stem + derivational suffix combinations do not easily break up in speech errors.

The prediction that follows from this processing argument can be straightforwardly derived. A good way to effect serial order would be to activate upcoming elements as a function of their distance from the unit currently being readied for production. Depending upon the order of the bound morphemes, the following two activational strategies are available. Strategy A would be appropriate for the order of the inflectional suffix preceding the derivational one, Strategy B for the inverse case. As can be seen from Fig. 1, the activation pattern in A is unsatisfactory because the unit to follow the stem is less highly activated than the next but one unit. This constellation is unstable because the derivational suffix, following its higher activation, is liable to interfere with the selection of the inflectional morpheme. There is thus an immanent drive towards moving the derivational suffix to the left. As a result, the processing system is likely to reach a stable state only when the derivational morpheme has temporal priority over the inflectional one. This is tantamount to a serial-ordering relationship of the kind depicted in Figure 1B.

There is no need to review the well-known data that bear out the psycholinguistic prediction. It is notable how strongly the processing constraint is obeyed by the linguistic structure; there are hardly any exceptions to it in English and German. A celebrated case in point is German *Kind-er-chen* 'little children' with the morphological structure 'stem + plural morpheme + diminutive morpheme'. This counterexample is highly idiosyncratic. It is worthy of note that the diminutive suffixes

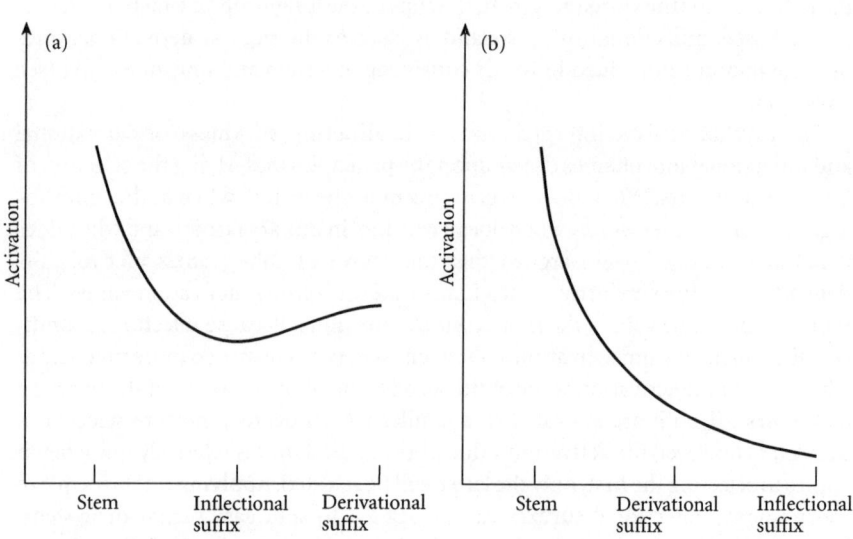

FIGURE 1. Activation pattern in stem + suffix structures at the moment of stem selection

cannot be preceded by a plural morpheme in other lexical items. Let us take the word *Schwein* 'pig', which is pluralized as *Schwein-e* 'pigs'. The diminutive suffix can only attach to the singular form, thus yielding *Schwein-chen*, not *Schwein-e-chen*. This word is inherently ambiguous, as it means both 'piggy' and 'piggies'. Therefore, the prohibition on the order 'inflectional + derivational morpheme' is generally effective. That it fails in *Kinderchen* may be put down to an anthropocentric bias in language. Human beings regard their offspring as more important than animals. Therefore, it is communicatively more important for them to formally distinguish between 'little child' and 'little children' than between 'piggy' and 'piggies' in German.

To conclude, a link has been established between the strategies of activation spread in the mental network and the ordering of morphemes within complex words. The activational principles give rise to certain privileged relationships between morpheme types. There is a psycholinguistically natural order which favours the placement of the derivational suffix before the inflectional one. This processing principle is claimed to mould the morphological structure of language.

4.19. Blending

Blending is a remarkable word-formation process in English whereby two independent lexical items are fused into (a new) one. Among the best-known examples is *smog*, a blend of *smoke* and *fog*. It is conceivable that such cases are intentionally generated. A speaker has a coherent idea in mind for which no word in the lexicon is available but which can be coded by drawing upon the semantic content of two independent lexicalized items. To express the reshuffling of semantic features, a parallel (i.e. iconic) reshuffling of segments takes place at the phonological level. A paradigm example is the cross-breeding of animals. The extralinguistic fact of cross-breeding is reflected in the structure of the language by 'crossing' two words, as in *geep*, a blend of *goat* and *sheep*. This example shows that blends can be deliberately planned. The extent to which speakers master and actually exercise this skill is not known. It is probable, though, that blending as a means of enlarging the lexicon is of limited productivity (but see Bryant 1974). Many instances that have been recorded are individual cases designed for specific purposes in specific contexts which do not enter the general language (Cannon 1986). Only a minority, such as *smog*, appear to have acquired full lexical status. In any event, blending as a process and as a product is an interesting principle of intentional synchronic word formation as well as a category of diachronic change.

Blends also occur as inadvertent behaviour. That is to say, speakers may, despite themselves, blend two independent words together, probably because they could not make up their minds as to which of the two provided the better match with their intentions. The nature of such slips of the tongue is determined by system-internal processing principles to which speakers have no conscious access. A genuine error cannot, in any reasonable sense of the word, be said to be planned.

The point of the foregoing discussion is to argue that intentional and unintentional blends are conceptually distinct. The first type is created to meet a particular communicative need, the second is a derailment of the psycholinguistic system without any communicative function or purpose. Hence there is no a priori reason to expect both phenomena to possess identical properties. It thus is an open question whether intentional and unintentional blends can be empirically distinguished. In intentional blends, speakers manipulate the flow of information in the processing network in accordance with their intentions. To a certain degree, creating a specific pattern of activation involves counteracting the system-internal processing principles. In speech errors, by contrast, the processing system resembles a machine that is left to its own devices. Because of the absence of any wilful intervention, errors may be expected more faithfully to reflect the network-internal constraints. An example may help to elucidate this point. One processing principle holds that words of the same syntactic category activate one another more strongly than words of a different category. Inadvertent blends thus exhibit an effect of identical syntactic category. However, it may be that speakers intentionally blend a noun and a verb just because this is dictated by their prelinguistic intentions. There is no reason to assume that the processing system is in principle too inflexible to make this happen.

Thus the prediction that can be formulated is twofold. On the one hand, if the processing system shapes the structure of intentional language, it is to be expected that intentional blends are subject to the same basic constraints as unintentional ones. On the other hand, these constraints should be less pronounced (but still be present) in wilful language patterns than in slips of the tongue. This is because speakers' intentions may reduce, but not annul, the impact of the processing principles. These predictions will now be put to the test.

The empirical evidence that serves as the database for all subsequent analyses comes from a corpus of intentional English blends collected by Pound (1914). It comprises 300 examples drawn from written and oral sources. Pound does not make a distinction between blends of a more passing or a more permanent nature. Her corpus includes contractions such as *prime minister* → *prinister*. Since it is debatable whether the underlying mechanisms are the same as in blends, all contractions are discarded from the analysis.

Let us begin with the example that was used to clarify the predictions that can be derived for the structure of intentional blends. As has repeatedly been reported in the literature, unintentional blends almost always involve interactants of the same word class, as in (121). When syntactically dissimilar units interact, the resultant form is not usually a blend, as in (122).

(121) *smever* (*smart* × *clever*)
(122) *three pulls of the* [mʌskəlz] (*muscles* × *muscular*) (both from Fromkin 1973)

The speaker in (121) hesitated between *smart* and *clever* and ended up producing *smever*. Case (122) is not a blend in the strict sense because only one of the two interactants, the noun, is appropriate in the syntactic frame. Errors like (122) therefore, are best characterized as interferences by a member of the same morphosemantic set to which the target appertains. In his corpus of English tongue slips, Harley (1990) finds only 4 out of 254 errors (1.5 per cent) in which the like syntactic category constraint is violated. Thus, the prediction for intentional blends is clear: they should also obey the like syntactic category constraint, albeit to a lesser degree than slips of the tongue.

This prediction is nicely borne out by Pound's (1914) data. Of the 280 blends in her sample, 244 (87 per cent) involve words from the same category and 36 (13 per cent) words from different categories. The former type is exemplified in (123), the latter in (124).

(123) *pomato* (*potato* × *tomato*)
(124) *wegotism* (*we* × *egotism*) (both from Pound 1914)

While two nouns are blended together in (123), a pronoun and a noun interact in (124). Going by the definition given above, it is possible to classify (124) as a blend because syntactic contexts are conceivable in which the two blending partners stand in a paradigmatic relationship. Clearly, the intentional blends closely match the inadvertent ones in this respect.

The next criterion on which intentional and unintentional blends will be compared is the addition effect. The interactants in slips of the tongue tend to be of equal length. When they are of differing length, however, the resultant error form takes after the longer rather than the shorter word. This complexification can be observed at all levels of linguistic analysis, two of which will be focused upon here—the segmental and syllabic levels. Words may begin with a vowel or a consonant. If a consonant and a vowel-initial word are involved in a blend, a decision has to be made as to whether a consonant should be added to the vowel-initial interactant or deleted from the consonant-initial interactant. Both possibilities are illustrated in (125) and (126).

(125) *This applies mownly to undergraduates* (*mainly* × *only*) (from Fromkin 1973)
(126) G: *Dann habe ich beim nächsten Mal wenigestens 'ne olle– tolle Geschichte zu erzählen* (*toll* × *ordentlich*)   [ɔlə tɔlə
    tɔl ɔrdɛntlɪç]
'After all, this will give me the opportunity of telling a great story next time'

The conflict between vowel- and consonant-initialness has been resolved in favour of the consonant in (125) but in favour of the vowel in (126). All other things being equal, both possibilities have the same baseline probability of occurrence.[26] There is a clear addition bias in my speech error corpus. Of 10 unambiguous cases, 8 begin

---

[26] However, all other things are not equal. While a particular vowel-initial interactant may be more or less common than a given consonant-initial interactant, vowel-initial words are generally less frequent than consonant-initial items. The consonant addition effect may therefore be regarded as a tendency towards more frequent items. However, the addition effect only happens to look like a frequency effect in this particular instance. It really is an anti-frequency effect, as argued by Stemberger (1991).

with a consonant and 2 with a vowel. Hence, the prediction regarding intentional blends is that they should follow the same trend, though to a lesser extent. This is precisely the case. In 39 out of 59 (66 per cent) relevant blends in Pound's corpus, consonant-initialness outcompetes vowel-initialness (127), whereas the reverse happens in only 20 (34 per cent) cases (128).

(127) *figitated* (*fidgit* × *agitated*)
(128) *austern* (*austere* × *stern*) (both from Pound 1914)

There is thus a clear preference for consonant-initialness, though it is less pronounced than in slips of the tongue.

Spontaneous blends are subject to a further complexification effect. The majority of slips of the tongue involve blending partners of equal length (as measured by syllable number), but a longer and a shorter word may also interact. In the latter case, the blend word tends to be modelled after the long rather than the short interactant. In Fromkin's (1973) published speech error data, 13 blends are of the additive and 6 of the subtractive kind.

(129) *edited* (*edited* × *annotated*)
(130) *pain kills* (*pills* × *killers*) (both from Fromkin 1973)

Whereas the erroneous form is as long as the long interactant in (129), it is as short as the short interactant in (130). It is to be expected that the same trend towards more complex outputs can be replicated for intentional blends. A second prediction is that the number of interactants of equal length will be noticeably lower in intentional blends because speakers choose the words they wish to splice for semantic, not for formal reasons. The length of a word is not the primary motive during the selection process in intentional blends, though it plays an important role in speech errors.

Before the results of the investigation are presented, a few words about the calculation procedure are in order. The first constellation is that two interacting words are of equal length. When the blend is longer than its interactants, it is classified as *additive*, when it is shorter, as *subtractive*. When the two interactants are of unequal length and one interactant is of the same length as the blend, the length of the blend is compared to the diverging interactant. When both interactants are of the same length as the blend, the item is assigned to the category *neutral*. Finally, there is the possibility that the one interactant, the other interactant, and the blend all differ from one another in number of syllables. When the blend is shorter than one interactant but longer than the other, it is categorized as *indeterminate*. When both blending partners are longer or shorter than the outcome of the blending process, there is no difficulty in labelling the blend as either additive or subtractive. Table 14, presenting a quantitative analysis of Pound's corpus, reveals a clear predominance of the additive blending type. The subtractive type is vanishingly rare. This trend holds across all word classes involved in blends. Two typical examples appear below.

TABLE 14. *Additive vs. subtractive tendencies in intentional blends (N = 280)*

	Additive	Neutral	Indeterminate	Subtractive
Noun	101	26	5	8
Adjective/adverb	39	21	2	7
Verb	29	42	0	0
TOTAL	169	89	7	15
%	60.4	31.8	2.5	5.4

(131) *prevaricaterer* (*prevaricate* × *caterer*)
(132) *preet* (*pretty* × *sweet*) (both from Pound 1914)

What is particularly noteworthy about Table 14 is that the addition/deletion asymmetry is even more pronounced than in slips of the tongue. Our general expectation has been that intentional blends are less strongly influenced by system-internal processing principles than are speech errors. However, the opposite is true in the case at hand. This suggests that there must be an additional factor at work which contributes to enlarging the numerical difference between blends of the additive and the subtractive type. Actually, one such factor stands out. A speaker who resorts to blending must be aware of the fact that listeners, who are expected to understand the word correctly, encounter it for the first time. The speaker must therefore be intent upon facilitating the listener's decoding process of a word which is not in his lexicon. An obvious way of alleviating the listener's workload is to preserve the integrity of the blending partners, which themselves are known to the listener, to as great an extent as possible. This strategy evidently favours additive over subtractive blends.

However, it is unlikely that the listener-oriented production principle accounts for the complexification tendency in full. Slips of the tongue are free of this production principle but still exhibit an addition bias. The most probable conclusion is, therefore, that the strong predominance of intentional blends of the additive type is brought about by both automatic (i.e. speaker-independent) and strategic (i.e. speaker-dependent) production principles.

It is often not possible in unintentional blends to unambiguously identify the end of one interactant and the beginning of the other, as in (133).

(133) *stuch* (*stuff* × *such*) (from Stemberger 1982)

This error may be interpreted as attesting to a recombination of either *st* + *uch* or *stu* + *ch*. Because the same vowel occurs in both interactants, it is difficult to determine their break-up point. The vowel, as it were, acts as a bridge between them (Crompton 1981), i.e. it appears to facilitate the switch from the one to the other blending partner. No. (133) is not at all exceptional. In Fromkin's (1973) published sample of English blends, a 'bridge' can be located in 62 per cent of cases. This is far above chance. The 'bridge effect' is clearly psycholinguistically motivated in that it contributes to the confusion between two linguistic items. This aspect should be irrelevant in intentional blends, because they involve no confusion in the narrow sense of the word but a deliberate fusion. So if the bridge effect also shows up in intentional blends, a strong argument can be made in favour of their psycholinguistic motivation.

An examination of Pound's corpus makes it quite plain that the bridge effect is characteristic of intentional blends as well. It is present in 59.6 per cent (167 out of 280) of the data. It is worthy of note that in more than one third of these cases, the bridge consists of more than one (identical) segment, as illustrated in (131) and (134).

(134) *vividity* (*vivid* × *avidity*) (from Pound 1914)

The statistical analysis reveals that intentional and unintentional blends do not differ significantly from each other in terms of their sensitivity to the bridge effect, which is only slightly stronger in slips of the tongue ($p > 0.1$). This suggests in the first place that the intentional word-formation patterns are created on the model of spontaneous errors—a model which undoubtedly is not consciously available to the speaker. In the second place, the bridge effect in intentional blends is more pronounced than might be expected. The most plausible explanation of this result is that identical elements are ideal points of splicing (parts of) words.

After having compared intentional and unintentional blends from the formal point of view, it is expedient to take a look at the semantic side. A *sine qua non* of spontaneous blend errors is the contextual synonymy of the interactants. Only in very few cases can a non-synonymous (e.g. antonymic) relationship be observed. In all cases, the two blending partners are semantically related (cf. (121) and (125)). The prediction for intentional blends is that they should be subject to the same constraint, though less so than the unintentional ones.

Testing this prediction presupposes a clear conception of what counts as semantically related. One might take the traditional approach, and consider as semantically similar all those word pairs which stand in any of the conventional semantic relationships (e.g. hyperonymic, meronymic). However, this procedure does not do justice to all items in the Pound corpus. Some blends do not enter into any of the above relationships and yet cannot be viewed as completely unrelated, as in (135).

(135) *hellophone* (*hello* × *telephone*) (from Pound 1914)

It is obvious that *hello* and *telephone* stand in a contiguous relationship. The telephone call creates a context in which *hello* as a phatic means of communication is legion. There is a certain percentage of such borderline cases where a relatively arbitrary decision for or against meaning-based similarity has to be made. In general, a rather conservative attitude has been taken, in that debatable items have been assigned to the category 'unrelated'. No. (136) exemplifies one such debatable case. Two clear examples are given in (137–8).

(136) *smokolotive* (*smoke* × *locomotive*)
(137) *barsolistor* (*barrister* × *solicitor*)
(138) *ballcony* (*ball* × *balcony*) (all from Pound 1914)

While in (137) *barrister* and *solicitor* are of cognate meaning, no semantic relationship exists between *ball* and *balcony* in (138). Owing to the inherent uncertainty in determining semantic similarity, no attempt is made to provide exact figures. A rough estimate, which is sufficient for our purposes, is that between half and two-thirds of the blending partners are meaning-related. This is clearly above chance, but also clearly less than the 100 per cent mark in inadvertent blends.

The reason for this lower rate of semantic similarity is easy to see. The volitional element in intentional blends is the rearrangement of semantic features from different lexical items so as to create a word with a new meaning. If these words are synonymous it is evidently no use recombining them, because the blend would not go beyond either of its source elements. A certain discrepancy between the blending partners is therefore basic to the very idea of an intentional blend. This discrepancy does not, however, lead to semantic unrelatedness. What is critical in blending as a word-formation process is the subsumption of hitherto independent semantic features under a common lexical unit. It is less important in which feature complexes they were originally embedded. As a consequence, the semantic similarity plays a lesser role in intentional blends than in speech errors. That it is nevertheless present can most plausibly be seen as the effect of system-internal processing constraints on the production of this kind of neologism.

Apart from the above, there are other parallels between intentional and unintentional blends. For instance, both types almost invariably draw upon two and only two interactants. Kubozono (1990) showed that speech errors and purposeful language patterns exhibit similar preferences for the point at which their interactants are broken up. All this is further evidence for the claim that the mechanisms underlying the generation of inadvertent and intentional blends are highly similar.

To conclude, on the basis of psycholinguistic data, predictions have been derived regarding the nature of intentional recombinations of lexical items (with momentary or more lasting impact). These predictions could be empirically validated. The basic similarity between intentional and unintentional blends notwithstanding, there are also certain differences between the two types, most of which were expected. All of these differences find fairly natural explanations in the differing production constraints to which slips of the tongue and intentional blends are subject. These differences are relatively minor compared to the large amount of commonalities. There is thus solid evidence that this word-formation process owes a great part of its characteristics to psycholinguistic processing principles.

4.20. Linear Distance Effects

As noted, serialization is one of the central tasks that have to be accomplished during language production. To work properly, the serialization mechanism must employ a strategy which allows it to pick out one element after another in the intended order. The simplest strategy one could imagine would be to activate upcoming units solely as a function of their linear distance to the one that is currently outputted. The next unit to be outputted would be more highly activated than the next but one, the next but one would be more highly activated than the next but two, and so forth. This may be dubbed the 'staircase strategy of serialization', as depicted in Fig. 2.

The advantage of this strategy would seem obvious. The activation level of a unit is gradually raised as the moment of selection approaches. This strategy avoids boosting a unit from resting level to production threshold all at once, and thus minimizes the risk of failing to reach the production threshold at the appropriate moment. It is striking to observe that, despite the apparent simplicity and efficacy of this activation strategy, the sequencer does not appear at first sight to resort to it. In fact, this is because the staircase strategy is largely camouflaged by two other activational principles. The first is the hierarchical organization of language, which leads to the activation of nodes according to their position in the hierarchy. This strategy may attenuate linear distance effects. The second activational principle is that units may have disparate inherent specifications and that the sequencer is sensitive to these differences. For example, segments divide into consonants and vowels and the activation levels of to-be-outputted units depend upon whether the current unit is a consonant or a vowel. This strategy produces no linear distance effects.

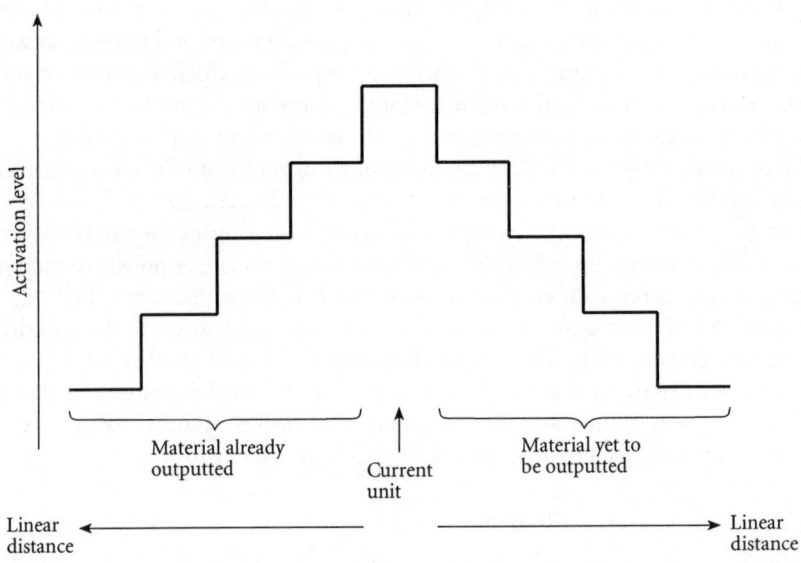

FIGURE 2. The staircase strategy of serialization

It is not altogether easy to insulate the staircase strategy from the other two and, in so doing, demonstrate its existence. The main problem is that the hierarchical strategy automatically captures most linear-distance effects. The closer two elements are together in a linear string, the greater the chance they stand of belonging to the same superordinate unit. However, there are at least two arguments which in combination speak strongly in favour of the staircase strategy. The most straightforward evidence comes from Arabic. Because this language has very little hierarchical organization below the word level (Berg and Abd-El-Jawad 1996), we should find here convincing evidence for the staircase strategy. If this strategy exists, the likelihood of error should increase with the proximity of source and target element. This is in fact the case. The majority of consonant errors involve either adjacent consonants or consonants which are separated by one vowel. The error 'skips' another consonant in only a minority of cases. The typical situation is illustrated in (139), the untypical one in (140).

(139) *takriib* for *takbiir*
 'glorification'
(140) *maraaʕiš* for *mašaaʕir* (both from Abd-El-Jawad and Abu-Salim 1987)
 'feelings'

In (139) the interacting segments are as close as they can be, the only intervening segment being a vowel. No. (140) exemplifies the exchange of two remote consonants which skip the pharyngeal fricative. The empirical fact that the error rate increases with the proximity of potential interactants is good evidence for the staircase strategy.

Since the error patterns look so different in the Indo-European languages, it might be objected that the staircase strategy is peculiar to Arabic and should not be considered a universal strategy of serialization. To meet this objection, it is imperative to show this strategy to be at work also in those languages in which hierarchical structures influence the activation pattern more strongly. One telling piece of evidence is the interaction between error type and average distance between the interacting elements. Bipositional error classes (shifts and exchanges) exhibit significantly shorter distances between the interactants than monopositional classes (anticipations and perseverations). Two pertinent examples are given below.

(141) *trimbel* for *timbrel* (from Shattuck-Hufnagel 1979)
(142) *Bach distinguishes three different bipes* for *types* (from Fromkin 1973)

Case (141) involves two positions—the rhotic disappears from one and resurfaces at another. The distance it travels is minimal. Indeed, it could not be less without violating the parallel syllable structure constraint. By contrast, the error process distorts the intended utterance in (142) at only one point. As can readily be seen, the distance covered by the bilabial stop is quite large. These examples, though extreme, illustrate the differing sensitivity of various error types to linear distance. The explanation for this difference rests upon the assumption that different error classes have different baseline probabilities of occurrence. Because bipositional slips distort an utterance twice, they have a lower baseline probability than monopositional slips. As a consequence, bipositional errors need to rely more strongly upon facilitators, one of them being linear distance. Monopositional errors have a higher baseline probability and may therefore more easily do without this facilitator. It may be inferred from this that the staircase strategy is operative in Indo-European languages as well. It is even probable that it is a processing universal.

Taking the reality of the staircase strategy for granted, we may now enquire what implications it might have for language structure. Quite straightforwardly, the interaction between elements that are linearly closer to each other should be stronger than that between elements that are more distant. Although various kinds of interaction are relevant, we will focus upon only one, agreement. In its most common form, agreement is a process whereby one element (the target) is matched with a property of another (the controller) (Corbett 1983). As it happens, the target may be under the influence of two controllers with disparate controlling properties. In that case, a decision has to be made as to which controller is given priority. It can be predicted on psycholinguistic grounds that the controller which is closer to the target will win out. The following pair of sentences, taken from Morgan (1984), bears out this prediction.

(143) There was a man and two women in the room
(144) There were two men and a woman in the room

The two sentences demonstrate that the two NPs *two women* and *a man* may individually control the verb. As can be seen, the number of the verb is determined by the number of the closest conjunct. The alternative agreement patterns in (143') and (144') are generally regarded as unacceptable.

(143') *There were a man and two women in the room
(144') *There was two women and a man in the room

Thus the order of conjuncts is critical for deriving the correct agreement pattern. Note that a hierarchical-structure account has difficulty coming to grips with sentences (143–4). It would have to be stipulated that the left-hand sister node of the conjoined phrase node is somehow more powerful than the right-hand sister node. However, this account is unworkable. Setting aside the fact that 'left' and 'right' are notions that are readily interpretable in a linear framework but are less natural in a hierarchical framework, this claim is falsified, at least as a universal principle, by data from other languages. Consider the following pair from Polish:

(145) Kobiety i meszczyzni sa dobrzy
 'Women and men are good (m-pl.)'
(146) Meszczyzni i kobiety sa dobre (both from Steinberg and Caskey (1988)
 'Men and women are good (f-pl.)'

Examples (145–6) show that the gender specification of the predicative adjective depends upon the gender of the nearest noun in these conjoined phrases. In (145) the nearest noun is masculine; hence the adjective takes on the masculine ending. In contrast, the feminine form is selected in (146) because the closest noun is of feminine gender. To account for this variation, it would have to be stipulated that the right-hand node dominates the left-hand node, which is in contradistinction to what has been claimed for the English examples above. The issue of directionality (i.e. left–right) thus does not appear to work as a general account of agreement. A better solution is provided by the linearity assumption. It simply holds that targets are more likely to be affected by close than by distant controllers (with distance being understood as *linear* distance in the surface structure).

It should be pointed out that the proximity principle is only one of the factors determining agreement, and that it may consequently be overridden by others. The psycholinguistic argument even predicts that linear distance should be a relatively weak principle because it is only weakly present in slips of the tongue (in Indo-European languages), being masked to a large extent by hierarchical effects. It is therefore not surprising to find violations of the proximity principle as in (147) and (148), taken again from Morgan (1984).

(147) A man and two women were in the room
(148) Two women and a man were in the room

This pair reveals that the order of the conjuncts is immaterial in simple SVO sentences in English. Irrespective of whether the predicate is directly preceded by a singular or plural noun, only the plural form is appropriate. This is because the conjoined phrase functions holistically as a plural subject. In (143) and (144), however, a different syntactic structure is at issue. Basically, there are two subjects, a grammatical one (*there*) and a logical one (*a man and two women*). Probably because of a conflict between the two subject types, the analysability of the conjoined phrase is enhanced in *there*-constructions. Although a detailed solution to this problem remains to be worked out, it is clear that agreement is determined by far more than the proximity principle alone, and that linear-distance effects can manifest themselves only within the confines defined by certain syntactic and semantic constraints. The important point in the present context is that it is possible to demonstrate the sensitivity of language structure to effects of linearity over and above effects of hierarchicalness.

4.21. Adjective/Noun Order in Noun Phrases

Languages tend to be very rigid about the position of adjectives relative to nouns. Adjectives are either preposed or postposed, with free variation being very uncommon. When there *is* variation it usually involves semantic/stylistic differences, as in French where the preposing of normally postposed adjectives may serve an emphatic function. The question that will be addressed in this section is whether this positioning is under the influence of psycholinguistic factors. As is generally agreed, there is a dependency relation between nouns and adjectives. The noun (the 'head') can stand on its own, whereas the adjective (the 'modifier') cannot. This one-sided dependence has clear implications for language processing. On the assumption that it is in principle possible to generate utterances in piecemeal fashion (Kempen and Hoenkamp 1987), nouns might be expected to be processed prior to adjectives. Evidently, the gender marker of an adjective cannot be generated unless information about the noun has been made available. It thus appears to be a useful strategy to access the noun first.

If this is the correct account of the time course of lexical access, the following prediction about the order of nouns and adjectives in NPs can be derived. Because nouns are needed earlier than adjectives, the former should also appear earlier than the latter in linearized utterances. This would be the more natural order, in that the linear order of production reflects the order of activation in the mental network. However, there is evidence to suggest that this description of the mental processes is flawed. If the access of nouns and adjectives proceeds in serial fashion, the speech error in (149) can while that in (150) cannot occur.

(149) F: *un des trèmes principaux* for *un des thèmes*
 [trɛm prɛ̃sipo   tɛm]
 'one of the major topics'
(150) *some kunny kind* for *funny* (from Fromkin 1973)

The analysis of (149) and (150) capitalizes upon the most compelling *conditio sine qua non* of syntagmatic slips of the tongue. The source and the target element can only interact when they have been activated at about the same time. Garrett (1976) speaks of 'computational simultaneity' in this connection. In (150), the onset of the noun tampers with the onset of the adjective. This is the expected pattern on the serial-access assumption. Being activated earlier, the noun can interfere with the production of the adjective, even if the former follows the latter. However, the serial-access hypothesis runs into difficulties when faced with cases such as (149). In this error, a segment from the adjective intrudes upon the noun which comes first. This event would be quite impossible if the adjective had not been accessed at the moment in time when the noun was about to be produced. By implication, this tongue slip is incompatible with the serial-access assumption. It presupposes the parallel access of adjectives and nouns in NPs.

It might be objected that the evidence from speech errors is weak because they may not be indicative of smooth, error-free processing. In fact, it may be argued that computational simultaneity is the *cause* of speech errors. That is to say, activational simultaneity is seen as a computational derailment which leads to slips of the tongue. In this view, the seriality assumption underlying the production of correct language might be upheld.

However, there are two pieces of evidence that argue against this conjecture. Motley (1973) showed that the adjective/noun constellation is very propitious to speech errors. Many more slips occur between a noun and an adjective than between a noun and a verb. This is particularly remarkable in view of the fact that the combined occurrence of nouns and verbs is higher than that of nouns and adjectives in general language usage. The implication of this result is that nouns and adjectives tend to be activated concurrently, at least more so than nouns and verbs. This conclusion makes good sense on the assumption that the shallower the syntactic boundary between two given lexical items, the more likely they are to be planned together.

And yet it could still be maintained that speech-error data do not make the strongest case for parallel processing. Hence, it would be essential to have information on the time course of lexical access in normal, error-free speech. This information has been provided by Schriefers (1992), who investigated Dutch noun phrases of the type DET + ADJ + N. He found in a picture–word interference task that the adjective and the noun in NPs are accessed in parallel,[27] despite the unilateral dependence between the two categories. There is thus a neat convergence of the experimental and naturalistic data, which lends credence to the claim that the mental processes underlying the generation of slips of the tongue are not radically different from those underlying the production of correct language. To be specific, it is reasonably safe to assume on the basis of (149) that the activation of a noun and a following adjective in French also occurs in parallel. Thus, the order of access in the mental network appears to be, at least partly, independent of the final order in the surface string.

Being based upon a number of different languages, this psycholinguistic result may be assumed to be of cross-linguistic validity. Therefore it has certain implications for universal patterns of adjective/noun order. In view of the claim that the dependence of the adjective upon the noun does not cause a delay in the processing of the modifier, it can be argued that both adjective/noun and noun/adjective orders are equally easy (or difficult) to process. Thus the somewhat counterintuitive prediction is that the adjective/noun order should be about equally common cross-linguistically as the noun/adjective order. If there is an asymmetry, it would be expected to be in favour of the postposed adjectives—simply by virtue of the head/modifier relationship between the two categories in question. However, this asymmetry would not be expected to be strong.

This prediction was tested against two language samples. The first is Greenberg's (1963) study of word-order correlations. By today's standards it is relatively small, comprising thirty languages from diverse areas and language families. The second is Dryer's (1992) monumental work on 625 languages which were fairly carefully selected with as little genetic and areal bias as possible. Table 15 is based upon Greenberg's and Dryer's findings. For various reasons, not all languages in Dryer's sample could be included in the analysis. For quite a few of them, the information

---

[27] The adjective was even in the lead compared to the noun but this was in all probability due to an experimental artifact.

TABLE 15. *Frequency of noun/adjective and adjective/noun order*

	Adjective/noun	Noun/adjective
Greenberg	11 (36.7%)	19 (63.3%)
Dryer	95 (42.4%)	129 (57.6%)

on adjective/noun order was not available or had not yet been extracted from the relevant sources.

As can be gathered from Table 15, the noun/adjective order is slightly more frequent than the inverse order. It appears from the percentages that this trend is more pronounced in the Greenberg than in the Dryer sample. However, the percentages are deceiving. Calculation of χ^2 indicates that the skewing in neither sample is statistically significant: $\chi^2(1) = 1.1$, $p > 0.25$ (Greenberg); $\chi^2(1) = 2.6$, $p > 0.1$ (Dryer). These results accord well with the research hypothesis. Languages do not clearly favour postposed adjectives, even though the noun/adjective order would appear more natural. The psycholinguistic explanation of this cross-language pattern is that the processing system operates in parallel (in the case of NPs), and is therefore in a position to accommodate both word orders (almost) equally easily. The noun/adjective order is only minimally advantaged because the processing system cannot completely neutralize the one-sided dependence between nouns and adjectives.

The claim that the postposition of adjectives is slightly more natural than their preposition entails the following prediction. In languages which principally allow both word orders, the prepositioning needs an extra facilitator in order to overcome its inherently lower probability of occurrence. In point of fact, French bears this prediction out. While it is predominantly postpositional, as noted above, a restricted number of adjectives, such as *grand* 'big' and *petit* 'small', appear before the noun. A common characteristic of these adjectives is that they are high-frequency monosyllabic items. As high frequency facilitates lexical access (see section 5.17), these words are available early in the production process. They therefore qualify well for prepositioning. Again, the structure of the language can be shown to be sensitive to principles of information processing.

This completes the discussion of psycholinguistic influences on language structure. An evaluation of the success of the processing approach will be deferred until all the empirical analyses have been performed.

5

Language Change

This part of the monograph presents an assessment of the impact that language processing makes upon language change. The procedure will be the same as in the previous part. As before, the order of the individual sections is from phonological to higher levels. To begin with, the most basic issue will be addressed. If the germ of language change lies in the psycholinguistic principles underlying speaking and listening—if, in other words, the key to diachrony is to be found within synchrony—we should expect the patterns of language change to mirror the patterns in speakers' and listeners' spontaneous behaviour. By 'patterns' is meant not only the classificatory system that is considered appropriate to the description of the data but also the more specific characteristics that can be observed. The term 'behaviour' also requires explication. Since our interest is in the dynamics of change and since change involves the deviation from a norm, it is instructive to study deviant processing events, i.e. those outputs which do not conform to the current norm. From the production perspective, these deviations are referred to as slips of the tongue, from the perception perspective, as slips of the ear. These psycholinguistic data therefore provide the starting-point for the majority of the analyses to follow.

5.1. Spontaneous Errors and Sound Change: A Macroscopic View

It has often been asserted but never convincingly demonstrated that language change originates in the inadvertent speech errors perpetrated by individual speakers. This view dates back to the last century and was voiced by Paul (1880), Meringer and Mayer (1895), von der Gabelentz (1891), and Eckhardt (1938) among others. The basic rationale is this. At any moment in time, a language possesses a system of norms (or rules) by which concrete utterances can be judged to be correct or incorrect, i.e. in conformity or non-conformity with the rules. A later stage in the evolution of a language is characterized by a different set of norms, to the effect that what used to be incorrect may have become part of the norm (or vice versa). According to this hypothesis, the change from stage 1 to stage 2 is brought about by a violation of norms at stage 1. In fact, as Cherubim (1980) argued, every correct utterance is a confirmation of the current set of norms while an incorrect utterance presents a challenge to these norms. Let us look at these violations in greater detail.

The major distinction drawn in the classification of slips of the tongue is that between contextually and non-contextually determined errors. In the former case the malfunction is instigated by material nearby, whereas no such influence is discernible in the latter. Contextual errors can be further divided into whether the interacting segments are more or less similar to each other as compared to the target utterance. Similarity-increasing tongue slips go by the name of 'anticipations' and 'perseverations', depending upon the direction of influence (i.e. right-to-left and left-to-right). Similarity-decreasing slips have received very little attention in the psycholinguistic literature, and therefore do not bear a widely accepted name. Non-contextual errors are of course neutral with respect to this similarity scale, as there is nothing to compare them with. These three categories capture everything that is theoretically possible. They are illustrated below by one English and two German examples.

(151) *crimicals* for *criminals* (from Stemberger 1985a)
(152) G: *der blaue Kraus*– Klaus
      [blauə kraus klaus]
      'the blue Klaus (proper name)'
(153) G: Muß sie es noch mal ticken– tippen?
      [mus ziː ɛs nɔx maːl tɪkən tɪpən]
      'Does she have to retype it?'

No. (151) is a within-word slip in which the velar stop erroneously shows up again and replaces the alveolar nasal. In this way, the similarity between the two segments is increased. The opposite happened in (152) where the two identical consonants in *blaue* and *Klaus* are dissimilated. Under the assumed influence of the first /l/, the second /l/ changes to /r/. In (153), it is impossible to locate a source element for the replacement of the bilabial by the velar stop. It took place for no apparent reason.

In view of these three psycholinguistic categories, the predictions for diachronic change are clear. If there is a connection between inadvertent errors and diachrony, one would expect the same categories in the description of language change. Diachronic developments at the phonological level are standardly described as assimilations, dissimilations, and 'spontaneous' sound changes. It is plain to see that these categories closely match those set up for the classification of slips of the tongue. Assimilations correspond to anticipations and perseverations, or, to be more precise, regressive assimilations correspond to anticipations and progressive assimilations to perseverations. Spontaneous changes correspond to non-contextual errors. Finally, slips such as (152) correspond to dissimilations in diachrony.

However, historical linguists have a wider conception of the term 'dissimilation' than is captured by (152). They take it to include not only dissimilations in the narrow sense of the word but also those cases in which one unit is lost under the influence of an identical element nearby. A pertinent example is Old French *flaible* → Modern French *faible* 'weak'. Comparable cases form a well-established class in speech error collections. They are referred to as 'masking' or, to use a theoretically more neutral term, 'repetition loss errors' (Stemberger 1990). A French example of this error type is provided in (154).

(154) F: des fluctuations pus– plus brusques
[fly:kty:asjõ py: ply: bry:sk]
'more rapid fluctuations'

The central assumption of slips such as (154) is that the lateral is lost in *plus* because it also occurred in the preceding word. The first /l/ blots out, as it were, the second.

The prototypical repetition loss error involves identity between the masking and the masked element. For instance, a /p/ will only obliterate another /p/, not a /b/ or a /x/. However, the empirical reality seems to be more variegated than is customarily acknowledged. The masking and the masked unit may differ in size and thus need not be identical. For example, of two different syllables, one may be lost when the onset consonant is the same in both. This process is illustrated in (155–6).

(155) *repetively* for *repetitively* (from Fromkin 1973)
(156) G: Nimmst du immer die schlechten Banen– Bananen?
[ba:nən ba:..na:..nən]
'Do you always take the bad bananas?'

Both slips of the tongue exemplify the loss of a whole syllable which seems to be instigated by an abutting similar syllable. /tɪv/ blots out /tɪ/ in (155) and /nən/ obliterates /na:/ in (156).

Interestingly, the same pattern can be replicated in the history of languages. In diachronic investigations, it has received the label 'haplology'.

(157) Hom. Gr. *amphiphoreus* → *amphoreus* 'two-handed pitcher'

No. (157) is strikingly similar to (155) and (156). The syllable /fi:/ disappears under the influence of the adjacent syllable /fo:/. Haplology is an instance of simplification. The reason for this tendency can be found in the constraints upon information processing. The processor has difficulty producing identical or near-identical elements or sequences of elements (see section 4.17). This type of linguistic change may therefore be understood as a reaction to this difficulty, i.e. as a drive towards eliminating problems for the processor.

The identity constraint on the repetition of phonological elements can be relaxed in yet another way. In some speech errors, the deletion of a segment appears to be occasioned by a non-identical, albeit highly similar unit. The prototypical case involves the liquids which are known to rank high on the interactivity scale. Consider (158–9).

(158) *split bain* for *split brain* (from Fromkin 1973)
(159) G: Weißt du, was hier unten so stinkt? Das ist diese Preßpa– platte.
[prɛspa platə]
'Do you know what stinks down here? It's this chip board.'

A plausible interpretation is that the rhotic is lost in the vicinity of a liquid in (158) and vice versa in (159). Of course, it cannot be ruled out that both slips belong to the category of non-contextual deletions, but the existence of a nearby liquid would then have to be regarded as haphazard. Interestingly, the same phenomenon recurs in language change, as shown in (160–1).

(160) Sp. *melrar* → *meldrar → *medrar*
(161) Lat. *astronomia* → OHel. *astrolomia*

As in (159), the liquid disappears under the influence of the rhotic in (160). Number (161) documents the dissimilation of the two non-identical nasals /n/ ... /m/ to /l/ ... /m/. Clearly, the similarity between the psycholinguistic and the diachronic categories is significant.

Apart from the basic error categories exemplified in (151–4), there is a more complex type which involves two positions at the same time. This error type, called exchange, divides into 'classical' exchanges and adjacent switches. Both are introduced below.

(162) *phisolophy* for *philosophy* (from Fromkin 1973)
(163) G: Ich stell mir froh– vor, du ...
   [fro: fo:r]
  'I imagine you ... '

Number (162) is a true exchange in that two non-contiguous segments swap places. The lateral moves into the position of the fricative and the fricative moves into the position of the lateral. Example (163) involves the reordering of the two contiguous segments /r/ and /o:/. Despite some similarity between exchanges such as (162) and switches such as (163), it is not appropriate to subsume the one category under the other because both display distinct properties.

Again, the match between diachronic and psycholinguistic categories is striking. Exchanges correspond to distant metatheses and adjacent switches to contact metatheses. An example of the latter category is given in (164), the former is illustrated in (165).

(164) OSax. *hros* → OE *hors* 'horse'
(165) Lat. *parabola* → s_p *palabra*

It is questionable whether the term 'metathesis' as a common label for both types of sound change is justified. Using the same term for both phenomena obviously implies that they are surface manifestations of the same underlying mechanism. This is not likely to be the case.

That exchanges form a distinct error category is not a logical necessity. It is theoretically possible that they evidence a concurrence of two separate error processes, viz. an anticipation followed by a perseveration. In this approach, (162) would be interpreted as a two-step malfunction. At first, the /s/ is anticipated and subsequently the /l/ is perseverated. There is clear indication that this analysis is inadequate. If it were correct, the properties of the so-called exchanges would be entirely reducible to those of anticipations and perseverations. It can, however, readily be shown that exchanges display unique properties which they share with no other category. For example, they occur more often in word-initial positions than do anticipations and perseverations (Shattuck-Hufnagel 1994). Exchanges may therefore be legitimately regarded as unitary phenomena.

This interpretation has a clear implication for diachronic metatheses. Theoretically, two historical scenarios are conceivable. Take the *parabola* example cited above. The transition to *palabra* may occur in one or two discrete steps. In the latter case, one would assume that the rhotic assimilated to the lateral, yielding something like *palab(o)la* as an intermediate result which achieved a certain stability for some time. At a subsequent stage, a second change would be presumed to have taken place whereby the two /l/s dissimilated to give rise to *palabra*. The psycholinguistic account rules out this possibility. It predicts that metatheses are actuated in one pass without any intermediate result. This prediction seems to be essentially correct. The vast majority of well-documented cases do not provide evidence of intermediate forms (Wanner 1989).

The final psycholinguistic category to be mentioned does not fit any of the above classes. It is called blending, and involves competition between two items for the same slot. It results in a compromise, in that an erroneous word or sentence is created through the recombination of parts of the contending units. This category was extensively discussed in section 4.19 and will therefore be touched upon only briefly here.

As expected, blending is also of diachronic relevance. It is a process by which the lexicon may be enlarged over time. That is, the status of blends may shift from ad hoc productions of an individual speaker to a part of the permanent vocabulary of a large portion of the linguistic community. A famous example from Lewis Carroll is *to chortle* (*chuckle* × *snort*), which has acquired full lexical status. The link between the psycholinguistic and the diachronic categories is particularly close in the case of blends (see section 4.19).

A first conclusion is that, at a general level, there is an almost perfect match between the categories that fit the description of spontaneous speech errors and those pertaining to sound change. This close resemblance between the two categorically distinct phenomena is significant. It lends credence to the conjecture that one origin of sound change lies in the imperfections of language use. Occasionally, speakers are unable to produce a sequence of segments in precisely the way that is prescribed by the norms of the language. By hypothesis, these slight mishaps may act as a starting-point for language change.

5.2. Spontaneous Errors and Sound Change: A Microscopic View

As has been argued in the preceding section, the errors that the processing system makes are similar to the patterns observed in language change. A similarity at the macroscopic level is not, however, enough to establish a causal link between the psycholinguistic and the diachronic processes. A similarity in general terms might not, after all, be very surprising because the set of categories are constrained by the logical possibilities, which are identical for processing malfunctions and historical developments. What has to be demonstrated, therefore, is that the two category types are more than just superficially similar. One would hope to find similarity even at the microscopic level. However, it is unrealistic to expect complete identity between the psycholinguistic and diachronic patterns. This is for a very simple reason. The psycholinguistic data are limited to spontaneous speech errors, and it would be foolish to reduce language change to speech errors. Clearly, there is more to language change than the occurrence of an error from an individual speaker on a particular occasion. The error has to be 'assimilated' by the linguistic community at large. Given that errors may cover only the first part of the itinerary of language change, differences between the two phenomena are a priori to be expected. It follows that individual discrepancies should not be taken to argue against the hypothetical connection between processing and historical change. However, matches between the two data types strengthen the claim that processing principles provide a partial explanation for the nature of language change.

Three areas have been selected for a more detailed comparison between psycholinguistic and diachronic categories—metatheses, assimilations, and dissimilations. These will be discussed in turn.

5.2.1. *Adjacent switches and contact metatheses*

Adjacent-segment switches represent an uncommon type of speech error. They mainly come in two varieties. When two consonants are switched, one of them is almost invariably /s/. When a consonant and a vowel are switched, the consonant most often is a liquid.

(166) *aks* for *ask* (from Fromkin 1971)
(167) G: Ich kann ihr da doch keine Frosch– Vorschriften machen
                                    [frɔʃ   foːrʃrɪftən]
    'I can't order her what to do'

In (166), the alveolar fricative takes the place of the neighbouring velar stop and vice versa. Case (167) documents an interaction betweeen /oː/ and /r/, with a concomitant shortening of the vowel.

If metatheses originate in spontaneous switches, the diachronic patterns may be expected to be similarly constrained. Hence, it is predicted that metatheses involve the same segment classes as slips of the tongue. This prediction is strikingly confirmed in the history of English. Consonant metatheses almost always involve an /s/ and a stop:

(168) OE *wæsp* → WSax. *wæps* 'wasp'
(169) OE *āscian* → WSax. *āxian* 'ask'

It is a noteworthy coincidence that the speaker of (166) unwittingly repeated the historical change illustrated in (169).

There is also a good number of liquid/vowel metatheses. These occurred in both directions. A following liquid was placed before the vowel or a preceding liquid was placed after the vowel, as in (170–1).

(170) ME þurk → Mod. E through
(171) OSax. brinnan → WSax. birnan 'burn'

Fundamentally different types of metathesis cannot be found in the historical records of English.

The commonalities between slips of the tongue and diachronic changes appear to go even further. The alveolar fricative does not metathesize with all consonants. Basically, only /k/ and /p/ are eligible, whereas examples involving /t/ are not attested. The same holds true of adjacent switches. Also, /r/ is affected by the switching process more frequently than /l/ in language change. The same can be said of spontaneous speech errors. However, these similarities are no more than suggestive because the numbers of pertinent slips of the tongue are too low to warrant firm predictions.

Furthermore, metathesis is traditionally regarded as a sporadic phenomenon. When it develops into a regular process, it lasts only for a limited time span in the history of a given language (Ultan 1978). This sporadicness is paralleled by the above-mentioned uncommonness of adjacent switches. The production mechanism strongly discourages the interaction of contiguous elements (see section 4.20). It makes sense to assume that the resistance of the psycholinguistic system to this type of error is one reason why metathesis has not become a major diachronic process.

Aside from these similarities, one possible difference should be noted. While vowel–consonant metatheses mostly involve a short vowel, adjacent switches are not so constrained; witness (167), where a long vowel is at issue. How should this disparity be rationalized? Note that metatheses seemingly involving long vowels do occur, but it is standardly assumed that a short vowel and a consonant were metathesized and that a subsequent lengthening of the vowel occurred (Stanley 1952–3). However, an alternative analysis appears more probable than the two-step account. Wieden (1983) argues that short vowels are much more susceptible to qualitative changes brought about by adjacent liquids than are long vowels. The stronger the coarticulatory effect, the less easy it is for the human ear to tell the individual segments apart, that is, the less perceptible a metathesis becomes. Because of the reduced coarticulation in long vowel/liquid sequences, a metathesis of these segments is more likely to be vetoed by the listener. It is for phonetic-perceptual reasons, then, that, unlike short vowels, long vowels are not involved in metathetic processes. The probability that both will be metathesized is assumed to be the same at the level of error generation, but the one type is immediately filtered out by the perceptual system while the other is not.

There is a high degree of convergence between the characteristic traits of adjacent switches and contact metatheses. Although categorically distinct, both processes operate upon the same segmental classes in similar positions. When a discrepancy arises, it can be shown to follow from the limited predictive value of slips of the tongue. As production phenomena, they of necessity cannot speak to perceptual processes. On the basis of the above results, it can be concluded that the principles governing the generation of metatheses are remarkably similar to the principles governing the generation of slips of the tongue. There is thus a strong psycholinguistic component to the reordering of adjacent sounds in the history of English.

5.2.2. Assimilation

While assimilations were examined from the synchronic perspective in 4.11, they will be treated as diachronic phenomena immediately below. As noted in the introduction to Chapter 4, the psycholinguistic predictions are inherently neutral with respect to synchrony and diachrony and principally apply to both. The focus of section 4.11.1 was on directionality. It was predicted on the basis of the speech error data that the regressive influence should outweigh the progressive one. This prediction was tested against synchronic data above, and will now be tested against the historical evidence.

The first test case is the process of umlaut, in which a vowel is changed under the influence of a non-adjacent vowel or glide. Umlaut counts as assimilation because the similarity between the interacting vowels is increased. Depending upon which phonological feature is borrowed, a distinction is customarily made between /i/, /u/, and /a/ umlaut:

(172) Goth. *sandjan* = OE *sendan* 'to send'
(173) AS *ebur* = OE *eafor* 'boar'
(174) AS *faran* = OE *færan → *fearan* 'fare'

In (172), the high palatal glide raises the /a/, thereby reducing the phonetic distance between the two. Numbers (173) and (174) are instances of diphthongization. Instead of a given feature being replaced by another, a whole feature bundle is juxtaposed to an already existing one. As the resultant compound vowel contains elements of the trigger, it is justified to treat these cases as assimilations.

As predicted by the psycholinguistic data, the umlauted vowel precedes the umlauting segment. It even appears that the direction of influence is always from right to left. In that case, the historical data display a more extreme tendency than the psycholinguistic evidence. This difference is relatively easy to account for. Since the probability of occurrence for a completed change such as umlaut is lower than for slips of the tongue, the former cannot occur under less than optimal facilitatory conditions. Being rather weak, the left-to-right influence is one such less-than-optimal condition. Hence, it is not powerful enough to induce perseveratory umlauting.

Apart from umlaut, there are two major types of assimilation. Let us call them nasal and obstruent assimilation, as illustrated in (175–6) and (177–8) respectively.

(175) Lat. *primu tempus* → F. *printemps* 'spring'
(176) OE *elnboga* → *elmboga* 'elbow'
(177) Lat. *met-sui* → *messui* 'I have moved'
(178) OE *bliþs* → *bliss* 'bliss'

The nasal accommodates to the place-of-articulation feature of the stop in (175–6). The /s/ replaces the alveolar stop in (177) and the dental fricative in (178). All four examples evince an anticipatory influence, and indeed this is highly typical of these types of assimilation. Nasal assimilation does not appear to operate from left to right whereas obstruent assimilation is not so tightly constrained.

(179) OE *met + de* → *mette* '(he) met'
(180) OE *cys + de* → *cyste* '(he) kissed'

It is obvious that the morphological structure interferes here. The past-tense ending *-de* and the verb do not enjoy equal status. The stem is the primary element, and thus has the power to impose itself phonologically upon the affix. Because the affix is a suffix, the influence perforce is of the perseveratory kind.

It is justified to conclude, then, that anticipatory assimilations predominate not only in synchrony but also in diachrony. This is exactly as predicted by the psycholinguistic evidence.

The second prediction is based upon a pervasive property of slips of the tongue. The probability of an error depends upon the similarity of the linguistic contexts in which the interacting units are embedded. Let us consider the interaction of the feature [velar] and the feature [bilabial]. One might expect there to be a certain constant probability of interference between them, but this is not so. The probability of interference is higher when the features are a part of otherwise identical segments (e.g. /b/ and /g/) and lower when the features are part of very different segments (e.g. /m/ and /k/). A feature change in the latter case would result in a feature error (e.g. /m/ ... /k/ → /m/ ... /b/) whereas a feature change in the former case would appear as a segment error (e.g. /b/ ... /g/ → /b/.../b/). In all available speech error corpora, feature slips (181) are far less common than segment slips (182).

(181) *hit the roop* for *hit the roof*
(182) *cuff of coffee* for *cup of coffee* (both from Fromkin 1973)

Both (181) and (182) evidence the interaction of the features [stop] and [fricative]. This interaction leads to a feature slip in (181) but to a whole-segment slip in (182). It does not matter for our present purpose whether cases like (182) are best classified as feature or segment slips, although Klatt (1981) convincingly showed the latter analysis to be preferable. The important point here is that the likelihood of error depends upon similarity constraints 'elsewhere'.

This psycholinguistic effect entails a clear prediction regarding the frequency of assimilation types in language history. Full assimilations should outnumber partial assimilations. A serious test of this prediction is hampered by the absence of a largescale quantitative survey of assimilatory phenomena. Some supporting evidence can be found in Hickey (1984). His report suggests that there is a predominance of complete assimilations in Old English. This skewing is particularly clear in manner assimilations. Complete assimilations are given in (183–4); a partial assimilation is shown in (185).

(183) *wifman* → *wimman* 'woman'
(184) *enleofan* → *ellefan* 'eleven'
(185) *wǣpn* → *wǣmn* 'weapon'

Examples (183) and (184) represent the predominant case of full assimilation. No. (185) is remarkable in showing how a less frequent type did not stand the test of time. The assimilated form has not established itself in the modern language.

However, two other types of assimilation appear not to bear out the psycholinguistic predictions. Both place assimilation in nasals and voice assimilation typically are of a partial nature. Examples of the former type were given in (175–6), examples of the latter in (179–80). While precise quantitative information on voice assimilation is lacking, it is clear that nasal assimilation is seldom complete.

Thus the empirical data do not unequivocally support the research hypothesis. The challenge is therefore to come to grips with the fact that some aspects are predicted by processing principles whereas others are not. The best way to rationalize this puzzling situation appears to be to question the complete parallelness of assimilations and speech errors. One possible assumption would be that slips of the tongue and diachronic assimilations arise at different processing levels at which different, though overlapping constraints are operative. This hypothesis receives independent support both from the empirical and from the theoretical perspective. As exemplified in (181–2), speech errors most usually involve non-adjacent sound units. Cases like (166) are truly exceptional. However, contrary to what might be expected, historical assimilations typically implicate abutting segments. Assimilations at a distance occur (as in umlaut) but consonantal assimilations at a distance are extremely uncommon. Examples such as (186–7) are sparse and rely upon reconstructed forms (Vendryes 1911).

(186) Lat. *barba* ← **farba*
(187) Lat. *prope* ← **prokw-*

Thus, there is a strong disparity between the speech error evidence and the historical data.

A moment's reflection reveals that this discrepancy is, after all, not too surprising. Diachronic assimilations are standardly seen to be caused by a relaxation of articulatory constraints. By contrast, speakers do not make slips of the tongue because of sloppy articulation.[1] Tongue slips are not less carefully articulated than error-free

---

[1] This is also true of adjacent switches as in (166) which resemble assimilations in terms of the adjacency of the interacting elements.

utterances. There is little doubt that assimilations are low-level, articulation-based phenomena whereas speech errors evidence non-articulation-based,[2] high-level processing.

If this localization is accurate, slips of the tongue might be held to have little to contribute to an explanation of diachronic assimilations. I maintain that this logic follows only in a discrete two-stage model which prohibits the interaction of high-level and low-level processes. This model is, however, inadequate. It predicts that the properties of slips of the tongue and diachronic assimilations should maximally diverge. But this is decidedly not the case. There are clear parallels between speech errors and diachronic as well as synchronic assimilations. It is necessary therefore to provide for a 'leak' between the high and the low level and to replace the discrete model by an interactive one. In this view, speech errors are at the very least indirectly relevant in an account of assimilations. Even though they may arise at a different level, the dynamics of the psycholinguistic system makes sure that processing principles at one stage are partly responsible for the properties of the output at a different stage.

On this account, different characteristics of the empirical data have to be allocated to different processing levels. The long-distance effect in speech errors would be assigned to high-level processing but the short-distance effect in assimilations would be assigned to low-level processing. The predominance of the right-to-left influence is one of the properties that leak down from the higher to the lower level. It thus is shared by the two levels, but this does not mean that it is of equal strength at both: it may be stronger at the higher than at the lower level. This supposition is compatible with the analysis of the synchronic assimilations carried out in section 4.11.1.

Even an interactive two-stage model appears oversimplified. It is conceivable that within one and the same stage, some assimilation types might arise earlier than others. For example, voicing assimilations might not occur at the same moment as place assimilations. This would inevitably lead from a two-level to a multi-level model. Only an in-depth quantitative study of assimilation phenomena can show whether such an extension is necessary and, if so, to what extent.

5.2.3. Dissimilation

There is no reason to expect dissimilations to be subject to the same constraints as assimilations. Therefore, the psycholinguistic predictions will have to be formulated anew and new diachronic tests have to be performed. As compared to assimilations, the investigation of dissimilations is facilitated by the availability of comprehensive surveys which allow for more precise testing.

In diachronic studies, the term 'dissimilation' covers both the substitution and the deletion of elements. Because these two phenomena may be conceptually and empirically distinct, it is useful to reserve separate labels for them. Substitutions will

---

[2] See MacNeilage et al. (1981) for an explicit defence of this view.

accordingly be referred to as 'diachronic dissimilations' and deletions as 'masking' in the analysis of language change. With reference to speech errors, substitutions will be termed 'synchronic dissimilations' and deletions 'repetition losses'.

Dissimilatory slips of the tongue have notable properties which mark them out among other error classes. Three of these properties will be discussed in some detail because they have not yet received any attention in the psycholinguistic literature—the direction of dissimilatory influence (anticipatory vs. perseveratory), the syllable positions in which the malfunctions preferentially occur, and the kind of segments that are the outcome of the dissimilatory process. The distinct profile of the two psycholinguistic categories will allow us to formulate clear expectations regarding the nature of sound change.

As has been noted in section 4.11.1, the anticipatory influence is generally stronger than the perseveratory one in slips of the tongue. However, there are a few exceptions to this pattern, two of which are dissimilations and repetition losses. One example of each is given below.

(188) G: *Die haben bei dem Lied sehr Deutsch-Engliss– Englisch gesprochen*
[dɔɪtʃ   ɛŋglɪs   ɛŋglɪʃ]
'They "spoke" the song with a heavy German-English accent'
(189) *below the gottis* for *the glottis* (from Fromkin 1973)

Both errors exemplify an influence from left to right. In (188), the sequence /ʃ/ ... /ʃ/ is dissimilated to /ʃ/ ... /s/. No. (189) provides a different solution to the problem of pronouncing recurrent elements. The second /l/ is 'masked' by the first. The quantitative analysis of both error types in my German corpus of slips of the tongue as a function of directionality is presented in Table 16. Synchronic dissimilations divide about equally into the anticipatory and the perseveratory subtype, while repetition losses display a slight predominance of the left-to-right influence. Even if the possibility of individual misclassifications cannot be excluded, it is clear that the strength of the anticipatory influence is undermined in dissimilations and repetition losses (see also MacKay 1969). Further support for this claim comes from Stemberger's corpus of English slips of the tongue, in which an even stronger perseveratory influence on repetition losses has been observed. The slight difference between dissimilations and repetition losses (i.e. the former are more or less symmetrical (48–52 per cent) whereas the majority of the latter (56 per cent) are of the perseveratory kind) does not reach statistical significance. However, it is not known whether a reliable difference would emerge if the number of errors was higher. The following order must therefore remain somewhat tentative.

(190) anticipatory dominance ⟵⟶ perseveratory dominance
(synchronic) assimilations—dissimilations—repetition losses

Placing dissimilations between synchronic assimilations and repetition losses makes sense because they share properties with both neighbouring categories. Dissimilations are similar to assimilations (in a way that repetition losses are not) in that both

TABLE 16. *Anticipatory and perseveratory influences in synchronic dissimilations and repetition losses*

Category	Consonants			Vowels		
	Anticipatory	Perseveratory	Both	Anticipatory	Perseveratory	Both
Dissimilation	33	31	5	4	9	1
Repetition loss	32	43	0	2	1	0

lead to the substitution of one unit under the influence of another. Dissimilations are also related to repetition losses (in a way that assimilations are not) in that both presuppose the existence of two identical elements in the syntagmatic context of which one disappears. If the 'two tokens of the same type' character is associated with the perseveratory influence and the substitutive character with the anticipatory influence, the hybrid nature of dissimilations becomes understandable.

The predictions that can be derived from the speech-error patterns are clear. In language change, perseveratory dissimilations and maskings should outnumber anticipatory ones. Further, the predominance of perseveratory processes might be stronger in maskings than in dissimilations.

To test these predictions, a set of historical data is required. Despite the sporadic and unsystematic nature of diachronic dissimilations, this is not a problem because both Grammont (1895) and Posner (1961) provide extensive lists of examples of dissimilations. Grammont (1895) contains data from the history of various Indo-European languages. Although it certainly falls short of being complete, Grammont has made an attempt to survey all the materials available to him. His book thus provides for a database which is large enough to allow general statements to be made. As to the criteria of data selection, only those examples are included in the ensuing analysis in which identical sound units are repeated.

As the strength of the perseveratory influence in synchronic dissimilations and repetition losses is expected to follow from processing mechanisms which are independent of any particular language, it is legitimate to subject several languages to analysis. Those languages have been selected for which Grammont was able to muster a sizeable number of examples, namely Germanic, French (*langue d'oïl*), and Slavic. In the appendix to his book Grammont lists a number of doublets, i.e. spelling variants of a word in which the same dissimilatory process has taken place. These have been counted once. Table 17 reports on the strength of the anticipatory/perseveratory influence in diachronic dissimilations and maskings which occurred in the history of Indo-European languages.

It is immediately apparent that the research hypothesis is *not* supported. In all languages, there is a strong preponderance of diachronic changes in which the dissimilatory element occurs on the right and the dissimilated one on the left. This asymmetry is very pronounced and is consistent across all the languages investigated. Furthermore, it holds for both synchronic dissimilations and maskings. A

TABLE 17. *Frequency of diachronic dissimilations and maskings as a function of direction of influence*

Language	Diachronic dissimilation		Masking	
	Anticipatory	Perseveratory	Anticipatory	Perseveratory
Germanic	29	15	1	0
French	46	7	12	2
Slavic	79	3	0	1
TOTAL	154	25	13	3

subsidiary result evident in Table 17 also conflicts with the psycholinguistic data. While the numbers of synchronic dissimilations and repetition losses are almost equal, maskings are appreciably less frequent than diachronic dissimilations.

That the predominance of the anticipatory influence in diachrony is a robust effect is further suggested by the best-known instance of dissimilation, Grassman's Law. It states that two aspirated stops are changed to the effect that one of them becomes plain (i.e. loses its aspiration):

(191) PIE *dhidhēmi → Gr. tithēmi 'to put'

Significantly, the direction of influence seems to be always of the anticipatory type in Grassman's Law, confirming the patterns summarized in Table 17. Note that the root would be destroyed if a perseveratory assimilation had occurred in (191). However, morphology plays less of a role in other examples.

We will now proceed to an examination of syllable position effects in synchronic dissimilations and repetition losses. Consonantal omissions tend to occur in relative syllable positions (i.e. post-initial and pre-final), while substitutions favour absolute ones (i.e. initial and final). The reason for this differential preference is a frequency effect (Berg 1988a). The change brought about by the malfunction leads to a syllable structure which is at least as frequent as, if not more frequent than, the error-free version. Because of this, repetition losses involve relative syllable positions significantly more frequently than do synchronic dissimilations. Two typical and two less typical examples are given in (192–5).

(192) *A great part of the brain dain in other countries is ...* for *brain drain*
(193) *Who tole the– stole the spoon?* (both from Stemberger 1990)
(194) G: *Bis gestern klaubte ich* for *glaubte*
       [gɛstɛrn klauptə   glauptə]
    'Until yesterday I used to believe ... '
(195) G: *Zwei Fliegen mit einer Knapp– Klappe schlagen.*
              [knap klapə ʃlaːgən]
    'to kill two birds with one stone'

Cases (192) and (193) exemplify repetition losses, (194) and (195) dissimilations. No. (192) involves an omission in a typical position (post-initial), (193) an omission in a less typical position (initial). This patterns is reversed in (194–5), where the initial position is more error-prone than the post-initial one. The analysis of the German data reveals that the difference between the dissimilations and the repetition losses in terms of their position sensitivity is statistically significant ($\chi^2(1) = 6.2, p < 0.02$).

On the assumption that diachronic dissimilations and maskings are historical fossilizations of spontaneous error processes, it can be predicted that similar constraints will hold in these categories. In particular, significantly more maskings than diachronic dissimilations should be found in relative syllable positions.

To test this prediction, Grammont's (1895) database was again turned to. The following languages were investigated: Germanic, French (*langue d'oïl*), Italian, and Spanish. Orthographic and/or pronunciation variants such as It. *curtello–cortello* were counted once. When the dissimilating and the dissimilated consonant do not occupy a parallel syllable position, the site of the dissimilated segment is given preference because this is the locus where the change took place. The historical masking process may be accompanied by other diachronic processes which lead to the rearrangement of the segments within the syllable or word. A consonant which used to be in initial position may thus turn up in final site, as in (196).

(196) Lat. *anima* → Sp., It. *alma*

In such cases the original form has always been considered, because it is to this form that the historical process was applied. An example of a diachronic dissimilation is given in (197); masking is illustrated in (198).

(197) Sp. *lintel* → *dintel*
(198) It. *deretro* → *dereto*

Table 18 presents the analysis of Grammont's data. Absolute syllable positions clearly predominate with dissimilations, while maskings occur more frequently in relative positions. This difference between the two diachronic categories is highly reliable: $\chi^2(1) = 56.5, p < 0.001$. It is also robust in that it recurs in all the languages examined. The preference for absolute, and the dispreference for relative, sites is very pronounced in dissimilations. The opposite trend in maskings appears to be less strong, although one notes that this is due to the influence of one language only.

TABLE 18. *Syllable position preferences in consonantal dissimilations and maskings*

	Diachronic dissimilation				Masking			
	Initial	Post-initial	Prefinal	Final	Initial	Post-initial	Prefinal	Final
Germanic	9	4	5	24	–	1	–	–
French	40	2	–	13	–	2	1	8
Italian	55	2	–	8	–	6	–	1
Spanish	29	2	–	12	–	7	–	1
TOTAL	133	10	5	57	0	16	1	10

French is aberrant in that it evidences an excessive number of maskings in final positions such as *herberger* → *héberger*. Notice that these maskings always occur in word-medial, syllable-final but never in word-final positions. This is a site where maskings can be reasonably well tolerated because it lends itself well to compensatory processes such as lengthening of the preceding vowel. Setting this deviation aside, the psycholinguistic prediction is clearly borne out by the historical evidence. Maskings and dissimilations exhibit diametrically opposed tendencies as far as their syllable-position involvement is concerned. The diachronic and psycholinguistic categories can thus be viewed as possessing similar properties.

A general characteristic of phonological slips of the tongue is the parallel syllable structure constraint. It describes the fact that the majority of errors arise through an interaction of two segments from like syllable positions. Indeed, one might say that this constellation goes a long way towards making slips possible in the first place. No. (192) above is an example of an interaction between the two homologous /r/s in *brain* and *drain*. The dissimilations in (194) and (195) also respect the parallel syllable structure constraint. However, this principle is not inviolable, as the following cases show.

(199) *They pace– place too little emphasis on their own results* (from Stemberger 1990)
(200) G: *Für mich sprick– spricht* [mıç ʃprık ʃpriçt]
 'What can be said in my favour'

The interaction in (199) takes place between an initial and a post-initial lateral. To be specific, the initial /l/ in *little* appears to blot out the post-initial /l/ in *place*. No. (200) exemplifies a dissimilation between two consonants stemming from non-identical positions. The prefinal /ç/ in *spricht* is dissimilated by the final /ç/ in *mich*. Such cases are not often found. They account for 5–10 per cent of the pertinent speech error data.

The prediction that can be formulated on the basis of the psycholinguistic evidence is straightforward: it is to be expected that the diachronic dissimilations and maskings will be subject to the parallel syllable structure constraint. However, exceptions are not categorically ruled out, as they can also be found in corpora of slips of the tongue.

This prediction has been tested against Posner's (1961) collection of diachronic dissimilations, by far the more frequent of the two processes under investigation (see Table 18). Because Posner's data base is quite extensive, the ensuing analysis is restricted to those words beginning with the letters <a>,<b>,or <c>. As in the preceding count, the syllable position of the interacting consonants is defined against the etymon. Ten unclear cases had to be excluded. The relevant results are summarized in Table 19, and leave little doubt about the sensitivity of dissimilations to position effects. 71 per cent of the data obey the parallel syllable structure constraint whereas 29 per cent do not. Chance depends upon the phonological nature of the language being examined and is therefore somewhat variable. A highly conservative estimate for all the languages in question is the 50 per cent mark, so the difference between the actual and the expected pattern is clearly significant (p < 0.001). It may be concluded therefore that the occurrence of two identical segments in the same position greatly enhances the likelihood of a diachronic dissimilation.

There is no denying that the rate of violations of the parallel syllable structure constraint is higher in the diachronic than in the synchronic dissimilations. In an effort to explore the possible reasons for this difference, a closer look has been taken at the historical data. In particular, the data have been analysed by consonant type. It might be the case that different consonant classes unevenly contribute to elevating the incidence of violations. To enlarge the data base, additional material from Posner (1961) has been investigated, i.e. all words beginning with the letters <d> to <o>. The exclusion of 17 unclear cases leaves us with 145 dissimilations from the same languages as in Table 19. Of these 145 examples, 106 agree with the parallel syllable structure constraint and 39 disagree with it (73 per cent as against 27 per cent). These percentages are very similar to those reported in Table 19, thus attesting to the robustness of the relatively high number of dissimilations involving consonants from non-identical positions. Table 20 breaks down the data by consonant type.

Transformed into percentages, obstruents follow the parallel syllable structure constraint in 95 per cent, nasals in 94 per cent, and liquids in only 38 per cent of

TABLE 19. *Parallel syllable structure effects in diachronic dissimilations*

	Syllable position identical	Syllable position non-identical
Italian	37	12
French	29	15
Portuguese	4	3
Spanish	30	10
TOTAL	100	40

TABLE 20. *Parallel syllable structure effects as a function of consonant type in diachronic dissimilations*

	Obstruents		Nasals		Liquids	
Position	Identical	Non-identical	Identical	Non-identical	Identical	Non-identical
Italian	17	–	12	–	15	17
French	14	2	8	2	3	15
Portuguese	4	1	2	–	2	1
Spanish	19	–	9	–	1	1
TOTAL	54	3	31	2	21	34

cases. It can be seen, then, that the degree to which the parallel syllable structure constraint is respected varies with the nature of the consonants involved. While dissimilating and dissimilated obstruents or nasals almost always occupy identical sites, liquids are much less constrained in this respect. The majority of liquids involved in dissimilations come from disparate syllable positions. This difference between nasals and obstruents on the one hand and liquids on the other is highly significant: $\chi^2(1) = 53.5$, $p < 0.001$. However, there is no difference between obstruents and nasals. Four typical examples follow. The first two cases respect the parallel syllable structure constraint whereas the latter two violate it.

(201) Lat. *phosphorus* → Sp. *fosporus*
(202) It. *Bononia* → *Bologna*
(203) Fr. *blialt* → Sp. *brial*
(204) *Margarita* → Po. *Magarida*

We may conclude that obstruents and nasals behave in diachronic dissimilations exactly as predicted by the psycholinguistic evidence. They rely quite heavily upon the parallel syllable structure constraint and only exceptionally allow violations. As regards the liquids, the psycholinguistic prediction fares less well. However, upon closer inspection, their behaviour is not totally unexpected. Note first of all that liquids are disproportionately often involved in diachronic dissimilations. Precisely the same can be said of liquids in slips of the tongue. In consonant confusion matrices, /r/–/l/ interactions are generally the most frequent (Berg 1988a). This finding may be interpreted as a heightened susceptibility to interaction. Once such an interactivity is acknowledged, it is easy to see that liquids are less dependent upon error-facilitating effects, of which the identical syllable position of the interacting segments is just one. Hence, liquids can interact in slips of the tongue as well as in diachronic processes even under less favourable circumstances. The heightened susceptibility to interaction allows a given liquid to dissimilate any other nearby liquid in the same word, irrespective of whether their syllable positions are identical or not. Thus, the special role of the liquids is also explainable in processing terms. Admittedly, their behaviour in diachronic dissimilations may be more extreme than could be expected, but the germs for their exceptionality can clearly be located in psycholinguistic constraints.

The next analysis centres around the relationship between the original consonant and the one into which it is transformed through the dissimilatory process. Sticking to the three-way division of consonants into obstruents, nasals, and liquids, the outcome of the dissimilation may be classified as category-preserving or category-changing. The former type subsumes those dissimilations in which, let us say, an obstruent is changed into another obstruent. The latter type involves a change from, say, an obstruent into a nasal or a liquid. This difference is illustrated by the following two synchronic dissimilations.

(205) G: *Eine Partei muß auch in den verschiedenen Gle– Gremien die Fragen der Zeit diskutieren* [gle: gre:miɛn fra:gən]

'A political party also has to discuss the current issues in its various committees'

(206) G: *wenn ich stecht schlafe* for *schlecht schlafe*
[ʃtɛçt ʃlaːfə ʃlɛçt]
'when I sleep badly'

Case (205) is category-preserving while (206) is not. In (205), the rhotic is replaced by /l/, but in (206) the lateral is supplanted by an obstruent. As shown in Table 21, category-preserving tongue slips outnumber category-changing ones in my German database.

It can be inferred from Table 21 that a consonant is replaced by another consonant of the same phonological category in 81 per cent of the dissimilations. The exceptions to this pattern form a minority of 19 per cent. The behaviour of the nasals is peculiar in that they apparently prefer to lose rather than keep their nasality feature. However, given the low number of relevant cases, it seems unwise to attach much significance to this point.

In light of this result, it can be predicted that dissimilations are likewise constrained. Category-preserving dissimilations should be the rule and category-changing ones exceptional. This is in fact the case, as made clear by Table 22, which is based upon the relevant Spanish words listed in Grammont (1895). Here are two pertinent examples, one category-preserving (207) and one category-changing (208).

(207) Sp. *arambre* → *alambre*
(208) Lat. *pulcella* → Sp. *poncella*

A liquid is dissimilated into another liquid in the first example but into a nasal in the second.

TABLE 21. *Frequency of category-preserving and category-changing dissimilations in a corpus of German speech errors*

	Obstruent		Nasal		Liquid	
turns into a(n)	Obstruent	Non-Obstruent	Nasal	Non-nasal	Liquid	Non-liquid
	44	6	2	4	8	3

TABLE 22. *Frequency of category-preserving and category-changing diachronic dissimilations in Spanish*

	Obstruent		Nasal		Liquid	
turns into a(n)	Obstruent	Non-obstruent	Nasal	Non-nasal	Liquid	Non-liquid
	0	3	3	5	20	5

An inspection of Table 22 uncovers similarities and differences between the diachronic and the synchronic data. Liquids tend to interact among themselves both in synchronic and diachronic dissimilations. The numbers in Tables 21 and 22 for this class of segments are quite similar. Interestingly, the same can be said of nasals. Although their behaviour is unexpected under the similarity constraint on interactants, nasals prefer to replace, and be replaced by, non-nasals rather than by other nasals in the psycholinguistic as well as the historical data. In all five cases, an alveolar nasal interacts with a liquid. Why this affinity between /n/ and /r,l/ is stronger than between /n/ and /m/ is an open issue.

A twofold disparity between the speech-error data and the sound changes reveals itself in the case of obstruents. For one thing, they are most commonly involved in slips of the tongue but only rarely so in sound changes. For another, while synchronic dissimilations of obstruents tend to be category-preserving, diachronic dissimilations of obstruents mostly result in non-obstruents. This divergence suggests somewhat different constraints to which the two data types are subject.

By way of conclusion, the psycholinguistic data are a fairly good predictor of the historical developments. Spontaneous speech errors thus contribute substantially to the explanation of diachronic dissimilations. The match between the two data sets is not, however, perfect. Many points of convergence notwithstanding, slips of the tongue and diachronic dissimilations differ on their directionality and certain preferences for consonant types. What might be the reasons for these divergences? In view of the very pronounced biases, a sampling error in the historical data appears highly unlikely. The same probably holds good for the speech-error patterns.

A further possibility would be that the speakers' deviations initially share all the properties of slips of the tongue but that not all potential sound changes stand the same chance of surviving. It might be imagined that the perseveratory dissimilations are filtered out whereas the anticipatory ones are retained. The net effect would be a predominance of the latter in the records of the language. While this scenario is not unthinkable, there is no evidence in support of it. That perseveratory slips are perceived as more deviant than anticipatory ones has never been demonstrated. If anything, the opposite is true (Nooteboom 1980; Tent and Clark 1980).

The perceptual-filter mechanism seems to fare better in accounting for the rarity with which obstruents are implicated and the commonness with which liquids are implicated in diachronic dissimilations. The hypothesis would be that changes within the liquid category are less easily noticed by listeners than changes within the obstruent category. One indirect measure of the probability of noticing an error committed by the speaker is the frequency with which listeners mistake a given segment for another. Such information can be obtained from segment confusion experiments. The more likely a segment A is to be confused with segment B, the less likely listeners are to notice a change from A to B. Consonant confusion studies (e.g. Wang and Bilger 1973) show that /r/ and /l/ are highly confusable. This might explain the listeners' tolerance *vis-à-vis* liquid changes. The fact that continuancy is a very stable feature on obstruents implies that listeners find it easy to identify continuancy changes as such and are likely to edit them out. This might contribute to explaining why obstruent dissimilations figure so seldom in the historical records.

5.3. Phonological Similarity in Sound Change: I

One of the ubiquitous principles of the psycholinguistic system is its sensitivity to similarity. It can be found in the domains of perception and production (as well as learning). To begin with pure production data, segmental speech errors are subject to the phonological similarity constraint. The commonest slips are those in which target and error unit differ in only one feature. Tongue slips become progressively less common when the substituting and substituted units are more dissimilar. One frequent and one infrequent consonantal slip follow.

(209) *That kid was eskorking us* for *escorting*
(210) *Michael Malliday* for *Michael Halliday* (both from Fromkin 1973)

Case (209) exemplifies a switch involving a minimum number of features whereas a maximum number of features is changed in (210). The difference between /k/ and /t/ in the first error can be stated as a change from [alveolar] to [velar]. In contrast, the segment change in the second error involves all relevant dimensions—place of articulation, manner of articulation, and voice.

The pattern for vowel errors is highly similar. Their occurrence is also promoted by a high number of features shared. This relationship between error rate and similarity of the interactants has been observed in all speech-error corpora regardless of the language being examined.

It is worth noting that consonants and vowels are very reluctant to interact in slips of the tongue. This reluctance may be viewed as evidence for their disparate phonological specifications. Because vowels and consonants belong to different feature sets (in most though not in all phonological theories), interactions between them would perforce involve feature switches on all dimensions and should thus be strongly discouraged. However, there is a second reason, at least equally strong, which prohibits the occurrence of vowel/consonant substitutions. Speech errors almost always produce well-formed linguistic patterns, e.g. they tend not to violate phonotactic constraints. A consequence of this is that consonants simply cannot move into vocalic positions, because this would create unacceptable or even unpronounceable segment sequences. The probability of consonants and vowels interacting can therefore be reliably assessed only when there is an opportunity for them to do so. This opportunity is only rarely given in English, so an infinitesimal number or even a complete absence of such errors can hardly be surprising. When there is such an opportunity and when certain facilitatory conditions are met, consonant and vowel interactions do occur, albeit at an extremely low rate. One example from English and one from German are presented below.

(211) *Big Bore Platty* for *Big Boy Platter* (from Stemberger 1983)
(212) G: *Da fand ich hollte im 'Spiegel'* for *heute im 'Spiegel'*
         [hɔltə   ʃpiːɡəl   hɔitə]
       'Today I found in the *Spiegel* (name of a news magazine)'

No. (211) is an exchange betwen /r/ and /ɪ/ which both appear in word-final position and therefore can be said to be extrinsically similar. The rhotic splits up the diphthong /ɔɪ/ and places itself at the position of the second constituent. The first constituent is lengthened concomitantly. The ousted /ɪ/ of *boy* has no difficulty surfacing in the original position of the /r/ because it has a non-syllabic and a syllabic variant. In view of all the constraints that have to be satisfied, it is understandable why such slips are so uncommon. Case (211) is paralleled by (212) in that a diphthong is broken up and a sonorant allies itself with the first constituent. The /l/ remains in final position despite its dislocation. It can be seen, then, that it is not in principle impossible for consonants and vowels to interact although they are very unlikely to do so.

With respect to slips of the ear, very similar observations can be made although the available data bases are smaller and have been less systematically analysed. From the many examples published in Bond and Robey (1983), it can be gathered that the phonetic/phonological similarity of two segments increases the likelihood of the one being misperceived as the other. An interaction between two similar consonants is reported in (213), two dissimilar consonants are involved in (214).

(213) *atnosphere* for *atmosphere*
(214) *goo* for *who* (both from Bond and Robey 1983)

In (213) the nasality is retained while only the place-of-articulation feature is changed. By contrast, all three dimensions (voicing, place, and manner of articulation) are affected in (214).

Vocalic misperceptions are also subject to the similarity constraint: the more similar the interactants, the greater the likelihood of error. As in slips of the tongue, monophthongs do not interact only with other monophthongs but also with diphthongs, as in the following misperception.

(215) *This blind guy in my class* for *This blond guy* (from Bond and Robey 1983)

Similarity is also a relevant factor in speakers' and listeners' evaluations of their own and others' output. Whether they regard a given message as erroneous or correct depends upon how great the disparity between intended and actual utterance is perceived to be. In a mispronunciation experiment, Cole (1973) had subjects detect consonants which were deliberately introduced in a spoken text (and which thereby distorted it). He manipulated the number of features changed and found a clear relationship between severity of distortion and detection rate. As a rule, one-feature changes went unnoticed while multiple-feature changes were readily detected. This result applies not only to the detection of other-produced errors but probably also to that of self-produced slips. In my corpus of naturally occurring speech errors, a trend similar to that reported by Cole (1973) in his more controlled study appears, though it fails to reach standard levels of significance.

From all the threads of evidence taken together, a very coherent picture emerges. Both from the listener's and the speaker's angle, there is a strong bias towards favouring minimal deviations from the norm. This may be self-evident from the listener's perspective, but it is certainly not self-evident when one looks at it from the production side. The listener's task is to reduce the infinite variety of different stimuli to a finite number of mental categories. Since this reduction operation is guided by the principle of similarity, listeners are more likely to ignore minimal than maximal distortions of the signal. There is no logical necessity for speakers to tend to perpetuate 'near-misses'. It suggests a particular architecture of the processing network in which lower levels may affect higher ones.

In any event, the predictions for language change are clear. If a segment undergoes a change, it should turn into its most immediate neighbour on the similarity scale. In principle, this does not have to be so in every single case because, as we have seen, the processing system is able to cope with multi-feature switches. We may therefore predict single-feature switches of consonants and vowels to be the rule and multi-feature switches to be exceptional. A further prediction is that monophthongization and diphthongization should be common historical processes. Yet another prediction concerns the interaction between consonants and vowels. Vocalization and devocalization may occur but should be quite rare.

Testing these predictions is a straightforward task. The major sound substitutions in the history of English, excepting those of very limited regional extension, have been catalogued and examined for the similarity between the earlier and the later form. It can be ignored in how many words a given change took place because only the probability of certain phonological developments is at issue. The analysis is hindered only by the uncertainty of reconstructing the pronunciations of some graphemes and, by implication, the adequate feature specifications of some segments. In regard to consonants, the list contains thirty-one changes which took place since Proto-Indo-European times. Of these, only two involve a two-feature switch, while the remaining twenty-nine are one-feature switches.

In this connection, it is appropriate to mention Grimm's Law with its three components, 'spirantization', 'devoicing', and 'deaspiration'. By means of spirantization, the stops turned into their homorganic fricatives. Thus, only one phonological parameter was affected. At first glance, the change from /p/ to /f/ looks like a two-feature switch (i.e. from [− continuant] to [+ continuant] and from [bilabial] to [labiodental]). However, there is both linguistic and psycholinguistic evidence to suggest that bilabials and labiodentals should be assigned the same place-of-articulation feature, namely [labial] (Gamkrelidze 1978; Berg 1989b). If this description is followed, the development from /p/ to /f/ can also be interpreted as involving a single feature. The devoicing rule of Grimm's Law turned the voiced stops into their voiceless congeners without any other modification. The deaspiration part is slightly more complicated in that it apparently engendered two forms in Proto-Germanic. By this rule, the voiced aspirated stops lost their aspiration. The resultant plain stops stood in allophonic variation with their homorganic fricatives, but this does not undermine the hypothesis that a one-feature switch is involved here. The most probable interpretation seems to be that two different phenomena are involved—the deaspiration of the stops as a diachronic process and the contextual accommodation as a 'synchronic' process. It is thus not necessary to assume the same direct link between, let us say, /dʰ/ and /ð/ as between /dʰ/ and /d/. In sum, all nine changes captured by Grimm's Law are describable as one-feature switches.

The subsequent stages in the development of the consonants are similarly supportive of the research hypothesis. In the history of English, only two changes may be amenable to a two-feature analysis. Firstly, <þ> developed into /d/ before the lateral, as in (216).

(216) Goth. *neþla* → OE *nǣdl* 'needle'

If <þ> is taken to represent the voiceless dental fricative, as is usually done, the change would be manifest on the voicing and the manner dimensions. However, the phonetic value of <þ> cannot be unequivocally determined. It might have been voiced due to the assimilatory influence of the following liquid. In that case, a one-feature switch would have happened.[3]

Secondly, palatalization turned /k/ into /tʃ/. Of course, the phonological distance between /k/ and /tʃ/ is not minimal, but it is most likely that the development occurred in several successive steps. Palatalization probably preceded assibilation and therefore the development is best characterized as a sequence of minimal changes rather than as one complex change. To conclude, consonantal changes overwhelmingly obey the similarity constraint. The so-called exceptions to this generalization are of doubtful value because they are open to alternative interpretations.

From Old English to Modern English, 53 major monophthongal changes have been recorded. This list includes neither centralization tendencies in unstressed syllables nor certain shortening or lengthening processes. Of the 53 changes, 44 (83 per cent) involve a one-feature switch and 9 (17 per cent) a two-feature switch. Among the latter, there are 7 in which the qualitative change is accompanied by a quantitative one, as in (217–18).

(217) Goth. *armōsts* → OE *earmŭst* 'poorest'
(218) OE *dŭru* → *dōre* 'door'

---

[3] The change along the place dimension can be ignored in this case because it is absolutely minimal. Although the most natural articulation for /d/ and /t/ is in the alveolar region, there is a certain latitude from post-alveolar to dental pronunciations. Since historical reconstruction cannot capture such fine phonetic detail, there is no basis for postulating a place change in addition to the manner change. The OE alveolar stops may have had a slightly fronted articulation. If this were the case, the manner change would be truly homorganic; if not, the concomitant place change would be fairly minor.

Most of these cases appear to be interpretable as 'phonologically natural' ones. Short vowels are generally more central than their long counterparts. As a result, lengthening and shortening processes tend to be accompanied by qualitative changes (and vice versa). So if the /o:/ is shortened, as in *armosts*, it moves closer in quality to /ʊ/. Conversely, if the /ʊ/ is lengthened, as in *duru*, it approaches the region of /o:/. Thus, the interdependence of vowel quality and length at the phonetic level is at the core of these so-called two-feature switches. Whether the classification as 'two-feature switches' is psycholinguistically adequate is a moot point. This classification follows from the assumption that vowels are independently specifiable on the qualitative and the quantitative dimensions. If this assumption is given up in favour of a specification in terms of vectors in an n-dimensional space, it would be possible to reanalyse these cases as minimal-distance switches.

The remaining two cases are /ã/ → /o:/ and /u/ → /ʌ/. The denasalization of OE /ã/ is peculiar, especially as the nasal vowel stems from a homorganic oral one (/a/) in Proto-Germanic. All other instances of OE denasalization conform to the minimal-distance principle. The other case is fairly recent. It involves a change along the backness and the height dimensions. The development from /u/ to /ʌ/ seems to have gone through the intermediate stage /ə/, in which case it can be postulated that the two features changed successively. At first, the vowel moved frontwards and was subsequently lowered. On this account, it would be more appropriate to speak of two one-feature switches rather than one two-feature switch. By way of internal summary, there is no doubt that vowel changes adhere fairly strictly to the minimal-distance principle. Although two-feature switches are not categorically excluded, they are rare and for the most part phonetically well motivated.

As in slips of the tongue, interactions between monophthongs and diphthongs are quite common in language change. Monophthongizations and diphthongizations are regular processes in the history of English. It is worthy of note that the proportion of diphthong-based errors among all vocalic slips of the tongue in Stemberger's (1992a) corpus is about equal to the proportion of monophthongizations and diphthongizations among the vocalic changes in the history of English (*c.* 33 per cent). This match may be coincidental because token frequencies have been completely ignored in the historical, though not in the psycholinguistic, data. On the other hand, this match may be taken to suggest that similar mechanisms are at work in both areas.

Since it is not obvious how similarity relationships between diphthongs and monophthongs can be defined, the analysis of monophthongizations and diphthongizations can only be of a preliminary nature. Including changes from one diphthong to another, there are 28 pertinent cases.[4] These can be compared in terms of whether the first, the second or neither constituent of the diphthong is identical to the monophthong (or to the other diphthong). Identity between the monophthong and one part of the diphthong is given in 19 of the 28 cases (68 per cent). They

---

[4] The ME developments such as /ɑw/ → /ɑʊ/ and /eġ/ → /ei/ do not enter into this calculation.

divide evenly between those with an identical first or second element. This is far more than can be expected by chance.

An interesting pattern emerges among the remaining nine cases, in which there is no identity between the segments involved. The monophthongizations appear to take individual features from both constituents of the diphthong and to recombine them in a monophthong. In Middle English, for example, the long and the short diphthongs /ēo/ and /ĕo/ yielded /ø:/ and /ø/, respectively. These monophthongs can be most naturally seen as recombinations of the frontness of the /e/ and the roundness of the /o/, yielding the front rounded vowel /ø/. The same holds for diphthongizations such as /æ/ → /ea/ in Old English, where the monophthong is roughly on the trajectory of the diphthong. The diphthongization process can thus be viewed as the breaking up of the vowel into two parts which are minimally distinct from the original monophthong. Hence, monophthongization and diphthongization processes are arguably governed by the principle of phonetic/phonological similarity.

With respect to the frequency of devocalizations, the agreement between the psycholinguistic and the historical data is perfect. As predicted, they are practically nonexistent. However, somewhat unexpectedly, vocalizations are not uncommon in the history of English. In Old English, the final semi-vowels /w/ and /j/ developed into their vocalic cognates /u/ and /i/, respectively, as in (219). This process gained ground in Middle English, creating a large number of diphthongs (220). It affected not only semi-vowels but also fricatives such as /ɣ/ (221), but it seems that the vocalization of fricatives occurred less frequently than that of semivowels.

(219) G: *bealwes* → *bealu* 'bale'
(220) OE *weȝ* → ME *wei* 'way' ([j] → [i])
(221) OE *dragan* → ME *drawen* 'draw' ([aɣ] → [au])

From the phonetic point of view, the transition from a semivowel to a vowel is absolutely minimal. So as soon as the semivowel stage is reached, the vocalization is almost complete. What is more difficult to come to grips with is the earlier stages. The development as a whole is clear: the stops began to spirantize, the fricatives became semivowels, and the semivowels turned into full vowels. The only link in this chain which is unexpected from the high-level psycholinguistic perspective is the substitution of fricatives by semivowels. Such changes do not occur in slips of the tongue. However, these changes can be motivated from the low-level phonetic perspective. The Old High German form *wega* 'way' testifies to a stop /g/ which was spirantized in Old English *weȝ*. It is probable that the OE sound began as the velar or palatal fricative /ɣ/ or /j/ and later lost its frication and developed into a semivowel. In the *dragan* example above, the change may therefore have taken the following form: [aɣ] → [aw] → [au]. My tentative conclusion is that fricatives are not immediately vocalized. They are semivocalized before they become full vowels. This provides a phonetically natural explanation for a phenomenon whose relative frequency is not exactly predicted by high-level psycholinguistic data.

To summarize, the prediction that sound change is sensitive to the principle of similarity has been fulfilled across the board. Within the levels of accuracy attainable in historical linguistics, it can be ascertained that changes preferentially affect only a single phonological dimension. The diachronic principle of minimal deviation from the norm derives from the way that information is processed in the mental network. In general, high-level phonological and low-level phonetic processes work hand in glove. That they do not always do so is suggested by the case of vocalization which is motivated by low-level though only weakly by high-level processes. All this is good evidence for the claim that diachronic change is shaped by high-level processing constraints.

5.4. Phonological Similarity in Sound Change: II

In the preceding section, the similarity constraint on sound change has been explored. It has been shown that phonological change proceeds in small steps, changing only one feature at a time. The similarity constraint was established on the basis of a model of phonological representation which encompasses various dimensions and which defines similarity in terms of the number of dimensions that are changed. For instance, the changes from /b/ to /g/ and from /d/ to /g/ are regarded as high-similarity substitutions because they occur along a single dimension: place of articulation. These two changes are treated in equivalent fashion because both involve a single-feature switch. This decision is debatable, however. It implies that the features on a particular dimension are an unordered set, which is not necessarily true. An alternative representation would express the articulatory distance on a straight line. In the case of consonants, this can be straightforwardly accomplished along the place-of-articulation dimension. From the front to the back of the oral cavity, the features would be aligned as follows: [bilabial], [labiodental], [dental], [alveolar], [palato-alveolar], [palatal], and [velar]. Phonological similarity is accordingly measured in terms of the linear distance between the distinctive features. The more features are 'skipped', the greater the dissimilarity. Thus, the distance from /b/ to /g/ is greater than that from /d/ to /g/. Hence, both substitutions cannot be treated in equivalent fashion even though they are one-feature switches.

The manner-of-articulation features can also be organized along a straight line according to their degree of sonority. The sound classes may be ordered as follows (from less to more aperture): stops, affricates, fricatives, nasals, liquids, glides. In the case of vowels, the height and backness dimensions lend themselves well to a linear-distance analysis of their features. The height dimension arranges its basic features in the following order: [high], [mid], [low], and, if necessary, certain intermediate values may be added. The backness dimension usually makes do with three features: [front], [central], and [back]. All the dimensions mentioned so far organize several features. In fact, this is a prerequisite for discovering subtler differences in phonological similarity. The binary features of length and voice are thus not amenable to closer scrutiny.

It is an empirical question whether the phonological representation is of the coarse- or the fine-grained type. There is no a priori reason why the phonological representation should be sensitive to the criterion of intra-oral distance, especially as a certain amount of phonetic detail has to be abstracted away in any case. In addition, information on intra-oral distance is redundant in the sense that it is not needed to distinguish one segment from another. This job is already done by the conventional feature matrices.

To arbitrate between the competing models, recourse will be taken to speech errors. They provide a suitable testing-ground because they are assumed to arise at an abstract phonological processing stage before low-level phonetic rules are applied (Mohanan 1982; Berg 1989b). If slips of the tongue are sensitive to the phonetic-distance principle, they should prefer to 'travel' the least distance. Consonant errors such as (222) should therefore occur more commonly than cases such as (223).

(222) *Tathy can type* for *Kathy*
(223) *gave the goy* for *the boy* (both from Fromkin 1973)

No. (222) illustrates an interaction between two adjacent features on the place-of-articulation dimension. There is no feature between [alveolar] and [velar] in the stop series of English. By contrast, (223) involves an interaction between the non-adjacent features [velar] and [bilabial]. The feature [alveolar] is skipped.

If, on the other hand, speech errors are not sensitive to the linear-distance principle, long and short distances should be covered equally often. As it turns out, the speech error data exhibit a sensitivity to the linear-distance principle (Berg, in preparation). The less the distance between two segments, the more likely they are to interact. The phonological representation can thus be claimed to incorporate articulatory phonetic information.

On the assumption that (a completed) sound change is phonological in nature, it can be predicted on psycholinguistic grounds that the phonological distance covered will be minimal. In the process of change, segments will not arbitrarily choose another feature on the same dimension. Rather, they are expected to prefer their next-door neighbour to the more remote ones.

This hypothesis will be tested against data from the history of the English language. It has to be borne in mind that the concept of phonological distance cannot be defined in general terms. It makes sense only when applied to individual phonological systems. In modern English, for example, there are vowels of a central quality, thus rendering the backness dimension ternary. However, the Old English vowel system did not contain central vowels. Hence, front and back vowels have to be treated as contiguous along the backness dimension for this period. This implies that when a change along this dimension occurs, it cannot help being phonologically minimal. The backness dimension has therefore to be left out of account in the ensuing analysis.

Let us begin with vowel height. Of 32 pertinent monophthongal changes, as many as 31 cover a minimal phonological distance. Typical cases include /e/ → /æ/ in Old

English, /i/ → /ɛ:/ in Middle English, and /o:/ → /u:/ in Early Modern English. The only seemingly exceptional case is Old English /ɑ/ → /e/, a standard example of palatal umlaut. On the minimal-distance hypothesis, the expected result would be /æ/ instead of /e/ because /æ/ is closer to /ɑ/ than /e/. Intriguingly, there is evidence to suggest that /æ/ occurred as an intermediate result during the transition from /ɑ/ to /e/. A ligature can be found in the oldest Anglo-Saxon texts, as shown in (224).

(224) Goth. *brannjan* ≐ OE *bærnan* 'to burn'

Such forms warrant the claim that /ɑ/ → /e/ is also a minimal-distance change. Thus, all monophthongal changes examined here move as little as possible in the vowel space.[5] The research hypothesis is fully supported.

Consonant change is less rewarding an area to study from the perspective of linear distance because the dimension that lends itself best to such an analysis, viz. place of articulation, is hardly affected by diachronic change (see next section). The changes along this dimension are too few to allow a test of the hypothesis under scrutiny. The manner-of-articulation dimension has been more productive of diachronic changes. A look at the pertinent data reveals that manner changes tend to abide by the minimal-distance principle. The most common manner switches are from [fricative] to [stop] or vice versa. At first sight these might look like non-minimal-distance changes because stops and fricatives are separated by affricates which involve an obstruction as well as a constriction gesture. However, this problem does not present itself in practice. Affricates, which have always played a minor role in the history of English, are found only in the palatal region. If anything, they could stand in the way of stop–fricative changes in that region. In all other regions, there are no affricates and hence no elements to skip. Thus the fricative/stop changes can legitimately be considered to respect the minimal-distance principle. With this proviso, the vast majority of the manner changes in English history can be claimed to cover a minimal phonological distance.

The only exception to this generalization appears to be the vocalization of consonants in Middle English. Vowels, especially glides and diphthongs, tend to originate from fricatives but never went through the nasal or liquid stages, as might be expected according to the alignment of features proposed above. However, no linguist would seriously expect transitional nasals or liquids from, let us say, [ɣ] to [w]. The great phonetic disparity between these sounds precludes such developments. At this point, the limitations of one-dimensional representations become apparent. In addition, a simple paradigmatic account does not do justice to the Middle English vocalizations. These are clearly context-dependent in that they are determined by the quality of the surrounding vowels. To take the above example, [ɣ] passed into [w] only after those vowels which, like [w], have a back quality, see (221). There is no consonant which is closer to /u/ than /w/, so the minimal-distance principle can hardly be said to be infringed.

---

[5] The Early Mod. English case /ʊ/ → /ʌ/ has been discussed in section 5.3.

A similar explanation is available for the Middle English development from /w/ to /v/ in the north of England. Regarding /w/ as a semi-vowel, the change from a semi-vowel to a fricative would not appear to be minimal in terms of the number of features that are skipped along the manner dimension. However, the labial component of /w/ makes it quite similar to /v/. No liquid or nasal, nor any other fricative can be claimed to be more similar to /w/ than /v/. Thus the change from /w/ to /v/ may be seen as involving maximally similar segments, even though one-dimensional approaches only inadequately express this similarity.

To conclude, the historical data support a fine-grained analysis of similarity relations between the earlier and the later sounds. Not all feature dimensions can be tested, either because they are binary or because they are largely immune to diachronic change. The dimensions that can be subjected to investigation almost invariably involve minimal-distance switches. The exceptions to this pattern are more apparent than real. They arguably disclose weaknesses in the conception of what is to be regarded as a minimal distance. It has transpired that only a multidimensional approach is adequate; the one-dimensional methods that have been employed here are therefore of limited descriptive value.

Thus all the available evidence is compatible with the hypothesis that sound change is constrained by two types of similarity: the number of features that are changed is kept to a minimum, and features change to adjacent positions along the relevant phonological dimensions. These two types of similarity reflect information-processing principles in the mental network, and can therefore be argued to derive from these.

5.5. Dimensional Preferences in Consonant Change

The standard way of classifying consonants is in terms of the dimensions of voice, manner, and place of articulation. These three dimensions generally suffice exhaustively to describe all consonants from the phonological perspective—with the possible exception of aspiration, which was not redundant with voicing at certain points in the history of the language under examination. Consonant gemination represents a further dimension which was relevant at certain historical stages. Since neither aspiration nor gemination has survived, it is difficult to determine how speakers and listeners would have treated these features in language use. They therefore have to be ignored in the subsequent analysis.

Not all three core dimensions are equally often involved in consonantal slips of the tongue. While voice appears to be relatively immune to change, manner and place of articulation regularly undergo modification in speech errors. MacKay (1970b) finds place of articulation to be the least stable. Also in my data, there is a slight predominance of single-segment errors involving the place dimension. About 50 per cent of the tongue slips change the place feature and about 40 per cent change the manner feature. The following examples may serve as an illustration.

(225) *Somebody will proceed to sow* for *to show*
(226) *farticle shift* for *particle shift*
(227) *Liverpool lullapie* for *lullabye* (all from Fromkin 1973)

All three segment errors involve a single featural dimension—place is changed in (225), manner in (226), and voice in (227). Multiple-feature changes may be analysed in similar fashion. They are also subject to the place–manner–voice order of decreasing vulnerability.

This pattern is almost exactly replicated by slips of the ear. According to Bond and Robey (1983), place errors (47 per cent) are somewhat more frequent than manner errors (37 per cent), while voicing slips are uncommon (4 per cent). An example of each is given in (228–30).

(228) *Do you want a Coke?* for *coat*
(229) *kutchion sole* for *cushion sole*
(230) *Will the glass* for *the class* (all from Bond and Robey 1983)

No. (228) involves a change from [alveolar] to [velar], a fricative becomes an affricate in (229), and the voiceless stop turns voiced in (230). As Bond and Robey (1983) note, many slips of the ear in their corpus implicate more than one feature at the same time. Unfortunately, they do not provide percentages for the single-feature changes. The above percentages thus have to be treated with some caution.

The congruence between the slips of the tongue and ear is striking. It suggests that voice is processed quite accurately while manner and place of articulation are relatively error-prone. However, the slips of the ear data are at variance with a number of reports which have all shown that voice is *less* perceptible than other consonantal features. Lackner and Tuller (1979) had subjects repeat a series of nonsense syllables. During this task the subjects made errors, and they were instructed to press a button when they had detected one. It was thus possible to determine which error types were detected how often. Lackner and Tuller found that subjects detected voicing errors significantly less often than place-of-articulation errors. The authors interpret this outcome in terms of the assumption that the accuracy of detection is a function of the grossness of the distortion created by the error. They argue that a change along the place dimension represents a gross distortion in that it involves a different gesture of the primary articulators, which leads to considerable differences in the structure of the acoustic signal. By contrast, a voicing change has only minor articulatory and acoustic consequences.

The second study worth discussing in this context reports on a standard mispronunciation experiment. Unlike the study mentioned above, the subjects had to detect errors in the speech of others. They were played a tape-recorded text which was filled with certain kinds of errors in certain locations. In several mispronunciation tasks, Cole et al. (1978) tested the perceptibility of place and voicing changes and discovered that the latter were significantly more likely to pass undetected than the former. This research is thus in full agreement with Lackner and Tuller's report.

Cole et al.'s findings have been replicated by Bond and Small (1983) using a shadowing task.

Thus all three studies converge in support of the claim that speakers and listeners are less sensitive to detecting changes along the voice dimension than along other dimensions. This conjecture makes sense on articulatory, acoustic, and linguistic[6] grounds. However, it is at odds with the data on slips of the tongue and ear. Since the conflict cuts across the production and perception studies, it cannot apparently be attributed to differences in the way the productive and perceptual systems process voicing information. The problem resides within perception alone: voice is kept constant in slips of the ear even though speakers and listeners tend not to notice voicing changes. In fact, there is one way of reconciling this conflict. What does a slip of the ear involving the voice dimension actually imply? A slip of the ear presupposes that the listener becomes aware of the fact that s/he has constructed an internal representation of the signal which is at loggerheads with what s/he supposes the speaker intended to say. A slip of the ear involving the voice dimension implies that listeners attend to this dimension closely. If they did not, their latitude in dealing with voice information would be greater, and hence the likelihood of their becoming aware of a misperception would be smaller.

It transpires, then, that the conflict is more apparent than real. Because listeners do not pay close attention to the voice dimension, they only rarely report having made a slip of the ear. As a consequence, error corpora will include few instances of the pertinent error type, as is indeed the case. We may conclude that voicing is not processed very reliably by the listener.

There remains, however, the problem of the stability of voicing in the productive domain and the instability of voicing in the perception data. It is possible that voicing errors are under-represented in the production data because the error collectors detect them less easily than other error types. Despite this possibility, it is improbable that perceptual biases alone can account for the difference between the productive and the perceptual evidence, because the trends apparent in naturalistic speech error data have been shown to be very similar to those obtained in more carefully controlled experimental situations (Berg 1992b; Stemberger 1992b). It seems that we face a genuine difference in the processing of voice between the production and the perception mechanism. We are forced to decide, therefore, which side should be given more weight. In general, the following strategy will be adopted. In case of a conflict between production and perception, the perceptual side is accorded priority. No matter what the speaker may produce, that which does not meet the listener's 'approval' is bound to fail. Listeners are more powerful than speakers because it is them whom the speakers must 'convince'. Since listeners are responsible for the diffusion of a change, they decide upon its eventual success.

The primacy of perception gives rise to the following prediction. Voicing switches should be a common diachronic phenomenon because listeners have

[6] Minimal pairs differing only in voicing (e.g. *beat–peat*) are less common than minimal pairs involving other phonological dimensions (Denes 1963).

difficulty noticing them. Both the perception and the production data lead to the prediction that manner switches should also be frequent, though less frequent than place changes. It is impossible to derive precise predictions regarding the frequency of voicing switches relative to others, for it is not known to what extent perceptual biases can offset productive ones.

A survey of the consonant changes in the Germanic languages yields a relatively clear picture: voicing and manner changes occur regularly, while place changes are rare. This pattern is fairly robust across epochs and languages. In Natural Phonology, consonant changes are often described as 'fortitions' and 'lenitions'. The course of a typical lenition is from a voiceless geminate stop to a simple stop, from a voiceless stop to its voiced counterpart, from a voiced stop to a homorganic fricative, from a supraglottal to a glottal fricative or a glide, and from there to zero (Hock 1986). This process may involve changes along all phonological dimensions, but the most commonly documented ones are voicing and manner switches. Virtually the same holds true of fortitions. Let us return to Grimm's Law. Leaving aside the deaspiration rule, it captures changes along the voicing and manner dimensions. The voiced stops are devoiced and the voiceless stops pass into their homorganic fricatives. The second Germanic sound shift also induced spirantization of simple voiceless stops. The geminates were affricated. So both changes took place along the manner dimension.

In the history of English, place changes are very infrequent while voicing and manner changes occur fairly often. One of the few place changes is the development from /x/ to /f/ in Early Modern English, as in (231).

(231) OE *dweorh* → Mod.E. *dwarf*

Voicing changes occur throughout the Old and Middle English periods. They are quite regular in the sense that they tend to affect all those words which fulfil certain structural conditions. Among the most well-known examples is the voicing of intervocalic obstruents. In initial positions voiceless fricatives became voiced, whereas at the end of monosyllabic words voiced fricatives were devoiced. Voicing and devoicing in individual lexical items persisted into Early Modern English.

Manner changes are also common throughout the history of English. The most typical development is from fricative to stop and vice versa. Due to the minimal-distance constraint (see sections 5.3 and 5.4), these changes almost always involve homorganic consonants. Manner changes tend to affect all obstruents to the same degree. The most regular changes are represented by palatalization and assibilation processes.

It can be seen, then, that the psycholinguistic predictions are only partly borne out by the historical data. As expected, voicing and manner changes occur frequently. Place changes, however, which were predicted to be most common of all, proved to be least common. From the psycholinguistic viewpoint, the historical instability of voicing finds an explanation in the way this feature is processed in perception. Because a voice switch has relatively minor perceptual consequences, listeners tend not to notice it.

By contrast, the diachronic instability of manner of articulation lends itself more appropriately to a speaker-based explanation. Given that speakers easily make manner errors, it is no wonder that manner switches are regularly observed in language change. The stability of place of articulation is still a complete mystery. We must therefore conclude that the dimensional preferences in consonant changes do not seem to be entirely under psycholinguistic control. Processing has a role to play, but not all players in this game are psycholinguists.

5.6. Dimensional Preferences in Vowel Change

Vowels are standardly classified along the dimensions of length (long–short), height (high–low), backness (front–back), rounding (rounded–unrounded), and nasality (oral–nasal). Not all dimensions need to be relevant at every point in time. When a language has no nasal vowels, for example, it is superfluous to use the label [oral]. However, the core dimensions of backness and height are applicable to all vowel systems. What will be explored in this section is whether vowels are more susceptible to change on one dimension rather than on another.

The investigation of speech error data from English clearly demonstrates that not all vowel parameters are equally vulnerable. Two results stand out in Shattuck-Hufnagel's (1986) analysis of English vowel slips. For one thing, the production of length is very reliably controlled. For another, the most common error type involves the dimension of backness. The other vowel parameters are of medium vulnerability. Here is one typical and one untypical example.

(232) We [riːtuːn]– routinely make
(233) the [hʌzi]– housing subsidy (both from Shattuck-Hufnagel 1986)

The two interacting vowels in (232) are of the same length. Their major difference is in terms of backness. The difference in roundedness probably can be considered irrelevant, as this feature is redundantly coded on back vowels. Case (233) is a rare instance of a substitution of a diphthong, which counts phonologically as a long vowel, by a short monophthong.

Interestingly, the slips of the ear do not agree with the speech error data. In Bond and Robey's (1983) corpus, vowel-height errors predominate. They constitute more than 50 per cent of all vowel misperceptions. Errors involving the backness dimension are much less common and the length changes are least common. Two pertinent examples are noted in (234–5).

(234) *How do you spell 'sense'?* for *How do you spell 'since'?*
(235) *a little peel box* for *a little pill box* (from Bond and Robey 1983)

In (234), the vowel was perceived as lower than what had actually been produced. Case (235) illustrates the misperception of vowel length.

Assuming that the error-proneness of certain dimensions during speaking and listening creates an instability in the long run, it can be predicted on the basis of both perceptual and productive evidence that long vowels should seldom be shortened and short vowels should seldom be lengthened. As regards the other dimensions, a conflict between perception and production arises. As discussed in the preceding section, perceptual influences may be expected to prevail over productive ones. Hence, the prediction is that vowel height rather than backness will be most susceptible to change in the history of the English language.

This prediction will be tested against the same data that have been used in the analysis of phonological-similarity effects, i.e. all major vocalic changes that have occurred from Old English up to now. We will look at qualitative changes first. It is not surprising to find that changes along the [oral]–[nasal] dimension are extremely rare. This is for the simple reason that the nasal vowels were denasalized in Old English and never came back. That there are very few changes involving the roundedness assumption is also to be expected, because front rounded vowels existed only for a limited time span in English. After their elimination roundedness became redundant, and may have been lost as a feature specification on vowels.

The most interesting result comes from the comparison of the height and backness dimension. In line with the psycholinguistic prediction, vowels undergo changes on the height parameter much more frequently than on the backness parameter. In fact more than 50 per cent of all monophthongal changes in English shift along the height axis, while the backness dimension is involved in approximately 10 per cent of cases. The diachronic evidence thus bears out the psycholinguistic prediction regarding the qualitative side of vowels.

With respect to the quantitative side, however, a discrepancy between the processing and the historical data cannot be overlooked. Contrary to expectation, vowel length proves to be very unstable over time. In the Old English era, no vowel was exempt from lengthening or shortening. However, a closer look reveals that the length changes are in the main syntagmatically motivated. Many such changes are of a secondary nature in that they may be construed as a response to a primary change. For example, short vowels were lengthened in Old English following the disappearance of <ȝ>, as in (236).

(236) O.E. *mæȝden* → *mǣden* 'maiden'

Such a repair process is but one instance of a more general phenomenon, which may be described as a tendency towards rime isochrony. According to this principle, long vowels tend to pair with a lower number of consonants while short vowels prefer to be followed by a higher number of consonants. Consequently, long vowels were shortened when followed by at least two consonants, compare (237). By contrast, two-consonant clusters such as [mb] and [nd], which form a certain unity, induced lengthening, as shown in (238).

(237) OE *blīþs* → *bliss* 'bliss'
(238) OE *lamb* → *lāmb* 'lamb'

These developments persisted into Middle English, where the dependence between stress, vowel length, and coda type gained ground. The vowels in open syllables were lengthened (239) whereas those in closed syllables were shortened (240).

(239) OE *wĭku* → ME *wēke* 'week'
(240) OE *sōfte* → ME *sŏfte* 'soft'

These were very general developments which affected a large number of words. Subsequent to the Middle English period, vowel quantity remained fairly stable. The Great English Vowel Shift did not implicate length. When a diphthong was created, it always developed from a long monophthong, thus holding the quantitative aspect constant.

In a bird's-eye view, the length change from Old to Modern English has been a radical one. While the Old English vowel system displayed a perfect balance between long and short monophthongs and even diphthongs, the Modern English system is very inconsistent. All short diphthongs disappeared, leaving the long ones without counterpart. Among the monophthongs, some have retained a short/long opposition (e.g. /i:/–/ɪ/) while others (e.g. /e/) have not. Generally speaking, length has lost its highly systematic function. It has been demoted from a major to a minor classificatory feature of the English vowel system.

In evaluating the correctness of the psycholinguistic predictions, we have to be clear about the domains for which the processing data are relevant and for which they are not. To a certain extent slips of the tongue are context-free phenomena, in the sense that they involve intrusions from elements which are not part of the *immediate* context. This is not to say that the neighbours of the error unit do not wield an influence on the probability and the shape of a malfunction, but this influence is only of secondary importance, especially in relatively neutral contexts such as CV structures. The speech-error data can thus be argued to speak to context-free, paradigmatic processes but to be less informative with respect to context-dependent, syntagmatic processes. This *post hoc* analysis forces us to narrow down the psycholinguistic prediction: length should be quite immune to context-free historical change, while nothing can be predicted about context-dependent changes.

If formulated in this way, the diachronic evidence is no longer incompatible with the psycholinguistic prediction. Context-free changes involving length are almost completely missing. Context-dependent changes can be argued to be motivated by rhythmic factors. Assuming that it is advantageous to the speaker and the listener to have rimes of equal length, the loss of a syllable-final consonant is likely to be compensated for by vowel lengthening. There is thus an interesting conflict between the two principles, the one stabilizing vowel length and the other indirectly leading to its destabilization. That the latter principle prevails is mainly a spin-off of the strength of syntagmatic influences upon sound change.

Even if length should prove unstable in context-free vowel change, it is not necessarily the case that the psycholinguistic account is falsified. It might be that vowel length, like voice, is one of the dimensions that listeners are not particularly careful about. Mispronunciation, shadowing, and other experiments might help to elucidate the role of vowel length in perception, but unfortunately the lack of pertinent studies precludes an assessment of this possibility.

One conforming and one neutral piece of evidence have been recorded. The expectation regarding the quality of vowels is fully satisfied. In line with the prediction, height is the most vulnerable dimension in diachronic vowel change. The instability of height can therefore be put down to a psycholinguistic principle whereby the height dimension is processed less reliably than the others. The predictions concerning vowel quantity could not be submitted to a serious test because they target a type of change that hardly occurs in the history of English. The changes that do occur respond to syntagmatic constraints about which the processing principle under examination here has nothing to say.

5.7. The Differential Susceptibility of Consonants and Vowels to Change

Consonants and vowels are quite different in various ways. In language production research, consonants have been found to be much more often involved in slips of the tongue than vowels. The ratio is about 3 : 1 in favour of the consonants. Consider (241–2):

(241) *poppy of my caper* for *copy of my paper*
(242) *a pope smiker* for *a pipe smoker* (both from Fromkin 1973)

Number (241) documents the transposition of consonants, (242) that of vowels. The predominance of consonant errors is expected in the case of additions and deletions because vowels cannot be easily inserted into, or excised from, a syllable without drastically altering its structure, which often leads to phonotactic abnormalities. In contrast, consonant additions and losses can be tolerated much more easily. However, in substitutions, the most common error type, vowels could theoretically be affected as easily as consonants. That they are not points to a greater inherent error-proneness of consonants as compared to vowels. Consonants and vowels also differ in the way they are perceived by listeners. Whereas consonants are perceived categorically, vowels tend to be perceived continuously. The showpiece of categorical perception is the discrimination of voiced and voiceless consonants. When presented with artificial stimuli in which voice onset time (VOT) is systematically varied, subjects identify bilabials as voiced below + 30 ms. but as voiceless above + 30 ms. VOT (Lisker and Abramson 1970). Thus from the perceptual point of view there is a sharp boundary between voiced and voiceless consonants. The area of indeterminacy is minimal. This shows that listeners perceive consonants in either/or fashion and that they are insensitive to variations above or below the critical + 30 ms. mark.

Remarkably, the picture is radically different for vowels which are perceived in continuous fashion (e.g. Studdert-Kennedy 1976). That is, the perceptual boundaries between two adjacent elements in the vowel space are fuzzy rather than sharp. By implication, listeners are not as consistent and confident in their decisions as to stimulus identity. It is important to point out that they are perfectly capable of perceiving even minor acoustic differences, but they are unsure of how to interpret them in phonological terms. This uncertainty makes the perception of vowels particularly susceptible to contextual influences.

The differential strategies with which listeners cope with consonants and vowels have certain implications for language change. Given that consonants are subject to categorical perception, fluctuations in their articulatory implementation are likely to be ignored or filtered out by the listener. In other words, even in the face of unstable productions, the listeners' perceptions remain stable (at least as long as the categorical boundaries are not crossed). This robustness means that listeners should hinder or even prevent the diffusion of an incipient change, i.e. their activity should preserve the nature of the consonants. In the case of vowels, by contrast, listeners cannot block the changes in such an efficient manner. Because clear perceptual boundaries are missing, a change from one vocalic category into another is relatively easy. If the speaker's deviation has certain systematic traits, which might derive from the syntagmatic context, listeners may 'make sense' of this variation, interpret it in systematic fashion, and in this way promote an incipient change. Thus the workings of the perceptual mechanism are such that the chances of a successful consonant or vowel change are vastly different. The prediction for language change from the perceptual perspective is that consonant change should be less common than vowel change.

Again, productive and perceptual principles lead to conflicting predictions regarding the nature of sound change. Given the assumed priority of perception, the bias of the perceptual mechanism serves as the basis for the formulation of relevant predictions. Although the perceptual constraints invoked here are assumed to be universal, the main focus in what follows will be upon English.

There is no question that, from Proto-Indo-European times to this day, vowels have changed in much more radical ways than consonants: the imbalance between vowel and consonant changes is overwhelming. Let us briefly retrace the history of English sounds.[7]

From West Germanic to Old English, the vowel system was drastically restructured. Breaking and umlaut not only produced new monophthongs and diphthongs but also changed the quality of many established vowels. A similar influence can be attributed to palatalization. Although contextually limited, monophthongization also contributed to a severe restructuring which involved almost all diphthongs. In addition, the length of the vowels was seriously affected (see section 5.6).

---

[7] The following standard manuals have served as sources of reference: Campbell (1959); Lehnert (1973); Jordan (1974); Mossé (1952); and Ekwall (1975).

In contrast, the consonantal changes were less numerous, applied less across the board, and were more contextually determined. Voiceless fricatives underwent intervocalic voicing while some voiced fricatives were devoiced in final positions. The velar stops were palatalized. Also, two new consonants, [tʃ] and [ʃ], came into being. The other changes are relatively minor.

This situation is essentially replicated during the transition from Old English to Middle English. If anything, the asymmetry was even more skewed. The consonant system survived the Middle English period virtually without modification. The very few changes that took place were regionally limited. This stability is all the more remarkable as there was a great influx of French loanwords, which were phonologically integrated into the English consonant system. However, the vowel system changed massively. The old diphthongs were monophthongized and many new diphthongs were created. The high front rounded vowels began to disappear. Some vowels were raised and, especially in unstressed positions, underwent merging. Not all length distinctions were retained. As in Old English, long vowels were shortened and short vowels were lengthened (under particular circumstances).

The phonological development from Middle English to modern times lends itself well to a more quantitative treatment. A major advantage over the older periods is the reliability of the data. The sixteenth century marks the beginning of the publication of works which provide information about the pronunciation of words. The evolution of each sound can therefore be traced relatively accurately. A list has been compiled of all the sounds which underwent a change and those which did not. The result is that 85 per cent of the consonants (22 out of 26) survived unscathed, whereas three-quarters of the vowels (13 out of 17) underwent a qualitative change. This is a rather conservative estimate because the amendments in the consonant system concerned items of very low type or token frequency. Granting each change the same weight, the disparate vulnerability of consonants and vowels is fairly obvious. The research hypothesis is thus fully supported.

Compared to English, other languages were typically slower in their development, but in general they also attest to the greater instability of vowels as compared to consonants. One minor exception to this pattern comes from the history of Continental Spanish, whose vowel system has remained virtually unchanged over the past 500 years (Penny 1991). However, it has to be added at once that the consonant system has also been fairly stable, and that the conservativeness of Continental Spanish is quite unusual. The Middle and South American varieties of Spanish are much more progressive as regards vowel development.

To conclude, the prediction that vowels are more subject to change than consonants has been shown to be borne out in the history of English. It is claimed, therefore, that the explanation for the differing vulnerability of consonants and vowels is rooted in psycholinguistics. More precisely, perceptual rather than productive constraints are argued to be responsible for this difference.

5.8. Repair Strategies in Sound Change

Almost by definition, segmental substitutions in speech errors as well as diachronic sound changes are isolated events which affect a particular element and leave its syntagmatic context unruffled. This is made possible by the fact that languages allow a certain degree of freedom in the way segments may be put together to form a linear string. However, there are limits to this freedom. The question therefore arises as to what happens when a paradigmatic choice conflicts with syntagmatic constraints. One theoretical possibility would be that such conflicts never arise because of some built-in avoidance mechanism. However, this is not so. As will be shown immediately below, phonotactic constraints are powerful enough to deal with these conflicts but they are not powerful enough to prevent them from occurring in the first place.

Two areas will be selected where a conflict between a paradigmatic decision and a syntagmatic constraint arises. One is the well-known prohibition on tauto- and heterosyllabic nasal + stop sequences (see section 4.11.1). Nasals adjust their place-of-articulation feature to that of the following stop. We thus have [nt] in *lint*, [ŋk] in *link*, and [mp] in *limp*. Other nasals are not allowed in these contexts. Note in passing that these phonotactic rules are less strict in German than in English: while German prohibits [ŋt], it licenses both [nt] and [mt]. Given these constraints, how does the context react to a nearby slip of the tongue? More precisely, does the nasal accommodate to an intruding stop which differs from the intended one in terms of its place feature? This question can be answered in the affirmative. A pertinent case is given in (243) below.

The other area concerns the alternation of palatal and velar fricatives in German. Omitting certain complications, the palatal fricative appears after front vowels whereas the velar fricative is appropriate after a back vowel. We thus have *Dach* [dax] 'roof' vs. *Dächer* [dɛçɛr] 'roofs'. This phonological process is not blocked by syllable boundaries. By analogy with nasal assimilation discussed above, it will be asked whether an error on the tone vowel is accompanied by a switch of the neighbouring fricative. This situation is illustrated in (244).

(243) *The* [rænd] *orker of the subjects* for [ræŋk] *order* (from Fromkin 1973)
(244) G: *Hast Du in Braunschwach– schweig einmonatige Kündigung?*
        [braunʃvax   ʃvaıç]
'Have you got a one month's notice in Brunswick?'

The stops /d/ and /k/ take each other's position in (243). If no concomitant repair had happened, this malfunction would have placed an alveolar stop next to a velar nasal. However, the sequence [ŋd] did not see the light of day, for the velar nasal turned into an alveolar one. In (244), the diphthong /aı/ is replaced by the monophthong /a/. This creates a velar context for the palatal fricative. The fricative adjusts itself to the back vowel and surfaces as [x]. Examples (243–4) are typical in that accommodation is the rule (albeit not exceptionless—see section 4.13).

These patterns allow the following predictions to be made regarding linguistic change. When a consonant change occurs near a vowel, the nasal should be changed as well. In other words, a secondary sound change should take place. Similarly, when a back vowel is changed to a front vowel (or vice versa) near a palatal or velar fricative, the latter should also be involved. It can also be predicted that the accommodatory process occurs concurrently with the primary change. Differently put, there should not be a stage at which the primary process has already taken place but the secondary process has not. Evidently, these predictions rest upon the assumption that the phonotactic constraints at issue were operative at the time to which the predictions are intended to refer. The more general hypothesis that emerges from the psycholinguistic results is that sound change should not normally[8] alter the phonotactic rules of the language.

There are three ways in which the critical context of a nasal (or a palatal/velar fricative, for that matter) may change. The critical segment may be replaced by another one, a new segment may be inserted between the dominant and the recessive element, and the deletion of the dominant element may promote a new segment into the critical position.

Unfortunately, these predictions are difficult to test, despite their clarity. This is because of the ambiguity of the written records. Since the digraphs <ch> and <gh> stood for both the palatal and the velar fricatives, there is no way of pinning down a possible change from the one sound to the other. By the same token, since the grapheme <n> represented both the velar and the alveolar nasal, a change from the one place specification to the other would not be detectable. In view of this state of affairs, the testing-ground is limited to the alveolar and bilabial nasals, for which separate symbols were in use.

(245) *hindber* → Mod.G. *Himbeere* 'raspberry'
(246) *anebo* → Mod.G. *Amboß* 'anvil' (both from Paul 1916)

In both cases, segment deletion created a new environment for the nasal. The alveolar consonant was dropped in (245) and the mid vowel in (246). These losses created an adjacency between an alveolar nasal and a bilabial stop. As predicted, the nasal took on the place feature of the stop even though the two segments were separated by a syllable boundary. Within-syllable influences are at a premium because final stops almost never change their place specification.

Though scant, the available data suggest that primary sound changes may be accompanied by repair strategies. This result is consonant with the psycholinguistic prediction. It seems that the repair strategies took place concurrently with the primary sound changes. There is no evidence attesting to spellings such as *Hinbeere* and *Anboß*.

---

[8] This qualification is necessary, as speech errors may violate phonotactic rules. Such cases are not common, but they attest to the fact that these rules may be overridden in processing for spontaneous speech. This is why they should not be sacrosanct in language change. This prediction, too, is in accordance with the empirical facts.

5.9. The Special Nature of /sC/ Clusters

It is a truism that there exist systematic relationships between phonological segments and the contexts that they occur in. Not all segments are equally appropriate in all positions. This is not only true of singleton segments but also of segment sequences both within and across syllables. Sequences such as /lk/ and /nd/ are common in intrasyllabic final sites as well as in intersyllabic medial sites, but not in word- or syllable-initial ones. One way of capturing phonotactic regularities is the 'sonority sequence principle'. It states essentially that less sonorous segments precede more sonorous ones in the prevocalic domain, whereas the opposite holds good in the postvocalic domain. Although this principle is of quite some generality, some recalcitrant data remain. In particular, /s/ + stop clusters have proven quite challenging. Despite the fact that they have a decreasing-sonority profile, they are not at all unusual in prevocalic positions.

The sonority sequence principle is a tentative generalization, not an explanation. However, it throws into relief the areas where one might begin to look for processing particularities. That English word-initial /s/ + stop clusters are indeed special has been shown by Stemberger and Treiman (1986). They examined both naturally occurring and experimentally elicited slips of the tongue, and found that generally the first constituent of a word-initial consonant cluster is accessed more reliably than the second. However, when the cluster begins with /s/, the incidence of loss of the first constituent is higher than when it does not. A pertinent example is provided in (247).

(247) *So I assume it's probably till cheaper* for *still cheaper* (from Stemberger and Treiman 1986)

The higher loss rate of the first part of /sC/ clusters testifies to a certain vulnerability of the alveolar fricative in this position and context. It is remarkable that the higher loss rate is not paralleled by a higher addition rate in the speech error data.

One reason for the vulnerability of the /s/ can be deduced from a set of syllabification experiments carried out by Treiman and Zukowski (1990), who compared the frequency with which, let us say, /st/ and /dr/ clusters were treated as a unit or split up in intervocalic positions. The authors found that the syllable boundary was placed before the /dr/ cluster whereas the /st/ cluster tended to be broken up. In a follow-up study, Treiman et al. (1992) examined the /sC/ clusters in greater detail. They reasoned that the specialness of these sequences might stem either from their inverted sonority contour or from the alveolar fricative itself. Therefore, other clusters such as /sl/ and /sn/ were included in the stimulus set. Treiman et al. discovered that *all* /sC/ clusters evinced a reduced degree of cohesiveness as compared to non-/sC/ clusters. The nature of the second element, and by implication the inverted sonority contour, appeared to be largely irrelevant. Thus, the alveolar fricative is at the heart of the instability of /sC/ clusters. This instability arguably follows from the tendency of the /s/ to associate itself with the preceding syllable. We may conclude, then, that /sC/ sequences display a certain degree of heterosyllabicity. Where possible, these clusters fall apart in that their individual consonants distribute across different syllables. This is possible in intervocalic but not in word-initial loci.

So what happens when /s/ + stop clusters appear at the beginnings of words? Granting that /s/ + stop combinations are subject to a force which destabilizes them, we may predict the occurrence of certain 'repair mechanisms' which work towards the elimination of these structures. Four problem-solving strategies suggest themselves. The cluster may be destroyed by deleting either the first or the second consonant. As argued above, the alveolar fricative is probably more vulnerable than the following stop because the former is mainly responsible for the instability of the cluster. The third possibility is to break up the cluster by inserting a vowel. Finally, a vowel can be added to the very beginning of a word, which would have the effect of shifting the cluster from initial to medial position. In this way, a new syllable is created to which the first constituent of the cluster may attach and the tautosyllabic cluster is eliminated. The prediction is, then, that whatever repair strategies are involved, they are applied to /sC/ clusters but not to others.

In fact, the expected repair mechanisms *have* made their appearance in the history of Indo-European languages. We will look at two areas, one involving vowel prothesis and the other the loss of the /s/. Perhaps the best-known relevant example is e-prothesis in Western Romance. Latin words beginning with /sp/, /st/ and /sk/ were regularly augmented by a front mid vowel on their way to the individual western Romance languages, as exemplified in (248).

(248)	Latin	French	Spanish	Portuguese	English gloss
	spiritus	esprit	espíritu	espírito	'spirit'
	studere	étudier	estudiar	estudar	'study'
	scribere	écrire	escribir	escrever	'write'

The examples given in (248) illustrate how the problematic clusters were dispensed with. The prothetic vowel created a new syllable to which the alveolar fricative could attach. The addition of the /ɛ/ to the beginning of the word is an ideal solution because it allows the alveolar fricative to enact its inclination to associate with the left-hand syllable, as was demonstrated in the psycholinguistic studies. An insertion of the vowel between the constituents of the cluster would have precluded this possibility, because the alveolar fricative would then have remained in initial position. Prothesis thus is better motivated than epenthesis in the case at hand. Note also that the choice of /ɛ/ might be connected with its high frequency.

The case of French is particularly interesting in that it shows both repair mechanisms in the same form. As the language that has progressed the furthest from Latin, it has lost the trouble-maker /s/ in all /st-/ and /sk-/ words (with concomitant lengthening of the vowel). There is thus a relative chronology in that the e-prothesis must have preceded the deletion of the fricative.

It is noteworthy that the e-prothesis affected /s/ + stop clusters but did not extend to other /sC/ sequences. This is not directly predicted by Treiman et al.'s

(1992) results. It is tempting to relate this difference to the sonority characteristics of the two cluster types. Whereas the /s/ + stop clusters have an inverted sonority contour, the sonority contour of the other /sC/ structures is unremarkable. Because of their violation of the sonority sequence principle, /s/ + stop clusters are more 'offensive' than other sequences and therefore have to be worked upon first. Although this explanation has a certain appeal, a much more straightforward one is available. The restriction of e-prothesis to /s/ + stop clusters follows from the nature of /sC/ clusters in Latin. Word-initial clusters beginning with /s/ almost invariably had a voiceless stop in second position. /s/ + sonorant clusters practically did not exist. Trivially enough, if there are no such clusters, there is no opportunity for them to be preceded by a prothetic vowel. As a consequence, the historical data do not argue against the general instability of /sC/ clusters in word-initial sites.

The second development to be dealt with focuses more directly upon the status of the alveolar fricative. Specifically, Proto-Germanic allowed the alternation of words with or without an initial /s/. This phenomenon goes by the name of *mobile /s/*. That these words are not independent lexemes but rather formal variants of the same lexeme is most evident from the semantic bond between them. Quite often, the two words are synonymous as in Lat. *taurus* vs. G *Stier*. The chronology of the development of this alternation is not known as both variants turn up in the earliest documentation available.

In congruence with the psycholinguistic findings, the alveolar fricative can be mobile in front of any following consonant; it did not matter whether the /s/ formed part of an orthodox or unorthodox cluster (as determined by sonority contour). However, the predictions for both cluster types are slightly different. Nothing unusual is expected for /s/ + sonorant sequences. One and the same sonorant may or may not be preceded by the alveolar fricative. By contrast, certain phonotactic constraints have to be observed for /s/ + stop structures. The alveolar fricative can only be followed by a voiceless, not by a voiced stop. So when an /s/ is placed before a voiced stop, a phonotactic conflict arises. This conflict may be resolved by changing the voicing feature, as can be observed in (249). It has been claimed that the stop following the /s/ is an archiphoneme unspecified for voicing (Stemberger 1983). This implies that when the fricative is removed from the onset cluster, a voiced stop may see the light of day. Again, this is what can be observed in speech errors such as (250).

(249) G: *Stocktor von Schmidt* for *Doktor von Schmidt.*[9]
   [ʃtɔktoːr fɔn ʃmɪt   dɔktoːr]
   'Dr Smith'
(250) *in your really gruffy– scruffy clothes* (from Stemberger 1983)

No. (249) attests the addition of the palato-alveolar fricative from [ʃmɪt] to the onset of [dɔktoːr]. The resultant cluster /ʃt/ shows that the second obstruent

---

[9] Note that the German palato-alveolar fricative and the English alveolar fricative are entirely parallel in their behaviour in these clusters (Berg 1994).

underwent devoicing. The opposite process is exemplified in (250). The deletion of the fricative from the /skr-/ cluster does not leave the sequence /kr/ behind. Interestingly, the velar stop undergoes voicing.

These production mechanisms allow for the following prediction. If the presence of /s/ alternates with its absence before a stop, the variant with /s/ should have a voiceless stop whereas the variant without /s/ should, at least sometimes, begin with its voiced congener.

The historical data bear out this prediction. The following word pairs are all taken from Siebs (1904). Cases (251–3) exemplify /s/ + sonorant clusters, (254–6) /s/ + stop clusters. The forms without /s/ appear in the left-hand column, those beginning with /s/ in the right-hand column.

(251) OE *meltan*—OHG *smelzen* 'to melt'
(252) OE *liccian*—ON *sleikja* 'to lick'
(253) OHG *weibôn*—OHG *sweibôn* 'to sway'
(254) OI *paśyati*—Av. *spasyeˊti* 'see (3 Sg.)'
(255) Lat. *cutis*—Lat. *scūtum* 'shelter'
(256) Gal. *tarvos*—OE *steor* 'bull'
(257) IG **bhelg*—IG **sphelg* 'split'
(258) Latv. *gīdrs*—Lith. *skaidrùs* 'bright'
(259) Goth. *danus*—OE *stéam* 'steam'

The examples give evidence of the 'neighbour-blindness' of the mobile /s/: it may be found before any consonant, be it an obstruent or a sonorant. As predicted by the speech-error data, there is not only an alternation between /s/ + voiceless stop vs. voiceless stop as in (254–6), but also between /s/ + voiceless stop vs. voiced stop, as in (257–9). This alternation is expected if an archisegmental representation of the stop in /st/, /sk/, and /sp/ clusters is assumed. This allows the stop to appear as a voiced variant in word-initial position. The parallel between the speech error in (250) and the historical data in (257–9) is striking indeed.

What is most important in the present context is that no consonant other than the alveolar fricative is able to alternate in this way. One interpretation of this fact is that the /sC/ clusters are not ideal word onsets. The problem that these clusters face is entirely due to the alveolar fricative which tries to distance itself from any following consonant. On this account, the most likely chronology is that the alternating word pairs came into existence through the loss rather than the addition of /s/. The addition would be unmotivated because singleton stops are good onsets and thus do not have to be repaired. In keeping with this, there was no significant tendency to add an /s/ in front of a stop in the Stemberger and Treiman (1986) study. The loss, in contrast, can be straightforwardly motivated by the inherent instability of the alveolar fricative before a consonant. While the reasons for this instability are controversial,[10] it is clear that the weakness has a psycholinguistic origin.

---

[10] Stemberger and Treiman (1986) link the instability of the /s/ in adult processing to a production difficulty of this sound in child language. This may not be correct, because the same reasoning would

Siebs (1904) assigns the /s/ the status of a prefix or at least the relic of a former prefix. This function would grant the alveolar fricative a certain independence from the following material (the 'stem') in that a morpheme boundary would then separate them. According to this view, the morphological independence of the /s/ would be at the core of its mobile nature. This hypothesis is difficult to verify because the historical sources do not allow us to pin down the meaning of the assumed prefix. Viewed in the light of the processing principles discussed above, the prefix hypothesis is not needed to explain the instability of the /s/. It appears less arbitrary to claim that the problem is located at the phonological rather than the morphological level. The alveolar fricative is inherently difficult to access in word-initial consonant clusters.

Summarizing, the point has been made that the germ of phonological changes of long ago can be found in certain characteristics of the speaker's processing system. It has been argued that the voiceless alveolar fricative suffers difficulties of access in language production in word-initial loci, difficulties which it shares with no other consonant. This property has repercussions for the way /sC/ clusters develop over time. The history of the Indo-European languages documents the problematical status of these clusters. The processing problem is solved either by obliterating the troublesome fricative or by distributing the cluster across different syllables and thereby placing the /s/ in a position where it is less difficult to access. No comparable repair strategies seem to exist for other consonants. The psycholinguistic prediction is thus confirmed.

One of the remaining puzzles is that the difficulty of access would let us expect that /sC/ clusters should be rather infrequent. However, this is not generally true. /sC/ clusters abound in the Germanic languages, with the inverted-sonority clusters (i.e. /s/ + stop) greatly exceeding the clusters with orthodox sonority contours (i.e. /s/ + sonorant) in frequency. In English, /s/ + stop clusters are among the most frequent consonant sequences in word-initial positions (Trnka 1966). They are thus much more common than the clusters with a reversed order of their constituents, to wit: /ts/, /ks/, and /ps/. Hence, a force must exist which is strong enough to oppose the tendency of eliminating /sC/ combinations. One possible explanation has been offered by Heike (1992). He attributes the frequency of /sC-/ and /ʃC-/ clusters and the infrequency of /Cs-/ and /Cʃ-/ clusters to differences in ease of articulatory control. While it is relatively easy to move from a fricative to a stop, it is more difficult to move from a release phase to a constriction which requires very precise articulatory control. The popularity and the instability of /s/ + stop clusters might thus be a spin-off of opposing forces at low and high levels of processing.

---

lead us to expect problems of access in adult language for all sounds that children find hard to acquire (e.g. velar stops). However, as argued in this section, the crucial aspect of the /s/ is that it possesses unique characteristics which it shares with no other consonant.

5.10. Palatalization

An interesting question in the psycholinguistic analysis of phoneme systems is whether some segments are inherently stronger than others. A good way to determine whether segment strength is a psychologically real concept is to explore substitution patterns in slips of the tongue. The argument is straightforward. If a given unit is stronger than another, it should replace others rather than being replaced by them. Such an asymmetry may be due to frequency of occurrence. If a given segment /A/ is more common than /B/ in general language usage, /A/ may be expected to supplant /B/ more often than vice versa. Frequency-based strength effects occur in processing (Levitt and Healy 1985), but they will not be dealt with here. The topic of this section is frequency-independent strength effects.

Shattuck-Hufnagel and Klatt (1979) published an analysis of a large corpus of English speech errors and examined it for possible asymmetries in the substitution patterns. They found that in general the likelihood of /A/ replacing /B/ is as high as that of /B/ replacing /A/. However, they noted one (and only one) major exception. Palato-alveolar segments are stronger than alveolar ones. In particular, the palato-alveolar fricative /ʃ/ replaces its alveolar congener /s/ significantly more often than vice versa.[11] A typical example is given in (260), a less typical one in (261).

(260) *And show she just cashed it* for *and so*
(261) *seventy percent to so– show that it's not random* (both from Stemberger 1991)

The palato-alveolar fricative ousts the alveolar fricative in (242) whereas the opposite happens in (243). In Shattuck-Hufnagel's corpus, /s/ → /ʃ/ errors are twice as frequent as /ʃ/ → /s/ errors. Exactly the same trend emerges in my German database. It may therefore be claimed to have some cross-linguistic validity.[12]

The prediction that can be erected upon this finding is obvious. The alveolar fricative should develop into its palato-alveolar cognate more frequently than vice versa.

The unequal strength of /ʃ/ and /s/ comes out very clearly in the history of German (Paul 1916). The alveolar fricative turned into the palato-alveolar one in word-onset clusters. This change occurred before sonorants (262) as well as obstruents (263–4).

(262) OHG *slahan* → Mod.G *schlagen* [ʃlaːgən] 'to slay'
(263) OHG *stein* → Mod.G *Stein* [ʃtaɪn] 'stone'
(264) OHG *skild* → Mod.G *Schild* [ʃɪlt] 'shield'

The developments exemplified in (262–3) affected the entire lexicon, such that /sl/ and /st/ are impossible word onsets in Standard German. The /sk/ clusters are

[11] There is a similar effect for the palato-alveolar affricate /tʃ/ and the alveolar /t/, which led Shattuck-Hufnagel and Klatt to refer to this asymmetry as a psycholinguistic palatalization mechanism which turns alveolar segments into palato-alveolar ones.

[12] This does not mean, however, that palatalization is of necessity universal in nature. It is quite possible that the psycholinguistic strength of palato-alveolar segments has a language-particular basis.

somewhat different. They also underwent palatalization, with concomitant loss of the velar stop, as in (264). However, /sk/ clusters are not completely absent from Modern German. They are mainly found in loanwords (e.g. *Skandinavien* 'Scandinavia') which entered the language when the historical palatalization process had come to a standstill.

The palatalization of /s/ was not restricted to word onsets. It can be found in other positions, though less consistently. The palatalization process also affected /ts/ which turned into /tʃ/ in some words, as illustrated in (265).

(265) MHG *rutzen* → Mod.G *rutschen* 'to slide'

It is significant that according to Paul (1916), no changes from /ʃ/ to /s/ occurred in the history of German.

English differs from German in that the change from /s/ to /ʃ/ before consonants did not take place. The palatalizations and affricatizations that did occur did not involve the alveolar fricative. However, one process is directly relevant to the research hypothesis. The palato-alveolar fricative was a newcomer to the Old English phoneme system. As in German, it evolved from the diphone /sk/, as exemplified in (266).

(266) OE *wascan* → Mod.E. *to wash*

This process took place in all positions, with the initial positions being slightly ahead of the others. Seeming exceptions are Modern English *school* and *scholar*. These are words in which the Latin pronunciation was deliberately preserved. That palatalization has survived to this day can be seen in words like *issue* and *tissue*, which are in the process of moving from /s/ to /ʃ/ in medial positions.

Paralleling the historical situation in German, English does not appear to have produced any changes from /ʃ/ to /s/.

In conclusion, the diachronic data are entirely compatible with the psycholinguistic prediction. While developments from /s/ to /ʃ/ are documented in both German and English, the reverse process is not. It is argued that underlying this asymmetry is the differential psycholinguistic strength of the two fricatives in question. This strength increases the likelihood of certain historical developments and decreases the likelihood of others.

The following afterthought might be in order. Given that the palatalization effect can be found in the speech errors made by speakers of current English, it may be expected to manifest itself in synchronic patterns as well. This is precisely what happens. Even in speech styles which cannot be regarded as sloppy, the palato-alveolar fricative supplants the alveolar one. This substitution is illustrated by an English example in (267) and by a German one in (268).

(267) *gas shortage* → [gæʃʃɔːtɪdʒ]
(268) *bloßstellen* [bloːsʃtɛlən] → [bloːʃʃtɛlən] 'to compromise'

The disappearance of the /s/ in (267–8) leads to a lengthening of the palato-alveolar consonant. It bears mentioning that a change from /ʃ/ to /s/ would be utterly out of the question. Nobody would say [gæssɔːtɪdʒ] unless a speech defect is involved or a comic effect is intended.

The unequal strength of /s/ and /ʃ/ also explains the absence of tautomorphemic /sʃ/ sequences in language structure. A search through the CELEX database reveals that not a single word in English has the sequence /sʃ/ either with or without a syllable boundary separating these consonants. Articulatory ease cannot fully account for the absence of /sʃ/, because this sequence is certainly not unpronounceable.

Note that the critical fricatives are separated by a word boundary in (267) and a morpheme boundary in (268).[13] In a way, this boundary serves to protect the alveolar fricative from its palato-alveolar cognate because different words or morphemes are not co-activated to the same extent as different syllables of the same morpheme or word. By contrast, the unequal strength of /s/ and /ʃ/, coupled with their high degree of coactivation within morphemes, implies that /sʃ/ structures are highly unstable. They should therefore be eliminated fairly rapidly (or rather should not arise in the first place). Thus, the prediction derived from processing principles is borne out not only by the diachronic but also by the synchronic evidence.

5.11. The Differential Vulnerability of Word Beginnings and Ends

In this section, the vulnerability of word beginnings and ends to diachronic change will be examined. The terms 'beginning' and 'end' have no morphological status. They divide the phonology of a word into a left-hand and a right-hand portion.

As was shown in section 4.2, slips of the tongue predominantly involve the beginnings of words while the ends are relatively free of them. The processing of word beginnings thus is carried out less reliably than that of word ends in language production.

It is appropriate to begin the discussion of perceptual biases with a purely structural concept—the uniqueness point. Determining the uniqueness point involves examining a word from left to right and finding the segment beyond which the word can be unambiguously distinguished from all others. Each word has its uniqueness point after the last segment or somewhere before (ignoring homophones). For example, the uniqueness point of *woo* occurs at the end of the word because the vowel is the segment which distinguishes *woo* from, let us say, *woe*. In contrast, the word *criterion* has its uniqueness point at the /t/ because there is no other word which begins with the segment sequence /kraɪt/. Luce (1986) carried out a computational analysis of uniqueness points in the English lexicon. His investigation of 20,000 individual lexical items indicates that the majority of words have their uniqueness point *before* the last segment, provided their length exceeds five

---

[13] Recall the discussion of the effects of linguistic boundaries in section 4.17.

segments. Rather unsurprisingly, with an increase in word length the uniqueness point is more likely to occur earlier in the word.

Psycholinguists are interested not so much in the uniqueness point but in the recognition point of a word, i.e. the moment at which a mental representation is retrieved on the basis of the acoustic signal. It was noted in section 4.12 that the process of word recognition is not delayed until the complete acoustic signal is available. It is therefore possible for recognition to take place before the entire word has been perceived. In point of fact, the uniqueness point has been argued to be a relatively reliable guide to the recognition point even if the former occurs before the last segment (Marslen-Wilson and Welsh 1978; Marcus and Frauenfelder 1985). Marslen-Wilson and Tyler (1975, 1980) showed that subjects were even able to recognize isolated monosyllabic words before their offset. Nouns with an average length of 0.4 sec. were identified at the 0.3 sec. mark.

The recognition point divides a given word into two unequal parts—the left-hand part or beginning, which extends up to the recognition point, and the right-hand part or end, which follows the recognition point. The beginning is of utmost importance because it guides lexical access. In contrast, the end is less essential for successful comprehension because the word has already been identified. In a word, it is redundant.

This difference has clear implications for language change. Since modifications at the beginning of words are more disruptive than those at the end, the perceptual system will tolerate changes in the left-hand part much less than in the right-hand part. The perceptual bias thus conflicts with the asymmetrical processing reliability in production. This conflict is resolved as in the previous sections. Listening strategies are expected to prevail because asymmetries produced by the speaker can be at least partly offset by the listener but not vice versa. These perceptual biases will be detailed below.

What kinds of historical change does the psycholinguistic analysis predict? Basically, the ends would be free to erode without compromising the listener's decoding task. In short, these parts may be lost. This development evidently has to be understood within the context of the speaker's drive towards economy of expression. Following the principle of least effort, no more is done in fulfilment of a particular aim than is necessary. So speakers may, and actually do, articulate the ends less carefully than the beginnings of words (e.g. Cooper and Paccia-Cooper 1980). This leads to a related prediction: apart from shortenings, the ends of words should undergo changes from articulatorily more difficult to less difficult segments. To look at it from the other side, changes which are neither productively nor perceptually advantageous should not occur at the ends of words. Another prediction is that longer words should be more receptive to change than shorter ones because the recognition point is further to the left in the former as compared to the latter.

For the beginnings of words, qualitatively and quantitatively different changes are expected. For one thing, they should be far less common; for another they should not be motivated by the speakers' desire to minimize their articulatory effort. These are all fairly constrained predictions which will be tested below.

Note that, in the parallel processing model assumed here, there is no need for beginnings to be entirely immune to change because parallel processing has the effect of relativizing the importance of any part of a word. A processing problem at the beginning, which may be brought about by language change, can be compensated for by parallel processing on the latter parts of the word (see section 4.12). Changes at the beginning thus are not impossible, but are appreciably more difficult to process than changes at the end.

It comes as no surprise that, in line with the psycholinguistic predictions, the ends of words display a greater instability than the beginnings in the history of the Indo-European languages (Gauthiot 1913). Also, the ends of longer words are less stable than those of shorter ones. Almost all Indo-European final consonants disappeared in Proto-Germanic polysyllabic words, but some were retained in monosyllabic ones, as in (269).

(269) PIE *$q\mu od$ → PGerm. $x\mu at$

Through this extremely general process, short vowels were placed in word-final positions and also underwent deletion, as in (270).

(270) PGerm. *$gastiz$ → *$gasti$ → OE $\mathfrak{z}(i)est$ 'guest'

It is interesting to note that the deletion process was contingent upon the weight of the preceding syllable. If this syllable was heavy (i.e. had a branching rime), the vowel in the final syllable was lost; if, however, the first syllable was light (i.e. had a non-branching rime), the final vowel was preserved. This is to be expected, because light syllables are shorter than heavy ones and therefore have their recognition point further to the right than do heavy syllables.

The great number of final vowels is severely cut down from Proto-Indo-European to Old English times. These developments may be seen as a consequence of fixing lexical stress, and have carried through the Old and Middle English periods to this day. In Middle English, the reduction of final vowels had the additional twist of causing the collapse of the inflectional system, which was carried by the endings. The short back final vowels merged into [e], which reduced to schwa and eventually disappeared completely.

(271) OE *sunu* → ME *sone* [sune] → [sunə] → [sun] 'son'

Subsequently, the segments and segment sequences which coded a morphological function followed suit. All these developments are readily interpretable as a reduction of articulatory effort.

In stark contrast, nothing of the kind happened at the beginning of words. Neither consonant or vowel reductions nor complete losses are recorded. The attested substitutions are of two types. The 'high-level' type is documented by Grimm's Law, which also applied to word-initial consonants:

(272) PIE pətēr → OE fæder 'father'

These changes are not triggered by contiguous segments, and respect the phonological similarity constraint between substituting and substituted element. They are neither obviously speaker- nor hearer-oriented in the sense that they facilitate neither the production nor the perception process.

The second 'lower-level' type involves influences between adjacent segments. For instance, the vowel may change the quality of the preceding consonant. In Old English, word onsets underwent palatalization and assibilation under the influence of a front vowel, as in (273).

(273) AS *kinni* = OE *ćin* → *čin* 'chin'

There is no obvious sense in which these developments can be linked to arguments drawing upon ease of production, in particular as affricates involve a more complex articulatory gesture than stops or fricatives. What happens at the beginning of words is thus very different in kind from what can be observed at the ends.

The preceding summary analysis has shown that the material preceding the recognition point proves quite stable historically, while the material following it is subject to erosion. The latter process is of remarkably long range. It dates back to Proto-Germanic times, and finds a natural termination point in the monosyllabicity of morphemes so prevalent today. Of course, not all languages are equally rapid in succumbing to this tendency.[14] English in Germanic and French in Romance are unmistakably in the vanguard of this development.

5.12. The Differential Strength of Reduction Processes in English and Spanish

Reduction processes are quite common in the history of languages. They run through a number of partly predictable stages between the endpoints of full articulation and complete disappearance. Consonant reduction has been found to be segment- and position-dependent. For example, segments in post-initial and pre-final sites are more vulnerable than those in initial and final sites. The weakening of vowels involves such steps as monophthongization, shortening, and bleaching (i.e. reduction to schwa). The final vanishment of a vowel may create syllabic consonants which may also fade out eventually. The starting-point of reduction processes is almost always the unstressed syllable.

These regularities invoke a theme that was discussed in connection with palatalization in section 5.10—the varying strength of linguistic units. In psycholinguistic

---

[14] Note that the psycholinguistic account of the differential vulnerability of word beginnings and ends makes some testable predictions regarding the variable strength of the erosion process. It is not unreasonable to speculate that the recognition point may generally occur earlier in some languages but later in others. The prediction would, of course, be that less erosion will take place in the latter than in the former type of language.

terms, the strength of an element may be construed as the amount of activation it receives during the production process. Evidently, elements which are insufficiently activated fail to be produced. Stronger elements rely upon more activational forces and are therefore more stable. However, the accumulation of activational sources is an energy-consuming task. When it is possible to make do with less, speakers tend towards reduction. That is, they shift to linguistic units which are easier to access because they require less expenditure of activational energy.

Hence, the psycholinguistic system introduces a bias to the effect that elements which are easy to access will gradually replace those which are more difficult to access. Furthermore, those units which implicate lower levels of activation are most likely to be lost over time. Whether such a bias makes an effect upon language change will be examined from the perspective of one activational source and its cross-linguistic variability. This source is lexical stress.

Three individual effects have to be kept apart in the psycholinguistic analysis of stress. First, a stressed syllable accords its segments an activation advantage which segments from unstressed syllables do not obtain. Secondly, vowels, be they stressed or unstressed, receive more activation from the syllable node than consonants because they are the most essential part of the syllable (Berg 1990a).

Thirdly, the allocation of activation to vowels depends upon the position of the syllable in the word. Various lines of evidence have led to the establishment of a pervasive psycholinguistic hierarchy. Initial positions are most reliably accessed, final positions less reliably, and medial positions least reliably. A good illustration of this comes from tip-of-the-tongue studies in which speakers are queried about the partial information that they can retrieve during the phase when they have a word on the tip of their tongue. Brown and McNeill (1966) showed that in these situations speakers provide most accurate information about the initial portion, less accurate information about the final portion, and least accurate information about the medial part of a word. A plausible interpretation of this finding is that the baseline activation for each position within the word is variable. Initial syllables reach the production threshold sooner than final syllables which in turn prevail over medial syllables. All these effects act upon a unit's activation level, which therefore is multiply determined.

It will be assumed that these activational determinants are cross-linguistically valid. The differences that exist among languages reside in their varying sensitivity to lexical stress. Berg (1991a) observed a notable disparity in the processing of stressed and unstressed syllables in English and Spanish. Spanish syllables are less sensitive to stress differences than English syllables. This claim is supported by the following empirical facts. If consonants have a lower stress sensitivity than vowels and Spanish a lower stress sensitivity than English, it should not make a processing difference whether a consonant in Spanish is stressed or unstressed. In fact, Berg reported that the frequency of Spanish consonant errors is not determined by the stress value of the syllable they occur in. Vowels, by contrast, should evince a stress sensitivity even in Spanish. Indeed, unpublished research reveals that vowel errors are more commonly found in stressed than in unstressed syllables in this language. True, consonants and vowels are also differentially treated in English, but because of its higher stress sensitivity this language implements the stress difference not only in vowels but also in consonants. Vowel as well as consonant errors are more frequent in stressed than in unstressed positions.

The processing difference between Spanish and English is best characterized as a gradual one. English displays a general, Spanish a more limited sensitivity to stress. In the latter language, there is less of a difference in the accuracy with which segments in stressed and unstressed loci are retrieved. Specifically, segments are less weakened by the fact that they occur in unstressed positions in Spanish than in English.

This processing difference has intriguing implications for language change. Because phonological units in unstressed syllables are stronger in Spanish than in English, they should be less likely to be worn off in the former than in the latter language. However, this does not mean that an identical development of segments from stressed and unstressed syllables is predicted. Because lexical stress makes an impact, albeit a limited one, upon phonological processing, we may expect that unstressed syllables are generally more subject to reduction processes than stressed ones. At the same time, the unstressed syllables in Spanish should be less subject to reduction than those in English. A further prediction is that the development of Spanish vowels should be sensitive to word position. The most reduction is expected to occur in medial positions, less reduction in final positions, and least reduction in initial positions.

A useful starting-point in the testing of these predictions is the prototypical reduced vowel, schwa. As a matter of fact, schwa is totally absent from Modern Spanish. Like their stressed counterparts, unstressed syllables always contain full vowels. There is no evidence that schwa was a member of the Spanish vowel system in earlier stages of the language. Although there have been vowel mergers and losses (see below), there is no indication that schwa showed up as an intermediate result.[15] In Modern English, however, schwa is the most common vowel occurring in unstressed syllables (Denes 1963).

The general distribution of vowels is the next criterion to be examined. The large differences in the distribution of English vowels in stressed and unstressed syllables were the subject of section 4.9 and will not be repeated here. In keeping with the general expectation, the distribution of Spanish vowels in stressed vs. unstressed syllables is more balanced, though not absolutely so. In contemporary Spanish, all five monophthongs may occur in stressed as well as unstressed sites. Only the complex vowels /iə/ and /ue/ are restricted to stressed syllables. This exception is fully expected because the generation of complex units requires more mental effort and can therefore be carried out more easily in positions which are more strongly activated.

[15] Of course, identifying schwa from the spelling is not an easy task because languages do not usually have a special orthographic symbol for representing its phonetic value.

During the time span from Vulgar Latin to Modern Spanish, the vowel system has remained fairly stable, both in stressed and unstressed syllables (Penny 1991); the few changes that did take place are as predicted. Initial positions were less subject to loss than final ones. Consequently, there is no difference between vowels occurring in stressed and unstressed initial positions. The full array of vowels was preserved in word-initial unstressed syllables. However, the word-final unstressed positions are weaker and therefore more susceptible to loss. Specifically, the two high vowels /i/ and /u/ were dispensed with, a process which had already begun in Vulgar Latin. Of the remaining three vowels /e/, /a/, and /o/, the latter two were almost entirely stable while /e/ was not. In two periods of the history of Castilian Spanish, the front mid vowel was lost in many words (in speaking though not in writing), but was later re-established and survives to this day. The permanent loss of /e/ took place in only a handful of lexical items (274). Similarly, the loss of final /o/ and /a/ was limited to individual words (275).

(274) Lat. *cake* → *coçe* → *coz* 'kick'
(275) *santo* → *san* 'saint'

Again in line with the psycholinguistic prediction, unstressed vowels in the middle of words proved least stable. With the possible exception of /a/, which remained quite immune to loss, all vowels in this position tended towards obliteration, a process whose origins date back to Vulgar Latin times, as in (276).

(276) Lat. *temporanu* → Sp. *temprano* 'early'

There is little doubt, then, that the word positions are differentially effective in protecting vowels from disappearing.

Clearly, vowel reduction and loss are much more prevalent in the history of English. In Early Old English, a process of vowel reduction in final unstressed syllables began whereby /a/, /o/, and /u/ merged in the neutral vowel [ə]. This process culminated in the complete disappearance of the syllable-bearer at the end of the Middle English period. Jordan (1974: 142) claims that the loss of final schwa took place 'in all cases', no matter whether the words were disyllabic or trisyllabic nouns or verbs. The <e> was also reduced and syncopated in medial syllables, as exemplified in (277). A nice example which epitomizes all these developments is given in (278).

(277) OE *fæderas* → ME *fadres* 'fathers'
(278) OE *þanone* → *þanene* → *þanne* → ME *þan* 'then'

It is worthwhile to note that the development from schwa to zero in medial positions is still an active process nowadays. Hooper (1976) showed that schwa in unstressed medial syllables is highly unstable in American English, witness (279).

(279) *history* [hɪstərɪ] → [hɪstrɪ]

It appears that the incidence of vowel reduction and loss is greater in final than in medial syllables in English. At first sight, this result is not exactly predicted on psycholinguistic grounds. However, it should be borne in mind that loss in medial positions has a much lower baseline probability of occurrence because it presupposes words that are at least three syllables long. In Modern English, words of this length are rather uncommon, accounting for no more than 4.6 per cent of the entire vocabulary (Roberts 1965). For this reason alone, it is to be expected that medial-position losses are less outstanding. We might even go a step further, and claim that the infrequency of longer words is evidence of the early demise of medial vowels.

It may be concluded that the differences in the historical development of Spanish and English come out as predicted. Both languages give evidence of the loss of vowels but differ sharply on the quantitative level. Whereas this is a full-scale process in English (in certain positions), it occurs on a much more reduced scale in Spanish. The psycholinguistic explanation of this disparity is that the Spanish processing system gives segments from unstressed syllables more activational power than does English. This makes the phonological structure of Spanish less subject to erosion.

Interestingly, the psycholinguistic account advanced in this section puts some limits on the plausibility of the principle of least effort which is customarily invoked as an explanation of the reduction processes observed in synchrony and diachrony. As English speakers reduce and obliterate on a larger scale than Spanish speakers, it would have to be argued that the former are lazier than the latter. This view cannot be seriously upheld. The alternative suggested by the above analysis is that speakers are 'caged' by the processing mechanisms of the language they speak. While all speakers regardless of language may be assumed to be equally lazy, languages differ in their tolerance of speaker-based reduction strategies. The amount of articulatory reduction allowed by the individual language is not completely under the control of the speaker. Rather, the individual language determines to a certain extent the amount of articulatory sloppiness that a speaker is allowed. To elaborate, the processing system determines on a language-particular basis how and to what extent the principle of least effort is instantiated.

5.13. The Differential Susceptibility of Open- and Closed-Class Items to Phonological Change

The distinction between open-class words and closed-class items is legion in linguistics: it is based upon their differing semantic, syntactic, and phonological properties. Although there are some boundary cases such as adverbs and prepositions, the criteria for assigning a given word (class) to the one or the other subset are generally clear and widely accepted. Bradley (1983) introduced this distinction into psycholinguistics. She argued that closed-class items and open-class words play a differing role in word recognition. In language-production research, function words have been found to be rather immune to error in a double sense. For one thing, they are reluctant to be misordered as wholes (i.e. at the lexical level) (Garrett 1975); for another they successfully defy distortion at the segment level (Dell 1990). Even though both effects are related, the main focus of this section will be on the latter. The general observation, then, is that open-class words are more prone to phonological errors than closed-class items. Two pertinent slips of the tongue follow.

(280)   *It's the red-bood* for *red book* (from Fromkin 1973)
(281)   *There's not as nu– much* (from Stemberger 1984b)

The phonological malfunction affects a noun (an open-class word) in (280) and an adverb (a closed-class item) in (281). The differential vulnerability appears to be independent of the language being examined. Two reasons have been proposed for this effect. On the one hand, the relative immunity of function words to phonological distortion may stem from an inherent difference between open-class words and closed-class items (Rosenberg et al. 1985). In this view, both categories undergo disparate processing operations during language production. On the other hand, the difference between open- and closed-class words may simply emanate from their widely divergent token frequencies. The type/token ratio in open-class words is far lower than in function words. As will be discussed in section 5.17, the processing system is highly sensitive to frequency. High frequency leads to greater reliability in lexical access. Therefore, processing errors on function words are less probable, both at the lexical and at the phonological level. According to the frequency hypothesis, there is no intrinsic difference between open- and closed-class items (Stemberger 1984b).

No matter which hypothesis turns out to be correct, the predictions concerning linguistic change are the same. Because the correct phonological representations of function words are built up with a minimum amount of interference from other items, it can be predicted that the phonological structure of function words should prove relatively stable over time. This prediction will be tested by comparing the Old and Middle English pronoun systems with those of Modern English. The section will be concluded by a brief look at prepositions.

The clearest case is probably that of personal pronouns. Table 23 summarizes the Old English system from which the modern forms are derived. It can readily be seen that this table contains many easily recoverable forms. In fact, quite a few of them are very similar to their modern descendants. This is particularly true of the dative form from which the modern object pronouns are derived. Many phonological discrepancies between the old and the modern forms go back to the Great English Vowel Shift, which did not spare the closed-class items. Some changes which have affected the Modern English forms can be shown to spring from variations which can be retraced to Old English times, such as the dropping of the final consonant in *mīn*. Significantly, most of the glaring differences between Old and Modern English are not induced by phonological change but by replacements of whole forms. For example, all of the 3rd person plural forms have been supplanted in their entirety.

Thus the Middle English system, reproduced in Table 24, is conspicuously close to Modern English. The Middle and Modern English pronoun systems are strikingly similar. Some of the few changes that did take place can be dated towards the end of the Middle English period, e.g. the dropping of /h/, the replacement of the southern forms *here* and *hem* by their northern counterparts *their* and *them* respectively, and the confusion of *thou* and *you* as well as that between *ye* and *you*. As noted, the Great English Vowel Shift turned the Middle English forms into their current pronunciations, while their spelling remained largely unaffected. The forms of the 2nd person plural have been extended to the 2nd person singular. However, this has not led to their complete disappearance. Even though *thou* and *thee* are unmistakably archaic, they still belong to the vocabulary of Modern English.

It transpires, then, that personal pronouns were extremely conservative in their development, more conservative in fact than open-class words in general. Phonological changes have been very slow in coming, with a long-standing fluctuation between (dialectal) variants of which one was closer to the modern form than the other. This conservativeness can also be observed at the morphosyntactic level. The personal pronouns retained the dual longer than the open-class words. While nouns, verbs, and adjectives got rid of it in Old English, the pronouns of the 1st and 2nd person continued to honour this category for some time. Note also that the distinction between subject and object forms has been retained to this day in the pronoun system though not anywhere else.

Personal pronouns could also be used as reflexives in Old English. In an effort to keep the two senses formally apart, *self* was added to the genitive forms of the personal pronouns. Lounsbury (1970) notes that the 1st and 2nd person forms *myself*, *thyself*, and *yourself* established themselves during the Old English period; they have preserved their orthographic structure to this day. For the 3rd person forms, the

TABLE 23. *The Old English personal pronoun system (from Lounsbury 1970)*

	1 sg.	2 sg.	3 sg.	1 pl.	2 pl.	3 pl.
Nominative	ic	þu	hē, hēo, hit	wē	gē	hī
Genitive	mī(n)	þi(n)	his, hire, his	ūre	ēower	hira
Dative	mē	þē	him, hire, him	ūs	ēow	him
Accusative	mec, mē	þē(c)	hine, hēo/hi, hit	ūs(ic)	ēow(ic)	hī

TABLE 24. *The Middle English personal pronoun system (from Lounsbury 1970)*

	1 sg.	2 sg.	3 sg.	1 pl.	2 pl.	3 pl.
Nominative	I	thou	he, she (h)it	we	ye	they
Genitive	mi(n)	thi(n)	his, hire, his	oure	youre	here
Object case	me	thee	him, hire, (h)it	us	you	hem

dative and accusative of the personal pronouns served as the basis for the creation of the reflexives, giving *himself, herself, itself,* and *hemself.* The formal coding of number on the reflexive pronouns, which began in Early Modern English, represents a morphological rather than a phonological innovation. Clearly, then, the reflexive pronouns are another illustration of the unwillingness of function words to undergo phonological change.

The modern English possessive pronouns have evolved from the genitive case of the personal pronouns. Setting aside the feminine and neuter 3rd person singular and the 3rd person plural forms, which underwent a special development, it is obvious from Tables 23 and 24 that the Old and Middle English forms are phonologically similar to the Modern English ones. This holds good of both the attributive and the predicative forms of the possessive. Their behaviour is thus akin to the other types of pronoun reviewed above.

The demonstrative pronouns exemplify an exceptionally high degree of phonological constancy. The Old English singular forms from which the modern ones developed have almost fully retained their phonological integrity. The paradigm case is Modern English *this*, which goes back to Old English *þis*. Apart from the voicing of the initial consonant which is so typical of closed-class items, nothing has changed. The case of Modern English *that* is similar. It also goes back to the neuter nominative/accusative form, namely Old English *þæt*. Like *þis*, it is subject to voicing in initial position. The identity of the vowel in the Old and Modern English forms is probably misleading. The Old English vowel underwent lowering and returned to its original position in Early Modern English. However, it is worth noting that the form *þaet* also existed in the southern dialects of Middle English.

Unfortunately, the Modern English plural forms *these* and *those* have no straightforward etymology. Modern English *these* and *those* appear to be retraceable to Old English *þis* and *þās*, respectively. Since *þis* was a singular form, it received *-e*, the plural marker of adjectives. Faiß (1989) argues that the vowel change in *þise* is motivated by the desire to increase the formal distinctness between the singular and the plural form. Old English *þās* developed into Middle English *þo(o)s*. Whether this is a forerunner of the Modern English form is doubtful (Faiß 1989). In any case, the system of demonstrative pronouns as it operates today has established itself only in Early Modern English. Thus, while the plural forms have seen a complex development, the phonology of the singular forms exhibits a remarkable robustness.

A number of relative pronouns in Modern English are not formally distinct from interrogative pronouns (e.g. *who* and *which*). In order to retrace their phonological development, a look at interrogative pronouns may therefore suffice. Interrogative pronouns are moderately susceptible to sound change. Modern English *who* goes back to Old English *hwā, whom* to *hwam, whose* to *hwæs, what* to *hwæt, why* to *hwy, which* to *hwik, whether* to *hwæðer,* and *how* to *hū.* In Middle English, the letters <hw> were reversed. The reduction of Old English [hw] to Middle English [w] certainly represents a minimal phonetic change, which affected all interrogative pronouns with the exception of *hwa*. The vowels were rather unstable. Some changes date back to Middle English, e.g. /æ/ → /a/ in *what*, others are fairly recent, e.g. /a/ → /ɒ/ in *what* and /iː/ → /aɪ/ in *why*. The consonantal changes are few and regular, such as the disappearance of the /l/ before /tʃ/ in *which*. It can be concluded that the interrogative pronouns are vulnerable to vowel change but that their consonantal structure remained largely the same.

The recognizability of Old English forms can also be seen in the case of indefinite pronouns. While many have died out or altered their function, the phonological forms of those which have survived can often be found to be similar to those in Old English. Here are some examples, all of which document a change from Old to Modern English: *all* → *all*, *sum* → *some*, *ǣni* → *any*, *nauht* → *naught*, *nān* → *none*. Of course, not all instances are as favourable to the research hypothesis as the ones mentioned, but it is clear that a strong potential for preserving their phonological shape cannot be denied for indefinite pronouns. This potential does not, however, exempt them completely from phonological change, especially in the vocalic domain.

Finally, prepositions will be briefly examined. As function words, they should follow the same trends as pronouns. Although the function of the forerunners of the Modern English prepositions was quite different in Old English, their phonology looks surprisingly modern. A good number of examples follow, all of which show the development from the Old to the Modern English form: *æt* → *at*, *æfter* → *after*, *from* → *from*, *under* → *under*, *bī* → *by*, *ofer* → *over*, *to* → *to*, *on* → *on*, *of* → *of*, *wiþ* → *with*. Even though the identity of spelling is slightly deceptive, the constancy of these forms over time is impressive. This constancy is also remarkable in view of the many semantic and syntactic changes that the prepositions have undergone.

By way of summary, a good deal of evidence has been marshalled in support of the claim that function words exhibit a high degree of phonological conservativeness. However, they are not immune to change—nor could they be expected to be, given such radical restructurings as the Great Vowel Shift and the fact that the basic principles of lexical access apply to open-class words and closed-class items alike.

5.14. Paradigmatic Pressure towards Pattern Symmetry

In the processing model that underlies the present work, the phonological component is organized into three separate levels—a suprasegmental, a segmental, and a subsegmental. Only the latter two are of interest in the ensuing discussion. Each level consists of a set of homogeneous units. Surprisingly perhaps, the elements at each level form an unstructured set. There is no intra-level organization; the only extant organization is of an indirect, inter-level kind. To be specific, the lower level imposes a structure upon the higher one. This is accomplished by vertical connections between the feature and segment levels. Each segment establishes connections with its features. The phoneme /b/, for example, connects to the features [bilabial], [stop], and [voiced]. Because each feature is represented by only one node, it is a junction of several connections. The node [bilabial], for instance, is linked to the segments /m/, /b/, and /p/.

Phonological features may differ on the number of connections that reach into the segment level. While [voiceless] has a dozen or so such connections, the feature [glottal] only has one in English. Given the principle that information spreads in parallel between the levels, the retrieval of a particular unit is not a local event but is influenced by the structure of the entire processing system. When a voiceless segment is accessed, it activates not only the feature [voiceless] but also, via this node, all other voiceless segments. These, in turn, return their activation to the feature level, thereby supporting the activation of the [voiceless] node as well as that of the segment node to whom they owe their activation in the first place. Obviously, the higher the number of connections, the greater the support for a particular unit. Thus, /p/ receives much support from the system (as there are other bilabial elements with whom it is connected) whereas /h/ receives little support (as there are no other glottal elements). Hence, the /p/ may be said to be well integrated and the /h/ ill integrated into the system.

Note that integration is a matter of degree (Martinet 1955) and depends upon the individual integrating feature being considered. Both the bilabial stop and the glottal fricative are well integrated in terms of the voice feature. However, the glottal fricative, though not the bilabial stop, is ill integrated on the place dimension. Each phoneme can therefore be said to have an individual integration index. It is not entirely clear how the integration index is best calculated. The easiest way would be to count the number of dimensions on which a given segment is well integrated or not so well integrated. However, it is not known whether all dimensions are equally important. Therefore, the integration index can only be derived approximately.

The degree of integration has important consequences for the access of linguistic elements. Since integration means support from the members of a given level, it is clear that the higher the integration, the easier the access will be. This argument is based upon theory-internal grounds but can also be substantiated empirically. A unit's activation level is standardly gauged by the likelihood with which it outweighs its competitors. Competition effects can be ideally observed in slips of the tongue. It was shown in section 4.15 that the length of the target vowel remains unchanged in German errors, while it may change in English ones. The retention of the length value in German and its modification in English attest to the differential strength of this feature in the two languages. In German, the length value of the target is more strongly activated than in English. This strength makes the target powerful enough to rebuff any intruding segment in terms of its quantity. In English, by contrast, the target's length feature is less strongly activated and therefore has to yield to the length specification of the error unit.

Berg (1988b) argued that this processing difference follows from the differential integration of length in the vowel systems of German and English. Length is perfectly integrated in German, where it exhaustively classifies the vowel system into seven long and seven short monophthongs. The situation is different for English, however, where length does not separate the monophthongs into two symmetrical sets. There are only a few correlational pairs, with one or two being of dubious status. Some long (or short) vowels do not have a short (or long) counterpart. The non-optimal classificatory nature of length is responsible for its lower activational strength and thus accounts for its relative weakness in slips of the tongue. We may conclude from this that the empirical data are in keeping with the basic assumptions of the processing model.

The notion of differential support for individual segments during their access has clear implications for the direction of language change. These implications can be subdivided into three parts according to the three logical possibilities of addition to, deletion from, and preservation in the lexicon. The deletion of a unit is all the more likely the less well it is integrated in the lexicon. Inversely, the probability of preserving a unit is higher when its integration index is also high. The likelihood of adding a unit is a function of its prospective integration index.[16] Let us look at the three possibilities in turn, beginning with the last.

At first glance it may appear paradoxical to relate the likelihood of addition to a *prospective* integration index. It hardly seems feasible to predict a development on the basis of a future state. However, such teleological reasoning is not foreign to parallel processing models. There are certain forces which work towards filling a gap provided this leads to a more balanced system. Due to the non-local nature of lexical access, 'integrated gaps' always receive a certain amount of activation. Imagine a system, modelled after the contemporary Dutch one, with velar, alveolar, and bilabial nasals as well as voiceless and voiced obstruents for all these places of articulation except for /g/. Accessing the voiceless velar stop involves the activation of the features [velar] and [voiceless], which pass their activation on to other velar segments such as /ŋ/. This causes the [voiced] node to be active, albeit to a low degree. The constellation is such that the three nodes [velar], [stop], and [voiced] are simultaneously active. This is a situation which is obviously propitious to the addition of the segment node /g/. Hence, the differential support from the system even applies to elements which are not (yet) there, giving stronger encouragement to the addition of would-be well-integrated elements and less encouragement to would-be ill-integrated ones.

The history of the English language provides a good example. By the end of the Old English period, the language had evolved the voiceless palato-alveolar fricative /ʃ/ from /sk/ via the intermediate stage /sx/. This addition created a gap in a system with many voiced/voiceless pairs such as /p/–/b/ and /ð/–/θ/. As noted, a gap is a paraphrase for a demand which arises through a sort of disharmony between the segment and the feature levels. While the three feature nodes for [fricative], [palato-

---

[16] Note that these predictions are very similar to what Martinet (1955) predicted on functional grounds.

alveolar], and [voiced] are simultaneously active (to a certain degree and at regular intervals), the corresponding segment /ʒ/ does not exist. There is thus a bottom-up pressure towards the creation of this node. This is precisely what happened. In Late Middle English times, the voiced palato-alveolar fricative developed from the voiced alveolar fricative /z/ followed by the palatal glide /j/. This combination of sounds provides an ideal basis for the creation of /ʒ/ because it assembles all the relevant articulatory features which are activated quasi-simultaneously. In addition to this favourable starting-point, the addition of the /ʒ/ is fostered by its endpoint, i.e. the effect it produces on the segment system as a whole. It fills a structural gap and thus leads to a more symmetrical system.

This analysis is strengthened by the fact that the voiced palato-alveolar fricative has been retained ever since. It appears to have found a permanent place in the segment system. This is all the more remarkable as it is by far the least common consonant in English (Denes 1963) and, unlike /ð/, occurs in words of very low frequency.[17] Finally, the palato-alveolar fricatives are rather difficult to pronounce, judging by the age at which they are usually mastered. Despite all these factors that work towards the loss of /ʒ/, it seems to enjoy a certain stability. Perhaps the best explanation for this robustness is its high degree of integration in the psycholinguistic system.

The rise of /ʒ/ has so far been described as a system-internal development. However, new sounds may also be introduced by language contact, i.e. borrowing. In the following, we will look at this problem more closely.

From the psycholinguistic standpoint, the likelihood of borrowing should be a function of how well the to-be-borrowed sound fits into the system of the recipient language. A large-scale test of this prediction is made possible on the basis of the data garnered in Maddieson (1986). Maddieson analysed 184 instances of borrowing in several dozens of languages and classified them into two basic sets according to the closeness of fit between the newcomer and the host language. A relation of close fit was found in 123 cases, one of remote fit in 61 cases. This difference is statistically reliable ($\chi^2(1) = 10.7$, $p < 0.005$). Maddieson's count is quite conservative in that he treats the integration of a borrowed segment in all-or-none fashion. However, various degrees of integration/desintegration have to be reckoned with. This leaves room for the possibility that the borrowed sounds are integrated to a different degree in the two sets. It would not be unreasonable to expect a lesser integration in the remoteness group than in the similarity group. In fact, this appears to be the case. As Maddieson notes, a 'relatively high proportion' of segments in the remoteness class have not made it into the core of the phonological system of the recipient language. The use of these segments is restricted to individual words, particular speech styles, registers, etc. It may therefore be inferred that the numerical asymmetry between the similarity set and the remoteness set is even larger than is expressed by the above figures.

[17] Note also that the development from /zj/ to /ʒ/ is not yet completed. The pronunciation of some words such as *azure* and *Asian* still vacillates between [zj] and [ʒ].

A further interesting result from Maddieson's study is that by far the most frequent subtype of borrowing is 'single-gap filling', which accounts for approximately half of the entire corpus. This is exactly what one would expect from the psycholinguistic viewpoint, because the pressure towards symmetry is highest when there is only one gap in a subset of the segmental system. When there are more gaps, the pressure on any one of them is appreciably lower. Inversely, it is not at all surprising to learn from Maddieson's report that the glottal consonants [ʔ] and [h] resist borrowing quite strongly. They exhibit a notorious tendency to remain largely unintegrated in the phonological systems of languages. This may be taken as evidence that there is no ready-made place for them whatever the structure of the system may be. In other words, the borrowing of these segments would not be conducive to higher pattern symmetry.

A further example of preservation is the set of dental fricatives. Both /ð/ and /θ/ have existed since Proto-Germanic times and have since shown no sign of disappearance from English, even though there is reason to expect them to. To begin with, they are relatively uncommon in the languages of the world (Maddieson 1984). According to Ingram et al. (1980) and others, they are among the last sounds to be acquired, a fact that attests to their extraordinary articulatory difficulty. Their frequency of occurrence is generally quite low, especially that of /θ/. The voiced congener occurs in a restricted number of words which, however, tend to have a high token frequency. The two dental fricatives have an interesting allophone-like distribution in word-initial positions. While /θ/ can be found only in open-class words, the occurrence of /ð/ is confined to closed-class items—contrast *thigh* and *thy*. The functional load carried by this opposition is minimal: a few minimal pairs can be found in noun/verb alternations like *the mouth–to mouth*. It is probable that the high token frequency of /ð/-initial words contributes to the stability of this consonant. However, this cannot be the whole story, as the voiceless counterpart is not so privileged but also quite stable. The most likely explanation for the stability of the dental fricatives is that they support each other and are supported by the system as a whole. The segmental system thus provides a good basis for the preservation of the dental fricatives.

The English language furnishes a particularly striking example of consonant loss. According to the psycholinguistic prediction, those segments which are ill integrated should be subject to loss. The glottal fricative has already been noted as a case of an ill-integrated obstruent because it is one of the very few obstruents which does not have a voiced phonemic counterpart and which is the only glottal element in the phonological system. We would therefore predict that /h/ should gradually disappear from the English inventory.

This is in fact the case. The history of English /h/ has been aptly traced by Lutz (1991). She has demonstrated persuasively how this sound developed over a period of more than a millennium from the velar fricative /x/ to zero. She documents the amazing systematicity of this phenomenon and shows that the gradual loss is mainly controlled by the following three factors—whether /h/ occurs in stressed or unstressed syllables, its position within the syllable, and its segmental context to the right. As was argued in section 4.9, stressed syllables are stronger than unstressed ones and impart their strength to their constituent segments. Therefore, the glottal fricative predictably is better protected against loss in stressed than in unstressed syllables. Indeed, as shown by Lutz, the loss of /h/ occurred first in unstressed and only later in stressed syllables.

As discussed in section 4.2, onsets are generally stronger than codas. Thus the enhanced support given to consonants in onset positions should make them less vulnerable than coda consonants to erosion. In point of fact, /h/ vanished in final positions earlier than in initial ones.

The third factor concerns the influence of the following segment. Lutz uncovers a correlation between the date of loss and the sonority of the following segment: the more sonorous it is, the longer the /h/ is preserved. The glottal fricative disappears first before sonorants, then before glides, and finally before vowels. Any segmental loss entails a change in the structure of the syllable. In the case of initial clusters such as /hn/, the deletion of the first element leads to a more preferred syllable structure because CVC syllables are generally more frequent than CCVC syllables. In the case of simple onsets, however, the obliteration of /h/ turns a CVC syllable into a VC syllable. Since empty-onset syllables are disfavoured as compared to filled-onset syllables, this is a change in the negative direction. Berg (1988a) showed that segment losses in slips of the tongue are more likely when the resultant syllable structure is more common than the original one. It is therefore to be expected that the /h/ is dropped first when this process is encouraged by the structure of the syllable and last when it is not. As Lutz demonstrates, this prediction is borne out by the historical data.

My conclusion is twofold. In the first place, in line with the psycholinguistic prediction, it is precisely the element which is least well integrated in the segment system which is subject to obliteration. In the second place, the disappearance of a sound is not an instantaneous process: it follows a slow, regular course which is determined by psycholinguistic principles. Because not all suprasegmental positions receive the same amount of activation, some are automatically better protected against loss than others. Elements in less favoured positions therefore disappear earlier than those in privileged positions.

The hypothesized interaction between diachrony and patterns of activation flow in the mental network can be amplified by looking at negative examples. Rather than asking why a given sound entered the phonemic inventory, it is also instructive to explore why other sounds did not. It would not be fruitful to enquire why a sound unit which is completely alien to a phonological system is not actually a part of it. The range of such sounds is virtually unlimited and the analysis hopelessly arbitrary. A starting-point is needed which provides a focus on one particular element which has a certain chance of gaining access to the system but fails to do so. A most natural starting-point for entering the segment inventory would be an allophonic variant, i.e. a segment which already exists at the periphery but has not quite made it to the centre. An illuminating case in point is the voiceless palatal fricative [ç], as occurring in words like *huge* and *humid*. The question that has to be addressed is why [ç] is not an established segment of the English language. Recall the prediction that only those segments will find their way into the system for which a well-integrated place is procured. Actually, English has no voiced or voiceless velar fricative (except in *loch*) and, more importantly, it also lacks the voiced palatal fricative. Thus the [ç] receives little support from the system and has a difficult time being integrated. In other words, there is no structural gap for it. Hence, the marginal status of [ç] in English can be put down to the low acceptance it meets with in the segmental system. This reluctance is a spin-off function of the way linguistic units are accessed in the processing network.

To summarize, the psycholinguistic theory of phonological retrieval predicts that well-integrated segments should be preserved, would-be well-integrated segments added, ill-integrated segments lost. It is also predicted that would-be ill-integrated segments are denied access to the system. Supporting examples from the history of the English language have been found for all four possibilities. Evidently, the possibility that individual examples may not fit this pattern cannot be excluded. However, this does not necessarily argue against the correctness of the research hypothesis. The claim that is being made here is that the degree of psycholinguistic integration of linguistic units is one factor (among numerous others) determining their stability over time. Other factors may of course have different effects. Take substrate or superstrate influences on segmental systems. These factors certainly have to be taken into account in a more comprehensive analysis. Because they are non-psychological in nature, they obviously cannot be covered by the present approach.

5.15. Resolving Phonological Problems at the Lexical Level

Continuing the argument of section 4.14, this section will examine the implications of the parallel flow of information between subordinate and superordinate levels, in particular between the lexical and the phonological levels. A major function of parallel information flow is that it enhances the 'visibility' of each processing level. Due to parallelness, the lexical level can 'look ahead', i.e. it learns through feedback what effect its processing outcome, whether preliminary or definitive, would have on the phonological level. In this way, the lexical level anticipates potential problems at the phonological level and takes them into account. Ideally, the lexical level allows its processing result to be influenced in such a way that the problem is alleviated or even overcome. Only two radical problem-solving strategies are conceivable in this system. Either the system works towards a change in the segmental structure of the word, or the desired word node remains inactive, following a problem at the phonological level. This would be a problem-avoidance strategy. It bears emphasizing that this strategy is an ineluctable consequence of the architecture and dynamics of the processing system. Given that phonological problems reduce the amount of feedback to the lexical level, lexical items are automatically less strongly activated.

Thus the parallel information flow in the mental network provides for the possibility of solving a phonological problem not only at the phonological but also at the lexical level. So when a phonological problem arises, we may predict that two repair strategies have operated during the historical development of a language. The claim that the problem may be attacked at the phonological level is certainly not novel. More interesting is the prediction that a word may pass out of the system because of phonological problems. Note that there is no compulsory element in this prediction, because the solution at the lexical level has to be viewed as secondary compared to that at the phonological level. After all, the problem is a phonological one, and it is clearly more natural for repair mechanisms to operate at the same analytical level as that at which the problem is located (rather than at a different one). Therefore, it cannot be expected that a lexical response to a phonological problem can always be obtained or that this response, when it takes place, is always strong.

In an attempt to test this prediction, three word-onset clusters have been scrutinized which have been simplified in the history of English, /kn/, /gn/, and /wr/. We presume that the first part of these clusters was lost as a reaction to a phonological problem.[18] The question to be addressed in this section is, then, whether there have been a disproportionate number of words which began with these clusters and which have dropped out of the language. To this end, the ratio of words that have survived to this day to those that disappeared was determined on the basis of the *Oxford English Dictionary* (*OED*).

The analysis to be presented below was confronted with the difficulty of which words count as independent and which as variants. I started out from the conviction that, no matter what the best answer would be, any decision is of secondary importance as long as the same criteria hold for the two word sets in question. It was decided to follow the *OED* as closely as possible. That is, each main entry was taken into account even if this involved including homonyms and formally identical words from different syntactic classes. Dialectal and rare items were included, spelling variants, erroneous spellings, and other kinds of variation excluded.

In order to carry out a meaningful analysis, it was necessary to compare the words beginning in <kn>,<gn>, and <wr> to those beginning with unproblematic clusters. My selection was guided by the principle of similarity. I reasoned that a cluster which shares one consonant with a troublesome cluster provides a safer basis for comparison because the conditions at the phonological level are as similar as is possible. My choice fell on /sn/, which shares the second element with <kn> and <gn>, and on /kr/, which shares the first element with <kn> and the second element with <wr>. Note that only those words of the /kr/ category were examined in which /kr/ corresponds to the letters <chr>. All in all, 1742 words were included in the analysis. This is an infinitesimal fraction of the words listed in the *OED*, but it

---

[18] Whether this problem is productive or perceptual in nature need not concern us here. It stands to reason that productive difficulties predominate in /kn/ and /gn/ whereas the perceptual side is of greater importance in the case of /wr/. How these problems arose in the first place is also not relevant to the present argument.

should be sufficient for making the point. Table 25 is preceded by three pairs of examples of which the upper word is extinct and the lower still in use.

(282) wr
- wrethe 'to support'
- wringan 'to wring'

(283) kn
- knapple 'to bite'
- cniht 'knight'

(284) gn
- gnidan 'to rub'
- gnaʒan 'to gnaw'

As can be gathered from Table 25, it is possible to draw a dividing line between the two sets on the basis of the percentages of losses. Taken as a group, 555 preservations oppose 219 losses in the problematic-cluster set, while there are 803 preservations as against 165 losses in the unproblematic-cluster set. This difference is highly significant ($\chi^2(1) = 31.1$, $p < 0.001$). Taken individually, only the comparison between /sn/ and <kn> does not reach standard levels of statistical significance. The difference between /kr/ and <kn> is marginally significant, whereas all others are highly reliable.

It is not surprising to find rather large differences among the individual categories. For example, the loss rate of <wr> words is twice as high as that of <kn> words even though both belong in the set of words with problematic onsets. The <wr> words thus turn out to be particularly prone to obliteration. The explanation of the differential loss rate is that there is almost certainly more than one reason which may promote the erosion of words, and these reasons may even differ from word

TABLE 25. *Rate of word loss as a function of onset cluster type*

Cluster	Preserved	Lost	% lost
/kr/ ($\triangleq$<chr>)	204	32	13.6
/sn/	599	113	15.9
/kn/	260	61	19.0
/gn/	76	24	24.0
/wr/	219	134	38.0

(type) to word (type). However, the results of Table 25 lend themselves well to the conclusion that one of the reasons for word loss can be identified at the phonological level.

To conclude, the empirical data provide support for the claim that speakers may resort to a radical means of solving phonological problems: they circumvent these problems by simply not using the words in which they crop up. This avoidance is a spin-off function of the claim that these words accumulate less activation than is necessary for a successful production. The generalized effect is that these words are likely to disappear from the language. Despite the fragmentary nature of the empirical data, it could be shown that this is indeed what happened in the history of English.

5.16. Verb Inflection

The inflection of English verbs has been the subject of many studies, both linguistic and psycholinguistic. Regular and irregular verbs have been found to be fundamentally different. The former are very large in number, constitute an open class, their phonological characteristics are irrelevant for their assignment to the regular group, and the regular inflection is used productively. By contrast, irregular verbs are small in number (about 200 at a maximum, with quite a few obsolete items), constitute a closed class, their phonological characteristics are critical for their assignment to the irregular group, and the irregular inflection is hardly used productively. Because the verb paradigm is narrowly circumscribed and the set of rules involved in the generation of inflected forms is small, with the rules having non-overlapping domains of application, it is possible to gain a relatively complete picture of the internal forces operating in the verbal system. The English verb inflection thus offers an ideal opportunity of measuring the past by the yardstick of the present.

Two major psycholinguistic works have looked into the error patterns of adult speakers of English—Stemberger's (1985a) analysis of naturally occurring slips of the tongue and Bybee and Slobin's (1982a) study of experimentally elicited errors. Their results are of relevance in that they allow us to formulate expectations as regards the course of linguistic change. To begin with, Stemberger finds that verb inflections involving a change of major category almost invariably shift from the irregular to the regular class but seldom vice versa. There are twenty-six cases of regularization as against a singleton error evidencing deregularization[19] in his corpus. Examples are provided in (285–6).

(285) *She's always goed– gone into weird things*
(286) *You have chown– chewed on ice* (both from Stemberger 1985a)

Both utterances involve the faulty production of a past participle form—a regular one in (286) and an irregular one in (285). In the first tongue slip, the irregular form

---

[19] There is one further type of irregularization in Stemberger's data base. It is introduced below in the main text.

gone was rendered as the regular form *goed*, and in the second, the regular verb *to chew* was treated as if it were irregular.

Because there is only one regular pattern as opposed to several irregular ones, the road from irregularity to regularity always leads to the same endpoint. The shift from regularity to irregularity is much more involved, however, as there are several ways in which a regular form may be deregularized. Which of these ways is chosen depends upon the phonological characteristics of the stem. The target *chew* closely resembles verb forms such as *knew*, *flew*, and *threw*. All these past tenses are irregular, and form their past participles on the /əʊn/ pattern. It is therefore not accidental that exactly this pattern was transferred to the regular verb *to chew*. This is a neat example of phonological constraints impinging on morphological decisions.

Stemberger's second relevant finding relates to regularization errors. When an irregular item is regularized, two operations have to be performed: the irregularity has to be dispensed with and the regular suffix has to be added to the stem. The possibility arises that only one of these operations is carried out, i.e. that the regular suffix attaches to an irregular stem, leading to the double marking of the past tense/past participle form. There is a second class of errors, given that the irregularity of inflected verbs may be based upon more than one (irregular) modification of the base. Again, it is possible that only one of these rules is applied and that the outcome is partly regular, partly irregular. These two error classes are named 'partial regularization'. Overmarking is illustrated in (287), undermarking in (288). Note the difference between partial and full regularizations, where an irregular verb is treated like any other regular verb. Such is the case in (285) where the vowel of the stem is preserved (/əʊ/ instead of the correct /ɒ/) and the regular verb ending is affixed to the base.

(287) *It tooked a while* for *took* (from Stemberger 1985a)
(288) G: *Ich dank– dachte, die essen jetzt erst groß*
[daŋk daxtə]
'I thought they are going to have a big meal now'

Both slips of the tongue exemplify an unorthodox mixture of regular and irregular elements. In (287), the regular past tense suffix was added to a form to which the ablaut rule had already applied. It is as if the speaker has overshot the target by marking the past tense twice instead of once. Number (288) is in a sense the opposite of (287) in that the speaker has undershot the target: instead of performing the two requisite segmental modifications, only one is carried out. To turn the infinitive *denken* 'to think' into the past tense, the tonic vowel as well as the following coda have to be changed (from /ɛ/ to /a/ and from /ŋk/ to /x/, respectively). However, only the vocalic alternation took place, with the consonantal part of the infinitive remaining unchanged.

In both Stemberger's and my own database, partial regularizations as in (287–8) are much less common than full regularizations as in (285). This may be surprising, because it would seem easier to carry out one modification rather than two. The empirical pattern appears to indicate that the two changes cannot be conceived of independently of each other, and that the process of irregular past tense/past participle formation is rather holistic in nature.

The next error pattern is one in which an irregular target is replaced by another irregular form. As noted, the irregular verbs can be divided into several subsets, so there is the possibility of switching from one subset into another. Such an interaction is encouraged among those irregular subtypes which are structurally similar. As a matter of fact, the various ablaut rules provide an opportunity for misapplication.

(289) *You wan– you won by fourteen points* (from Stemberger 1985a)
(290) *to sting* → *stang* for *stung* (from Bybee and Slobin 1982a)

Although (289) occurred naturally and (290) was elicited in a laboratory situation, both errors are fairly similar. The two infinitives *to win* and *to sting* have an /ɪ/ which is erroneously transformed into an /æ/ even though an /ʌ/ would have been appropriate. There are of course verbs that have an /ɪ/ in their base and an /æ/ in their past tense form, such as *to swim*, *to ring*, and *to sink*. This similarity creates competition between the /ʌ/ and the /æ/ rules—the ideal precondition for malfunction.

It is noteworthy that errors in the opposite direction occur as well. Bybee and Slobin (1982a) report a number of cases in which the past tense of *to swim* and *to ring* was rendered as *swum* and *rung* in lieu of *swam* and *rang*, respectively. Going by Bybee and Slobin's results, this direction of influence appears to be stronger than that evidenced in (289–90).

Mention should also be made of the deregularization of verbs whose bases end in an alveolar stop. The regular way of deriving past tenses from these verbs is to add the syllabic allomorph /ɪd/. This would seem unproblematic, but there are two interference factors. For one thing, some (irregular) verbs ending in /t/ or /d/ do not take a suffix at all to form their past tenses; examples include *to shed* and *to set*. The problem created by these verbs is that a regular verb may be mistaken for an irregular one on account of its partial formal similarity. For another, English has /t/ and /d/ as regular past tense markers which occur far more frequently than the syllabic allomorph. Given that infinitives may also end in an alveolar stop, /t/ and /d/ are functionally ambiguous. They may signal the final part of the base or the past tense. There is thus the danger of mistaking a base verb for a past tense form. These two interference factors may jointly lead to a situation in which the past tense marker is not applied to regular verbs where it should have been. The result is what has been called a 'no-marking' error, of which two examples are given below.

(291) *So we test'em on it* for *tested* (from Stemberger 1985a)
(292) *to crash* → *crash* for *crashed* (from Stemberger and MacWhinney 1986b)

In both cases, the regular past tense marker *-ed* fails to show up. It is clear from the context that the speaker intended to utter the past tense form. In (291), the speaker related an event that happened in the past and in (292), the speaker's task was to produce a past tense form under experimental conditions. The base verb ends in an alveolar stop in (291) but not in (292). In light of what has been said above, it is to be expected that no-marking errors will occur most often on /d/ or /t/-final verb stems but only rarely on other verbs. This is in fact the case. Stemberger (1985a) has twenty-five slips of the former and four of the latter type in his speech-error collection.[20]

Precisely the opposite situation is also conceivable. It has been noted that verbs ending in an alveolar stop may have regular and irregular past tenses, with the regular forms taking the syllabic allomorph and the irregular forms taking nothing. While the previous paragraph documented irregular suffixing of regular verbs, regular suffixing of irregular verbs also occurs, as shown in (293).

(293) *to hit* → *hitted* for *hit* (from Bybee and Slobin 1982a)

Here, the correct no-marking pattern has been supplanted by the incorrect regular past tense rule. Such regularizations are particularly common on /d/- and /t/-final verbs. They therefore preferentially occur also on a similar subtype of irregular verbs, i.e. those whose infinitives end in /d/ and whose past tenses are formed by devoicing the alveolar stop, e.g. *to build, to spend*. Bybee and Slobin give no concrete examples but a typical error would be (294).

(294) *to send* → *sended* for *sent*

As in (293), the irregular verb *to send* is treated as a regular one. This error process is triggered by the fact that the phonological structure of this irregular verb is suspiciously close to that of regular verbs such as *to mend* and *to tend*.

It can be seen, then, that the English verb system has interesting dynamics which show quite a few competitive effects. At the most general level of explanation, the reason for these system-internal pressures lies in the way linguistic items are represented in the psycholinguistic network and in their phonological structure. Thus, problems arise mainly on two fronts. The representation of linguistic items ensures that larger classes put pressure on smaller classes; so if a language has both regular and irregular verbs, the former will attract the latter rather than vice versa. The distinction between regular and irregular classes is particularly difficult to maintain when the difference between them is not phonologically encoded. That is, when regular and irregular verbs are formally similar, there is a heightened danger of interference. Actually, similarity is the overriding index of competition. It not only helps to cross the boundary between regular and irregular verbs but also determines the frequency with which individual sets of irregular verbs interfere with one another. The more similar any two sets are, the more likely the wrong rule is to be applied. Thus all category shifts are subserved by the same psycholinguistic mechanism (see also Hare and Elman 1992).

---

[20] Whether cases like (292) are generated by exactly the same mechanism as cases like (291) is not at issue here. All that matters is frequency information.

On the premiss that these system-internal forces influence the course of language change, it is to be expected that the psycholinguistic patterns are an accurate predictor of the historical development. In fact, given the clear processing results, fairly precise predictions regarding linguistic change may be formulated. These are enumerated below. First, diachronic regularizations should outnumber irregularizations. Secondly, partial regularizations should be less frequent than full regularizations. Thirdly, in the case of irregular verbs, ablaut rules should be replaced by other ablaut rules rather than by other irregular changes such as final-consonant modification. In particular, the /ʌ/ and /æ/ rules are expected to interact heavily. The influence between /ʌ/ and /æ/ may be both ways, with /æ/ → /ʌ/ predominating. Fourthly, deregularization is expected on regular verbs ending in /t/ or /d/. These verbs should not be marked for past tense at all—in other words, they should lose their past tense suffix over time. Fifthly, because of their phonological form, shape-invariant irregular verbs should be particularly prone to regularization. Sixthly, the same fate should be reserved for those verbs whose irregularity is characterized by a change of the stem-final voiced alveolar stop into its voiceless cognate.

Note that all these predictions are particular to English. Other languages might exhibit different spontaneous-error patterns and thus lead to the setting up of different predictions. This is especially likely in the case of the irregular verbs, whose phonological structures may produce different types of interaction. However, the strength of regular verbs and the attendant weakness of the irregular verbs is presumably a language-independent effect.

These six predictions will be tested by looking at the morphological evolution from Old English to Modern English. The analysis will be based upon Jespersen's (1942) diachronic grammar, which retraces the history of many verbs in sufficient detail. The first prediction, that irregular verbs tend to convert into the regular group rather than vice versa, is clearly borne out by the historical facts. Already in Old English, the weak (i.e. regular) verbs formed the most important verb class. Its size has grown ever since, as many strong verbs became weak or died out and almost all newcomers to the language entered the weak class. By contrast, only a few verbs which were originally weak turned strong. In addition, irregularity was progressively banned from the Old English weak verbs, as evidenced by the loss of stem alternations and inflectional variants (Stark 1982). Regularization is exemplified in (295), deregularization in (296).

(295) OE *helpan—h(e)alp—(hulpon)—ʒeholpen* →
 ME *helpe—halp—(holpen)—(y)holpen* →
 Mod.E *to help—helped—helped*
(296) OE *werian—werode—ʒewerod* →
 ME *weren—ware/wore—wore* →
 Mod.E *to wear—wore—worn*

The examples given by Jespersen (1942) are not exhaustive, so it is difficult to quantify the extent of regularization as against that of deregularization. The cases of regularization appear particularly under-represented, probably because they are less interesting than the reverse development. All in all, Jespersen's book contains 21 instances of deregularization as against 45 cases of regularization. This conservative count yields a statistically reliable difference ($\chi^2(1) = 4.5$, $p < 0.05$). Thus, regularization outweighs irregularization—just as has been predicted on psycholinguistic grounds.[21]

The second issue brings to the fore an even more extreme pattern. The expectation that full regularizations have a higher frequency of occurrence than partial ones is unmistakably fulfilled. As far as can be determined on the basis of Jespersen (1942), there is not a single instance of partial regularization to be found in the history of English. Neither the overmarking of past tenses as in (287) nor the undermarking of past tenses as in (288) can be observed. Concretely, *ated and *cat are not viable past tenses of to eat and to catch, respectively. It follows from this that whenever a verb undergoes regularization, it assimilates completely to the regular class. A compromise is apparently out of the question.

Why partial regularizations are entirely absent is more readily understandable in the case of overmarking than in the case of undermarking. Overmarking means that a regular suffix is added to a past tense verb. That is, it arises from a confusion between the present and the past tense form. Because competent speakers are not liable to confuse these forms, they will not accept such errors; hence the probability of a change in this direction is virtually zero. Undermarking presupposes that the base and the inflected form are related to each other by at least two rules. This process is less unlikely a priori; nonetheless, it fails to show up, probably because partial regularizations occur extremely seldom in naturalistic speech error data. As argued above, the two rules do not operate in ignorance of each other. Consequently, irregular past tense forms may convert *as wholes* into the regular group, though not *aspects* of their irregularity.

Prediction No. 3 is concerned with the competition between the two subtypes of irregular verbs which change their base vowel /ɪ/ into /ʌ/ or /æ/ in the past tense. These verbs are very similar phonologically in that they all end in a non-velar nasal or a velar nasal + homorganic stop. This may be one of the reasons why these classes have attracted new members over time, such as *to fling* and *to ring*. In the history of the English language there has been quite an exchange between the two verb classes in question. The boundary between them has always been permeable, allowing verbs to belong to both classes at the same time. For example, the past tense of *to swim* vacillated between *swam* and *swum* in Old English. Also, the formal distinction between the past tense and the past participle was not very well respected. The form *began*, for instance, could serve both functions. Below are listed all the relevant verbs in Jespersen (1942) whose past tense forms of yesterday diverge from those of today. The forms in which the former /æ/ has now been replaced by /ʌ/ are given

---

[21] The same development can be observed in the history of the German language (see Theobald 1992).

under (297a), those in which the former /ʌ/ has given way to /æ/ under (297b). The past participle (PP) forms are also provided.

(297) a. Present Past   PP   b. Present Past   PP
          cling   clang clung   swim   swum   swam
          fling   flang flung   begin   begun   began
          sling   slang slung   ring   rung   rang
          slink   slank slunk   sing   sung   sang
          swing   swang swung   spring   sprung sprang
          spin   span   spun   drink   drunk   drank
          win   wan   won   shrink   shrunk shrunken
                                     sink   sunk   sank
                                     stink   stunk   stunk

As is apparent from (297), English verbs have shifted rather freely from one category to the other but not to a third. This is precisely the expected pattern. The /ʌ/ → /æ/ verbs are slightly more common than the /æ/ → /ʌ/ items (9 : 7), but the numbers are obviously too low to be more than suggestive. What they might suggest is that the pull towards /ʌ/ in the past tense is somewhat stronger than that towards /æ/, again in agreement with the psycholinguistic predictions. It is notable that the verbs listed under (297b) have 'inverted' past tense and past participle forms as compared with the Modern English standard. This switch-over is undoubtedly facilitated by the fact that some /æ/ forms are past tenses while others are past participles. This ambiguity has led to confusion, and might eventually even lead to the abolition of the formal distinction between past tenses and past participles. In fact, some modern verbs such as *to win* and *to spin* have already done so. Previously, these verbs formally distinguished their past tenses and past participles (see 297a). Why the neutralization did not take place in the verbs given in (297b) remains an open question.

The fourth working hypothesis states the conditions under which deregularization is expected to occur. Regular verbs ending in an alveolar stop should be zero-affixed in the past tense, on the analogy of verbs like *to put* and *to split*. We would thus predict an increase in the number of invariable verbs. This in fact happened at some stage in the history of English, though it does not occur nowadays. According to Jespersen, this deregularization process was strongest in Early Modern English. He gives the following five verbs that started out as weak verbs, deregularized and subsequently regularized again: *fast, fret, lift, start,* and *waft*.[22] Occasionally, the irregular form did not succeed in supplanting the regular one. That the number of such verbs is apparently not higher is not unexpected. It follows directly from the

---

[22] Apparently the only verb that used to be regular, then deregularized and preserved its irregularity to this day, is *to build*. Jespersen states that the regular form, *builded*, has not been completely eliminated, and is occasionally encountered still in this century. Note that this verb does not belong to the no-change class but to one which will be discussed below.

claim made earlier that deregularization should represent a much weaker tendency than regularization. Consonant with this, the deregularization process was rather short-lived. The above words regained their status as regular verbs. It is worth adding that no verbs are known which turned invariable and did not end in an alveolar stop.

The preceding discussion has already hinted that the opposite trend should play a more important role in the history of English. Invariable words should have tended towards regularization. Indeed, this is what they did. In addition to the five verbs given in the preceding paragraph, there are at least ten verbs of which either the past tense or the past participle, or both, used to be invariable but which now take regular endings. Among them can be found *to dread, to shred, to roast,* and *to wed*. This is probably a conservative estimate. Only those verbs have been counted for which Jespersen provides sufficient information. There may be regional differences such as between British and American English, grammatical differences such as when the regular form tends to function as a past tense and the irregular one as a past participle, and semantic differences such as when the regular form codes a more general meaning and the irregular one a more specific sense. Sometimes the invariable form has fossilized in more or less fixed expressions, e.g. *roast beef*. These may be considered relics of forms which used to be more productive. They thus are not counterexamples of the general trend towards regularization.[23]

All the verbs mentioned so far are monosyllabic. In point of fact, all Modern English no-change verbs have only one syllable. This was not always so. A number of polysyllabic /t/-final words which entered the language as past participles underwent functional extension without formal change, and accordingly joined the category of no-change verbs. Pertinent examples are *to complete, to content, to select,* and *to separate*. As predicted, all these verbs have gradually shifted to the regular class as far as verb inflection goes, even though some of the invariant forms have persisted as adjectives to this day, e.g. *a select group of people, a complete set*. This makes good sense, because the system of verb inflection is under tighter constraints than the adjectival system. There is more paradigmatic pressure in the verb system and thus a greater drive towards regularization in the case of verb inflections than in the case of the phonological structure of adjectives.

The final prediction is concerned with a similar verb type which forms its past tense by devoicing the stem-final consonant with no suffixation at all. Like the no-change verbs, these verbs should be especially prone to regularization—which is what has actually happened to this class of verbs. Jespersen lists the following five verbs which used to be irregular but have largely regularized nowadays: *to blend, to*

---

[23] The preceding argument may be extended to strong verbs which end in an alveolar stop and which undergo formal change in the past tense. Since the alveolar stop is the past-tense marker of regular forms, these verbs are prone to being misidentified as weak. This leads to the prediction that strong verbs ending in /d/ or /t/ should be particularly apt to be attracted by the weak category. This is precisely what happened. As shown in Krygier (1994), regularization is more likely in verbs with root-final alveolars than in verbs ending in other consonants.

wend, to gird, to gild, to geld. Others like *to build* and *to spend* have, however, preserved their irregularity. Whether or not they did so is clearly a function of frequency (see section 5.17). The more frequently the verbs occur, the greater the chance they stand of resisting the attraction of the regular set. In exceptional cases, a verb may be so infrequently used that it passes out of the language before it has had time to undergo regularization. One such example is *to shend* 'to shame', for which Jespersen gives the past tense *shent* but which is no longer listed in dictionaries of current usage. The regular past *shended* is not apparently on record.

In conclusion, the parallelism uncovered between slips of the tongue and language change is quite astonishing. All of the six predictions derived from the speech-error patterns are borne out by the diachronic data. Although the absolute numbers of the irregular verbs in each subset are too low to develop a statistical argument—that they are so low is, ironically, formulated as one of the predictions—the trends are always in the expected direction. There is thus something fascinating about the inadvertent derailments of the language production system. These derailments, which are of a purely synchronic nature, lay bare the constraints, principles, and pressures to which the system is subject. One would be tempted to add immediately 'pressures to which the system is subject *at the moment of speaking*'. However, the preceding analysis suggests that the pressures of the present are identical to those of the past. It thus does not seem exaggerated to say that speech errors do not only project the current system and its future changes, as Bybee and Slobin (1982a: 287) note, but also provide a key to its historical evolution. Of course, it cannot be predicted on the basis of the error data just when a given change begins and how fast it proceeds. What can be predicted—or rather retrodicted—and quite successfully so, is the direction that the change will take or, rather, has taken.

5.17. Local Frequency Effects

Frequency is a concept of central importance in psycholinguistic research and has been shown to pervade practically all facets of human behaviour. Its effect is adequately captured by the following characteristics: it makes processing easier, faster, and more reliable. All three aspects are intimately related. The greater the processing ease, the higher its speed and the less its error-proneness. Actions that are performed often are carried out more easily, more quickly and more accurately.

Let us briefly look at the empirical evidence for this claim and consider the following slips of the tongue.

(298) *It's a meal mystery* for *real mystery*
(299) *telefathic fox* for *telepathic* (both from Fromkin 1973)

Both errors document a distortion of the phonological structure of the target word. By a segment substitution process, *real* is changed into *meal* in (298) and *telepathic* into *telefathic* in (299). *Meal* is a high-frequency word while *telepathic* is a low-frequency item. Stemberger (1984b) showed that phonological errors on high-frequency words are significantly less common than on low-frequency items. This finding indicates that phonological access is more reliable with high than with low-frequency words. A straightforward explanation of this difference in connectionist models is that high-frequency units at the lexical level spread more activation to the phonological level and thus are in a better position to protect their segmental constituents against their competitors (Stemberger and MacWhinney 1986a). It does not really matter exactly how frequency is coded (in the linkages or in the nodes) as long as provision is made for an information flow of variable strength in the network.

The increased processing reliability of high-frequency words is not confined to the phonological level. It also applies to the access of morphological units. Stemberger and MacWhinney (1986a) showed that morphological errors occur more often on low- than on high-frequency lexical items. They examined the frequency of 'no-marking errors' on verbs where the present tense is produced instead of the requisite past tense form, as in (300).

(300) *What was it you just sing?* for *sang* (from Stemberger and MacWhinney 1986a)

That such errors are less often found in high-frequency items suggests that morphological access is also sensitive to frequency. The benefit of lexical frequency thus accrues to all processing levels that are subordinated to the word level.

Frequency makes an impact not only upon processing but also upon representation. This aspect is irrelevant in monomorphemic words but takes on a great deal of significance in more complex items. A word like *waiting* may be stored holistically, analytically, or even in both ways (see section 4.17). There is some evidence for an interaction between the representational format and the frequency of the item to be represented. By their very nature, high-frequency units are more often used in speaking and listening than low-frequency items. It stands to reason that what is often needed is most directly accessible. That is, frequently occurring words may be expected to be stored in unanalysed fashion because it is easier to use a ready-made unit than to put the unit together through the application of certain rules to the stem. For less frequently occurring words, there is simply less need (or perhaps less opportunity) to build up a holistic representation. This theoretical expectation has been confirmed by Stemberger and MacWhinney (1986a). They present experimental evidence in favour of the view that regularly inflected words of high frequency are stored both in holistic and in decomposed fashion in the lexicon, whereas only the latter alternative appears appropriate for low-frequency items.

Thus frequency increases the robustness of lexical items as regards their phonological and morphological representations. The prediction that follows from this conclusion is obvious. Because of their psycholinguistic stability, high-frequency items should be less subject to historical change than low-frequency items. When a change takes place, it should manifest itself first in low- and subsequently in high-frequency units.

However, there is another, less obvious prediction that can be derived from the way the processing machinery works. During the production of an utterance, the relevant nodes at all levels have to be fully activated. These include the intended words, segments, and features. If these units do not attain the requisite level of activation, their production is compromised. The top-down information flow in production is of a divergent nature (MacKay 1987). One higher-level unit activates many lower-level units. Because of this 'multiple responsibility', the superordinate node has to have a fairly high activation level so as to be able reliably to access all subordinate nodes.

As MacKay (1987) argued, the picture is somewhat different in perception. The bottom-up information flow in perception is of a convergent nature: many lower-level nodes conspire to activate one higher-level node. Because of this summed effect, the activation of higher-level units in perception is easier than the activation of lower-level units in production.[24] One implication of this claim is that the activation of individual subordinate elements is less important for the activation of the superordinate element in perception. MacKay (1987) dubbed this asymmetry the 'principle of higher-level activation'. Taking into account the fact that the activation of lower-level nodes in perception is only a means to an end, it becomes understandable why the processing system can allow itself to be less careful about the activation of lower-level units. The same result can be obtained with less expenditure of energy.

The perceptual principle of higher-level activation opens up an interesting possibility for the speaker. Given that articulation requires physical effort, and given a certain inertia on the part of the articulators, speakers are naturally intent on minimizing the energy expenditure. They may allow their articulations to become more sloppy. What is beneficial to speakers taxes the decoding process. The less careful the speakers' articulations, the higher the listeners' workload in the recovery of the information contained in the signal. Since speakers are also listeners, they have no difficulty in making up for a certain degree of sloppiness.

One of the factors by which the degree of articulatory sloppiness may be influenced is word frequency. It has been shown that speakers are able to make fairly reliable judgements about the frequency of occurrence of lexical items (Shapiro 1969), so that this information can be safely assumed to be at their disposal. Frequency effects make themselves felt in both perception and production. It has been empirically demonstrated that frequency speeds up the word-recognition process (Oldfield and Wingfield 1969). If speakers exploit this principle, they can be more sloppy about the pronunciation of high-frequency words than about that of low-frequency items, while still achieving the same degree of communicative success. In fact, this is precisely what speakers do: the higher the redundancy of a word, the less accurately it is articulated (Lieberman 1963).

---

[24] This hypothesis rationalizes the intuition that listening is less effortful a task than speaking and the fact that speakers' passive vocabularies are always larger than their active ones.

We may now derive the following prediction for linguistic change. On the premiss that one incentive for language change is the speakers' desire to reduce their articulatory effort, it can be predicted that low-frequency items should resist language change more successfully than high-frequency ones. Hence, diachronic change should affect more frequent units before less frequent ones.

We are thus confronted with what looks like a paradox. Language change is predicted to be both positively and negatively correlated with frequency of occurrence. This paradox is more apparent than real, however, because the two conditions have different domains of application. As argued above, the positive condition (i.e. higher frequency—faster change) is limited to those changes which crucially implicate the articulatory component, i.e. those which make articulation easier. In contrast, the negative condition (i.e. higher frequency—slower change) refers to those changes which are independent of articulatory constraints, i.e. those which do *not* make articulation easier. There are thus two distinct areas where linguistic change may originate: on the one hand the processing network, which is subject to high-level constraints, and on the other the 'articulatory bottleneck', which is subject to low-level constraints.

Before the two predictions can be put to the test, a word about the notion of articulatory ease is in order. Clearly, there is no received theory of articulatory ease which may serve as a reference point for determining which diachronic changes alleviate the articulatory effort and which are neutral in this respect. However, even in the absence of such a theory, quite a few pieces of the puzzle have been identified through the study of allegro speech in adults, language acquisition, and breakdown. For instance, the sounds which are acquired first are generally regarded as involving little articulatory difficulty. To play safe, only the relatively uncontroversial cases of articulatory ease will be focused upon in the following.

Let us begin with the high-level constraints and examine the prediction that low-frequency items display less stability over time than high-frequency ones. One area which is undoubtedly unrelated to problems of articulation is the morphology of verbs. English verbs form their past tenses and past participles in either regular or irregular fashion. It was argued in the preceding section that irregular verbs tend to undergo regularization. Importantly, there cannot be a phonetic motivation for this pull because there is no difference in articulatory difficulty between *fought* and *fighted* or *dreamt* and *dreamed*. If anything, the irregular past tenses appear to be phonologically simpler than their (contrived or real) regular counterparts. Our prediction is, then, that high-frequency irregular verbs resist the pull of the regular verbs more successfully than low-frequency irregular verbs.

This issue was addressed by Hooper (1976). She retraced the development of the strong verbs from Old English to Modern English, and examined their tendency to convert to the weak class as a function of their frequency of occurrence. The frequency of the Old English verbs was determined on the basis of Kučera and Francis's (1967) quantitative analysis of Modern English. As Hooper herself recognizes, this is a less than ideal procedure, as there is no reason to expect lexical frequency to be immune to diachronic change. With this caveat in mind, Hooper's results may be summarized as follows. The strong verbs that have remained strong over the past millennium (N = 15) have an average frequency of 304.2, whereas those that have become weak (N = 18) have an average frequency of 26.1—a highly significant difference.

To exemplify this difference, we may compare the development of the Old English verbs *ridan* and *weaxan*. Both used to form their past tenses by dint of a vowel change. At least in Modern English, they differ greatly in terms of frequency. The Modern English counterpart of *ridan* occurs often but that of *weaxan* seldom. While *ridan* has remained in the class of strong verbs (*to ride–rode–ridden*), *weaxan* converted into the class of weak verbs and now is regular (*to wax–waxed–waxed*). We may conclude that frequency affords 'endangered' words a certain robustness and thus prevents them from being assimilated into the class of weak verbs. To put it differently, frequency is a counteracting force to analogical levelling.

The positive relationship between frequency and stability is found in many other areas. One way in which irregularity comes about is through defiance of a general change. Irregularity should therefore correlate with high frequency because high-frequency items are predictably less resistant to change. This is in fact so. Morphological and phonological irregularity is found most commonly with high-frequency words.

There even is a correlation between 'height' of frequency and degree of irregularity. The most extreme form of morphological irregularity, suppletion, is mostly found with the commonest items of a language.[25] Given that sensitivity to frequency is viewed as a general trait of processing systems, independent of the particular information to be processed, we would expect this correlation to hold cross-linguistically. Take as a paradigm case the auxiliary *to be*. Its extreme frequency is beyond doubt. Whether we consider Latin *esse*, German *sein*, Spanish and Portuguese *ser*, or Dutch *zijn*, they all exhibit suppletion in their declension. The other auxiliary, *to have*, exemplifies irregularity on the level of pronunciation. Although the sequence <-ave> is usually pronounced [eɪv], as in *cave* and *shave*, this is not true for *have*. The situation is similar in the other irregular verbs, which are less frequent and accordingly less likely to have suppletive forms than auxiliaries. Pertinent examples are English *go–went*, French *aller–vais*, and Spanish *ir–voy*. Modal auxiliaries also deserve to be mentioned in this connection (cf. English *will–would, may–might*, etc.). Bybee and Slobin (1982a) note that of the thirty most frequent English verbs, twenty-two belong to the irregular category.

That it is frequency more than anything else which resists the pressure of the majority group can be seen by comparing phonologically similar material. A particularly telling example comes from French. This language displays a difference in the declension of base verbs and those that are derived from them. That is, identical stems admit of two different declensions. The regular type is found with the derived

---

[25] The link between frequency and irregularity is even accepted by Mayerthaler (1981), who tends to play down the role of frequency in diachrony and synchrony.

verb and the irregular type with the base verb. It is significant that the base verb is generally of far higher frequency than the derived verb. An interesting example is *dire–contredire–médire* 'to say–to contradict–to curse'. The 2nd person plural present tense indicative form is irregular in the base verb (*vous dites*) but quite regular in the derived verbs (*vous contredisez, vous médisez*).

This example is not particular to French. In English we find *to come* and *to have* as irregular verbs but *to welcome* and *to behave* with regular inflections. Interestingly, *to become* is also irregular, even though it has a complex structure diachronically. The reason, again, is its high frequency. All this shows that it is not the phonological form *per se* that encourages or discourages a certain linguistic change.

Of course, this correlation is not confined to verbs. It can be found in any other word class, such as adjectives and nouns. The comparison of adjectives furnishes further examples. Suppletion in comparatives occurs only in the most frequent adjectives, such as English *good–better*, German *gut–besser*, French *bon–meilleur*, Danish *god–bedre*, as well as English *little–less*, French *peu–moins*, Danish/Swedish *liten/lille–mindre*. This list of examples could be easily extended.

In the noun class, irregular plural formation can be shown to correlate with frequency. The plural of *foot* is irregular while that of *tenderfoot* is regular. Almost invariably, the singular form is more common than the plural form. An exception to this rule is *child* with its double plural *child-r-en* (see Tiersma 1982 for more examples). Notably, the low-frequency item *brethren*, which is the irregular plural form of *brother*, is in the process of dropping out of the language.

Given the assumption that high frequency tends to make linguistic items immune to change, it is to be expected that low frequency should act to destabilize linguistic items. In point of fact, a hint of such an effect can be found in Jaberg (1937), who observed that uncommon words tend to display a great deal of variation in their phonological and morphological shape. For example, the regular plural morpheme may coexist with an irregular one, as in English *lexicons–lexica*.

A further example which clearly does not make articulation easier is the phenomenon of diachronic stress shift. English has quite a few noun/verb pairs, known as diatones, whose main difference resides in the placement of stress. Verbs have main stress on the ultimate but nouns on the penultimate syllable, as in *to transpórt–the tránsport*. Sherman (1975) showed that the number of such diatones has been steadily on the increase over the past few centuries. While he found only eight diatones at the onset of Early Modern English, the English language of today is estimated to have approximately 100 such pairs. This change is usually brought about by stress retraction on nouns—i.e. nouns are more likely to move their main stress to the left than are verbs to move their main stress to the right. Since stress shift is definitely unconditioned by articulatory ease, it can be hypothesized that this diachronic change will affect the less frequent words first and the more frequent ones last.

Phillips (1984) investigated this hypothesis and found strong support for it. She compared the average frequency of diatones and noun/verb pairs which do not involve a stress alternation, such as *to review* and *the review*, after having eliminated several subsets that are principally opposed to stress variation (e.g. all words beginning with *mis-*, as in *to mistáke–the mistáke*). Her results reveal that identically stressed noun/verb pairs are on an average three times as common as differently stressed ones (15.8 : 5.3). It seems that high frequency increases the robustness of word forms and thus makes them less vulnerable to prosodic change. Again, this finding bears out the psycholinguistic prediction.

Turning to the low-level constraints, we will enquire whether historical changes which incur an articulatory benefit are also affected by lexical frequency, albeit in a way opposite to the cases discussed above. We will look at two examples whose articulatory motivation can be reliably established. The first involves the omission of the unstressed vowel [ə] in word-medial position. The deletion of schwa by its very nature reduces the articulatory effort because it leads to a shortening of the word by one syllable. Hooper (1976) examined the possible relationship between frequency and vowel deletion and focused upon the status of schwa in words ending in [(ə)rɪ] such as *memory* and *surgery*. She presented eight linguistically trained subjects with a list of more than 100 words and asked them whether they would normally pronounce or not pronounce the schwa. The author excluded all those cases where there was no option of schwa deletion for phonological reasons. For example, the neutral vowel cannot be dropped in *burglary* because it would create the phonotactically illegal sequence /glr/. Hooper asserts that her data point to a frequency sensitivity of the vowel-deletion process: the rate of schwa deletion correlates negatively with the frequency of the word in which this vowel occurs.

Unfortunately, Hooper's method is so seriously flawed that the validity of the results is at stake. First of all, it has been shown that the judgements of linguists and linguistically naïve people in matters linguistic tend not to be identical (Spencer 1973). Hence the fact that Hooper's subjects were linguistically trained may have made a natural and spontaneous reaction impossible and the outcome questionable. Much more problematic, however, is the task that the subjects were engaged in. Hooper had them perform a metalinguistic task in which they were asked to provide information on how they think they speak. That is, she did not tap the subjects' actual behaviour but rather their conception of how they behaved. In fact, she herself unabashedly concedes that her test 'does not reveal any phonetic reality' (Hooper 1976: 96). It is imperative to check, therefore, whether the metalinguistic judgements are an accurate reflection of linguistic reality.

We have made an attempt to replicate Hooper's findings using a more suitable methodology. With the intention of replacing the metalinguistic by a linguistic task, my student Lutz Vogt ran a reading experiment. Subjects were instructed to read complete sentences, half of which contained words ending in [(ə)rɪ] and the other half filler items. Neither position of the critical items within the sentence nor speech rate was systematically manipulated. Neither the age of the subjects nor their socioeconomic background were monitored.

The main problem that is standardly associated with the reading task does not apply in the case at hand. By its very nature, reading relies upon orthography in a way that speaking does not. Unlike spoken language, read language may therefore be influenced by orthographic convention. However, as the spelling remains constant in all critical items—all of them have a grapheme representing schwa—the preservation or loss of schwa cannot be attributed to the graphemic structure.

Vogt selected for analysis the twenty-five most frequent words (at least eighteen occurrences in Kučera and Francis, 1967) and the twenty-five least frequent words (all occurring only once in Kučera and Francis) from Hooper's list. The number of subjects was twice as large as in the Hooper study. Almost all of them were speakers of American English. Those subjects who had difficulty with reading aloud were discarded from the analysis.

Vogt analysed the data spectrographically and found appropriate a three-way classification in 'schwa retained', 'schwa dropped', and 'unclear cases'. The unclear cases involve realizations intermediate between full schwa and no schwa at all, which may be phonetically described as 'voiceless schwas'. These voiceless schwas account for 9.5 per cent of the data, and exhibit no particular sensitivity to frequency. By contrast, there is a highly significant interaction between lexical frequency and rate of schwa deletion. The more commonly a word occurs in the language, the more liable it is to lose its medial schwa. This confirmation of Hooper's results is exactly what would be expected on the basis of the psycholinguistic predictions formulated above.

The second example is related to the first, in that it focuses upon the stage preceding vowel deletion. There seems to be a natural sequence of intermediate stages for phonological segments which are doomed to disappearance. To be specific, vowels tend towards centralization prior to obliteration. This process, known as vowel reduction, is also articulation-based, since it is easier to utter a neutral vowel, which requires hardly any articulatory gesture, than a non-reduced vowel, whose articulatory parameters have to be precisely set. Because of this articulatory grounding, it is expected that vowel reduction occurs first in frequent and last in infrequent words. Fidelholtz (1975) addressed this issue by examining the reduction of lax vowels followed by a consonant cluster in initial unstressed syllables. This environment allows for vowel reduction and therefore provides a basis for establishing a contrast between words that tend to undergo this process and those that do not. For instance, despite their similar phonological structure, the vocalic beginning in *astronomy* is usually pronounced in reduced form, whereas the initial vowel in *gastronomy* preserves its colour. Fidelholtz determined the pronunciation normatively by consulting standard pronouncing dictionaries of American English such as Kenyon and Knott (1953). The lexical-frequency data were taken from Thorndike and Lorge (1944). As predicted, Fidelholtz found a significant correlation between vowel reduction and lexical frequency: the more frequent a given item is, the more likely it is to have its first vowel reduced. The example of *astronomy*, which is 22.5 times as frequent as *gastronomy*, illustrates this difference well.

Beyond the cases discussed above, there are many other historical changes that fall in line with the psycholinguistic predictions. To name only a few further examples,

Ferguson (1978) finds that the intervocalic dental stop is spirantized to [ð], especially in high-frequency words. Janson (1977) reports that final /d/ deletion in Swedish is particularly common among frequent lexical items. Leslau (1969) reviews a number of processes in Ethiopian languages, including spirantization, elision, assimilation, and shortening, which affect frequent though not infrequent words. In Amharic, for instance, the commonly used form *dagmo* 'again' is assimilated to *dammo*. In all these cases, the change makes the sequence of segments more pronounceable.

It should not go unnoticed that not all sound changes fall neatly into either the 'articulation-sensitive' or the 'articulation-neutral' category. In some cases, it can only be determined *a posteriori* whether a sound change has or does not have an articulatory basis. Two developments may illustrate this difficulty. Phillips (1980) makes the case that the Old English raising of /a/ before nasals is sensitive to frequency. It occurs mainly in common words (e.g. *ond*) but rarely in uncommon ones (e.g. *panne*). Therefore, this process should be articulatorily driven. Even though it may not be obvious at first sight, the change from <an> to <on> can be regarded as an assimilation process in which the tongue is raised in anticipation of the following alveolar nasal (Phillips 1984), thus increasing the second formant of the vowel. However, the same explanation does not hold for bilabial nasals, before which no such raising occurred but which have the same effect on the preceding vowel.

The other development is more recent, and concerns the status of the glide /j/ before /u/ and after an alveolar consonant. Phillips (1981) investigated the rate of glide deletion in Southern American English in words like *nude*, *duke*, and *tune*. She found that this process is more common in infrequent than in frequent words: thus words like *new* tend to retain the glide while words like *tube* tend to lose it.

The truncation of phonological segments is a prototypical case of the reduction of articulatory effort, so it would be expected on the above logic that the glide should undergo elision in more frequent words more often than in less frequent ones. The opposite is, however, the case. Can glide deletion therefore be shown to have a non-articulatory motivation? Phillips (1984) indeed argues that the loss of /j/ is not a true assimilation process, but should rather be viewed as a phonotactic rule change. Taking Cooley's (1978) lead, she suggests that the emergence of /ju/ in Middle English violated abstract phonotactic constraints, and that the phonological system has striven to abolish this disruption ever since. The glide was first dropped after the liquids and is now in the process of disappearing after alveolar consonants.

For what it is worth, this hypothesis does not rule out the possibility that glide deletion is advantageous from the articulatory viewpoint. It just suggests an alternative which gives a satisfactory account of the empirical data and thus obviates the need to regard glide deletion as evidence failing the psycholinguistic predictions. My conclusion is, therefore, that the majority of historical developments follow the course predicted by the processing considerations.

Finally, it is instructive to compare the psycholinguistically based theory tested here with previous accounts in the literature. Actually, the only proposal that incorporates the dual role of frequency in language change is that of Phillips (1984). Her model centres around the distinction between physiological and non-physiological motivations for change. Changes that affect the most frequent words act first on surface forms and are physiologically motivated. In contrast, changes that diffuse from the less to the more frequent words act on underlying forms and are non-physiologically, or conceptually, motivated. While both theories bear an undeniable resemblance to each other, they differ in terms of basic assumptions, explicitness, and explanatory adequacy. The distinction between underlying and surface forms as two different phonological levels of representation, which is central to Phillips's model, is not invoked here. All that is required is the distinction between a phonetic (i.e. articulatory) and a phonological level, which is needed anyway and about which Phillips would certainly not disagree.

In addition, the terms 'physiological' and 'conceptual' in reference to motivations for language change are rather opaque. Although there is little doubt that 'physiological' must refer to speakers and their articulatory apparatus, Phillips (1984: 336) insists that 'physiologically motivated sound changes should not be confused with phonetically conditioned changes'. Thus it is not quite clear what exactly is meant by referring to physiological factors. Similarly, 'conceptual' is mainly defined in opposition to 'physiological', i.e. as 'non-physiological'. This procedure does not serve to elucidate the precise meaning of the term. Unless clear reference is made to the notion of articulatory ease, both these adjectives are bound to remain vague.

What is more, Phillips's theory leaves the most interesting question open. Why is it that frequency has two opposite effects on linguistic change? Apart from a passing reference to Anttila (1972), who invokes memory failures as a reason for analogical levelling, Phillips does not address this issue. As argued above, an answer to this question can only be found in a detailed examination of the processing characteristics underlying the behaviour of speakers as well as listeners. The model developed here thus purports to provide a deeper understanding of the mechanisms of linguistic change than is possible in terms of Phillips's account.

5.18. Global Frequency Effects

In the preceding section, frequency was regarded as a property of individual linguistic units. It was investigated what effect a unit's frequency has on its 'life-span'. The distinction between type and token frequency was hinted at rather than explicitly elaborated upon. While token frequency refers to individual items (e.g. *to be*), type frequency refers to classes of items (e.g. the set of irregular verbs). Such group effects will be examined in more detail in this section.

Effects which are based not upon individual elements but upon a set of elements are an emergent feature of connectionist processing systems. The basic principle is that all information is represented only once, but not on all elements for which it is relevant. As a consequence, all elements that share a particular property are connected via this property. Similarity among units thus functions to create sets of related items. For instance, all regular verbs form a set because they are linked via the appropriate past tense node. So when one regular verb is activated, all others also receive some activation and in this way reinforce one another.

Lexical items are not only connected via their phonological segments (the melody) but also via their structural representations in terms of C and V units (the skeleton). To be more specific, the two lexical elements *kick* and *pen* are more similar to each other than *kick* is to *on*, because the former pair has an identical CVC structure whereas the latter does not. This similarity metric is entirely independent of the segmental make-up of a word.

How should the connection between structural representations be conceived of? For the melody level, this is a straightforward task. The two words *kick* and *cool* are connected via the common /k/ node at the segment level. For the skeleton level, the issue is more complicated. It will be assumed that words are connected via structural nodes such as onset and nucleus. So, for example, all monosyllabic words are connected via the nucleus node. Via the onset nodes, all consonant-initial words are linked. The linking is more fine-grained, however. Two words beginning with a single consonant are more closely linked than two words of which one begins with a singleton and the other with a cluster. This is because the former word pair shares two nodes (i.e. the onset node and the C-node) whereas the latter shares only one (i.e. the onset node).

The connectivity of structural representations is conducive to particular biases in the processing system. Focusing upon word onsets, languages may differ in their rate of V-initial, C-initial, CC-initial etc. words: one language may have relatively few cluster-initial and relatively many vowel-initial words, whereas another language may show the reverse pattern. The principle of structural connectivity leads to processing biases which are more favourable to vowels in the former language but more favourable to consonants in the latter. The basic effect is one of a global situation exerting an influence upon a local decision—the so-called 'gang effect'. The global situation (i.e. the structure of the lexicon) may differ from language to language, and may therefore favour different solutions to one and the same problem.

The massive connectivity in the processing system has clear implications for linguistic change. Languages with heavy onset structures (i.e. many C-, CC-, CCC-initial words) should be more propitious to changes which increase onset weight. On the other hand, languages with light onset structures (i.e. many V-initial words) should be propitious to changes which decrease onset weight. This prediction will be tested against a diachronic phenomenon which was dealt with in section 5.9—e-prothesis in Romance. I will proceed by estimating the average onset weight in a selection of languages, derive predictions on this basis as to the probability with which each language should be willing to accommodate this change, and eventually examine whether the predictions hold.

The calculation of the average onset weight in a language is not an easy matter. Ideally, all words should be taken into account. However, this is a time-consuming task for non-computerized dictionaries. Restricting oneself to a representative sample is generally sufficient, as significant differences tend to emerge fairly rapidly. More serious is the weighing of the individual words. Should they all be given the same weight? One argument that militates against this method is the widely divergent token frequencies of individual words. It would be reasonable to give more weight to high-frequency than to low-frequency items. One difficulty of implementing this strategy is that it is unclear exactly how the weighing should be effected. Should a given item which is twice as frequent be given twice as much weight? In view of this and other more practical difficulties, it was decided to leave token frequency out of account. A major justification for this decision is that token frequency is a property of the lexical level, while the linguistic issue under debate is a phonological one. Effects from other levels may be safely assumed to be of secondary importance as compared to effects from the same level. A further problem of weighing should be noted: to derive an average onset weight, the 'distance' from one level of complexity to the next higher or lower one has to be gauged. The null hypothesis would hold that the distance from ø to C equals that from C to CC and that the distance from C to CC equals that from CC to CCC. Although this hypothesis is entirely unproven, it will be assumed here for simplicity's sake because the distance always involves one additional consonant. It is quite possible, however, that subsequent research may reveal that the distance from CC to CCC is greater than from C to CC.

Finally, the same problem arises that we encountered in the preceding section, in connection with Hooper's (1976) claim that infrequent verbs are more subject to regularization than frequent ones. As will be recalled, Hooper's basis for deriving frequency information was modern language, although it would have been methodologically more adequate to calculate the frequency of the verbs before they underwent regularization. This procedure is defensible only to the extent that the frequency of the words in question has not changed radically over time. I will make the same assumption, i.e. I will take it that the average onset weight is a property which is relatively resistant to change. In fact, word-onset consonants prove to be rather stable in diachrony: when a change takes place, it occurs at the melody level, turning, let us say, a voiceless obstruent into a voiced one. However, it rarely affects the skeleton level by adding new or deleting old material. Of course, only changes at the skeleton tier affect the weight of an onset.

The languages that were subjected to scrutiny are Italian, Spanish, Portuguese, and Romanian. For Spanish, recourse could be taken to a quantitative analysis of the entire vocabulary published by Lloyd and Schnitzer (1967). As the authors report percentages only, the raw numbers had to be reconstructed. This introduced a very minor degree of imprecision. For the other three languages, I have selected three medium-sized dictionaries[26] and extracted the first entry in each column. Each

---

[26] The three dictionaries consulted are: Livescu and Savin (1979); *Langenscheidts Großwörterbuch Italienisch* (1979); Irmen (1968).

page of each dictionary is divided into two columns. With a minimum length of 500 odd pages, this procedure yielded approximately 1000 words per language (or more). This sample is large enough for comparative purposes. Each word was categorized according to whether it began with a vowel or with one, two, or three consonants. The results of the analysis are reported in Table 26.

On the basis of this table, the average word-onset weight can be calculated. The following patterns emerge for the four languages.

(301) Spanish: 53690:70000 = 0.77
      Portuguese: 896:1146 = 0.78
      Romanian: 850:959 = 0.89
      Italian: 1482:1544 = 0.96

It is plain to see that the four languages differ considerably in their word-onset weight. Spanish word onsets are the lightest of all (closely followed by Portuguese), with an average of 0.77 consonants, whereas Italian word onsets are the heaviest, with an average of 0.96 consonants.

On the logic outlined above, Italian onsets should be most receptive to consonant-oriented change while Spanish onsets should be most receptive to vowel-based change. Since our focus is on e-prothesis, it can be predicted that Spanish will be most likely and Italian least likely to accommodate this process. It is not known, however, exactly how heavy a word onset must be on average for it to reject e-prothesis. It cannot therefore be predicted how many of the four languages will undergo this change. It is likely, though, that Spanish and Portuguese will behave identically, as their onset weights are practically indistinguishable. The psycholinguistic prediction is still rather constrained, in that if a language with a certain onset weight possesses e-prothesis, all languages with lighter onsets must also have it.

As it turns out, the processing prediction is borne out by the data. Both Spanish and Portuguese accommodated e-prothesis in their history, whereas Romanian and Italian did not. A few pertinent examples follow (see also (248)).

(302) | Spanish | Portuguese | Romanian | Italian | English gloss |
|---|---|---|---|---|
| escuela | escola | scoala | scuole | school |
| estrella | estrela | stea | stella | star |
| esplendor | esplendor | splendoare | splendore | splendour |

TABLE 26. *Word onset weight in four Romance languages*

Language	V	C	CC	CCC
Spanish	21,070 (30.1%)	44,170 (63.1%)	4,760 (6.8%)	– (0.0%)
Portuguese	330 (28.8%)	736 (64.2%)	80 (7.0%)	– (0.0%)
Romanian	262 (27.3%)	554 (57.8%)	133 (13.9%)	10 (1.0%)
Italian	317 (20.5%)	989 (64.1%)	221 (14.3%)	17 (1.1%)

It may be claimed, then, that the linguistic structure of the entire lexicon is responsible for the occurrence or non-occurrence of a particular diachronic development. Note that this explanation is not a linguistic one. Even though it draws upon linguistic structure, the critical aspect is the mechanism which endows the linguistic structure with the power to encourage or discourage certain changes. This mechanism is psycholinguistic in nature. It unites all elements of the lexicon in the form of a background which creates expectations about what is likely or unlikely to happen in a given language.

It is clearly not possible to argue that the difference in onset weight among the four languages originates from the fact that the lighter ones underwent e-prothesis while the heavier ones did not. This diachronic process affected only a small portion of the lexicon, that is, only those words which met the structural conditions for this change. It is therefore legitimate to say that the domain of application of this process is too narrow to affect the average onset weight of a language. There is no mistaking what is the cause and what is the effect.

It should, finally, be pointed out that the gang effect as an emergent property of connectionist models also makes predictions concerning the time course of linguistic change. Let us imagine a language which undergoes final consonant deletion. At first, relatively few words are affected because words ending in a final consonant are still in the majority and reinforce one another's structure. However, this resistance to change is weakened as more and more words succumb. We would therefore predict that a change in progress should not have constant speed but gain momentum as it progresses. This accords well with the available empirical evidence (e.g. Wang and Cheng 1977).

5.19. The Differential Stability of Word Class and Grammatical Gender

One of the characteristic traits of language is the principle of linking. Intonation contours may be linked with syntactic structures, the feature [+ stress] may be linked with syllables, and grammatical gender may be linked with words. In this section, a closer look will be taken at two categories which are typically linked with the lexical level—word class and grammatical gender. These two properties are part of the long-term representation of lexical items. Word class is the major criterion by which lexical items are assigned to distinct categories. Its principal function is to create a connection between the lexical and the syntactic component. Grammatical gender is primarily associated with nouns, but it may also be coded on pronouns and adjectives. It leads to a subclassification of nouns on a largely formal basis. Nouns thus constitute a particularly interesting class, in that they allow for a direct comparison of the status of two properties connected with lexical items.

Such a comparison was carried out by Berg (1992c), who investigated the role of word class and grammatical gender in language production. Because English lost (or gave up) the gender distinction on nouns, the analysis was focused upon German, where the three genders (masculine, feminine and neuter) are preserved.

In an attempt to determine the processing vulnerability of these properties, Berg turned to speech errors and examined the relative frequency with which these properties are changed in a malfunction. The less often this is the case, the more robust a given feature can be argued to be. In the case of word class, it was ascertained how often a noun interacts with another noun or with a lexical item of a different syntactic category. In the case of gender, it was ascertained how often two nouns of like gender and two nouns of unlike gender interact. The following four slips of the tongue serve as an illustration. Cases (303) and (304) refer to the word-class problem, cases (305) and (306) to the gender problem. A phonetic transcription can be dispensed with, given that the issue is not a phonological one. A morpheme-by-morpheme translation is offered instead. 'N' and 'A' abbreviate noun and adjective, respectively. 'm', 'f', and 'n' stand for masculine, feminine, and neuter, respectively.

(303) *weil Meer das Seehunde lieben* for *weil Seehunde das Meer lieben*
       because sea (N) the seals (N) love
       'because seals love the sea'
(304) *Ich bin doch Lamm– fromm wie ein Lamm*
       I am (intensifier) lamb (N) pious like a lamb
       'I am as gentle as a lamb'
(305) *Laß doch den Safe– den Schmuck im Safe*
       leave (intensifier) the safe (m) the jewellery (m) in the safe
       'Do leave the jewellery in the safe'
(306) *Die haben wohl Keller im Wasser* for *Wasser im Keller*
       they have probably cellar (m) in the water (n) water in the cellar.
       'Their cellar seems to be flooded.'

Number (303) exemplifies the standard case. A noun interacts with another noun. In (304), the noun *Lamm* 'lamb' intrudes upon the adjective *fromm* 'pious'. The interacting nouns are of like gender in (305) but of unlike gender in (306). A masculine noun replaces another masculine noun in (305), whereas a neuter and a masculine noun exchange places in (306).

The empirical data revealed a very clear picture. Nouns almost always replaced other nouns. To be exact, word class preservation could be observed in 95.6 per cent of cases. This result indicates that 'nounness' in particular and word-class information in general are very reliably accessed in language production. A similar but less strong trend emerges in the analysis of gender. Of all unambiguous cases, 72.0 per cent were like-gender and 28.0 per cent cross-gender errors. As argued in Berg (1992c), the rate of like-gender slips is significantly above chance. It can therefore be concluded that gender is not irrelevant during lexical access. However, the roles of word class and gender are not identical: word class constrains lexical access more severely than grammatical gender.

I take it as a working assumption that the processing reliability of particular linguistic features has repercussions upon stability in diachronic change. If this hypothesis is correct, the following prediction should hold: word class should be virtually immune to historical change, while cross-gender developments should not be all that uncommon. In other words, word-class changes should be significantly less frequent than gender changes. This prediction will be tested against German, although it is also applicable to other languages with a gender distinction on nouns.

Before the analysis proper, it is necessary to remove a linguistic red herring. The psycholinguistic prediction pertains to insidious changes which do not involve any conscious, purposeful activity on the part of the speakers. However, language is also susceptible to wilful manipulation, at least at the level of the individual speaker. A typical example of this is the functional extension of words as found in the language of advertising and poetry. Like English, German has at its disposal a number of morphological means of forming words on the basis of already existing words from different syntactic categories. This may happen without any formal modification at all (zero derivation). For example, all verbs may be turned into nouns in German (e.g. *sein* 'to be' → *das Sein* 'the being') while the development from noun to verb is more common in English (e.g. *the detail* → *to detail*) (Clark and Clark 1979). Similarly, adjectives may be easily turned into nouns in German (e.g. *unmöglich* 'impossible' → *das Unmögliche* 'the impossible'). These synchronic principles of word formation have diachronic implications to the effect that the syntactic versatility of words may be enlarged over time.

Although the existence of fuzzy edges is not disputed, there is a certain disparity between such changes and the ones targeted by the above prediction. The major difference lies in the fact that word-class enlargements are not changes in the sense that a word of the category X develops into a word of the category Y. Rather, the category Y word is created *in addition to* the category X item. In contrast, what is at stake here is true changes, i.e. the replacement of one feature by another, e.g. when a particular word gives up its use as a noun in favour of its use as an adjective. Hence, issues of word formation are irrelevant in this section.

It seems fair to say that nouns do not appear to convert into other word classes. Nouns may drop out of the language or be added to the word stock by processes of word formation, but they do not seem to arise from, let us say, verbs which have lost their verb specification and adopted the noun specification. Most diachronic examples that can be found are different from the ones at issue here. In the history of English, for instance, the definite article developed from the demonstrative pronouns. Even though this development cannot be captured by the standard rules of word formation, it is an expansion rather than a genuine change (as understood above) because the pronouns retained their demonstrative usage. It may thus be concluded that the psycholinguistic patterns correctly predict the virtual absence of word-class changes in language history.

Turning now to gender changes in German, it soon becomes apparent that gender has proved relatively unstable over time. Examples are plentiful in which a noun gives up a particular gender specification for another. Attendant upon this change is a period of uncertainty during which two genders may be acceptable for a given noun. However, this is very different from the cases mentioned above. The fluctuation accompanying the change of grammatical gender is a transitory phenomenon which emanates from the fact that diachronic change in general is a gradual rather than an abrupt process. Once the new form has been settled upon, the old one fades out of the system. By definition, this is not the case with lexical enrichment.

With three genders in German, there are six theoretical possibilities of shift: m → f, f → m, m → n, n → m, f → n, and n → f. All six cases are recorded in the history of the language. One example of each is furnished below. All are taken from Paul's (1916) historical grammar.

(307) m → f: OHG *seito* (m) → *die Saite* (f) 'string'
(308) f → m: Goth. *fralusts* (f) → *der Verlust* (m) 'loss'
(309) f → n: MHG *aventiure* (f) → *das Abenteuer* (n) 'adventure'
(310) n → f: OHG *bini* (n) → *die Biene* (f) 'bee'
(311) m → n: *der Bündel* (m) → *das Bündel* (n) 'bundle'
(312) n → m: *das Gips* (n) → *der Gips* (m) 'plaster'

Although these individual cases may suffice to defend the hypothesis that gender change occurs more frequently than word-class change, it would be instructive to gauge the extent of gender change in the history of German. A more quantitative approach is possible on the basis of Polzin (1903), who presents an extensive collection of material. His lists appear to be exhaustive, so the picture that can be gained from his study may be regarded as relatively accurate. Polzin distinguishes between gender change in the native vocabulary on the one hand and in loanwords and foreign words on the other. Unfortunately, he does not note how many native words did not undergo a change in gender specification. The pertinent results are displayed in Tables 27 and 28. Polzin also lists the gender changes taking place in each century from the fourteenth century onwards. Because it is not clear how these relate to the gender changes in Modern High German, they have been left out of account. In any event, they are quite similar to the data reported in Table 28.

Beginning with the loanwords and foreign words, the overall rate of gender change is 29.0 per cent. 149 nouns changed while 513 nouns preserved their gender specification. This percentage is quite high, but it has to be borne in mind that there is nothing extraordinary about loans accommodating themselves to the recipient language. Of course, the recipient language may possess the same gender distinctions

TABLE 27. *Gender change in native German nouns*

Period	m → f	f → n	n → m	m → n	n → f	f → m
OHG	14	10	24	18	5	16
MHG	27	4	15	7	6	16
Mod. HG	51	9	18	9	13	15
TOTAL	92	23	57	34	24	47

TABLE 28. *Gender change and preservation in loan and foreign words in German*

Period	Change						Preservation			% change
	m→f	f→n	n→m	m→n	n→f	f→m	m	f	n	
Pre-OHG	8	3	6	3	3	3	39	29	2	27.1
OHG	7	2	7	3	5	3	39	54	9	20.9
MHG	8	5	12	3	6	29	65	66	10	30.9
Mod. HG	9	1	5	5	2	11	19	26	6	39.3
TOTAL	32	11	30	14	16	46	162	175	27	

as the donor language, but this is no guarantee of the stability of gender because the principles of gender assignment may differ from one language to another.

Table 27 is more difficult to interpret, as precise data on the number of nouns are not available to me. Let us assume, as a rough estimate, that 3000–6000 nouns have to be reckoned with. Hence, between 5 per cent and 10 per cent of all native nouns were subject to gender change in the history of German. This is a non-negligible proportion of the native vocabulary, and provides empirical backup for the claim that gender shift is a regular process in linguistic change. A further document of the non-exceptional nature of this phenomenon is that it occurred at all times in the history of the language. That the native vocabulary is less prone to gender change than loanwords and foreign words is an obvious consequence of the fact that the latter, though not the former, have to be integrated into the system of the recipient language.

The conclusion prompted by the preceding analysis is that gender shift represents a more probable type of language change than a shift from one word class to another. This result conforms well with the psycholinguistic prediction. We may therefore assign these patterns of linguistic change a psycholinguistic cause. The instability of gender and the stability of word class in the history of German ensue from the instability of gender and the stability of word class in language processing. To be more specific, because gender is a less reliable feature in lexical access than word class, the access procedure may remain relatively undisturbed in case of a gender shift. The processing system thus allows for a latitude which may be capitalized upon by forces which push a particular noun from one gender category into another.

6

Poetic language

In the preceding two parts of this monograph, attention has been focused upon the implications of language processing for language structure and change. A third area to which processing aspects can be applied is the structure of poetry, which is not identical to what is standardly referred to as 'linguistic structure'. The reason for this non-identity is simply that (traditional) poetry, in its accentuation of the formal side of language, employs devices which play a very limited role in everyday language use. The most salient of these devices is rhyming, which is highly characteristic of poetry but untypical of ordinary speaking.

It is an open question whether poetic patterns are also subject to psycholinguistic constraints. My working assumption is that rhymes are the final product of a mental process, and as such shaped by the psycholinguistic mechanisms which have given rise to them in the first place. To be more specific, particular processing strategies are expected to produce particular rhyming patterns. This is in fact a strong claim, because the relationship between language processing and poetic structure is certainly not a direct one. Poets might be argued to be especially remote from, but not out of touch with, what is normally considered to be linguistically unmarked and psycholinguistically natural. One would expect poets to manipulate language in accordance with their individualistic if not idiosyncratic thoughts and emotions, such that little room is left for discovering the effects of general processing principles. However, traditional poets at the same time abide by general conventions, especially in rhyming, and it is against these conventions that the predictions from psycholinguistics will be tested.

Three different aspects of rhymes will be investigated—the phonological structure of rhymes (section 6.3), the starting-point of the rhyme (section 6.2), and the 'quality' of the rhyme (section 6.1). The languages under analysis will be German, English, French, and Arabic.

6.1. Imperfect Rhymes in German[1]

This section centres around the existence and nature of imperfect rhymes in German poetry. The perfect rhyme consists of two words which are identical in their phonemic make-up from the first stressed vowel onwards. This corresponds almost always

---

[1] The data reported in this section have been examined from a different theoretical perspective in Berg (1990b).

with the phonological notion of rime or super-rime (Berg 1989a). Both possibilities are exemplified below. Following is the second part of a poem by Christian Morgenstern entitled *Täuschung* 'Deception'. The phonetic transcription of the rhyming words appears at the end of each line. The rhyming strings are given in italics.

(313) Alles ist vielleicht nicht kl*ar*, [klaːr]
       nichts vielleicht erkl*ärlich*, [ɛr.kléːr.lıç]
       und somit, was ist, wird, w*ar* [vaːr]
       schlimmstenfalls entb*ehrlich*.[2] [ɛnt.béːr.lıç]

The identical structures comprise the phonological rime (i.e. nucleus and coda) in lines 1 and 3 but the super-rime (i.e. stressed vowel, coda and unstressed syllable) in lines 2 and 4. This difference is designated by the terms '*masculine* and *feminine rhyme*' in literary criticism.

The perfect rhyme rests upon the integrity of the phonological units that make up the rhyme. That is to say, the segments are implicitly taken to be indivisible units. We know from phonological speech errors that feature slips are uncommon and that indeed segments move as wholes, i.e. a segment that is driven out of position reaches its new location unscathed. However, there are two (and only two) error categories in German in which the segmental integrity is regularly destroyed. The one involves consonants, the other vowels. Since the latter category was given extensive treatment in section 4.15, only the essentials will be briefly recapitulated. The empirical observation is that when a long and a short vowel are substituted for each other, the length feature almost invariably stays put. The interacting segments behave as if length was not a part of their featural representation. Consider (314).

(314) *Mutterschühle* for *Mütterschule*
       [mutɛrʃyːlə   mytɛrʃuːlə]
       'prenuptial school'

The extraordinary feature of this error class is that it attests to a dissociation of vocalic length from its 'segmental core'. It might even be claimed that length is not specified at the representational level at which vowel slips come about. No other vocalic feature behaves like length.

In the consonantal domain, a comparable phenomenon can be observed. While consonantal features are generally faithful to the segment to which they belong, voice can be shown to display an exceptional behaviour (see Berg 1985). Two subcategories have to be distinguished according to the position in which the error occurs. In word- and morpheme-initial sites, the pattern to be reported below is optional; but as rhymes do not involve these positions, this subcategory can be ignored for the present analysis. Our focus will therefore be upon the pertinent errors in non-word-initial, syllable-initial loci, as exemplified in (315).

---

[2] Here is a rough translation for those non-German readers who cannot resist the urge of seeking a link between the contents of this poem and this book. 'Everything may not be clear, nothing perhaps explainable. As a consequence, that which is, will be, or was is in the worst case dispensible.'

(315) Die hätte mir die Ausen– Augen ausgekratzt
       [au.zən au.gən aus.gə.kratst]
       'She would have scratched out my eyes'

As in the case of vocalic length, consonantal voice is separated from the migrating segment during the error process. What has happened in (315) is that the /s/ from *ausgekratzt* is inadvertently shifted into a position which was originally destined for the voiced velar stop /g/. Rather than remaining intact, the /s/ surfaces as its voiced congener, /z/. In all the available examples, the error segment agrees in voicing with the target element, so that this metamorphosis cannot be regarded as fortuitous. This suggests that the target segment is not completely absent, but imposes its voice feature upon the intruding unit. There is thus a dissociation between voice and the 'rest' of the segment.

It was argued in Berg (1985; 1988b) that voice and length are best characterized as suprasegmental features. What predictions can be derived from this hypothesis regarding the structure of poetic rhymes? Given that the error process is blind to the voicing value of consonants and the length specification of vowels, it may be expected that the rhyming process operates in similar fashion. In other words, if voice and length differences are ignored in errors, they should also be ignored in rhymes. Two quite specific claims can be made on the basis of the psycholinguistic data. It is predicted that deviations from the perfect rhyme pattern are possible, and that these imperfect rhymes are brought about by a discrepancy in the voice or the length specification. A discrepancy involving other features is not allowed.

These predictions may be tested in one of two ways. Either portions of the works of a large number of poets or the complete work of a single author can be investigated. It was decided to concentrate upon one well-known poet who may be considered representative of the German rhyming tradition and whose language is close to its current state. The choice fell upon Wilhelm Busch (1832–1908), whose complete rhymed poetry was subjected to analysis. The corpus thus collected comprises approximately 10,000 rhyme pairs, which were examined with a view to determining the existence and nature of imperfect rhymes. This is a straightforward task in Busch's poems, because it is almost always clear how the graphemic sequence is to be phonologically interpreted and when the author resorts to rhyming and when he does not.

In concert with the predictions, imperfect rhymes can be found in Busch's poems. Among the 10,000 rhyme pairs I only found four exceptional cases, which I have left out of my analysis. All imperfect rhymes implicate a divergence in only one phonological feature (i.e. they are maximally similar) and divide into three subclasses. These are characterized by a disparity in voice in the case of consonants and of length and roundedness in the case of vowels. The three types of imperfection are illustrated in (316–18). The lines are taken from the Busch edition by Bohne (n. d.).

(316) Oh, was macht der Besenstiel [beː.zən.ʃtiːl]
       Für ein schmerzliches Gefühl! [gə.fyːl]

(317) Doch wie er schnell den Rückzug sucht, [zuːxt]
   Hemmt's Stubenmädel seine Flucht. [fluxt]
(318) Kaum hat er dies als wahr befunden, [bə.fun.dən]
   So kommt ein Stich direkt von unten.[3] [un.tən]

These rhyming patterns are not perfect because the tonic vowels disagree in roundedness in (316) and in length in (317). The non-word-initial, syllable-initial consonants disagree in voicing in (318). Specifically, [iː] vs. [yː] are paired off in (316), [uː] vs. [u] in (317), and [d] vs. [t] in (318). The analysis of the entire data set reveals that the imperfection is not restricted to any particular segments. All of them can in principle contribute and most of them actually do.

The next step is to determine whether the three subclasses of imperfect rhymes are real, i.e. whether the observer's perspective is congruent with the author's intention. In other words, the possibility has to be ruled out that Busch did not use these rhymes as freely as he used the perfect rhymes. If he had felt the so-called imperfect rhymes to be completely acceptable, it would be pointless to stigmatize them as 'imperfect' and to draw conclusions from their putative existence. Only if Busch can be shown to have discouraged the occurrence of rhymes such as (316–18) does it make sense to speak of imperfections in a theoretically significant way. This means that imperfect rhymes should occur with significantly less than chance frequency; therefore, a frequency count of all imperfect rhymes in the corpus is needed. Table 29 presents both the raw data and the normalized ones. The normalization procedure is necessary because the segments which are responsible for the imperfection are not equally common. The differing frequencies of occurrence have been eliminated by a method which is described in Berg (1990b). For the normalized set, only the percentages can be viewed as meaningful.

It is immediately apparent from Table 29 that the three imperfect rhyme types distribute very unevenly. Whereas length- and voice-induced imperfections are very rare, imperfect rhymes involving roundedness are extremely frequent, a tendency which comes out even more clearly through the normalization procedure. The extreme commonness of the roundedness category relative to the others should make us suspicious about its alleged status. Is it not too frequent to be regarded as an imperfection?

TABLE 29. *Frequency of imperfect rhymes in Busch's poetry according to rhyme type*

	Roundedness	Length	Voice
Non-normalized	914 (90.1%)	71 (7.0%)	29 (2.9%)
Normalized	5,557 (97.5%)	114 (2.0%)	29 (0.5%)

[3] Translation: (314) 'Oh what painful feeling the broomstick gives.' (315) 'But when he quickly took to retreat, the chambermaid thwarted his flight.' (316) 'No sooner had he discovered this to be true than a poke came directly from underneath.'

To clarify this issue, a subset of the data (450 rhyme pairs) has been analysed in terms of imperfect rhymes and, more importantly, in terms of perfect rhymes in which an imperfection might have been possible, i.e. where the phonotactic constraints of the language do not prohibit the potential occurrence of an imperfect rhyme. The subset at hand comprises 79 (73 per cent) perfect and 29 (27 per cent) imperfect rhymes of the roundedness category involving high front vowels. Chance can be calculated by comparing the number of perfectly rhyming vowel pairs with that of the imperfectly rhyming vowel pairs. There are four high front vowels in German: /i:, ɪ, y:, y/. These can be grouped into four perfect pairs (/i:/–/i:/, /ɪ/–/ɪ/, /y:/–/y:/, /y/–/y/) and two imperfect pairs involving roundedness (/i:/–/y:/, /ɪ/–/y/). This means that about one third (2/6) of all high front vowel pairs can be expected to be imperfect by chance. This percentage is not significantly different from the actual number of imperfect rhymes in the subset ($\chi^2 < 1$). It can thus be concluded that Busch treated /i:/–/i:/ and /i:/–/y:/ pairs indifferently: for him, both pairs were equally licensed. The implication is clear: rhymes whose imperfection is brought about by a difference in roundedness cannot legitimately be construed as imperfect rhymes. They may be imperfect in the eyes of the detached observer, but they were not imperfect in Busch's conception of poetry. We are thus left with length-induced and voice-induced imperfection—precisely the types for which an imperfection has been predicted. The special status of consonantal voice and vocalic length in slips of the tongue is paralleled in poetic rhymes.

However, it would be fallacious to believe that rhymes are utterly blind to voice and length specifications. If they were, they would be as common as perfect rhymes, contrary to fact. Voice and length divergences are only allowed as exceptions. Hence, information on the length of vowels and the voicing of consonants is available during the rhyming process, but it is less central in that it is the first to be ignored when a deviation from the ideal form appears inevitable. There is thus a gradualness in how central a given feature is to a segment. A very similar inference can be drawn from the speech-error corpus. Looking at the entire data, it can be easily seen that voice and length are not 'switched off' during the error process. In point of fact, they severely constrain the occurrence of errors in that the interaction of vowels of like quantity is strongly encouraged while the interaction of vowels of unlike length is strongly discouraged. The same applies to consonants and their voice feature. Voice and length are therefore available, though not at the same level as other features. In this view, length and voice are the first to be overlooked because they are the furthest away from their segmental core.

To conclude, there is a fair amount of convergence between the speech error and the rhyme data. In the majority of cases, both errors and rhymes agree in terms of consonant voice and vowel length. When they do not, the discrepancy is ignored in both cases. The speech errors behave as if voicing and length are simply not there, and the rhyme data also imply a disregard for differing voice and length specifications. Thus the poetic structures are in full agreement with the predictions derived from the psycholinguistic observations.

6.2. The Onset of Rhymes in English and French

It has been noted in the preceding section that German rhymes typically begin with a stressed vowel. For monosyllabic words, the break between the initial consonant(s) and the vowel is virtually the only way of constructing rhyme pairs. If the rhyme began earlier, it would coincide with the word boundary. The undesirable consequence would be that the selection of one rhyme candidate would compel the poet to use the same word again (or a homophone) in one of the following lines. It is self-evident that this strategy stands in the way of a neat progression in the poem, leads to excessive repetition on the formal and content side, and is ultimately detrimental to the quality of the work. The onset of the rhyme at the word boundary can thus be expected to be unpopular with poets. If, on the other hand, the rhyme began later, it would coincide with the coda. As the coda constitutes the final part of the word, the rhyme would end when it has only just begun. Not only the shortness but also the consonantal structure of such a rhyme would lessen its perceptual salience considerably. Evidently, a rhyme which is not salient cannot perform its task of highlighting the formal side of language. A rhyme beginning at the nucleus/coda boundary is therefore also disfavoured. The only remaining possibility, then, is the onset/nucleus boundary as the starting-point for the rhyme.

For polysyllabic words, the situation is different. In disyllabic words, two loci for the onset of a rhyme can be identified which do not run into any of the above-mentioned problems. The beginning of a rhyme may coincide with the first (stressed) vowel, as in the case of the monosyllabic words. Alternatively, the beginning of a rhyme may coincide with the syllable boundary. The decision for or against either possibility might be a function of the phonological structure of disyllabic words, i.e. whether the first (major) break separates the two syllables or the word onset from the rest (in typical two-syllable words). In the first case a syllabic representation would be built up, but not in the second.

Whether or not a syllabic representation is constructed might be a decision taken on a language-particular basis. A comparison of the syllable's role in the perception of English and French suggests that this is in fact so. Cutler et al. (1986), continuing earlier work of Mehler et al. (1981), explored the issue of whether the acoustic signal is translated into chunks of syllable size which serve as an access code to the units in the mental lexicon. If a syllable-based level of representation is constructed during on-line processing, it must be possible to tap information which is syllabically represented. In an attempt to do so, Cutler et al. used a phoneme-monitoring task in which subjects had to detect a prespecified sound or sound sequence among a list of stimulus words. The dependent variable was the time it took them to react, the independent variable was the particular relation between the (visually presented) prespecified sounds (targets) and the (aurally presented) stimuli. Basically, two possibilities were tested. The target sequence either corresponded or did not correspond to a syllable of the stimulus word. Let us take some examples from French. The sequence /pa/ corresponds to a full syllable in *palace* 'palace' where the syllable boundary falls between the first /a/ and the /l/. In *palmier* 'palm tree', by contrast, it does not correspond to an entire syllable because the syllable boundary divides the word into [pal] and [mje]. The opposite situation holds for the target sequence [pal].

Cutler et al. reasoned that if the speech signal is segmented into syllable-sized chunks, subjects should respond more quickly in the congruence than in the incongruence condition. This hypothesis was tested on both French and English speakers, because a priori considerations led the authors to expect differences between the two languages. English is notoriously difficult to syllabify. Quite often, it is simply not clear whether a syllable boundary is to be inserted before or after a medial consonant, as in *melon*. This uncertainty has led phonologists to introduce the notion of ambisyllabicity, i.e. the claim that one and the same segment may belong to two syllables at the same time. French does not pose such problems, at least not to the same extent (see below). Because it is a final-stress language and the onset of a stressed syllable is clearer than that of an unstressed syllable (contrast *listen* and *resist*), medial consonants in disyllabic words are generally unambiguous as to which syllable they are dominated by. This difference has encouraged the expectation that the French subjects in the experimental situation might react differently from the English subjects. In its strongest form, the hypothesis would hold that French listeners build up a syllable-based representation while English listeners do not.

Intriguingly enough, this is exactly what the monitoring experiments showed to be the case. French subjects reacted more quickly to targets which were congruent with the first syllable of the stimulus word than to targets which were not. In contrast, the reaction of the English listeners was not systematically influenced by the congruence or incongruence of the target and the first syllable of the stimulus word. Although the /pa/ targets did not elicit the same reaction times to stimuli such as *palace* as the /pal/ targets did to stimuli such as *palpitate*, there was no reasonable way of interpreting these results in terms of a syllabification strategy. Cutler et al. conclude that during the process of language comprehension, French listeners segment the speech stream into syllables whereas English listeners do not.

What predictions follow from this cross-linguistic processing difference regarding the structure of English and French rhymes? On the assumption that English listeners do not construct a representational level featuring syllables, it is highly unlikely that English rhymes comprise syllable-sized units, i.e. that the rhymes begin at the syllable boundary. The logic is simply that if a break is not made in the mind, it should not be made 'on paper'. For French poetry, the opposite prediction can be formulated: on the assumption that French listeners build up a syllabic representation, i.e. that the syllable boundary introduces a natural partitioning of French words, it is to be expected that French poets make use of this option and allow their rhymes to begin at the syllable boundary.

However, this prediction in no way implies that the onset of a French rhyme must always coincide with a syllable boundary. This is just an additional possibility which arises because of the way the speech stream is segmented in French. It does not preclude the possibility that the division between onset and (phonological) rime may also be real in French because the two breaks are located at different hierarchical levels (at and below the syllabic level).[4]

It was felt unsuitable to test the predictions pertaining to English against a single author. Since we are on the lookout for a specific rhyme type (or rather absence thereof), it is always possible that one poet has forgone using this particular rhyme for whatever reason. Certainly it would not be justified under these circumstances to ascribe any theoretical significance to this result. Therefore, preference was given to the option of having a wide spectrum of English poets at one's disposal. An anthology was considered best, and so I browsed through Hayward's (1956) edition of samples of English verse. As it turned out, I could not find a single example of a rhyme beginning at a syllable boundary (even when the syllable boundary was blurred by ambisyllabicity). I may of course have overlooked some pertinent cases, but there is no question that this rhyme type is of extremely low frequency, if it exists at all. It may be concluded, therefore, that the predictions concerning English poetry are borne out by the empirical data.

The predictions regarding French were tested against the writings of two great poets—Jean de la Fontaine (1621–95) and Arthur Rimbaud (1854–91). Rather than focusing upon the complete works of a single writer, it was deemed preferable to examine extracts from more than one author. This decision helped eliminate possible idiosyncratic influences and provided a basis for a comparison between the authors. Contrary to English, an anthology was regarded as inappropriate because detailed quantitative information was needed on the prevailing rhyme patterns. Such information could not be furnished by short passages from diverse poets.

The selection of La Fontaine and Rimbaud was motivated by the desire to examine two representatives of (almost) Modern French who are a fair time span apart. La Fontaine is the best-known French fabulist, whose fables are all rhymed. He has served as a model for others and is undubitably a good starting-point. Rimbaud wrote more than two centuries later, and used rhyme schemes in most of his works. The ensuing analysis is based upon the entire first book of fables and the first thirteen fables of the second book in the 1966 edition of La Fontaine. Rimbaud's rhymes were taken from the first thirty-five pages of his *Poésies* (pp. 25–59 of the 1964 edition of his poetic works). This yields a total of 1037 rhymes, a number large enough to permit a test of the above predictions.

Before the results are presented, a few methodological details should be noted. Only perfect rhymes were taken into account. The number of imperfect rhymes, all of which involved quantitative differences in the vowels, was extremely low. Rhyme triplets, which are not uncommon in La Fontaine's poetry, were counted twice, i.e. the first and the second rhyming word were counted as one pair and so were the second and the third rhyming words. Since the purpose of the following analysis was to determine the onset of the rhyme, a difficulty arose in those cases where the word

---

[4] Whether this is at odds with the onset/super-rime division remains to be seen.

or the syllable began with a 'zero consonant'. When 'something' contrasted with 'nothing' in a certain position, it was decided to treat this constellation as being non-identical. The same applies to contrasts between 'nothing' and 'nothing'. That is, formal identity can only be realized through audible segments.[5]

A further problem concerns the proper definition of the syllable in French. This issue has to be settled because, as argued at the beginning of this section, monosyllabic words may be expected to exhibit a behaviour different from that of polysyllabic ones. It is therefore necessary to set forth the principles whereby the number of syllables is established. There are two groups of controversial cases in French. The first is illustrated by words like *sable* [sabl(ə)] 'sand' and the second by words like *miette* 'crumb'. On one definition of the syllable, it can have only one peak in sonority. According to this definition, *sable* has to be counted as disyllabic because both the /a/ and the /l/ are more sonorous than the /b/. On the other hand, there is an absolute law in French which states that all words are stressed on the last syllable (leaving aside special cases such as emphatic stress). However, the assumed second syllable in *sable* never receives stress, which militates against the bisyllabicness of such words.

The item *miette* allows the two pronunciations [miɛt] and [mjɛt]. The first is disyllabic and involves adjacent vowels, while the second is monosyllabic and has a glide before the vowel. Furthermore, it is unclear whether /j/ belongs to the onset or the nucleus. The decision for one or the other pronunciation depends upon a number of factors, one of which being speaking rate. The slower it is, the more likely *miette* is to be rendered as [miɛt].

I submit that these problems cannot be resolved by arbitrarily giving more weight to one phonological criterion than to another. The ideal solution would appear to be to answer these questions on the basis of criteria which can be shown to be germane to poetic rhyming itself. As Rimbaud rhymes *cieux* [sjø:] 'skies' with *frileux* [fri:lø:] 'chilly', and as imperfect rhymes are the exception to the rule, it was decided to include this pair in the category of perfect rhymes, thereby implicitly assigning the on-glide to the syllable onset. Words like *sable* and *miette* were treated as monosyllabic because, under the two-syllable analysis, *sable* would have to be rhymed on *cycle* [sikl(ə)] 'cycle' and in this way form a rhyme from the nucleus of the second syllable onward. Such rhymes do not, however, occur, suggesting that these words function as monosyllabics in French verse.

With these preliminaries settled, we may move on to the analysis proper. Table 30 presents the results for the two authors separately. In line with the main objective, the table is divided into rhymes beginning at the onset/rime boundary (in the stressed syllable) and those that begin earlier.[6] Subdivisions are according to where exactly

---

[5] This is not as self-evident as it might sound. For example, Leech (1969) notes that vowel-initial word pairs qualified as an alliterative pattern in Old English verse. That is, identity is defined on the absence of a segment, i.e. on 'nothing'.

[6] Rhymes beginning later than this are not expected given the suprasegmental structure of French words (and the rhyming principles outlined above).

268 *Linguistic Structure and Change*

the rhyme begins and whether mono- or polysyllabic words are involved. As argued above, this leads perforce to different predictions, since monosyllabics cannot be broken up at the syllable boundary. Note that tokens rather than types were counted.

Table 30 calls for the following explanations. The mixed category comprises those rhymes of which the one word is monosyllabic and the other polysyllabic. The *pars in toto* category describes those rhymes in which the one rhyming word is phonologically identical to a part of the other, as exemplified in (325). It is also possible for the rhyme to be based upon phonologically identical words, either by exact repetition of the first word or by the use of homophones (see (326) below). Several illustrative examples follow. (Three points indicate that the next line has been skipped as it is irrelevant to the rhyme.)

(319) Nous nous sentions si forts, nous voulions être doux!   [du:]
       Et depuis ce jour-là, nous sommes comme fous!   [fu:]
       (Rimbaud, p. 38)
(320) Elle alla crier famine   [fa.mi:n]
       Chez la Fourmi sa voisine,   [vwa.zi:n]
       (La Fontaine, p. 51)
(321) Elle eut un doux rire brutal ...   [bry:.tal]
       Un joli rire de crystal.   [krɪs.tal]
       (Rimbaud, p. 44)
(322) L'Idéal, la pensée invincible, éternelle,   [e:.tɛr.nɛl]
       Tout; le dieu qui vit, sous son argile charnelle,   [ʃar.nɛl]
       (Rimbaud, p. 30)
(323) De linges odorants et jaunes, de chiffons ...   [ʃi:fõ]
       De fichus de grand' mère où sont peints des griffons;   [gri:fõ]
       (Rimbaud, p. 56)
(324) Quand, sous les poutres enfumées,   [ã.fy:.me:]
       Chantant des croûtes parfumées   [par.fy:.me:]
       (Rimbaud, p. 49)
(325) Quand un autre Dragon, qui n'avait qu'un seul chef ...   [ʃɛf]
       Me voilà saisi derechef   [dǝ.rǝ.ʃɛf]
       (La Fontaine, p. 61)
(326) Les sombres vêtements ne jouchent plus la terre,   [tɛr]
       La bise sous le seuil a fini par se taire ...   [tɛr]
       (Rimbaud, p. 27)

The first two examples document rhymes beginning at the onset/rime boundary. While (319) involves monosyllabic words, disyllabic words are rhymed in (320). The rhyme in (320) begins in the second, not in the first syllable. Rhyme (321) begins at the syllable boundary. In trisyllabic and longer words, the onset of the rhyme most usually coincides with the last syllable boundary. An exception to this is given in (324), where the rhyme begins at the last but one syllable boundary. In (322) and (323), the onset of the rhyme can be located within the penultimate syllable.

TABLE 30. *The onset of rhymes in French poetry*

Rhyme	Beginning at onset/rime boundary			Earlier, beginning at				Special cases	
Rhyme words	Monosyllabic	Polysyllabic	Mixed	σ Boundary	P. coda	P. nucleus	P. onset	*Pars in toto*	Identical words
La Fontaine	94	126	158	98	1	16	0	31	3
Rimbaud	140	53	131	77	3	29	4	60	13

Note: P. = previous; σ = syllable

Depending upon the structure of the syllable, the rhyme may begin with the coda (if any), as in (322), or with the nucleus, as in (323). Rhymes in which both nucleus and coda are identical in the penultimate syllable occur extremely seldom. Numbers (325) and (326) illustrate two special cases. In (325), one rhyming word is contained in the other. In the majority of cases, the shorter word begins at a syllable boundary of the longer one. In (326), phonologically identical words are rhymed. These need not be monosyllabic, as in (326), but may also consist of more than one syllable.

The foremost conclusion that can be drawn from Table 30 is that there are rhymes which do *not* set in at the onset/rime boundary. In fact, rhymes beginning at the syllable boundary are by no means few in number (16.9 per cent at the very least). How important they actually are numerically depends upon whether the rhymes beginning before the last syllable boundary of the word are taken into consideration, and to which category/categories of 'English' rhymes they are compared. Let us address the second point first. Trivially enough, rhymes commencing at the syllable boundary presuppose at least disyllabic rhyme words. To derive a fair estimate of the numerical importance of rhymes beginning at the onset/rime boundary and those beginning at the syllable boundary, it is imperative that both types stand the same chance of occurring. Therefore, it is only legitimate to compare the syllable-based rhymes against the polysyllabic 'English' rhymes. Even the mixed category of Table 30 has to be excluded because it involves one-syllable words.

The first point is harder to deal with. The crux is that the status of the material preceding the syllable boundary in the non-English rhyme type is unclear. The critical question is whether the identical material to the left of the last syllable boundary occurs at or above chance level. Chance was estimated on the basis of Juilland's (1967) inverse dictionary of French. It was determined how often the coda or the nucleus (or both) of the penultimate syllable of the two rhyming words are identical conditional upon their final syllables being already identical. Because the identical-coda category comprises very few instances indeed, attention was limited to those rhymes beginning with the vowel of the penultimate syllable. The following procedure was adopted. It was calculated for words with identical final syllables which vowel precedes the identical syllable in how many cases. This yields a frequency-of-occurrence value (expressed in percentages) for each vowel in this position. By squaring these percentages, we derive an estimate of how often two given words with identical vowels in the penultimate syllable will co-occur by chance. When these squared percentages for each vowel are added up, we obtain an index of the likelihood with which two words with identical final syllables happen to have the same vowel in the penultimate syllable. Let us take a concrete example. Juilland's dictionary lists 134 words ending in [ke:] such as *communiqué* and *fabriquer*. As shown in Table 31, the vowel /ɔ/ has a probability of occurring in the penultimate syllable of 29/134 = 21.6 per cent. The combined frequency of occurrence of two such words is $(21.6 \text{ per cent})^2 = 4.7$ per cent. That is to say, in almost 5 per cent of all these cases potential rhyming words have a half-open back rounded vowel in the penultimate syllable by chance. This procedure is repeated for all vowels. All squared

TABLE 31. *Frequency distribution of vowels in penultimate syllables of words ending in [-keː]*

Vowel	a	ā	e	ɛ	ɛ̃	i	ɔ	u	y
Instances	25	6	7	3	2	55	29	3	4

percentages sum up to 25.5 per cent. This means that vowels happen to be identical in about a quarter of all cases. With respect to the issue under debate, the implication would be that the poetic rhymes can be claimed to begin with the vowel of the penultimate syllable only if this percentage is significantly exceeded. Ideally, the entire lexicon would have to be subjected to such an investigation, but for practical reasons the analysis was restricted to twenty of the most common final syllables in French. These include [teː], [riː], [tiːk], [tɛ̃], [seː], [sɑ̃] and [tœr]. In any case the exclusion of the less frequent cases is not a serious drawback, because low-frequency items are, by their very nature, less likely to form rhyme words.

To calculate a general chance level, the percentages for all twenty word sets (comprising a total of 5799 words) have been averaged. This step is justified to the extent that there is no interaction between the size of the word set and the percentage of identical vowels in penultimate syllables. More specifically, if the percentage in question is deviant in small word sets, the results would be distorted because these word sets are under-represented in the data. However, there is no consistent relationship between set size and percentage of identical vowels. In the sets containing fewer than 100 words, the mean is 27.1 per cent while it amounts to 25.7 per cent for the sets containing more than 100 items. This is not a significant difference. We may conclude therefore that it is legitimate to average the percentages for sets of unequal size. Doing so, we arrive at a general chance level of 26.0 per cent. That is, the structure of French words is such that in word pairs with identical final syllables, the vowels of the penultimate open syllable happen to be the same in slightly more than a quarter of cases. Given that 20.5 per cent (45/220) of the rhymes begin with the vowel of the penultimate syllable (see Table 30), it can be shown that the empirical pattern does not significantly differ from chance ($\chi^2(1) = 0.6, p > 0.3$). If anything, the chance level is higher than the percentage actually observed. One way of rationalizing this trend might be to assume that the poets have made a deliberate effort to keep the vowels in the penultimate syllables distinct so as to increase the salience of the syllable boundary as the starting-point for the rhyme.

It can thus be concluded that French rhymes do not begin with the vowel of the penultimate syllable. The identical material preceding the last syllable is mainly a consequence of the phonological structure of French words. Neither the onset/rime nor the nucleus/coda boundary of the penultimate syllable can be considered a natural starting-point for rhymes.[7] On the other hand, there is no denying that an

---

[7] That rhymes begin much more often at the onset/rime boundary than at the nucleus/coda boundary is fully expected given the hierarchical structure of the syllable according to which the division into nucleus and coda presupposes that into onset and rime.

'excess' of phonological identity is not discouraged. This comes out most clearly in the special cases which involve a maximum of formal likeness. Either the rhyming words are completely identical or the one is identical to a part of the other. This should not be taken to mean that the greater the formal similarity between the rhyming words, the more highly valued the rhyme. Nevertheless, it does suggest that the criteria for what is an acceptable rhyme are less rigorous in French than in English or German.

We are now in a position to assess the significance of the rhymes beginning at the last syllable boundary. All rhymes beginning at the last syllable boundary or earlier were compared to all rhymes involving at least disyllabic rhyme words and beginning after the consonantal onset. Two calculations were performed, the one including and the other excluding the special cases (termed 'conditions I and II' respectively). Pooling the data from La Fontaine and Rimbaud, we get 64.7 per cent syllable-based rhymes in condition I and 56.0 per cent in condition II. A breakdown of the data by poet yields 54.2 per cent in condition I and 47.7 per cent in condition II for La Fontaine, and 77.8 per cent in condition I and 68.1 per cent in condition II for Rimbaud. That the percentage of syllable-based rhymes is significantly higher in Rimbaud than in La Fontaine follows from the fact that the former author uses relatively few 'English' rhymes involving polysyllabic words. Naturally, this gives more importance to the 'non-English' rhymes.

These percentages may be interpreted as follows. When the structural preconditions for non-syllable-based and syllable-based rhyme types are met, the latter are at least as likely as, if not more likely than, the former to occur. As argued above, there is no reason to believe that the syllable-based type eliminates the 'English' one entirely. In view of this non-exclusive situation, a largely equal partitioning of the territory is all one may reasonably expect.

The reality of rhymes beginning at the last syllable boundary can thus be taken for granted in French. This result is in perfect agreement with what has been predicted on psycholinguistic grounds. For English poetry, rhymes beginning at the syllable boundary were predicted to be non-occurring, and this was found to be true of the samples studied. For French, however, precisely these rhymes were predicted, and not only attested but actually found to be an outstanding type. The differing rhyming practices of French and English poets can thus be claimed to have to do with the differing processing strategies employed by speakers of these languages during language comprehension.

The following objection to this hypothesis may be raised. Rather than invoking psycholinguistic causes, it might be possible to find the reasons for the disparity between English and French rhymes in the structural differences between the two languages. By implication, this would obviate the need to look for processing explanations. English words tend to have stress on the first syllable while French words are always finally stressed. Because the beginning of stressed syllables is acoustically more prominent than that of unstressed syllables, it is easier to mark syllable boundaries in finally than in initially stressed words. As a consequence, French words are bound to have more clear-cut syllable boundaries than English ones. French poets, so one might argue, capitalize upon this opportunity which is not available to their English colleagues. In this view, the additional option in French would be a simple spin-off function of differences in stress placement between the two languages.

The problem with this account is not that it is wrong but rather its fragmentary nature. The mere establishment of a linguistic fact is not a sufficient explanation for a particular rhyming pattern. If the linguistic fact had no effect upon the processing system, that is, if the medial consonants in English *balance* vs. French *balance* were processed alike, there would be no genuine basis for expecting them to be differentially treated in poetic rhyme. There is reason to believe that the relationship between psycholinguistic processing and linguistic structure should not be conceived of in such a way that every single linguistic effect must have repercussions upon processing. Note that syllable boundaries are not always more clear-cut in French than in English. The stressed syllable in final position disambiguates only the medial consonants in disyllabic words. In longer words, the ambiguities increase with the number of syllables, especially as French also has short vowels which foster the occurrence of ambisyllabicity. Ambisyllabicity, then, is not a concept which is inapplicable to French. For example, the /l/ in *collaborer* [kɔlabo:re:] 'to collaborate' is no less ambisyllabic than that in English *colony*. Since ambisyllabicity is less wide-spread in French than in English, the difference between the two languages is only gradual.

I submit that there is no cogent reason why the processing system must take advantage of the more precise syllable boundary information in French. After all, this information is of limited utility. English listeners, who do not have this option at their disposal, are perfectly capable of comprehending fluent speech without it. The linguistic structure of French words can therefore be viewed as a necessary though not a sufficient reason for the deployment of this strategy. There must be something additional in the psycholinguistic mechanism which makes it responsive to the information in the linguistic structure. Only if this psycholinguistic principle can be shown to exist may we hope to arrive at a better understanding of the cross-linguistic differences under scrutiny.

To conclude, recourse to linguistic differences between English and French does not suffice to explain the differing rhyming patterns in the two languages. What is needed is an account which is based upon psycholinguistic representations which must be real and valid for poets during the construction of their rhymes. It is quite possible that the psycholinguistic mechanisms have evolved in response to linguistic structures, but this does not in any way weaken the claim that the structure of the rhymes is related to the operating principles of the processing system. It might even be argued that the processor functions as an intermediary between the linguistic and the poetic structures. The account of the rhyming patterns offered here is clearly psycholinguistic in nature, but it is readily acknowledged that the processing principles upon which it relies may at least in part be motivated by particular linguistic structures.

6.3. Rhymes in Arabic Verse

It was extensively argued in section 4.6 that the structure of the syllable in Arabic is predominantly flat. No evidence could be found for the phonological notion of rime as an intermediate constituent between the syllable/word and the segment nodes. On the premiss that poets draw upon the structural patterns of the language when engaging in their art of writing, it is possible to make a prediction which is quite astonishing from the Germanic viewpoint. In contradistinction to the Germanic rhyme tradition, which relies heavily upon rimes, it can be predicted that Arabic rhymes are *not* rime-based. The logic of the argument is very simple. If the notion of rime does not exist, poets cannot exploit it to their ends. Note nonetheless that despite this simplicity, the outcome of the analysis is anything but self-evident. The relationship between unintentional speech errors and intentional rhyming patterns, which are part of the cultural heritage of a linguistic community, is as remote as can be. A priori, there is no reason to expect poets to be constrained in the same way that speakers are when making slips of the tongue.

In addressing the psycholinguistic prediction, we will begin with a general qualitative examination of the issue and move on to a more detailed quantitative analysis afterwards. The following brief outline of the rhyme patterns in Classical Arabic is based upon Grotzfeld (n. d.). In line with the above prediction, the most important element in the Arabic rhyme is the rhyming *consonant*. It alone suffices to create a rhyming word pair. Of course, this is prima facie evidence against the rime as the rhyme-bearing unit. Two examples follow.

(327) darāb–rakib 'to hit'–'to ride'
(328) ʔaʕmaal–ʔihmaal 'deeds'–'carelessness'

The rhyme consonant is /b/ in (327) and /m/ in (328). As can be seen from these examples, the position of the rhyme consonant is variable. It may occur in onset or in coda position. In the latter case, the rhyme consonant terminates the rhyming words. In the former case, all elements following the onset have to be identical. Thus, basically the same two concepts are here at work that can be found in the Germanic literary tradition. For one thing, the concept of continuity states that the elements which constitute a rhyme must not be discontinuous (i.e. segregated by non-rhyming units). For another, the rhyme extends from left to right rather than vice versa: that is to say, the rhyming part cannot end until the end of the word (but see below). Given the morphological structure of Arabic, the rhyme consonant is usually preceded by an identical vowel, as in (329).

(329) 'atab–ḍarab 'blaming'–'to hit'

This is most commonly the low vowel /a/, which is by far the most frequent one. The high vowels /i/ and /u/ are used too infrequently as morphological markers to qualify for repetitive use in rhymes. It is important to point out that this vocalic identity is not considered an essential ingredient of the rhyme. Rather, it is 'externally' conditioned by the structure of the language.

In addition to rhyme consonants, there are also rhyme vowels. These are secondary in that they cannot occur in the absence of rhyme consonants. The rhyme vowel may either precede or follow the rhyme consonant. Therefore, the rhyme may begin almost anywhere. Going from right to left, rhymes may comprise codas, rimes (nuclei and codas), syllables (open and closed), and even larger units such as rhymes beginning with the nucleus of the penultimate syllable.

There is no doubt, then, that the phonological rime constitutes *one* linguistic basis for the poetic rhyme. It cannot, however, play a pre-eminent role because the nuclei, which are the obligatory parts of syllables, need not be identical in rhyme words. Still, the importance of the rime can only be adequately assessed through a quantitative analysis of rhyming patterns. It cannot, however, be ruled out that, although the rime might play a very limited role in theory, it is most commonly used in practice. An attempt was made therefore to examine the frequency of occurrence of the rime schemes in Arabic poetry. This necessitated a decision on which poems to select. In order to ensure a certain degree of representativeness, five poems or sets of poems from different authors and different epochs have been scrutinized. The first is taken from the oldest Arabic anthology, *Muʕallaqat*, which consists of seven long poems. The *Delectus* is a cross-section of shorter poems from different sources, and reproduces material from the old anthologies. These two corpora cover the pre-Islamic era. The third set of materials comes from the ninth-century poet Ibu al Muʕtazz, who is considered 'modern' by Arabic standards. Ibu Zaydūn is a poet from the eleventh century whose work is greatly appreciated. In contrast, Buhtūri's poetry (ninth century) is generally regarded as stilted and overdone. It was included to see whether this purportedly deviant way of dealing with literary norms was reflected in differing frequency patterns of the rhyme schemes. In this way, the range of quantitative variation may be delimited.

Table 32 gives the absolute numbers and percentages of rhyme types in the five poetic sources. All in all, more than 9000 rhymes have been subjected to investigation. The rhyme schemes can be divided into four basic categories according to the size of the linguistic unit they draw upon. These are coda rhymes, rime rhymes, syllable rhymes, and (preceding) nucleus + syllable rhymes.

One complication is relevant to the Arabic rhyme tradition but largely irrelevant to the issue under debate. Arabic rhymes may be discontinuous in that the rhyme is not only made up of identical segments in the last syllable but also of the low vowel, /a/, appearing in the penultimate or antepenultimate syllable, with non-identical material in-between. This constellation is illustrated in (330).

(330) maɣruur–maṡruur 'arrogant'–'happy'

Such cases have not been treated separately because they are uninformative with respect to the aim of this analysis. In any event, they are quite rare. Only Buhtūri uses them in appreciable numbers (see Table 32).

The results displayed in Table 32 are straightforward. The syllable and nucleus + syllable rhymes are the standard rhyme types from the quantitative point of view,

TABLE 32. *Frequency of occurrence of rhyme patterns in Arabic poetry*

	Coda r.	Rime r.	Syllable r.	Nucleus + syllable r.	Total
Muʕallaqat	–	–	322	286	608
	0.0%	0.0%	53.0%	47.0%	100.0%
Delectus	28	27	584	702	1,341
	2.1%	2.0%	43.5%	52.3%	99.9%
Ibu al Muʕtazz	152	61	1,141	1,147	2,501
	6.1%	2.4%	45.6%	45.9%	100.0%
Ibu Zaydūn	42	342	1,135	989	2,508
	1.7%	13.6%	45.3%	39.4%	100.0%
Buhtūri	45	4	1,331	826	2,206
	2.0%	0.2%	60.3%	37.4%	99.9%
TOTAL	267	434	4,513	3,950	9,164
AVERAGE	2.9%	4.7%	49.2%	43.1%	

Notes: r. = rhyme.
These data have been kindly placed at my disposal by Heinz Grotzfeld.

together accounting for more than 90 per cent of the data. The coda and rime rhymes are distinctly disfavoured. It was argued above that the rarity of coda rhymes follows from their lack of perceptual salience. However, no such explanation is available in the case of rime rhymes. That they are so uncommon cannot be put down to perceptual reasons, because this would wrongly imply that the standard Germanic rhymes are difficult to perceive.

Note from Table 32 that the frequency distributions are relatively constant across the various sources. The texts may therefore be considered fairly homogeneous despite their different origins. With respect to the central hypothesis, it is clear that the phonological rime is not a major option available to Arabic poets. If it plays a role at all, it is an extremely limited one. This is precisely what one would expect if a single consonant is the main carrier of the rhyme. Hence, the quantitative analysis fully confirms the qualitative approach.

It is safe to conclude that, quite unlike the Germanic tradition, Arab poetry does not use the rime as a linguistic unit on which to erect rhymes. One might be tempted to relate this difference between Germanic and Arab poetry to different literary traditions or aesthetic norms. However, this does not explain how these different traditions might have originated in the first place. The claim put forward here is that what may look like an arbitrary poetic convention is in fact strongly determined by the psycholinguistically relevant units of the language. Languages may differ in their choice of these units. Arabic has not availed itself of the rime, therefore poets cannot use it in their work. By contrast, the Germanic languages are more richly structured: they have evolved the rime to which poets may take recourse.

It has been suggested above that the rime is a good compromise between too much and too little phonological identity. Too much identity severely curtails the poets' freedom of word choice, while too little identity produces rhymes which are not salient enough to be identified as such. In this light, it is understandable why the rhyming chunks are in practice somewhat larger in Arabic than in the Germanic languages. Because the rime is not available in Arabic, Arab poets rely upon the next larger or the next smaller unit, i.e. the syllable or the individual segment. Both options are legitimate but, as shown in Table 32, the former is clearly preferred.

It is worth stressing finally that this account of the literary traditions holds that rhyming is a cognitive activity which is constrained by the psycholinguistic representation of the language to be processed. This representation may be assumed to be relatively invariant across activities speakers might engage in. Therefore, it functions to provide a link between such disparate activities as writing poetry and making slips of the tongue.

7

Discussion

7.1. Overall Results

It is now time to put together the results of the empirical work that lies behind us, to produce an overview. Overall, 45 major analyses have been performed (21 synchronic, 21 diachronic, and 3 poetic). These major analyses may be divided into 83 subanalyses (41 synchronic, 42 diachronic). (Subdivisions of the poetic sections were not made.) None of the major analyses failed completely. The psycholinguistic predictions were borne out either in part or totally. Of the subanalyses, 79 (92 per cent) matched the predictions while 7 (8 per cent) did not. Even without a precise null hypothesis, there is no question that the obtained results cannot be attributed to chance.

The overwhelming majority of analyses strongly support the following main conclusion: *The structure of language is shaped by the properties of the mechanism which puts it to use.* This link between the processor and the final product allows us to take the former as an explanation of the latter. Language is the way it is because it satisfies processing constraints in probabilistic fashion. Psycholinguistics thus qualifies as one likely[1] approach to the explanation of linguistic structure.

The explanatory value of the psycholinguistic approach has to be seen at two levels. At the global level, the processing account gains in strength as a general explanatory principle for language structure. That is, whenever an explanation for a given linguistic phenomenon is sought, psycholinguistics is one promising area to turn to. Of course, this is not to say that psycholinguistics is the best of all explanatory approaches, but it is one that has proven quite successful over a wide range of data. At the local level, the uncertainty surrounding a processing account of an individual phenomenon is somewhat reduced. Alternative explanations are always conceivable; however, the success of the psycholinguistic approach at large increases its plausibility as an account of individual patterns. Again, there is no guarantee that it will provide the best explanation in every single case, but at least there is good reason to assume that it provides a probable one. With respect to future analyses, linguists might feel encouraged to look to psycholinguistics for explanations of language structure and change.

---

[1] It is not possible to make any stronger or more precise claims beyond that of 'likelihood'. All explanations of necessity are hypothetical in character. Hence, all one can do is argue for or against the *likelihood* of certain theoretical accounts.

7.2. The Theoretical Significance of the Recalcitrant Data

It may very well be asked at this point whether it is surprising to find that the overwhelming majority of the psycholinguistic predictions were supported by the empirical data. Could it have been otherwise? After all, human beings rely in everything they do upon internal (i.e. psychological) states and representations. Granting this, one might be inclined to believe that every single aspect of language is determined by processing mechanisms. In that case, the main conclusion would be foregone and the original question banal.

This view is unacceptable for several reasons. Note at the outset that it is unpopular with the large number of linguists who stress the autonomy between language and processing (see Introduction). Ignoring matters of general attitude and persuasion, this criticism misses the most interesting point. In my opinion, the issue is not so much to find out whether there is a relationship between linguistics and psycholinguistics but primarily to discover how strong it is. Certainly, everything between 'virtually nonexistent' and 'almost deterministic' is conceivable a priori. Moreover, this view is unscientific because it takes for granted certain results which are not known until they have been obtained through a large-scale project. Only after this work has been done is it justified to argue one way or the other. Now that the first results are available, the above criticism can be rejected on empirical grounds. Not all psycholinguistic predictions were borne out. It is somewhat ironic that the negative findings are valuable in themselves. They contradict all criticisms to the effect that the results are artifactual. There *is* a certain independence between psycholinguistics and linguistics. Because the former does not completely tie down the latter, negative findings are to be expected. Processing thus manifests itself as one powerful factor; but this conclusion does not, of course, negate the relevance of other factors.

From a strictly methodological point of view, it would be premature to infer from a negative result that there is no relationship between language structure and processing. A number of possibilities have to be ruled out before such an inference can be regarded as valid. First, the psycholinguistic predictions may be wrong. It is conceivable that, by way of faulty reasoning, the correct psycholinguistic data and/or theory have been misinterpreted. Also, the processing data and/or theory may be wrong in two ways. For one thing, the wrong theoretical conclusions may have been drawn. As a consequence, it is unavoidable that the wrong psycholinguistic predictions would have been made. Such a case was encountered in the discussion of Cutler's (1986) claims about the processing of words which are only distinguished by lexical stress. Also, the data may be unreliable due to all sorts of methodological or theoretical difficulties. For another, it has to be borne in mind that the processing data do not form a homogeneous set. Processing principles may work against one another because of conflicting needs that have to be satisfied. It is easy to imagine that one such principle (A) has been isolated and has served as a basis for predictions while an opposing principle (B) has not been identified. If, for some reason, principle B overrides principle A in its effect on language structure, the psycholinguistic prediction is bound to fail.

This problem might be considered to be particularly acute in this study because many empirical sections started out from speech errors. Evidently, a single source of data, no matter how much insight it may offer, cannot claim to cover all the relevant aspects of high-level processing. Given the limited knowledge of processing principles currently at our disposal, it is quite possible that certain predictions will have to be modified in the face of new psycholinguistic evidence. On the other hand, it is quite surprising how many of the predictions were fulfilled although they were derived from a single data type.

Secondly, the empirical tests themselves may be inadequate. Like the psycholinguistic evidence, the linguistic data may be subject to sampling or other problems. It is also possible that the expected results did not turn up because the data were contaminated by some unrecognized interference factor whose existence could not be predicted on the basis of the processing principle invoked.

Thirdly, an error may reside in the assumed connection between psycholinguistics and linguistics. If the psycholinguistic and the linguistic evidence are impeccable but the processing mechanism fails to exert an influence upon linguistic structure, it might be that the connection between the two disciplines has been misconceived. That is to say, the connection may be real but take a form different from what has been hypothesized.

There is thus a plethora of possible explanations for the recalcitrant data. In light of this long list, it may even come as a surprise that the percentage of problematic cases is so small. I take this to mean that none of these pitfalls is of major importance and that the recalcitrant data should be treated as exceptions rather than as systematically opposing the main conclusion of the present study. Indeed, no systematic pattern emerges from a reconsideration of those analyses where the psycholinguistic predictions failed. For instance, the unexpected directionality of diachronic dissimilations might occur by analogy with the directionality of assimilations (Ohala 1992), but this is entirely ad hoc. Psycholinguistic explanations are as much at a premium as non-psycholinguistic ones. The same disappointing statement applies to the vulnerability of the place feature in language processing and its invulnerability in language history. The differences that were found between psycholinguistic and diachronic assimilations highlight in exemplary fashion one of the abovementioned limitations on the processing data. Granting that language production is best conceived of as a multi-level process, an assimilatory influence may take different shapes depending upon which level it occurs at. Given that speech errors arise, *ex hypothesi*, mainly at one particular level, it is obvious that the processing principles which they bring to the fore can account only for some of the properties of diachronic assimilations. A similar conclusion might be appropriate for vowel length in Dutch. The stability of this feature in the ablaut verbs and its instability in speech errors need not be contradictory on condition that both phenomena arise at different levels at which length is differentially represented. Obviously, more research is necessary to ascertain precisely which levels of processing are responsible for which property.

It seems, then, that highly individualistic explanations have to be sought for the exceptional cases. Whatever their ultimate cause, they are too diverse to argue against the postulate of a general link between psycholinguistic processing and linguistic structure. This link is quite strong but certainly not so strong as to be deterministic. Processing exerts a probabilistic influence upon language structure. That it is not deterministic is a natural spin-off of the fact that there are other factors, discussed in Chapter 2, which impinge on language and which relativize the importance of every single factor. It is quite conceivable that the exceptional cases attest to the influence of these non-psychological factors.

8

A Psycholinguistic Model of Language Structure and Change

8.1. How Processing Biases Penetrate Language

The overall objective of this work has been to establish a relationship between language processing and language structure. Thus far, all the attention has been focused upon identifying linguistic patterns which are predictable on psycholinguistic grounds. The weakest interpretation of this procedure would be to say that *correspondences* have been uncovered. For example, iconicity corresponds to parallel information processing. In a similar vein, the regularization of irregular verbs in history corresponds to the 'majority rule' in language processing. While interesting in themselves, it might be held that these correspondences do not suffice to demonstrate the relationship between process and product. What has to be specified is the exact mechanism whereby processing principles impinge upon the linguistic system. This is what Clark and Malt (1984) termed the linkage problem. According to them, an essential requirement of a theory is that it specify precisely how a given psychological constraint brings about a particular linguistic phenomenon. How important this requirement is can be seen from the fact that a processing principle may be a necessary though not a sufficient cause. As it alone cannot be held responsible for the existence of a given linguistic pattern, a certain indirectness between assumed cause and effect has to be acknowledged.

This indirectness is particularly apparent in attempts to relate non-psychological factors to language. Let us take two examples. In discussing the impact of sociological variables on linguistic behaviour, Dressler and Moosmüller (1991) make the claim that it is not enough to set up sociological parameters in a first step, linguistic variables in a next step, and finally to correlate the two. They caution that there is no *direct* relationship between social role or status and language use; rather, this relationship is an indirect one which is mediated by psychological factors. The authors claim that, whatever the social role or status of a speaker, what counts is not so much the role that is assigned to an individual by society but rather the speaker's internalization of this role. Clearly, only what is part of the speaker's mental representation can exercise an influence on language.

The other example comes from the analysis of colour terms. In section 2.1, Kay and McDaniel (1978) were cited as an attempt to explain linguistic patterns in neurological terms. As will be recalled, the evolution of colour terminology was argued to be constrained by certain principles of neurological processing. This argument involves quite a strong claim: that neural activity is *directly* linked to linguistic patterns. Precisely this underlying assumption has been questioned by Wierzbicka (1990), who argues that there is no such direct linkage and that it is cognitive processes such as conceptualization by which neurological and linguistic factors are mediated. These concepts derive from our everyday experience. For example, the colours blue and yellow originate from our perception of the sky and the sun, respectively.

It is perhaps no coincidence that the mediator in both examples is psychology. All kinds of information must pass through this level of representation, and are consequently moulded by its constraints (to an unspecified degree). In a sense, psychology acts like a relay station which mediates between many (or all?) relationships between linguistic and non-linguistic variables. Are we entitled to infer from this that psychology enjoys a privileged status, and that the linkage problem evaporates when it comes to establishing a relationship between psycholinguistics and linguistics? The answer is no. Although it may be possible to argue that the relationship between psychological processing and language structure is less indirect than between, let us say, neurological processing and language structure, psycholinguistics and linguistics are two conceptually distinct fields. Therefore, any assumed link between them has to be explicitly argued for.

How should this link, then, be conceptualized? How is language structure made to conform to processing principles? The account that will be detailed below is erected upon the claim that the relationship between process and product is doubly indirect. For one thing, processing does not directly act upon linguistic structure in the synchronic sense, but leaves its imprint on language as a diachronic phenomenon. For another, processing does not directly act upon linguistic structure but rather affects it through the intermediary of language use. Since language change is change of language use, the two aspects are obviously related.

Beginning with the first, an argument will be taken up from Hall (1988), who construes diachrony as the essential link between language structure (the explanandum) and language processing (the explanans). Hall discusses the role of diachrony in relation to one particular linguistic problem (i.e. the suffixing preference—see section 2.3). In the following, an attempt will be made to develop a theoretical account in more general terms.[1] Our starting-point is the uncontroversial assumption that the present linguistic structure reflects an interim stage in a historical process. Like all cultural phenomena, language is in a constant flux: at any given point in time it is susceptible to change. That is, a decision is made about being conservative or progressive and, if the latter, in which direction to move.[2] There are always various options available, and not all options are equally probable. In fact,

---

[1] Hall's specific proposal will be treated below (Section 8.4).
[2] Of course, it is not implied here that this decision is in any way consciously made by the individual speaker or the linguistic community. Although the language users are clearly involved in this process, they cannot be assumed to plot or plan language change (see Keller 1994).

each option has its own pros and cons. It is subject to a unique set of influences which, taken individually, may increase or decrease the likelihood that one option rather than another will be taken. These forces can be of diverse nature (e.g. psychological, sociological) and of variable strength and durability. Whenever a decision has to be made (i.e. virtually always), these factors make themselves felt and influence it.

Given the time span over which psycholinguistic predictions could be shown to hold, processing principles can be assumed to be of a relatively constant and permanent nature. Let us construct, albeit in highly simplistic and schematic form, a conceivable scenario of language change. There are two possible routes, A and B, which a language, or rather a particular property of language, may take. Let us assume (rather unrealistically) that the two routes would be equally probable if it were not for a psychological argument which tips the scale in favour of A but against B. This would basically mean that route A creates less processing problems than route B. Because of this bias, the language moves in one direction rather than in another. The net effect is that the structure of the language (as the outcome of the change) has become more 'psychological' on its transition from $stage_n$ to $stage_{n+1}$. In this way, processing aspects insinuate themselves into language structure. Note that in this conception the psychological principles are not the ultimate cause of language change. Rather, they act as facilitators which make certain developments more likely than others (see section 8.5 for an elaboration of this point).

This scenario applies not only to two different routes between which a linguistic change may choose but also to the decision of whether a change is to take place at all. At any given moment in time, any linguistic property is more or less stable. It may be stable because it is easy to process. When, however, it creates a processing difficulty, it may be viewed as less stable. Let us begin with a description of what the processing situation is *not* like. One might imagine that the production of language involves the activation of all the intended units and nothing but. If this were the case, there would be no competition between alternative ways of expressing a given idea. Although different ideas may vary in how easily (and quickly) they can be formulated, the formulation of each individual idea is an all-or-nothing process. In this view, the processing system would lack any kind of dynamics and it would be difficult to see from where it might derive its susceptibility to change.

As we now know, the processing system does not operate this way. Owing to the connectivity of the system and the parallel information flow, many more elements are active than are eventually needed for production or comprehension. This is the system's strategy of homing in on the best solution. By more or less automatically activating many different elements, the system considers many different possibilities at the same time. The different degrees of activation of these possibilities correspond to the differing 'qualities' of the hypotheses under consideration. A spin-off of parallelism and connectivity is competition in the processing system. Each utterance, whether perceived or produced, is the 'winner' in a struggle among various competitors of unequal strength.

The critical aspect of competition in the present context is that it is the prerequisite for change. When more than one solution is considered, a situation arises which may lead to different resolutions at different times. The strength of a particular solution is a function of its congruence with psychological principles (besides others). When the current norm conforms to these principles, it is unlikely to undergo a change. When, however, the current norm does not conform, it is in danger of being outweighed by a different solution which pays closer heed to processing constraints and which is always available as an alternative. The outcome of this constellation of competing factors may be linguistic change. In this conception, language change is fostered by two factors working in tandem—the relative weakness of the current norm and the relative strength of one alternative among others.

Let us illustrate the above claims by an example. It was shown in section 5.17 that ablaut verbs in English and German tend to change to regular (suffixed) verbs. However, they do not do so in a uniform manner. Infrequent verbs yield to majority rule more readily than frequent ones. Thus, two factors have to be reckoned with—token and type frequency. Both have their effect on the level of activation of a given hypothesis and influence the final outcome. As sketched above, the crucial feature of the connectionist processing model is the generation of multiple hypotheses or solutions. The generation of the 'best' solution is accompanied by the (lesser) activation of less optimal solutions. So when an ablaut verb is intended, a regular alternative is activated concurrently. For example, when the past tense of *to freeze* is prepared for output, *froze* will usually be the solution the system settles on, but the incorrect form *freezed* will be activated along the way. This is because the semantic feature PAST leads to the partial activation of all past tense forms. As the regular past tense verbs form the majority, the activation level of the *-ed* rule is not negligible at the moment when the past tense of *to freeze* is planned. The regular verbs try to impose their solution on the verb in question, and thus the system proposes *freezed* as one solution to the past tense problem. Under normal circumstances, however, this joint effect of the regular verbs remains 'below the surface' because the correct form *froze* accumulates more activation and thus manages to suppress the majority vote. That the conspiracy of the regular verbs is real, albeit not generally audible, is strongly suggested by the speech-error patterns of adults and the acquisitional data from children (Marcus et al. 1992). Additionally, it has been demonstrated in computer simulations of connectionist networks.

The type frequency of English verbs is only one half of the story. The other half is constituted by token frequency. The mechanism is quite simple: the more often a given verb is used, the more easily it can be activated and the more accurately it can be accessed. As a consequence, high-frequency verbs, be they regular or irregular, are less assailable than low-frequency ones, and prove more stable over time. The combined effect of type and token frequency upon activation levels is graphically represented in Fig. 3. The target, marked by an arrow, is a high-frequency irregular verb in (3A) and a low-frequency irregular verb in (3B). As can be seen, the difference in activation levels between the low-frequency irregular target and its competitors is smaller than that between the high-frequency irregular verb and its contenders. Thus, high frequency protects an irregular verb against the mass action of the regular verbs while low-frequency tends to make it vulnerable. So when a change takes place it will affect the low-frequency items before the high-frequency ones. The impetus and consequence of such a change is that the problem of morphological processing is alleviated.

The second backbone of the psycholinguistic account of linguistic structure is language use. It is claimed to act as a link between the process and the product. Here a few words on the difference between language use and structure are in order. By linguistic structure is meant the inventory of citation forms as can be found, for example, in a dictionary. These are represented in as neutral a fashion as possible, i.e. they are free from external sandhi and other processes. In contrast, language use refers to the actualization of structure in specific speaking situations. Because so many factors impinge upon actualization, quite a number of forms have to be reckoned with—such as the relationship between the speaker and the listener or the formality of the situation—which affect the speaking rate, the carefulness of pronunciation, and so on. Accordingly, one basic form may give rise to different variants. All these forms have different probabilities of occurrence in different contexts.

Language use is a performance phenomenon and as such subject to processing constraints. Whether one or another variant is selected depends, among other things, upon psychological factors. Let us resume the above example of a processing conflict between regular and irregular past tense verbs. As explained above, during the generation of a form such as *froze* for instance, the incorrect form *freezed* is activated at sub-threshold level. When *froze* is insufficiently activated for some reason, the likelihood of regularization increases. At some point in time the probability of occurrence of the two forms is more nearly equal, such that it is no longer

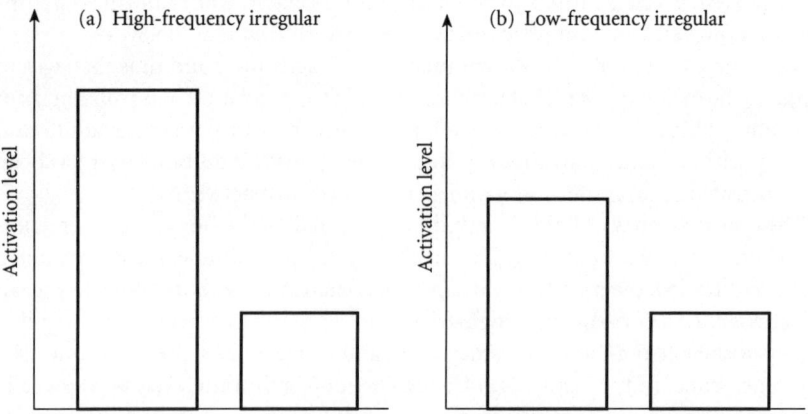

FIGURE 3. Activation levels during the generation of high- and low-frequency irregular verbs

possible to regard the one as right and the other as wrong. Which of the two wins out in any particular case also depends upon factors from outside the system. At this moment, language use would be called 'unsettled'. Contemporary examples from the domain of verbs are *to dream* and *to spell*, which allow both regular and irregular past tenses. This period of indecision may, but need not, be short-lived. Even though the processing system is in principle capable of supporting indecision,[3] it prefers unequivocalness and therefore ultimately settles on a more stable state. One major factor responsible for this tendency is the existence of inhibition in the psycholinguistic network (Berg and Schade 1992). Inhibition functions to enhance the contrast between competitors, and therefore contributes to an unequivocal decision in favour of one solution. At the end of the process, language use may be said to be settled. A state of variation has given way to a single basic form. The change from an irregular to a regular past tense verb has been completed.

Let us look at another example which highlights the competition between opponent forces and which illuminates the relationship between language structure and language use from a different angle. Over the past 500 years or so, voiceless word-final fricatives underwent voicing in words of extremely high frequency such as *his* and *of*. Two factors are at issue in this development. On the one hand, there is a phonetic factor working towards the preservation of the status quo. For both perceptual and productive reasons, voiceless obstruents are preferred to voiced ones in postvocalic positions. On the other hand, there is a semiotic factor working towards the change of the status quo. Frequent words tend to be shorter than infrequent ones (see Zipf's principle of least effort). Voiced obstruents are phonetically half as long as their voiceless cognates. Voicing thus implies shortening. The impetus for this change may therefore be the optimization of the relationship between lexical frequency and word length.

Evidence in support of this interpretation comes from the empirical observation that frequency is an excellent predictor of whether a change does or does not take place. As shown in Berg (1995a), the ends of low-frequency words such as *off* and *thus* remained voiceless. The endings of medium-frequency words such as *if* and *as* began to change, so there was a period of vacillation during which two variants were in use, (e.g. [ɪf] and [ɪv]). However, the new form was too weak to replace the old one and finally disappeared. In contrast, the change was carried through in high-frequency words such as *is* and *has*. Here, the new form was strong enough to replace the old one and a new pronunciation norm came to be established.

---

[3] One line of evidence in support of this contention comes from language acquisition. Because children do not delay the generation of words and sentences until they have completely mastered the segment system, they are permanently struggling to revise their sound production. As shown in a recent case study, it may take a long time before a new sound is entirely mastered (Berg 1995b). During this period, the child correctly produced a given sound in one word but incorrectly in another, or even produced one and the same word correctly at one moment but incorrectly the next. This shows that the psycholinguistic system can endure a state of indeterminacy for quite a while. Although language change in childhood and adulthood is certainly not the same thing, there are enough parallels to warrant the conclusion that the processing system is perfectly able to cope with variation (within certain limits).

It has been argued that psycholinguistic principles act upon language structure through the intermediary of language use. These principles act directly upon language use by enlarging the range of variation. An alternative develops to the basic form, and gains in strength because it meets certain (psychological) requirements which the original form does not meet. That such an alternative arises in the first place can be traced back to a processing system which is inherently dynamic and competitive, and which is geared towards generating more than one solution to a problem simultaneously. Differently put, the alternative is latent before it manifests itself audibly.[4] Then follows a period of indeterminacy which is ended by the gradual triumph of the new over the old form. A change along these lines has the effect of replacing a psychologically less motivated by a more motivated form. Through their impact upon language use, psycholinguistic principles influence the direction of linguistic change which results in the synchronic structure of a language. In this way, language structure is infiltrated by psycholinguistic constraints.

This influence is to the obvious advantage of the processing system. The linguistic structure is the material on which the processor has to work. When this static material incorporates psycholinguistic biases, it is easier to process. This is highly desirable, because the basic form is needed most frequently or perhaps even in every single case. It may thus be regarded as optimal to have the underlying representation in such a form that it conforms to (or anticipates) on-line processing demands to the greatest extent possible. This view presents linguistic rules and restrictions in a new light. Linguistic patterns and the rules associated with them can now be understood as the fossilized product of performance constraints. These constraints unfold spontaneously (i.e. in the act of speaking and listening), but they can be put to more permanent use by shaping language structure accordingly.

8.2. Three Ways of Conceiving the Explanatory Role of Processing

There are several ways in which processing may be claimed to explain language structure, depending upon the directness and the reciprocity of the link that is assumed to obtain between psycholinguistics and linguistics. Three basic types of link are distinguishable; examples of all three can be found in the empirical work above. The first type assumes that processing is independent of the particular information to be processed. This independence is not because the psycholinguistic machinery is impervious to linguistic structure; rather, certain psycholinguistic principles have to be deployed in all languages because all languages share certain basic features. For instance, all languages exploit the principle of linear order in subordinate units. By implication, a serialization mechanism is required which may function quite independently of the information to be serialized. In this sense, processing furnishes explanations which are of a universal nature.

---

[4] It should be underscored that this happens all the time and is a cost-free, automatic process in the psycholinguistic model used in this study.

The psychological mechanism which is necessitated by linear order as a design feature of natural languages has to have particular properties if it is to function efficiently. One of these design features is the activation advantage that is given to imminent elements as compared to those which have already been outputted. This imbalance has been used to explain assimilation patterns in language. Any psycholinguistic explanation which relies upon processing principles such as this one may claim to be of maximum generality and independence.

The second type of link assumes a relatively strong interdependence between linguistics and psycholinguistics. A certain processing principle is used to explain a certain linguistic fact, while the processing principle itself is a more or less immediate consequence of this linguistic fact. The critical issue here is the proper interpretation of the word 'immediate'. The most extreme form of 'immediacy' would be triviality, but such a situation is rarely given. In actual fact, the influence is less direct than one might think. Let us take the example of the differing phonological weight of word onsets in Spanish and German. It was suggested in section 4.4 that this linguistic difference is due to a difference in activation flow. But then, one may legitimately wonder, where does the psycholinguistic difference come from? It may be suspected that it follows from nothing else but the structural difference. This is not self-evident, however, and requires careful argumentation, because there is no logical necessity for a linguistic difference to entail a psycholinguistic one. In general, we would even expect a linguistic difference to have *no* implication for processing because of the one-to-many relationship between psycholinguistic principles and linguistic facts. Not every linguistic fact requires a processing strategy or principle of its own. If it did, it would certainly render the processing task intractable.

However, let us assume that the relationship between linguistics and psycholinguistics is not only reciprocal but also relatively direct. This would mean that a neat separation between explanans and explanandum is impossible. In fact, the psycholinguistic process and the linguistic product would be at the same time explanans and explanandum. In the face of such a state of affairs, could it be maintained that processing acts as an explanation for language structure? My answer is in the affirmative. Although it must be conceded that this type of explanation is 'impure', it may count as an explanation to the extent that psycholinguistics plays an active role in this game. It does so because of the reciprocity assumption. The processing system reinforces a linguistic structure by ensuring its optimal perception and production. The least that can be said, then, is that processing contributes one part of the explanation of linguistic patterns.

The third type of link similarly accepts the assumption of interactivity between linguistics and psycholinguistics, but differs from the second in that the linguistic problem to be explained is not identical to the linguistic fact that has brought forth the processing principle invoked. The diagrams in Fig. 4—all highly schematized and oversimplified—attempt to explicate the difference between all three types of link.

The claim illustrated in Fig. 4C is that processing may connect different linguistic structures. There is thus a certain independence between explanans and

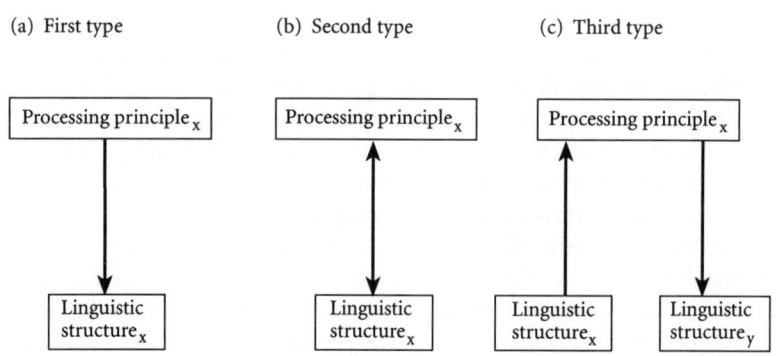

FIGURE 4. Three types of link between psycholinguistic processing and linguistic structure

explanandum which allows for the relatively pure use of the term 'explanation'. Consider the example of the morphophonemic difference between English and German. As discussed in section 4.15, English is less resistant to quantitative changes of the ablaut vowel than German. The explanation proffered was that more activation is spread along the pathways connecting long or short vowels to the feature level in German than in English. This processing difference cannot have been brought about by the explanandum, i.e. the differing patterns of morphophonemic alternation in the two languages. The primary motivation behind this claim is that the morphophonemic alternants are so few in number that they are incapable of acting upon the processing principles. A much more probable reason for the processing principles to be as different as they are is that the vowel systems of the two languages are so different. The segment system is undoubtedly the most basic aspect of phonological structure and therefore the most likely candidate to influence processing.

On this account, we have two distinct linguistic phenomena (i.e. the segment system and the morphophonemic alternations) which are related by processing. Psycholinguistics functions as a joint between separate linguistic facts and, in so doing, provides an explanation which is largely independent of the phenomenon to be explained. The psycholinguistic explanation is independent of the linguistic pattern under study, but not necessarily independent of other linguistic patterns. Note that it would be indefensible to leave the processing mechanism out of consideration and simply explain the cross-linguistic difference in linguistic terms, i.e. with recourse to differing phonological systems. Such an account would be grossly insufficient because it fails to explicate the critical link between the two linguistic phenomena (termed X and Y in Fig. 4C). That these are related is not a spin-off of linguistic constraints; rather, it follows from processing principles which serve as a general framework for the organization of linguistic patterns.

Of the three types of link discussed, the first would generally be most and the second least highly valued. Universal accounts are widely preferred to language-specific ones. Explanations which rest upon a less than neat separation of explanans and explanandum are commonly regarded as 'messy' and less satisfying (aesthetically?). I consider the basis for these value judgements questionable, and prefer to regard all three types of explanation as well worth pursuing. Rather than attaching more significance to universal than to language-specific accounts, I prefer to view both as complementary. Evidently, taken by themselves the two are of limited value. The one cannot deal with between-language variation and the other fails to explain between-language constancy. It should also be noted that explanations of language-particular facts are no less challenging than those of universal patterns. Both require the best of our minds. Finally, a warning should be directed at those who are anxious to find 'pure' explanations (e.g. Frazier 1985). It may be that this type of explanation occurs less often in nature than one might wish. I have the feeling that the majority of explanations are 'messy' (in the above sense), and that it might therefore be more rewarding to put up with messiness rather than to hunt chimeras.

Three types of link have been discussed, in terms of three ways in which processing may affect linguistic structure. It has been argued that all three have a certain explanatory value. Even the putatively weakest type is neither artifactual nor tautological because a considerable conceptual distance between linguistics and psycholinguistics remains to be covered. This distance guarantees that an attempt to explain language in psycholinguistic terms is meaningful. All three types of link have been encountered in the present study.

8.3. Further Aspects of the Theory

The psycholinguistic account that has been developed of language structure has several characteristics which deserve special mention. The first question that will be posed concerns the falsifiability of the theory. As noted, everything human beings do has to pass the psychological 'filter'. It might therefore be argued that there is no real alternative between a psychological influence and a lack thereof. However, one of the results of this work is the conclusion that this is not so. It is not a priori clear where an influence makes itself felt and where it does not. This is because the psycholinguistic factor is only one among other factors acting upon language, and it is not known beforehand which wins out in any particular circumstance. Clearly, the impact of processing upon language structure is an empirical issue. Any psycholinguistic theory can thus in principle be falsified by showing that alternative, and perhaps better, explanations are available for the phenomena which have been ascribed to processing principles. We may conclude that the proposed theory meets the criterion of falsifiability in that it can in principle be shown to make the wrong predictions. There is certainly no logical necessity for processing to make an impact upon language structure.

Another aspect of the psycholinguistic theory is its generality. It is conceived as a model which makes relevant statements about all levels of linguistic analysis. Processing principles are claimed to pervade the phonological, morphological, syntactic, and semantic levels. Equal attention has not been paid to all of these areas in this book: phonology has figured most prominently, less has been said about morphology, little about syntax, and nothing about semantics. Two factors are mainly responsible for this imbalance. For one thing, psycholinguistic theory, in particular those parts which are of relevance to linguistics, has not progressed to the same extent on all fronts. For example, much more relevant information is available on phonological processing than on syntactic processing. For another, the degrees of freedom, and hence the predictability, vary widely from one field to another. For instance, relatively precise predictions can be formulated in the area of sound change, but the psycholinguistic theory makes virtually no predictions regarding the direction of semantic change. One might be inclined to think that this represents a weakness of the psycholinguistic approach. However, I would argue that the contrary is true. The lack of pertinent predictions is in fact a virtue because semantic change is basically unpredictable (but see Williams 1976; Geeraerts 1985; Sweetser 1990). One reason for this is that the semantic system is less tightly organized than the phonological one, such that a particular change in the semantic domain is less constrained and can take place as an isolated event whereas a change in the phonological domain is more highly constrained and can often be construed as one part of a more global development. When the structure in a semantic field is tighter, however, one would predict changes at one place to have repercussions throughout. If, for example, a change in kinship terminology occurred (e.g. *aunt* being extended to male referents), it is not unlikely that this would upset the whole subsystem and similar changes would follow.

Further psycholinguistic predictions concern the semantic distance between the old and the new form as well as the incidence of iconicity. As regards the former, the obvious prediction is that only one semantic feature should be changed at a time (see the analogical claim regarding phonological change). Iconicity should in general be fostered. *Ceteris paribus*, developments which entail a higher degree of iconicity should be preferred to those that do not. Similarly, more iconic patterns should prove more stable over time than less iconic ones. When a group of words is not only semantically but also phonologically linked, the individual members should be less subject to loss. A case in point is the <wr-> words in English expressing the concepts of twisting, bending, and contortion.[5] The <wr-> words in Modern English are quite old, and one reason for this stability may be the mutual support that these words provide to one another: when one such word is activated, the others are activated not only via the semantic pathways but also via the phonological ones. This heightened activation gives them the requisite strength which protects them from erosion.

[5] This example brings to light an interesting conflict between two effects stemming from one processing principle. On the one hand, the principle of iconicity (i.e. parallel information flow) predicts a stability of <wr-> words having to do with 'twisting'. On the other hand, the dependence of lexical items upon phonological activation (i.e. parallel information flow) predicts a general instability of <wr-> words (which was actually documented in section 5.15). Remarkably, the two predictions are not at all mutually contradictory. For the <wr-> words which code the meaning of 'twisting', it would simply be assumed in an activation model that the disadvantage which accrues to them from the phonological level is at least in part offset by the advantage that accrues to them from the iconic principle.

Apart from these relatively minor constraints, however, the processing mechanism does not restrict the direction of semantic change. In other terms, it allows the linguistic sign to be largely arbitrary. This is as it should be if the system is to serve its users to a maximum degree. Speakers need a system that is maximally flexible, i.e. that allows them to express all their ideas which evolve constantly. If the system were inherently constrained in its adaptability, it would sooner or later lose its utility.

Finally, the proposed psycholinguistic theory blurs the distinction between synchrony and diachrony.[6] Although this distinction is clearly useful as a methodological principle, it plays no major role in the view of language advocated here. The psycholinguistic system continuously exercises its influence upon language, be it today, yesterday, or tomorrow. Obviously, not all processing principles are timeless; many of them are certainly subject to change. Others, however, such as the greater strength of majority over minority patterns, may have something like a timeless quality. A psycholinguistic influence on language is only possible when the diachronic and synchronic aspects work together. From the diachronic perspective, the processing principles facilitate the rise of a given effect, while from the synchronic perspective these principles contribute to its maintenance. Evidently, both rise and maintenance of a linguistic phenomenon are equally essential components in a psycholinguistic theory of language.

Indeed, some cases in the empirical sections were studied from both the synchronic and the diachronic angles. That similar results were obtained substantiates the claim that the processing principles impinge largely indiscriminately upon synchrony and diachrony. Note, however, that the match between synchronic and diachronic forces need not be perfect. It may well be that a phenomenon used to be supported by a processing principle but that this support vanished over time because a competing principle took over. Such a shift will not lead to instant modification of the entire linguistic system. Naturally, a change takes its time in order not to endanger communication in the period of instability. A case in point might be umlaut, where there seems to be a discrepancy between its vitality and its psycholinguistic support. It may be that at least part of this vitality stems from the days when it had a stronger phonological motivation. The extent of the mismatch between synchrony and diachrony remains to be determined, but in view of the slow change of psycholinguistic principles it is unlikely to be very large.

8.4. The Suffixing Preference Revisited

The cross-language preference of suffixation over prefixation was one of the first linguistic phenomena linked to an explicit psycholinguistic model. Cutler et al. (1985) claimed that this morphological asymmetry is a spin-off function of a processing asymmetry (see section 2.3). Their serial model appeared to account successfully for the linguistic facts, even though the serialness assumption was called into question.

---

[6] In this respect it is not unlike the philosophy expounded by Bailey (1982). A similar proposal is made by 'ecologists of language' (e.g. Fill 1993).

A curious implication ensues from this apparent contradiction; unless there is something wrong with the parallel model, Cutler et al.'s account must be flawed, although it provides a good fit with the linguistic evidence. This problem will be approached in the following.

Of course, a parallel model assumes that the processing of morphemes within a word occurs largely simultaneously. What are the arguments in favour of parallelism? The first is a theoretical one of internal consistency. Since it has been claimed that the processing of segments within morphemes as well as the processing of words within NPs occurs in parallel, it would be only natural to expect the morphological level between the two other levels to behave likewise. This expectation is grounded in the assumption that a psycholinguistic mechanism will find cross-level consistency easier to deal with, and thus preferable to cross-level inconsistency. What is more, empirical arguments also support the parallel view. The serial model rules out two types of speech error. Segments from prefixes cannot perseverate into stems, nor can segments from suffixes anticipate into stems. These error types would be impossible, because they presuppose that affixes are already activated at the time of stem processing. As a matter of fact, such slips of the tongue do see the light of day. Because the rather impoverished morphology of English makes these slips unlikely in the first place, two examples from German are reported in (331–2).

(331) *überflütet* for *überflutet*
       [y:bɛrfly:tɛt y:bɛrflu:tɛt]
       'inundated'
(332) auf der anderen Seite die Konsumheil– geilheit
                         [kɔnzu:mhaɪl gaɪlhaɪt]
       'on the other hand, the lust for consumption'

In (331), the vowel from the prefix *über-* 'over' distorts the stem *flut* 'flood' to give rise to the non-word *flüt(et)*. In (332), the prevocalic consonant of the nominal suffix *-heit* replaces the beginning of the stem *geil* 'wanton'. These interferences could not have been produced if the processing on the stem had preceded that of the affixes. In contrast, tongue slips like (331–2) are fully expected in a parallel framework. I therefore conclude that the empirical data require a parallel-processing model.

Without further elaboration, this psycholinguistic model embodies the claim that the processing and representation of stem + suffix combinations should be quite similar to that of prefix + stem complexes. Hence, the expectation as to linguistic structure would be that prefixes and suffixes should pattern with stems in symmetrical fashion. However, there is a problem with this prediction. It relies exclusively upon phonological arguments and does not take into account other relevant psycholinguistic facts such as evidence from morphological processing. In particular, it has to be enquired whether there are any differences in the way prefixes and suffixes are treated by the processor. What we find is that prefixes are more susceptible than suffixes to displacement. This can be seen most directly in syntagmatic movement errors such as (333–4), again from German.

(333) *daß man so ein Bekind, das man nicht gewollt hat, bekommt* for *Kind*
  [bəkɪnt   bəkɔmt   kɪnt]
  'that you get an unwanted child'
(334) *Da müßte man mal genauer in die Klatschspaltungen der Zeitungen schauen* for *Spalten*
  [ʃpaltən klatʃʃpaltuŋgən   tsaituŋgən]
  'You would have to take a closer look at the gossip columns of the newspapers'

No. (333) exemplifies the addition of a prefix, (334) that of a suffix. To be specific, the affix breaks loose from its original location and docks onto a different word which may be at quite a distance and which may belong to a different syntactic category. In (333), for example, the prefix *be-* of the verb form *bekommt* 'gets' attaches to the noun *Kind* 'child', with error and source being separated by an entire relative clause. The main constraint on these errors is that prefixes and suffixes never violate their morphological status. Prefixes are always placed before a word, suffixes always come after. Importantly, prefix errors greatly outnumber suffix errors in my corpus of German slips of the tongue.

How may the greater moveability of prefixes as compared to suffixes be understood? One way of rationalizing this difference is to posit that morphologically complex words are hierarchically organized. A prototypical word consisting of a prefix, a stem, and a suffix, such as *unbelievable*, would have the following constituent structure.

(335)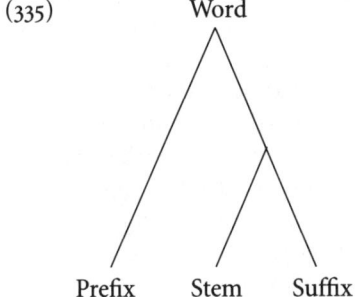

According to this model, the stem and the suffix form immediate constituents. Because the prefix and the stem do not, the former can detach more easily from the latter. This hypothesis is not only supported by the empirical data given above but also by evidence from blending errors. Blends break up morphologically complex words at the prefix/stem boundary rather than at the stem/suffix boundary. Note that the psycholinguistic representation depicted in (335) does not seem to agree with the linguistic evidence. Spencer (1991), in an extensive review of the linguistic literature, comes to the conclusion that there are hardly any convincing arguments for hierarchical structure in inflected and derived words. No attempt will be made here to reconcile this conflict.

Two further points should be mentioned in connection with (335). The right-branching structure is meant to be a *general* model of morphological organization. That is, *all* words with this make-up are assumed to be structured alike. If this assumption were not made, no general claims could be formulated. Besides, the representation in (335) has a limited empirical basis in that it draws exclusively upon German data. To make the following argument, it has to be claimed that the right-branching hierarchical structure is cross-linguistically preferred. Clearly, both the cross-linguistic preference and the general validity across all words of the lexicon of a particular language are very strong claims which are inadequately defended here, pending a great deal of further research. For the sake of the following prediction, the correctness of these claims will provisionally be taken for granted.

Before the psycholinguistic argument for right-branching can be brought to bear upon the structure of language, it has to be asked where affixes come from. I therefore agree with Hall (1988) that the diachronic dimension supplies the answer. There is a general consensus that, as far as the time window allows us to determine, affixes evolve from free-standing morphemes (e.g. Givón 1971; Bybee 1988). During this development, the morphological units run through a stage in which they are neither completely free nor completely bound. This affixoidal status is found in the current language in forms like *tax-free* and *clockwise*. The typical development thus is top-down rather than bottom-up in the linguistic hierarchy. Word boundaries turn into morpheme boundaries whereas segment boundaries do not normally turn into morpheme boundaries.

Taking this historical path as given, it can be predicted that free-standing morpheme + word structures will be less likely to develop into prefix + stem complexes than word + free-standing morpheme structures are to develop into stem + suffix complexes. The motivation behind this prediction is that, because of right-branching, the psycholinguistic system is predisposed towards activating right-hand material more strongly than left-hand material during processing on the stem. As a consequence, right-hand material is more readily integrated into the stem than left-hand material. This is effectively the prediction that agrees with the empirical facts: suffixes are more common than prefixes across languages.

This account is similar to that of Hall (1988), who also views the preference for suffixes as a reflex of a processing asymmetry. However, the two accounts differ in the assumptions they make about the underlying basis of this asymmetry. Following Cutler et al. (1985), Hall works with a serial processing model in which the beginnings of words are accessed before, and are more important than, their ends. To facilitate processing, left-hand material must preserve more of its independence *vis-à-vis* the stem than right-hand material. The weak point of this explanation is Hall's adherence to serial processing. The account developed here provides a different explanation for the processing asymmetry, which is claimed to emanate from a preference for right-branching over left-branching structures. This preference is quite compatible with parallel processing, and therefore fits well into the general framework advocated here.

8.5. Causality in Language Change

The empirical analyses have established that there are far-reaching parallels between the characteristic traits of slips of the tongue and language change. Commonalities have been found at both the macroscopic and the microscopic level. Although this is no proof that language change is *caused* by slips of the tongue, the massive similarities suggest that more than coincidence is at stake here. One conceivable interpretation of these commonalities is that slips of the tongue attest to the variation to which the processing system is subject (including the limits of this variation), and that language change capitalizes upon this variation and is constrained by the limits of variability. On this hypothesis, language change and slips of the tongue share so many properties because they originate in the same system, which therefore imposes the same constraints upon them.

This parallelism gives good reason to suppose that the causality of tongue slips is not completely unlike that of linguistic change. It may therefore be instructive to assess what can be learned from the origin of spontaneous speech errors for the explanation of language change. Slips of the tongue are the product of system-internal processing biases and noise, which is conceived of as randomly fluctuating activation levels inherent to all neurological and quasi-neurological systems. By definition, noise introduces unpredictability into the system, but this does not mean that it is 'lawless' and cannot be taken into account in computer simulations. The system-internal processing biases result from the architecture and dynamic properties of the processor. These principles, which exist independently of the noise component, favour one particular output at the expense of another.

It is of the utmost importance to stress that the likelihood of error increases with the number of processing biases. The function of these biases is best expressed by the designation 'facilitator'. One facilitator is usually not enough for the occurrence of a tongue slip which, typically, is multiply determined. That is, a number of facilitators contribute to an error. Noise serves to amplify the effect of the facilitators. All these facilitators, noise included, have an additive effect. Thus it is not generally possible to pinpoint *the* cause of a speech error. The slip occurs by virtue of a conspiracy of a set of facilitators none of which is necessarily decisive on its own.

This situation is readily translated into an activation-based model. Each facilitator influences the activation levels to a certain degree. If a number of facilitators conspire, a non-intended unit may amass more activation than the intended one, and an error is outputted. An important point to note is the way the activation model captures the difference between quality and quantity. A speech error is undoubtedly a qualitative phenomenon in that one element in an utterance is changed into another. However, the reasons for this qualitative change are of a quantitative nature. Each facilitator contributes some quantity of activation to a given error node. Taken together, the facilitators make the error node surpass the activation level of the target and lead to a tongue slip. Hence, a qualitative effect is conceptualized in this model as resulting from the joint action of quantitative factors which would be unnoticeable if they acted individually.

It is my contention that this conceptualization of speech errors can be more or less directly transferred to language change, despite the fundamental differences between the two phenomena. There is no denying that linguistic change represents the replacement of one intention by another whereas slips of the tongue represent a violation of an intention. Additionally, while noise is one important factor in the generation of inadvertent speech errors, its function is less than clear in linguistic change. None the less, the role of the facilitators in speech errors and language change appears to be comparable. In both areas, the competitor has to accumulate more activation than the norm. The advantage that accrues to the innovative form comes from a set of facilitators which may be of social, psychological, or any other origin in the case of language change. A change thus involves the strengthening of facilitators which increase the activation levels of competing forms. On this account, it is not possible to identify a single cause of language change. Rather, attention must be focused upon a specific constellation of facilitators which are of a quantitative nature when viewed in isolation but may have qualitative effects when acting in combination. Consequently, the search for a single cause of language change is futile. This phenomenon is more adequately understood by identifying as many of the relevant facilitators as possible and examining their interaction. Because of its misleading connotations, it may be expedient to replace the term 'cause' by 'facilitator' in the diachronic study of language. This shift from causes to facilitators may reduce the amount of frustration besetting some of those active in this area (e.g. Lass 1980) and lead to the formulation of more realistic research goals.

The preceding analysis elucidates the relationship between spontaneous errors and historical developments. In much the same way that a facilitator cannot cause an error, slips of the tongue cannot be viewed as causing language change. Their value lies more in revealing the processing principles that prevail in the psycholinguistic system. These principles introduce biases to which both slips of the tongue and language change are subject. Their common origin serves as an explanation for why speech-error patterns may be brought to bear so profitably upon the study of language change.

8.6. The Psycholinguistic Basis of Poetry

Poetic traditions, in particular the structure of rhymes, were incorporated in this study with a view to determining how far the influence of processing reaches into a language. Rhyming patterns might be deemed to be a cultural artifact or an artistic device which is predominantly shaped by aesthetic considerations. One might therefore expect to find a great deal of idiosyncrasy and arbitrariness in this field. The empirical analyses revealed, however, that the rhyming patterns are not as inexplicable as might have been expected. Indeed, they are subject to language-particular processing constraints in much the same way as everyday language is. The psycholinguistic influence extends to the size of the rhyming unit as well as to what counts as a permissible rhyme in a language. This is all the more remarkable as the situation in which poetry is created is vastly different from normal language use. Poets have practically unlimited time to produce their language, and can focus upon the formal side of language in a way that is quite untypical of ordinary language.

How can this surprising result be understood? It stands to reason that poets have an intuitive feel for what is possible or 'palatable' in their native language.[7] As particularly language-minded people, they may be attributed a heightened awareness of the aesthetic opportunities offered by their language. It is my conjecture that the poets' conception of aesthetics is unconsciously influenced by psycholinguistic constraints: what runs counter to psycholinguistic principles can hardly give pleasure, because these principles are so deeply entrenched in the speakers' minds that the consumers of the poems would not appreciate any deviations. In contrast, what is in conformity with psycholinguistic constraints is likely to be more appealing. I would suggest that speakers are not free in their aesthetic judgements; these are influenced by the psycholinguistic representation of the individual language which biases the choice for certain poetic structures rather than others.

It may be concluded that the pervasiveness of processing constraints is such that even the highly planned and self-conscious language found in verse is penetrated by them. More than that, poets unconsciously rely upon these constraints to achieve maximal aesthetic success. The emergence of literary norms and traditions is thus not only a cultural artifact but also a predictable consequence of the way language is represented and processed in the human mind.

---

[7] We may safely exclude the possibility that poets have constructed rhymes with a psycholinguistic theory in mind.

9

Implications for Psycholinguistic Theory

Although the major thrust of this work is a linguistic one, it may not be off the mark to touch briefly upon the psycholinguistic significance of the empirical findings. This excursion is justified by the assumed interactivity between linguistic structure and language processing. It was argued in Chapter 3 that in order to derive the 'best' predictions it is essential to rely upon the 'best' psycholinguistic theory. Which theory is the 'best' is, of course, a matter of dispute. The standard method of seeking confirmation (or disconfirmation) of a scientific theory is to adduce arguments from the domain to which the theory appertains. For instance, a psycholinguistic theory is built upon psycholinguistic considerations. This methodology is perfectly acceptable; however, there is no reason not to extend the argumentative basis to areas beyond the home domain and in so doing, broaden the coverage of the theory. Linguistic findings may thus be used to adjudicate between alternative psycholinguistic theories. Clearly, one psycholinguistic theory is superior to another when the linguistic data are compatible with the one but incompatible with the other.

For the past twenty years or so, psycholinguistic theorizing has been dominated by the controversy about the serial modular vs. the parallel interactive approach (see Garrett, 1990 for a review). Both theories make radically different predictions about what is possible in language structure and what is not. The serial approach is more restrictive than the parallel one and can therefore be more easily tested. Let us consider the two backbones of the serial model, 'vertical' serialness and 'horizontal' serialness, the former referring to the information flow in the hierarchical organization of language and the latter to the linear order of smaller units within larger ones (e.g. segments within words).[1] Because of the strictly top-down information flow in production, the serial model predicts an independence between the higher non-phonological and the lower phonological levels. Similarly, because of the strictly left-to-right strategy, processing on 'later' units can start only after the processing of 'earlier' units has been completed.

These two predictions are undermined by the structure of natural languages. If the phonological level was blind to what goes on at the lexico-semantic level, the relationship between the 'signifiant' and the 'signifié' of the linguistic sign would

---

[1] Butterworth (1989) and Levelt et al. (1991) are proponents of vertical serialness; Meyer (1990) is one proponent of horizontal serialness.

have to be arbitrary. While this was the prevailing thinking not long ago, it is now becoming increasingly clear that iconicity is an important design feature of language (even though it is not among the most powerful ones). As shown in the empirical section, the phonological similarity in morphophonological alternations is a faithful reflection of the semantic similarity holding between the members of a morphosemantic set. The serial model fails to predict this interaction. Thus the conclusion seems unavoidable that the existence of iconicity provides a strong argument for parallel-interactive processing.

Further, the serial model imposes constraints upon the phonological and morphophonological structure of words. The form of a particular segment may be determined by the unit preceding but not by the unit following. This is clearly falsified by the existence of regressive assimilation which indeed is even more powerful than the progressive type (see section 4.11.1). In addition, morphophonological accommodation such as is found in the allomorphy of the indefinite and definite articles in English should not occur under the serialness assumption. This model is also challenged by consonant mutation in the Celtic languages. The serial model must claim that mutating segments occur at the end of words. They cannot occur at the beginning, because the processing of the following material depends upon the nature of the initial segment. If this identity is not known, the following material and hence the whole word is unprocessable. The fact that consonant mutation occurs in word-initial positions (and that it poses no insuperable processing problem—see Boyce et al. 1987) is thus strong evidence against the serial model. Only a parallel model is capable of accommodating this phenomenon.

Similarly, the empirical finding that words are particularly susceptible to loss when the access of their phonological form is problematic is exactly what a parallel model leads us to expect. This result is difficult to reconcile with a serial approach, which can only predict a phonological but not a lexical repair strategy. Thus the diachronic data also reinforce the viability of the interactive activation model.

We may conclude, then, that there is a great deal of evidence to suggest that languages take more liberty in their structure than is granted by serial processing. The serial model imposes constraints upon the linguistic structure which are repeatedly violated. This means that it is not powerful enough to deal with the complexity that effectively exists in language. The parallel model, by contrast, fares much better. On account of its interactive nature, it can explain top-down and bottom-up as well as left-to-right and right-to-left influences. Because such effects are highly typical of language, more can be said in favour of the parallel model. I take this to be a significant coincidence: the parallel interactive framework is to be preferred not only on psycholinguistic but also on linguistic grounds.

10

The Overall Perspective: Reductionist or Non-reductionist?

The central question addressed in this work is how far the psycholinguistic approach takes us in explaining language. The overall conclusion is that it takes us quite a long way. Of course, this does not mean that the psycholinguistic approach is omnipotent: language cannot be reduced to psychology, in much the same way as phonology cannot be reduced to phonetics. This is because language is more than a psychological phenomenon. All the other facets discussed in Chapter 2 also have a role in this game. Unfortunately, it is not known how far these non-psychological approaches take us, because their impact upon the structure of language has not yet been investigated systematically and comprehensively. We are even more in the dark as to the multifarious interactions that may exist among the various dimensions of language. There are two reasons why relatively little explanatory work has been forthcoming. For one thing, the relevant disciplines have not progressed to the point where a direct and systematic link with language can be established. The paradigm case exemplifying this state of affairs is the neurosciences. For another, researchers in the disciplines in question have been intent on setting themselves off against the philosophy of autonomous linguistics; their attempts to establish their relative independence from formal linguistics have distracted their attention from issues of language structure. Therefore, the results of their research are often not directly transferable to the issues that are of major concern in the present study.

To put this work in a wider perspective, a vision of language and linguistics will be outlined which may serve as a research programme as well as a metatheory. Let us embark upon the following *Gedankenexperiment*. Suppose all disciplines have advanced to such a stage that it is possible to carry through a large-scale investigation of the impact that all external approaches make upon language structure. The next step would be an examination of the effects that the approaches produce, not in isolation but in combination. After this work has been completed, one would be in a position to reliably assess the contributions of each discipline individually and all disciplines collectively to the explanation of language structure. What might be the outcome of this assessment? Either all these external approaches provide a comprehensive account of language structure or there remains a significant portion of linguistic patterns that cannot be so explained. It goes without saying that there is currently no rational basis for anticipating which alternative will eventually turn out to be the correct one.

Curiously enough, many linguists, especially those of the generative persuasion, appear to assume that we already have the final answer, and that the fallacy of the external approach to language has been proven. It is equally curious that virtually none of these scholars has subjected this view to critical evaluation. Instead, they have indulged in the autonomous, formal approach to language and linguistics and have defended their conviction by discrediting the alternative view as reductionist. The opposition between reductionism and non-reductionism deserves closer scrutiny.

The issue is not whether it is reductionist to view the explanandum exclusively in terms of *one* explanans, e.g. the human mind in terms of the brain or language in terms of processing. The real issue is whether it should be called 'reductionist' to construe language as a joint result of all the external influences that have been considered in Chapter 2, and nothing else. It should be made quite clear that this conception leaves no room for system-internal, formal factors acting upon the structure of language. Formalisms may find a place in this conception only insofar as they effectively capture an external reality, even though they are presented in the guise of system-internal principles. This point will be expanded upon below.

There are two or even three positions that can be taken with respect to reductionism. Let us begin with the group of (mostly) theoretical linguists who tend to consider the external perspective reductionist. Their basic assumption is that there is something inherent to language ('the true nature of language') that cannot be covered by any other discipline. Of necessity, these scholars are strictly opposed to the external perspective because it nullifies what they regard as the core of language. As one example of this way of thinking one might cite Fodor (1978), who claims that there is a 'competence grammar' independent of a 'performance grammar'. The former refers to the 'linguistic core of language', the latter to the psychological mechanisms of language production and comprehension. Fodor argues that there are certain movement and deletion rules in syntax which make life more difficult for the processor than other rules would—which are not, however, found. On the assumption that there is nothing but the processor, the existence and generality of these rules would be hard to explain. Fodor goes on to argue that the existence of such rules is less surprising once it is assumed that they are more highly valued than their alternatives in an autonomous system of well-formedness conditions. The existence of these rules is thus taken as evidence for the reality of a competence grammar. This is not the moment critically to assess this argument. Fodor was merely cited as one explicit view against reducing competence to performance.

Those linguists who would not regard the external perspective as reductionist are likely to come from the interdisciplinary front. I find it virtually impossible to specify how many 'interdisciplinarists' would subscribe to this point of view. Most of them devote themselves to their interdisciplinary approach, and refrain from judging the significance of work in theoretical linguistics. One of the few students of language who have taken a definitive stance on this issue is Ohala (e.g. 1990). His argument is essentially this. The formal theoretical approach to language does not do justice to the nature of the object under investigation. Phonological patterns are best described and explained in terms of anatomical, perceptual and other constraints, rather than in terms of constraints on the well-formedness of formal representations. The former type of constraint can be shown to exist on independent grounds, whereas the latter type cannot. In short, Ohala sees no need for postulating a competence grammar over and above a performance grammar. Hence he espouses the view that there is nothing reductionist about exclusively focusing upon the latter.

A noteworthy intermediate position has been taken by Clements (1992), whose work would clearly group him with the 'formalists'. And, indeed, he criticizes Ohala's approach as reductionist. On the other hand, he acknowledges the possibility that what has here been called the 'external perspective' may ultimately turn out to be correct. That is, it may well be that all characteristics of language are derivable from non-linguistic principles. Clearly, this position is quite close to Ohala's. However, it does not lead Clements to reject the formalistic approach. Rather, he sees the formal method as a tool which is needed to compensate for the lack of advancement in the other scientific disciplines. Although he does not explicitly say so, the implication would be that once the other disciplines have reached the necessary level of sophistication, formalisms in linguistics can be dispensed with. As one advantage, Clements notes that formal models, on account of their explicitness and predictiveness, can even serve the function of clarifying the relation between linguistic and extralinguistic facts.

At first sight, Clements's prudent stance appears to be well taken. However, it seems to me that his conception of the role of formalisms does not tally with their actual use in linguistics. To Clements, formalisms are a matter of research tactics, a means to an end, whereas to many other linguists the construction of formal models is the ultimate goal of their research, the end *tout court*. It is not generally recognized or intended that formal models help bridge the gap between linguistic and extralinguistic facts (or intended that they should), simply because the extralinguistic aspects are not taken into consideration. Clements's anti-reductionist position appears justifiable to the extent that formalisms are seen as intermediate steps, to be replaced by explanations in the long run. As far as I can see, however, most generative linguists are not willing to take such steps. Note as well that there is nothing in Clements's argument that prevents one from trying to establish a direct link between the explanans and the explanandum without such intermediate stages.

Is there any way of establishing which of these conflicting views is more likely to be correct? In light of our immense lack of knowledge in this field, it is immediately apparent that any attempt to answer this question can be no more than suggestive and preliminary. However, there are arguments that can be brought to bear upon this issue. To begin with, there is an a priori argument put forward by Fodor (1978) himself. The reality of a performance grammar can be taken for granted, whereas the existence of a competence grammar has to be demonstrated by scientific argumentation. Without psychological mechanisms for speaking, understanding, and learning, language could not be used and could not have evolved. In contrast, there is no such argument for a competence grammar. One might even go so far as to claim that the reality of a competence grammar is doubtful a priori, because its function is uncertain and may even hinder the smooth running of the performance machine (see above). It is well known from biology that functionless or antifunctional properties either do not affirm themselves in the first place or tend to disappear (over long stretches of time).

The following research strategy seems to be the most productive at the present time. When an abstract, formal competence principle has purportedly been discovered, an attempt should be made to find out whether this principle can be shown to be related to one or more external (i.e. non-linguistic) constraints. Once an alternative explanation is available, it would be incumbent on the researcher to carry out a comparison of the two accounts with an eye to finding out whether one fares better than the other. Pitting one against the other will not be an easy task, partly because the evaluation criteria for competence grammars are somewhat ad hoc and subjective. In some happy circumstances, it may be possible to find different predictions or different degrees of specificness which might help in arbitrating between the two approaches empirically. Even if both approaches should turn out to be equally powerful, it might be argued that the language-external account is to be given preference over the language-internal one, because the former relies upon principles which are needed for independent reasons (see preceding paragraph).

Of course, it is not feasible to treat all competence principles that have been proposed in the linguistic literature, and it would be presumptuous to claim that all of them can be readily given an extralinguistic interpretation. I will therefore restrict myself to discussing a limited number of examples. Thus, the following analysis has an exemplary function. Its main objective is not definitively to decide the issue but rather to argue that there is no need to stop short at formalisms, and that the search for their extralinguistic bases is worthwhile. The first example has been selected to show that it is hazardous to assign to certain aspects of linguistic competence the quality of being unlearnable (i.e. innate) and in this way implicitly claim that it is futile to enquire into their extralinguistic motivation. The second and third examples examine formalisms which are widely recognized in the linguistics literature. All three examples attack grand issues of linguistic theorizing. There is thus no danger that we become lost in quibbles about paraphernalia.

The first issue to be tackled is one of the most popular theories of morphology known as Lexical Phonology (Kiparsky 1982; 1985). In fact its name is slightly inadequate, as part of its primary motivation comes from the analysis of morphological processes. Since these will be our major concern, the term 'Lexical Morphology' will be used henceforth. The core idea is the organization of the lexicon into levels or strata. Each level has a representation of its own and allows a unique set of rules to be applied. Kiparsky distinguishes three levels which are strictly ordered with respect to one another. The first level takes as its input so-called 'base forms', i.e. underived lexical entries. It deals with stem-changing morphology, in particular irregular inflectional rules such as ablaut and umlaut. The second level takes care of word-based processes, in particular word formation such as compounding and certain derivational rules. The third level is also word-based. It is responsible for regular inflection (e.g. the plural 's' in English). This level completes the morphological build-up of words. Its output is fed into the postlexical component. Note that, although this model could principally be a psycholinguistic one, it is not conceived as such; Kiparsky devised it as a model of linguistic competence.

Serial models have the virtue of making clear predictions about what is possible and what is not. Let us briefly look at two test cases. The level-ordering assumption imposes a strong constraint on the order of affixes. For example, word-based suffixes must follow stem-based suffixes. The inverse order is not possible because it would require level 1 to operate after level 2, thus violating the level-ordering assumption. Accordingly, *lugubriousness* is acceptable, because *-ous* is a level 1 and *-ness* a level 2 suffix. By the same logic, *beautifulity* is an impossible word, as a level 2 suffix precedes a level 1 suffix.

Constraints on compounding constitute the other test case. Since regular inflection follows compounding, a compound cannot have a regularly inflected form as its determinans. Thus, *rats-infested* is ruled out. However, since irregular inflection precedes compounding, a compound can have an irregularly inflected form as its determinans. Hence, *lice-infested* is impeccable.

On the basis of acquisition data, Gordon (1985) as well as Clahsen et al. (1992) argued that level-ordering in the lexicon is genetically coded and therefore that neonates enter this world with a blueprint of Kiparsky's model.[1] Note that the claim as to innateness entails a claim as to universality. If this conjecture is correct, the search for explanations, no matter of which kind, would be doomed to failure. However, there is good reason to be sceptical about the innateness hypothesis.

Let us ask first of all what it actually means to say that a model as specific as Kiparsky's is part of our genetic endowment. If the predisposition for level-ordering is genetically coded like the colour of our eyes, then we lack control over it. By implication, the level-ordering constraint must be inviolable. Not only must it be inviolable in language use but it must also be impossible to think up morphologically illicit forms. However, it is no problem to 'outwit the genes' by inventing such words as *rats-infested*. What is more, we only have to turn to actual language use to find numerous counterexamples. Contrary to the prediction of Kiparsky's model, level 2 affixes may precede level 1 affixes, as in *govern-ment-al* and *organ-iz-ation* (see Szpyra, 1989 for a summary of criticisms of Lexical Morphology from the linguistic angle). One way out of this problem is to create a category of affixes which simultaneously belong to levels 1 and 2. Clearly, this move is counter to the spirit of the strict separation of levels and severely undermines the theoretical significance of the serial model.

---

[1] It should be stressed that Kiparsky himself does not explicitly state that his model is unlearnable and therefore must be part of the innate knowledge children bring to the task of language acquisition. I do not know whether he would want to commit himself to such a view.

A further cogent criticism of level-ordering has been voiced by Fabb (1988). He shows that level-ordering rules out only a small subpart of all the unattested combinations of affixes in morphologically complex words. This means that the problem of what is and what is not attested is not adequately handled by the level-ordering assumption. Fabb argues that selectional restrictions mainly determine what is allowed and what is not, and that these restrictions are needed on independent grounds. Because of their wider scope, the selectional restrictions embrace, and thus make redundant, the level-ordering principle.

Similarly, contrary to the innateness hypothesis, regular inflection inside compounds is not unattested in actual language usage. Two relevant examples are *systems analyst* and *arms race*. Rastall (1993) notes that this type of word formation is on the increase, and even that a lexical opposition between singular and plural compounds begins to establish itself. Thus we find *account manager* alongside *accounts manager*, with the choice depending upon whether responsibility is held for one particular or more than one account. All these cases are incompatible with the level-ordering assumption.

Thus inflection inside compounds is not banned, although it should be noted that it is not particularly common. It is appropriate therefore to look for factors which discourage the occurrence of internally inflected compounds but not for factors (such as genetic ones) which categorically rule them out. Indeed, such probabilistic factors are not hard to find. It will be argued that three such factors are sufficient to explain the infrequency of the linguistic pattern under scrutiny. All of them are not only plausible psycholinguistically but can also be independently motivated. The first principle states that children find it harder to detect morphological markers in irregular than in regular forms. The second principle assumes that children's representations are more holistic than those of adults. The third principle holds that children prefer word-final inflection to word-internal inflection. Viewed together, these three principles are able to account for the data that Gordon (1985) and Clahsen et al. (1992) have taken to motivate the innateness hypothesis.

The first principle is based upon the assumption that morphological markers are easiest to identify when they are formally separate from the stem. Thus, the regular <-ed> past tense should pose less of a problem than ablaut changes. Given this, there is the real danger that children fail to detect irregular morphological markers and consequently misanalyse such complex forms as *bought* as simplex forms. This is one explanation of children's utterances like the following.

(336) *What did you bought?* (from Hurford 1975)

Significantly, such errors are particularly frequent with irregular verbs. The thrust of this argument is that children are less likely to recognize opaque than transparent morphological markers.

The second factor revolves around the claim that children progress from holistic to more analytical representations during the course of language acquisition. They tend to analyse linguistic patterns from top to bottom. Thus there is a stage at which words are unanalysed as to their segments and a stage at which segments are unanalysed as to their phonological features. By the same token, compounds may be treated in holistic fashion before they are broken down into their constituent parts.

The third factor embodies a very general principle which holds good of all languages with a concatenative morphology. Inflections appear at the margins rather than in the middle of words. This is an obvious consequence of processing ease (see section 4.16). Suffixing and prefixing preserve the integrity of the stem while infixing requires the breaking-up of a cohesive unit.

Taken together, the three principles account for the rarity of compounds of the type *systems analyst* in both child and adult language. If children tend to treat compound words holistically and if they favour word-final over word-medial inflection, they will automatically produce the observed patterns. Let us retrace this process in more detail. The main result of the Clahsen et al. study is the correlation they find between children's overgeneralizing certain plural markers and omitting these compound-internally. Precisely the suffixes -*s* (in normal-developing children) and -*n* (in most dysphasic subjects) that are overextended in simplex words (e.g. G *Indianern* for *Indianer* 'Indians') do not appear within compounds (e.g. G *Blumevase* for *Blumenvase* 'vase'). Clearly, the extent of overgeneralization can be viewed as a reliable index of the degree to which a given morphological marker has been identified as such. This is all the easier the more regular the marker is. In German, most plural allomorphs are not regular in the sense that English {-s} is. As a consequence, only the so-called regular allomorphs are left out compound-internally by German children. The children's dispreference for word-internal marking is a strategy which they develop from their experience with the language: they discover that the shape of words is generally left intact and transfer this experience to the compound words. The irregular allomorphs are not identified as such, and may therefore appear compound-internally (from the adult's point of view).

In conclusion, it may be hypothesized that there is no need to attribute genetic reality to Kiparsky's model. However, an even stronger claim seems justified. I maintain that it is completely wrong to consider level-ordering innate. Recourse to genetics imposes severe constraints that are met neither by child nor by adult language; thus this approach is empirically inadequate. The data can be straightforwardly explained by the joint effect of three psycholinguistic strategies which are independently motivated and which can be readily assumed to be learned through experience.

The second and third examples are the two most fundamental and solid principles that modern phonological theory has brought forth. These are the Obligatory Contour Principle (OCP) and the no-crossing constraint on association lines which were introduced at the very beginning of this monograph. By resuming this discussion we come full circle. It was argued in section 1.1 that to assess the explanatory power of formal-linguistic principles it is necessary to give them an extralinguistic interpretation. As it is now clear that the psychological approach is quite fruitful and powerful, it is fitting to interpret the two phonological principles in psycholinguistic terms. Our working hypothesis will be that the well-formedness conditions shown in the diagrams do not just exist on the linguist's paper but also in the head of the 'naïve' user of the language. On this assumption, the linguistic principles are formal analogues of psychological mechanisms and represent, however obliquely, a mental reality. What evidence is there in favour of this view? Auer (1991: 30) states laconically: 'Of course, speakers and listeners do not draw association lines' (my translation). This is trivially true at the most concrete level. In the act of speaking and listening, language users evidently do not sit down and draw association lines. However, there is a deeper metaphorical sense in which speakers and listeners may indeed be presumed to draw these lines as a psychological process. Taking for granted that the skeleton and the melodic tiers are psychologically real (Stemberger 1990), this might be conceived of as associative links that are established between units from different levels of analysis. For this operation to be carried out, an exchange of activation is necessary. From the psycholinguistic point of view, it is reasonable to assume that the linking process depends upon the activation levels of the units to be linked. Specifically, those units which are most highly activated at a given point in time will associate with each other. Let us now come back to the non-linear phonological representations, and bear in mind that the skeleton level codes timing units which impose serial order upon the string of segments (Clements and Keyser 1983; McCarthy 1989). To make the time dimension explicit, the critical part of (6) above has been expanded as (337).

(337)
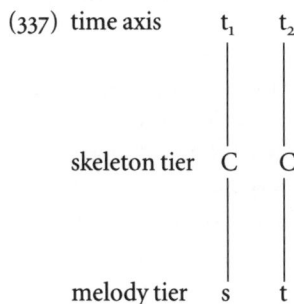

time axis t_1 t_2

skeleton tier   C   C

melody tier   s   t

The function of the skeleton tier is to make sure that the coronal fricative is produced at t_1 and the coronal stop at t_2. This is made possible through the following principle. At t_1, the /s/ is more strongly activated than the /t/ and accordingly associates with the first timing unit. At t_2, in contrast, the activation pattern is reversed and the /t/ can be linked to the next slot. In this way, the correct serial order is effected.

Now let us consider what would happen if the association lines crossed, as depicted in (338). Two variants are considered, depending upon whether the skeleton units connect to one (338a–b) or two (338c) elements at the melodic level.

(338)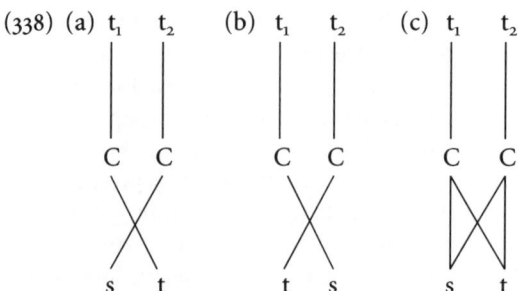

There is only one way to interpret (338a). At t_1, the stop is produced while the fricative wins out at t_2. Because of the ill-formedness of (338a), Bagemihl (1989) was led to argue that this representation is immediately repaired to (339a). This presupposes that the crossing of association lines was introduced in the first place. However, this is neither necessary nor possible from the psycholinguistic angle. Either the stop reaches its activational peak before the fricative, for which (339a) would be appropriate, or vice versa, for which (339b) would be appropriate. There is no room for crossed association lines because the elements at the melodic level are by definition unordered. In other words, the no-crossing constraint is an empty notion.[2]

Representation (338c) implies that exactly the same event takes place at t_1 and t_2. At both moments in time, /s/ and /t/ reach such a high level of activation that they can link to the timing unit. This situation is impossible, because it implies that mutually contradictory commands are issued to the articulators. Continuing the psycholinguist's perspective, this representation is defective in another way. If the events are identical at t_1 and t_2, there is no sense in which an ordering relation can be imposed upon them. Therefore, the need to postulate two separate timing units completely disappears. Again, one might be tempted to argue that the well-formedness can be restored by changing (338c) into (339c), in which the two timing units of (338c) are collapsed into one. However, it is not only more parsimonious but also less shaky to claim that representations such as (338c) do not arise in the first place.

(339)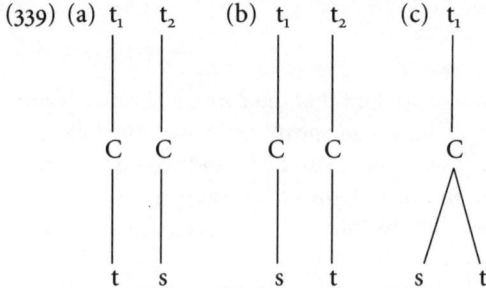

[2] This radical conclusion comes close to Coleman and Local's (1991) evaluation of the no-crossing constraint. Starting out from the claim that linguists have profoundly confused the phonological repre-

Diagram (339c) may now be the representation appropriate for affricates.

How does the OCP fare when interpreted in psycholinguistic terms? Is there a psycholinguistic sense in which the adjacency of two identical elements at the melodic tier can be said to be ill-formed? In the connectionist model which is at the heart of this investigation, segments are represented only once (see section 3.2.1). The second relevant aspect in the present connection is the claim that a segment that has just been outputted undergoes self-inhibition for about 200 ms. (MacKay 1986). This means that it is not available for reselection during this period of time. When these two psycholinguistic components are viewed together, it emerges quite clearly that the production of two identical segments in immediate succession poses a processing problem. Due to psycholinguistic constraints, one would expect the first production to run off smoothly (albeit too quickly or too early) and the second production to fail. Such a constellation may thus be assumed to be eliminated or prevented from occurring at all. This describes precisely what the OCP is about.

The central conclusion that may be drawn from the preceding analysis is this. When linguistic principles such as the OCP and the no-crossing constraint are placed in a psychological context, it is possible better to assess their real significance and their explanatory power. Specifically, it can be evaluated whether a linguistic principle has any relevance beyond constraining the form of diagrams. The OCP could be shown to originate from a psycholinguistic constraint or, rather, a set of psycholinguistic constraints. On a very charitable interpretation, the no-crossing constraint can also be interpreted as expressing a psycholinguistic constraint. The (ill-formed) crossing of association lines describes a psycholinguistic impossibility. The primary use of this principle lies in its power to rule out alternative interpretations. However, these alternatives are only *theoretically* possible (i.e. on the paper of the linguist). To all intents and purposes they are not serious contenders to the no-crossing condition, because no psycholinguistic situations are conceivable in which they could occur at all. Viewed in this light, the no-crossing constraint loses much of the significance it is attributed in linguistics. Be that as it may, the major point to be made is that a deeper understanding of the linguistic principles, in particular an evaluation of their role outside diagrams, can be reached by interpreting them in psycholinguistic terms.

Given the conclusion that the OCP makes sense from the psycholinguistic perspective, we face the following situation. On the one hand there are performance principles such as the impossibility of accessing one and the same unit in immediate succession. On the other hand there are the competence principles such as the OCP. We might be satisfied with this result, and close the case by stating that both types of principle are needed for different purposes and that they capture different

sentations and the diagrams intended to illustrate them, they argue that the no-crossing constraint is a vacuous concept. In fact it is no constraint at all, because it applies to diagrams, not to the representations themselves. In three-dimensional space, all diagrams can be drawn such that association lines do not cross. This trenchant criticism from the set-theoretical angle tallies to a certain extent with my psycholinguistic critique.

aspects of what we conveniently call 'reality'. However, we should perhaps strive to be more ambitious, and ask whether there is a way of pitting the linguistic and the psycholinguistic approach against each other. The best method would be to find areas where the two approaches differ in their predictions or their empirical coverage. If the one approach can be shown to do more than, while at the same time including, the other, we would have a rational basis for applying Occam's Razor, i.e. for arguing that only one approach is necessary and the other can be dispensed with.

How can we distinguish between the OCP as a formal competence principle and the psycholinguistic mechanisms invoked above? Fortunately, the two do not make identical predictions about empirical reality. As a general principle of phonological representation, the OCP is quite a rigorous and absolute notion: either a given sequence of elements is prohibited or it is not. There is thus room neither for intermediate shades such as probabilistic outcomes nor for other factors (e.g. positional ones) to influence the linguistic patterns. By contrast, the performance mechanisms are more malleable: they may coexist with other processing factors and they are probabilistic rather than deterministic in nature. These criteria allow us to directly contrast the two approaches.

Given that one motivation for the OCP came from the study of the non-concatenative morphology of Arabic, it is fitting to take the structure of consonantal roots as the critical test. As was argued in section 4.6, the patterning of root consonants is highly constrained in Arabic. For convenience, the pertinent findings are reproduced in Table 33. I contend that this pattern of results cannot be adequately captured by the OCP. Neither the vertical nor the horizontal axis in Table 33 is accounted for. Beginning with the latter, while the OCP deals very well with C_1–C_2 at the segment level, it fails in the case of C_1–C_3. This is because it stands and falls on the criterion of adjacency. Since C_1 and C_3 are by definition non-adjacent but on the same phonological tier, the OCP predicts no restrictions on segment repetition. The fact that these restrictions occur is thus roundly incompatible with the essence of the OCP. This is because of an interesting interaction between the OCP and the no-crossing constraint. The repetition of non-contiguous segments cannot be prohibited, as this would involve crossing association lines between the consonantal root tier and the melodic tier.

As regards the relationship between segments and features, it can be gathered from Table 33 that restrictions at the former level are generally tighter than those at

TABLE 33. *Restrictions on the repetition of identical elements in triconsonantal Arabic roots*

	C_1–C_2	C_1–C_3	C_2–C_3
Segment level	r. impossible	r. strongly discouraged	r. encouraged
Feature level	r. strongly discouraged	r. discouraged	r. discouraged

Note: r. = repetition.

the latter.[3] Of course, prohibitions on the repetition of identical elements can be established at any level, so it is not at all difficult to account for absolute restrictions at the feature level. What we find, however, are probabilistic restrictions which are incompatible with the OCP as a deterministic principle. There is a further problem to be noted. The restrictions at the feature level and those at the segment level appear to be related. The OCP is principally unable to express this between-level similarity. It remains purely accidental. The conclusion seems inevitable that the OCP as a formal phonological principle fails to account for the results displayed in Table 33. In a word, it is empirically inadequate.

By contrast, the psycholinguistic approach is flexible enough to come to grips with the Arabic data. Here, it will suffice to provide a thumbnail sketch of a possible processing account. Basically, such an account rests upon two assumptions. For one thing, all processing effects are scalar. In the case at hand, the repetition of identical elements in immediate succession is unlikely, though not impossible. How unlikely it is depends upon such factors as speech rate and the linguistic boundaries intervening between the identical units. For another, the repetition of identical segments puts a greater strain upon the processing system than the repetition of identical features. This difference is a natural consequence of the hierarchical organization of language. Segment identity involves a greater amount of identity than feature identity because the former includes the latter while the latter does not include the former. Segment identity presupposes feature identity at all feature dimensions (i.e. voice, manner and place), while only one feature dimension is implicated in feature identity. Given that identical units pose a general problem for the processor (Stemberger and MacWhinney (1986b)), it is understandable why Arabic is more liberal with feature repetition than with segment repetition. In this view, the conditions at both levels are intimately connected.

The preceding comparison invites the conclusion that the OCP and the psycholinguistic account are not separate concepts which exist in their own right in their respective conceptual frames. Rather, they are best viewed as competing theoretical proposals for certain linguistic patterns. It is therefore legitimate directly to contrast the two in terms of their descriptive and explanatory adequacy. It may be concluded that the psycholinguistic account fares better than the formal-linguistic one, and that the latter should be abandoned in favour of the former.

There is a more general lesson to be learnt. If we are bold enough to generalize from the few examples discussed, we might claim that there is no competence grammar over and above a performance grammar. I am convinced that this is more than wild speculation, although I painfully realize that it is virtually impossible to prove that something does *not* exist.

---

[3] The C_2–C_3 column will be ignored, as it involves several complications which have been discussed in section 4.6 but which are not central to the argument made here.

References

ABD-EL-JAWAD, H., and ABU-SALIM, I. (1987). 'Slips of the Tongue in Arabic and Their Theoretical Implications'. *Language Sciences*, 9: 145–71.
ALEXANDER, J. D. (1988). 'Aphesis in English', *Word*, 39: 29–65.
ANDERSON, S. R. (1981). 'Why Phonology Isn't "Natural" ', *Linguistic Inquiry*, 12: 493–539.
ANTINUCCI, F., DURANTI, A., and GABERT, L. (1979). 'Relative Clause Structure, Relative Clause Perception, and the Change from SOV to SVO', *Cognition*, 7: 145–76.
ANTTILA, R. (1972). *An Introduction to Historical and Comparative Linguistics*. New York: Macmillan.
AUER, P. (1991). 'Zur More in der Phonologie'. *Zeitschrift für Sprachwissenschaft*, 10: 3–36.
BAGEMIHL, B. (1989). 'The crossing constraint and "backwards languages" ', *Natural Language and Linguistic Theory*, 7: 481–549.
BAILEY, C.-J. N. (1982). *On the Yin and Yang Nature of Language*. Ann Arbor, Mich.: Karoma.
BARON, N. S. (1977). *Language Acquisition and Historical Change*. Amsterdam: North-Holland.
BAUER, L. (1991). 'Scalar Productivity and "-lily" Adverbs', *Yearbook of Morphology*, 4: 185–91.
BEAUGRANDE, R. DE (1996). 'The Pragmatics of Doing Language Science: The "warrant" for Large-Corpus Linguistics', *Journal of Pragmatics*, 25: 503–35.
BERG, T. (1985). 'Is Voice a Suprasegmental?' *Linguistics*, 23: 883–915.
—— (1987). *A Cross-linguistic Comparison of Slips of the Tongue*. Bloomington: Indiana University Linguistics Club.
—— (1988a). *Die Abbildung des Sprachproduktionsprozesses in einem Aktivationsflußmodell. Untersuchungen an deutschen und englischen Versprechern*. Tübingen: Niemeyer.
—— (1988b). 'The Whys and Wherefores of Suprasegmentalization', *Lingua*, 74: 283–302.
—— (1988c). 'Zur Leistungsfähigkeit linguistischer Konstrukte in der Beschreibung psycholinguistischer Daten: Untersuchungen an phonologischen Versprechern aus mehreren indoeuropäischen Sprachen', in B. Spillner (ed.), *Angewandte Linguistik und Computer. Kongreßberichte der 18. Jahrestagung der Gesellschaft für Angewandte Linguistik*. Tübingen: Narr, 197–9.
—— (1989a). 'On the Internal Structure of Polysyllabic Monomorphemic Words: The Case for Superrimes', *Studia Linguistica*, 43: 5–32.
—— (1989b). 'How Phonetic Is a Phonological Feature Representation? The Case of Labiodental Fricatives', *Speech Communication*, 8: 329–46.
—— (1989c). 'Intersegmental Cohesiveness', *Folia Linguistica*, 23: 245–80.
—— (1990a). 'The Differential Sensitivity of Consonants and Vowels to Stress', *Language Sciences*, 12: 65–84.
—— (1990b). 'Unreine Reime als Evidenz für die Organisation phonologischer Merkmale', *Zeitschrift für Sprachwissenschaft*, 9: 3–27.
—— (1991a). 'Phonological Processing in a Syllable-Timed Language with Pre-final Stress: Evidence from Spanish Speech Error Data', *Language and Cognitive Processes*, 6: 265–301.
—— (1991b). 'Redundant-Feature Coding in the Mental Lexicon', *Linguistics*, 29: 903–25.
—— (1992a). 'Umrisse einer psycholinguistischen Theorie der Silbe', in P. Eisenberg, K. H. Ramers, and H. Vater (eds.), *Silbenphonologie des Deutschen*. Tübingen: Narr, 44–99.

—— (1992b). 'Productive and Perceptual Constraints on Speech Error Correction', *Psychological Research*, **54:** 114–26.
—— (1992c). 'Prelexical and Postlexical Features in Language Production', *Applied Psycholinguistics*, **13:** 199–235.
—— (1992d). Review of M. Hellinger (1990), *Linguistische Berichte*, **137** (1992): 68–74.
—— (1993). 'The Phoneme through a Psycholinguist's Looking-Glass', *Theoretical Linguistics*, **19:** 39–76.
—— (1994). 'More on Intersegmental Cohesiveness', *Folia Linguistica*, **28:** 257–78.
—— (1995a). 'Word-Final Voicing in the History of English: A Case of Unnatural Phonology?' *English Studies*, **76:** 185–201.
—— (1995b). 'Sound Change in Child Language: A Study of Inter-word Variation', *Language and Speech*, **38:** 331–63.
—— (in preparation). 'Phonological distance'.
—— and ABD-EL-JAWAD, H. (1996). 'The Unfolding of Suprasegmental Representations: A Cross-linguistic Perspective', *Journal of Linguistics*, **32:** 291–324.
—— and SCHADE, U. (1992). 'The Role of Inhibition in a Spreading-Activation Model of Language Production', I: 'The Psycholinguistic Perspective', *Journal of Psycholinguistic Research*, **21:** 405–34.
BERLIN, B., and KAY, P. (1969). *Basic Colour Terms: Their Universality and Evolution*. Berkeley: University of California Press.
BEVER, T. G., and LANGENDOEN, T. (1971). 'A Dynamic Model of the Evolution of Language', *Linguistic Inquiry*, **2:** 433–63.
—— —— (1972). 'The Interaction of Speech Perception and Grammatical Structure in the Evolution of Language', in R. P. Stockwell and R. K. S. Macauley (eds.), *Linguistic Change and Generative Theory*. Bloomington: Indiana University Press, 32–95.
BIBER, D. (1988). *Variation across Speech and Writing*. Cambridge: Cambridge University Press.
BIRD, S. (1995). *Computational Phonology: A Constraint-Based Approach*. Cambridge: Cambridge University Press.
BLOCH, BERNARD (1947). 'English Verb Inflection', *Language*, **23:** 399–418.
BOHNE, F. (ed.) (n. d.). *Wilhelm Busch. Gesamtausgabe in vier Bänden*. Wiesbaden: Emil Vollmer.
BOND, Z. S., and ROBEY, R. R. (1983). 'The Phonetic Structure of Errors in the Perception of Fluent Speech', in R. Lass (ed.), *Speech and Language: Advances in Basic Research and Practice*, ix. New York: Academic Press, 249–83.
—— and SMALL, L. H. (1983). 'Voicing, Vowel, and Stress Mispronunciations in Continuous Speech', *Perception and Psychophysics*, **34:** 470–4.
BOOMER, D. S., and LAVER, J. (1968). 'Slips of the Tongue', *British Journal of Disorders of Communication*, **3:** 1–12.
BOTHA, R. P. (1989). *Challenging Chomsky: The Generative Garden Game*. Oxford: Basil Blackwell.
BOYCE, S., BROWMAN, C. P., and GOLDSTEIN, L. (1987). 'Lexical Organization and Welsh Consonant Mutations', *Journal of Memory and Language*, **26:** 419–52.
BRADLEY, D. C. (1983). *Computational Distinctions of Vocabulary Types*. Bloomington: Indiana University Linguistics Club.
BRAITHWAITE, R. B. (1968). *Scientific Explanation*. Cambridge: Cambridge University Press.

BRAUNMÜLLER, K. (1984). 'Morphologische Undurchsichtigkeit—ein Charakteristikum kleiner Sprachen', *Kopenhagener Beiträge zur Germanistik*, **22**: 48–68.
BROSELOW, E., and MCCARTHY, J. J. (1983–4). 'A Theory of Internal Reduplication', *The Linguistic Review*, **3**: 25–88.
BROWN, R., and GILMAN A. (1960). 'The Pronouns of Solidarity', repr. in J. A. Fishman (ed.), *Readings in the Sociology of Language*. The Hague: Mouton, 252–75.
—— and MCNEILL, D. (1966). 'The "Tip of the Tongue" Phenomenon', *Journal of Verbal Learning and Verbal Behavior*, **5**: 325–37.
BRYANT, M. M. (1974). 'Blends Are Increasing', *American Speech*, **49**: 163–84.
BUTTERWORTH, B. (1983). 'Lexical Representation', in B. Butterworth (ed.), *Language Production*, ii: *Development, Writing and Other Language Processes*. London: Academic Press, 257–94.
—— (1989). 'Lexical Access in Speech Production', in W. D. Marslen-Wilson (ed.), *Lexical Representation and Process*. Cambridge, Mass.: MIT Press, 108–35.
BYBEE, J. L. (1985). *Morphology: A Study of the Relation between Meaning and Form*. Amsterdam: John Benjamins.
—— (1988). The Diachronic Dimension in Explanation', in J. A. Hawkins (ed.), *Explaining Language Universals*. Oxford: Basil Blackwell, 350–79.
—— (1991). 'Natural Morphology: The Organization of Paradigms and Language Acquisition', in T. Huebner and C. A. Ferguson (eds.), *Crosscurrents in second language acquisition and linguistic theories*. Amsterdam: John Benjamins, 67–91.
—— and MODER, C. L. (1983). 'Morphological Classes as Natural Categories', *Language*, **59**: 251–70.
—— and SLOBIN, D. I. (1982a). 'Rules and Schemas in the Development and Use of the English Past Tense', *Language*, **58**: 265–89.
—— —— (1982b). 'Why Small Children Cannot Change Language on Their Own: Suggestions from the English Past Tense', in A. Ahlqvist (ed.), *Papers from the 5th International Conference on Historical Linguistics* Amsterdam: John Benjamins, 29–37.
CAMPBELL, A. (1959). *Old English Grammar*. Oxford: Oxford University Press.
CANNON, G. (1986). 'Blends in English Word Formation', *Linguistics*, **24**: 725–53.
CARSTAIRS, A., and STEMBERGER, J. P. (1988). 'A Processing Constraint on Inflectional Homonymy', *Linguistics*, **26**: 601–17.
CHEN, M. Y. (1972). 'The Time Dimension: Contribution Toward a Theory of Sound Change', *Foundations of Language*, **8**: 457–98.
—— and WANG, W. S.-Y. (1975). 'Sound Change: Actuation and Implementation', *Language*, **51**: 255–81.
CHERUBIM, D. (1980). 'Abweichung und Sprachwandel', in D. Cherubim (ed.), *Fehlerlinguistik. Beiträge zum Problem der sprachlichen Abweichung*. Tübingen: Niemeyer, 124–52.
CHOMSKY, N. (1965). *Aspects of the Theory of Syntax*. Cambridge, Mass.: MIT Press.
—— (1972). *Language and Mind* (enlarged edn). New York: Harcourt Brace Jovanovich.
—— (1986). *Knowledge of Language: Its Nature, Origin and Use*. New York: Praeger.
—— (1988). *Language and Problems of Knowledge*. Cambridge, Mass.: MIT Press.
—— (1992). 'On the Nature, Use and Acquisition of Language', in M. Pütz (ed.), *Thirty Years of Linguistic Evolution*. Amsterdam: John Benjamins, 3–29.
CLAHSEN, H., ROTHWEILER, M., WOEST, A., and MARCUS, G. F. (1992). 'Regular and irregular inflection in the acquisition of German noun plurals', *Cognition*, **45**: 225–55.
CLARK, E. V. (1993). *The Lexicon in Acquisition*. Cambridge: Cambridge University Press.

—— and CLARK, H. H. (1979). 'When Nouns Surface as Verbs', *Language*, **55**: 761–811.
CLARK, H. H., and CLARK, E. V. (1977). *Psychology and Language: An Introduction to Psycholinguistics*. New York: Harcourt Brace Jovanovich.
—— and HAVILAND, S. E. (1974). 'Psychological Processes as Linguistic Explanation', in D. Cohen (ed.), *Explaining Linguistic Phenomena*. New York: John Wiley, 91–124.
—— and MALT B. C. (1984). 'Psychological Constraints on Language: A Commentary on Bresnan and Kaplan and on Givón', in W. Kintsch, J. R. Miller, and G. Polson (eds.), *Method and Tactics in Cognitive Science*. Hillsdale, NJ: Lawrence Erlbaum, 191–214.
CLEMENTS, G. N. (1992). 'Comments on Chapter 7', in G. J. Docherty and D. R. Ladd (eds.), *Papers in Laboratory Phonology*, ii. Cambridge: Cambridge University Press, 183–9.
—— and KEYSER, S. J. (1983). *CV Phonology: A Generative Theory of the Syllable*. Cambridge, Mass.: MIT Press.
CLUMECK, H. (1979). 'A Parallel between Child and Adult Language: A Study in the Phonetic Explanation of Sound Patterns', *Journal of Child Language*, **6**: 593–8.
COHEN, A., EBELING, C. L., FOKKEMA, K., and VAN HOLK, A. G. F. (1961). *Fonologie van het Nederlands en het Fries*. 's-Gravenhage: Martinus Nijhoff.
COLÉ, P., BEAUVILLAIN, C., and SEGUI, J. (1989). On the Representation and Processing of Prefixed and Suffixed Derived Words', *Journal of Memory and Language*, **28**: 1–13.
COLE, R. A. (1973). 'Listening for Mispronunciations: A Measure of What We Hear during Speech', *Perception and Psychophysics*, **11**: 153–6.
—— JAKIMIK, J., and COOPER, W. (1978). 'Perceptibility of Phonetic Features in Fluent Speech', *Journal of the Acoustical Society of America*, **64**: 44–56.
COLEMAN, J., and LOCAL, J. (1991). 'The "No-crossing Constraint" in autosegmental phonology', *Linguistics and Philosophy*, **14**: 295–338.
Collins English Learner's Dictionary (1974). By D. J. Carver, M. J. Wallace, and J. Cameron. London: Collins.
COMRIE, B. (1993). 'Language Universals and Linguistic Typology: Data-Bases and Explanations', *Sprachtypologie und Universalienforschung*, **46**: 3–14.
COOK, V. J. (1974). 'Is Explanatory Adequacy Adequate?' *Linguistics*, **133**: 21–31.
COOLEY, M. (1978). 'Phonological Constraints and Sound Change', *Glossa*, **12**: 125–36.
COOPER, W. E., and PACCIA-COOPER, J. (1980). *Syntax and Speech*. Cambridge, Mass.: Harvard University Press.
—— and Ross, J. R. (1975). 'World Order', in R. E. Grossman, L. J. San, and T. J. Vance (eds.), *Papers from the Parasession on Functionalism*. Chicago: CLS, 63–111.
CORBETT, G. G. (1983). *Hierarchies, Targets and Controllers: Agreement Patterns in Slavic*. London: Croom Helm.
COULMAS, F. (1981). 'Introduction: The Concept of Native Speaker', in F. Coulmas (ed.), *A Festschrift for Native Speaker*. The Hague: Mouton, 1–25.
CROMPTON, A. (1981). 'Syllables and Segments in Speech Production', *Linguistics*, **19**: 663–716.
CULICOVER, P. W. (1984). 'Learnability Explanations and Processing Explanations', *Natural Language and Linguistic Theory*, **2**: 77–104.
CUTLER, A. (1980). 'Productivity in Word Formation', in *Papers from the 16th Regional Meeting of the Chicago Linguistic Society*. Chicago: CLS, 45–51.
—— (1981). 'Degrees of Transparency in Word Formation', *Canadian Journal of Linguistics*, **26**: 73–7.
—— (1986). '*Forbear* Is a Homophone: Lexical Prosody Does Not Constrain Lexical Access', *Language and Speech*, **29**: 201–20.

CUTLER, A., HAWKINS, J. A., and GILLIGAN, G. (1985). 'The Suffixing Preference: A Processing Explanation', *Linguistics*, **23**: 723–58.

—— MEHLER, J., NORRIS, D., and SEGUI, J. (1986). 'The Syllable's Differing Role in the Segmentation of French and English', *Journal of Memory and Language*, **25**: 385–400.

—— —— —— —— (1992). 'The Monolingual Nature of Speech Segmentation by Bilinguals', *Cognitive Psychology*, **24**: 381–410.

DAUER, R. M. (1983). 'Stress-Timing and Syllable-Timing Reanalyzed', *Journal of Phonetics*, **11**: 51–62.

DAVIS, S. (1984). 'Some Implications of Onset–Coda Constraints for Syllable Phonology', in *Papers from the 20th Regional Meeting of the Chicago Linguistic Society*. Chicago: CLS, 46–51.

—— (1989). 'Cross-Vowel Phonotactic Constraints', *Computational Linguistics*, **15**: 109–10.

DELL, G. S. (1986). 'A Spreading-Activation Theory of Retrieval in Sentence Production', *Psychological Review*, **93**: 283–421.

—— (1990). 'Effects of Frequency and Vocabulary Type on Phonological Speech Errors', *Language and Cognitive Processes*, **5**: 313–49.

—— and REICH, P. A. (1981). 'Stages in Sentence Production: An Analysis of Speech Error Data', *Journal of Verbal Learning and Verbal Behavior*, **20**: 611–29.

DEL VISO, S., IGOA, J. M., and GARCÍA-ALBEA, J. E. (1987). 'Corpus of Spontaneous Slips of the Tongue in Spanish'. MS, University of Oviedo, Spain.

DENES, P. B. (1963). 'On the Statistics of Spoken English', *Journal of the Acoustical Society of America*, **35**: 892–904.

DERWING, B. (1973). *Transformational Grammar as a Theory of Language Acquisition*. Cambridge: Cambridge University Press.

DE SAUSSURE, F. (1916/1978). *Cours de linguistique générale*. Paris: Payot.

DEWEY, G. (1923). *Relative Frequency of English Speech Sounds*. Cambridge, Mass.: Harvard University Press.

DINNSEN, D. A. (1980). 'Phonological Rules and Phonetic Explanation', *Journal of Linguistics*, **16**: 171–91.

DRACHMANN, G. (1978). 'Child Language and Language Change: A Conjecture and Some Refutations', in J. Fisiak (ed.), *Recent Developments in Historical Phonology*. The Hague: Mouton, 123–44.

DRESSLER, W. U. (1977). 'Phono-morphological Dissimilation', in W. U. Dressler and O. E. Pfeiffer (eds.), *Phonologica 1976*. Innsbruck: Innsbrucker Beiträge zur Sprachwissenschaft, 41–8.

—— (1984). 'Explaining Natural Phonology', *Phonology Yearbook*, **1**: 29–51.

—— (1985a). 'On the Predictiveness of Natural Morphology', *Journal of Linguistics*, **21**: 321–37.

—— (1985b). *Morphonology: The Dynamics of Derivation*. Ann Arbor, Mich.: Karoma.

—— (1986). 'Explanation in Natural Morphology, Illustrated with Comparative and Agent–Noun Formation', *Linguistics*, **24**: 519–48.

—— (1988). 'Preferences vs. Strict Universals in Morphology: Word-Based Rules', in M. Hammond and M. Noonan (eds.), *Theoretical Morphology: Approaches in Modern Linguistics*. San Diego, Calif.: Academic Press, 143–54.

—— (1990). 'The Cognitive Perspective of "Naturalist" Linguistic Models', *Cognitive Linguistics*, **1**: 75–98.

—— and Moosmüller, S. (1991). 'Phonetics and Phonology: A Sociopsycholinguistic Framework', *Phonetica*, **48**: 135–48.
Dretzke, Fred I. (1974). 'Explanation in Linguistics', in D. Cohen (ed.), *Explaining Linguistic Phenomena*. New York: John Wiley, 21–41.
Dryer, M. S. (1992). 'The Greenbergian Word Order Correlations', *Language*, **68**: 81–138.
Duden (1973). Vol. iv: *Grammatik*, ed. G. Drosdowski. Mannheim: Bibliographisches Institut.
Dyson, A. T. (1986). 'Development of Velar Consonants among Normal Two-Year-Olds', *Journal of Speech and Hearing Research*, **29**: 493–8.
Eckhardt, E. (1938). 'Die konsonantische Dissimilation im Englischen', *Anglia*, **62**: 81–99.
Ekwall, E. (1975). *A History of Modern English Sounds and Morphology*. Oxford: Basil Blackwell.
Elman, J. L. (1990). 'Finding Structure in Time', *Cognitive Science*, **14**: 179–211.
Enkvist, N. E. (1979).' "What" and "Why": On Causal Explanation in Linguistics', *Folia Linguistica*, **13**: 1–21.
Fabb, N. (1988). 'English Suffixation Is Constrained by Selectional Restrictions', *Natural Language and Linguistic Theory*, **6**: 527–39.
Faiß, K. (1989). *Englische Sprachgeschichte*. Tübingen: Francke.
Fenk–Oczlon, G. (1989). 'Word Frequency and Word Order in Freezes', *Linguistics*, **27**: 517–56.
Ferguson, C. A. (1978). 'Phonological Processes', in J. H. Greenberg, C. A. Ferguson and E. A. Moravcsik (eds.), *Universals of Human Language*, ii: *Phonology*. Stanford, Calif.: Stanford University Press, 403–42.
Fidelholtz, J. L. (1975). 'Word Frequency and Vowel Reduction in English', in R. E. Grossman, L. J. San, and T. J. Vance (eds.), *Papers from the 11th Regional Meeting of the Chicago Linguistic Society*. Chicago: CLS, 200–13.
Fill, A. (1993). *Ökolinguistik*. Tübingen: Narr.
Fischer, L. E., and McDavid, R. I. (1976). 'Aphaeresis in New England', *American Speech*, **48**: 246–9.
Fodor, J. D. (1978). 'Parsing Strategies and Constraints on Transformations', *Linguistic Inquiry*, **9**: 427–73.
Fox, B. A., and Thompson, S. A. (1990). 'A Discourse Explanation of the Grammar of Relative Clauses in English Conversation', *Language*, **66**: 297–316.
Frauenfelder, U. H., and Schreuder, R. (1991). 'Constraining Psycholinguistic Models of Morphological Processing and Representation: The Role of Productivity', *Yearbook of Morphology*, **4**: 165–83.
Frazier, L. (1985). 'Syntactic Complexity', in D. R. Dowty, L. Karttunen, and A. M. Zwicky (eds.), *Natural Language Parsing*. Cambridge: Cambridge University Press, 129–89.
—— and Rayner, K. (1988). 'Parameterizing the Language Processing System: Left- vs. Right-Branching Within and Across Languages', in J. A. Hawkins (ed.), *Explaining Language Universals*. Oxford: Basil Blackwell, 247–79.
Fromkin, V. A. (1971). 'The Non-anomalous Nature of Anomalous Utterances', *Language*, **47**: 27–52.
—— (1973). 'Appendix', in V. A. Fromkin (ed.), *Speech Errors as Linguistic Evidence*. The Hague: Mouton, 243–69.
—— (1977). 'Putting the EmPHAsis on the Wrong SylLABle', in L. M. Hyman (ed.), *Studies in Stress and Accent*. University of California, Los Angeles: Department of Linguistics, 15–26.

GAMKRELIDZE, T. V. (1978). 'On the Correlation of Stops and Fricatives in a Phonological System', in J. H. Greenberg, C. A. Ferguson, and E.A. Moravcsik (eds.), *Universals of Human Language*, ii. *Phonology*. Stanford: Stanford University Press, 9–46.

GARRETT, M. F. (1975). 'The Analysis of Sentence Production', in G. H. Bower (ed.), *The Psychology of Learning and Motivation*, ix. New York: Academic Press, 133–77.

—— (1976). 'Syntactic Processes in Sentence Production', in R. J. Wales and E. C. T. Walker (eds.), *New Approaches to Language Mechanisms*. Amsterdam: North Holland.

—— (1990). 'Sentence Processing', in D. N. Osheron and H. Lasnik (eds.), *An Invitation to Cognitive Science*, i: *Language*. Cambridge, Mass.: MIT Press, 133–75.

GAUTHIOT, R. (1913). *La Fin du mot en Indo-européen*. Paris: Paul Geuthner.

GEERAERTS, D. (1985). 'Cognitive Restrictions on the Structure of Semantic Change', in J. Fisiak (ed.), *Historical Semantics: Historical Word-Formation*. Berlin: Mouton, 127–53.

GEERTS, G., HAESERYN, W., DE ROOIJ, J., and VAN DEN TOORN, M. C. (1984). *Algemene Nederlandse Spraakkunst*. Groningen: Wolters-Noordhoff.

GIVÓN, T. (1971). 'Historical Syntax and Synchronic Morphology: An Archaeologist's Field-trip', in *Papers from the 7th Regional Meeting of the Chicago Linguistic Society*. Chicago: CLS, 394–415.

—— (1979). *On Understanding Grammar*. New York: Academic Press.

—— (1995). *Functionalism and Grammar*. Amsterdam: John Benjamins.

GOLDSMITH, J. (1979). *Autosegmental Phonology*. New York: Garland.

—— (1990). *Autosegmental and Metrical Phonology*. Oxford: Basil Blackwell.

—— (ed.) (1993). *The Last Phonological Rule*. Chicago: University of Chicago Press.

GOPNIK, M. (1990). 'Feature-Blind Grammar and Dysphasia', *Nature*, **344:** 715.

—— DALAKIS, J., FUKUDA, S. E., FUKUDA, S., and KEHAYIA, E. (1996). 'Genetic Language Impairment: Unruly Grammars', *Proceedings of the British Academy*, **88:** 223–49.

GORDON, P. (1985). 'Level-Ordering in Lexical Development', *Cognition*, **21:** 73–93.

GRAMMONT, M. (1895). *La Dissimilation consonantique dans les langues indoeuropéennes et dans les langues romanes*. Dijon: de Darantière.

GREENBERG, J. H. (1950). 'The Patterning of Root Morphemes in Semitic', *Word*, **6:** 162–81.

—— (1963). 'Some Universals of Grammar with Particular Reference to the Order of Meaningful Elements', in J. H. Greenberg (ed.), *Universals of Language*. Cambridge, Mass.: MIT Press, 73–113.

—— (1965). 'Some Generalizations Concerning Initial and Final Consonant Clusters', *Linguistics*, **18:** 5–34.

GREENLEE, M., and OHALA, J. J. (1980). 'Phonetically Motivated Parallels Between Child Language and Historical Sound Change', *Language Sciences*, **2:** 283–308.

GROSU, A., and THOMPSON, S. A. (1977). 'Constraints on the Distribution of NP Clauses', *Language*, **53:** 104–51.

GROTZFELD, H. (n. d.). 'Reimformen in der klassisch-arabischen Dichtung'. Ms, University of Münster.

HAIMAN, J. (1983). 'Iconic and Economic Motivation', *Language*, **59:** 781–819.

HALL, C. J. (1988). 'Integrating Diachronic and Processing Principles in Explaining the Suffixing Preference', in J. A. Hawkins (ed.), *Explaining Language Universals*. Oxford: Basil Blackwell, 321–49.

—— (1992). *Morphology and Mind: A Unified Approach to Explanation in Linguistics*. London: Routledge.

HAMMARSTRÖM, G. (1978). 'Is Linguistics a Natural Science?' *Lingua*, **45:** 15–31.

HAMMOND, M. (1993). 'On the Absence of Category-Changing Prefixes in English', *Linguistic Inquiry*, **24**: 562–7.
HANKAMER, J. (1989). 'Morphological Parsing and the Lexicon', in W. D. Marslen-Wilson (ed.), *Lexical Representation and Process*. Cambridge, Mass.: MIT Press, 392–408.
HARE, M., and ELMAN, J. L. (1992). 'A Connectionist Account of English Inflectional Morphology: Evidence from Language Change', in *Proceedings of the 14th Annual Conference of the Cognitive Science Society*. Hillsdale, NJ: Lawrence Erlbaum, 265–70.
HARLEY, T. A. (1990). 'Environmental Contamination of Normal Speech'. *Applied Psycholinguistics*, **11**: 45–72.
HARRIS, M. (1982). 'On Explaining Language Change', in A. Ahlqvist (ed.), *Papers from the 5th International Conference on Historical Linguistics*. Amsterdam: John Benjamins, 1–14.
HAWKINS, J. A. (1988). 'On Explaining Some Left–Right Asymmetries in Syntactic and Morphological Universals', in M. Hammond, E.A. Moravczik, and J.R. Wirth (eds.), *Studies in Syntactic Typology*. Amsterdam: John Benjamins, 321–57.
—— (1990). 'A Parsing Theory of Word Order Universals', *Linguistic Inquiry*, **21**: 223–61.
—— (1994). *A Performance Theory of Order and Constituency*. Cambridge: Cambridge University Press.
—— and CUTLER, A. (1988). 'Psycholinguistic Factors in Morphological Asymmetry', in J. A. Hawkins (ed.), *Explaining Language Universals*. Oxford: Basil Blackwell, 280–317.
—— and GILLIGAN, G. (1988). 'Prefixing and Suffixing Universals in Relation to Basic Word Order', *Lingua*, **74**: 219–59.
HAYES, B. (1982). 'Extrametricality and English Stress', *Linguistic Inquiry*, **13**: 227–76.
HAYWARD, J. (ed.) (1956). *The Penguin Book of English Verse*. Harmondsworth: Penguin.
HEIKE, G. (1992). 'Zur Phonetik der Silbe', in P. Eisenberg, K. H. Ramers, and H. Vater (eds.), *Silbenphonologie des Deutschen*. Tübingen: Narr, 1–44.
HELLINGER, M. (1990). *Kontrastive feministische Linguistik*. Ismaning: Hueber.
HEMPEL, C. G. (1965). *Aspects of Scientific Explanation and Other Essays in the Philosophy of Science*. New York: Free Press.
HENTON, C. (1990). 'One Vowel's Life (and Death?) Across Languages: The Moribundity and Prestige of /ʌ/', *Journal of Phonetics*, **18**: 203–27.
HERMKENS, H. M. (1969). *Fonetiek en Fonologie*. 's-Hertogenbosch: Malmberg.
HICKEY, R. (1984). 'Remarks on Assimilation in Old English', *Folia Linguistica Historica*, **5**: 279–303.
HOBERMAN, R. D. (1988). 'Emphasis Harmony in a Modern Aramaic Dialect', *Language*, **64**: 1–26.
HOCK, H. H. (1986). *Principles of Historical Linguistics*. Berlin: Mouton de Gruyter.
HOOPER, J. B. (1976). 'Word Frequency in Lexical Diffusion and the Source of Morphophonological Change', in W. M. Christie, JR. (ed.). *Current Progress in Historical Linguistics*. Amsterdam: North Holland, 95–105.
HOPPER, P. J., and THOMPSON, S. A. (1984). 'The Discourse Basis for Lexical Categories in Universal Grammar', *Language*, **60**: 703–52.
HOSPERS, J. (1946). 'On Explanation', *Journal of Philosophy*, **58**: 337–56.
HUDSON, G. (1986). 'Arabic Root and Pattern Morphology Without Tiers', *Journal of Linguistics*, **22**: 85–122.
HURFORD, J. (1975). 'A Child and the English Question Formation Rule', *Journal of Child Language*, **2**: 299–301.
HURFORD, J. R. (1991). 'The Evolution of the Critical Period for Language Acquisition', *Cognition*, **40**: 159–201.

INGRAM, D., CHRISTENSEN, L., VEACH, S., and WEBSTER, B. (1980). 'The Acquisition of Word-Initial Fricatives and Affricates in English by Children between 2 and 6 Years', in G. H. Yeni-Komshian, J. F. Kavanagh, and C.A. Ferguson (eds.), *Child Phonology*, i: *Production*. New York: Academic Press, 169–92.

IRMEN, F. (1968). *Langenscheidts Taschenwörterbuch*, i: *Portugiesisch–Deutsch*. Berlin: Langenscheidt.

ITKONEN, E. (1978). *Grammatical Theory and Metascience*. Amsterdam: John Benjamins.

—— (1981). Review of R. Lass, *On Explaining Language Change* (Cambridge: Cambridge University Press, 1980), *Language*, **57**: 688–97.

—— (1996). 'Concerning the Generative Paradigm', *Journal of Pragmatics*, **25**: 471–501.

JABERG, K. (1937). 'Sprache als Äußerung und als Mitteilung', in K. Jaberg, *Sprachwissenschaftliche Forschungen und Ergebnisse*. Paris: Droz, 137–85.

JANSON, T. (1977). 'Reversed Lexical Diffusion and Lexical Split: Loss of -d in Stockholm', in W. S.-Y. Wang (ed.), *The Lexicon in Phonological Change*. The Hague: Mouton, 252–65.

JESPERSEN, O. (1922). *The Philosophy of Grammar*. London: George Allen & Unwin.

—— (1942). *A Modern English Grammar on Historical Principles*, iv: *Morphology*. London: George Allen & Unwin.

JORDAN, R. (1974). *Handbook of Middle English Grammar: Phonology*. The Hague: Mouton.

JUILLAND, A. (1967). *Dictionnaire Inverse de la Langue Française*. The Hague: Mouton.

JULIÀ, P. (1983). *Explanatory Models in Linguistics. A Behavioral Perspective*. Princeton, NJ: Princeton University Press.

KAY, P., and MCDANIEL, C.K. (1978). 'The Linguistic Significance of the Meanings of Basic Color Terms', *Language*, **54**: 610–46.

KEENAN, E. L. (1979). 'On Surface Form and Logical Form', repr. in E.L. Keenan, *Universal Grammar: 15 Essays*. London: Croom Helm, 1987, 375–428.

KELLER, R. (1994). *On Language Change: The Invisible Hand in Language*. London: Routledge.

KELLY, M. H., and BOCK, J. K. (1988). 'Stress in Time', *Journal of Experimental Psychology: Human Perception and Performance*, **14**: 389–403.

—— —— and KEIL, F. C. (1986). 'Prototypicality in a Linguistic Context: Effects on Sentence Structure', *Journal of Memory and Language*, **25**: 59–74.

KEMPEN, G., and HOENKAMP, E. (1987). 'An Incremental Procedural Grammar for Sentence Formulation', *Cognitive Science*, **11**: 201–58.

KENSTOWICZ, M. (1994). *Phonology in Generative Grammar*. Oxford: Basil Blackwell.

KENYON, J. S., and KNOTT, T. A. (1953). *A Pronouncing Dictionary of American English*. Springfield, Mass.: G. & C. Merriam.

KING, R. D. (1967). 'Functional Load and Sound Change', *Language*, **43**: 831–52.

KIPARSKY, P. (1968). 'Linguistic Universals and Linguistic Change', in E. Bach and R. T. Harms (eds.), *Universals in Linguistic Theory*. New York: Holt, Rinehart & Winston, 170–202.

—— (1972). 'Explanation in Phonology', in S. Peters (ed.), *Goals of Linguistic Theory*. Englewood Cliffs, NJ: Prentice-Hall, 189–227.

—— (1982). 'From Cyclic Phonology to Lexical Phonology', in H. van der Hulst and N. Smith (eds.), *The Structure of Phonological Representations*, i. Dordrecht: Foris, 131–75.

—— (1985). 'Some Consequences of Lexical Phonology', *Phonology Yearbook*, **2**: 85–138.

KLATT, D. H. (1981). 'Lexical Representations for Speech Production and Perception', in T. Myers, J. Laver, and J. Anderson (eds.), *The Cognitive Representation of Speech*. Amsterdam: North-Holland, 11–31.

KÖHLER, R., and ALTMANN, G. (1986). 'Synergetische Aspekte der Linguistik', *Zeitschrift für Sprachwissenschaft*, **5**: 253–65.
KOHLER, K. (1974). 'Koartikulation und Steuerung im Deutschen', in U. Engel and P. Grebe (eds.), *Sprachsystem und Sprachgebrauch. Festschrift für Hugo Moser zum 65. Geburtstag*. Düsseldorf: Schwann, 172–92.
KÖPCKE, K.-M. (1988). 'Schemas in German Plural Formation', *Lingua*, **74**: 303–35.
KROCH, A. S. (1978). 'Toward a Theory of Social Dialect Variation', *Language in Society*, **7**: 17–36.
KRYGIER, M. (1994). *The Disintegration of the English Strong Verb System*. Frankfurt a.M.: Lang.
KUBOZONO, H. (1990). 'Phonological Constraints on Blending in English as a Case for Phonology–Morphology Interface', *Yearbook of Morphology*, **3**: 1–20.
KUCERA, H., and FRANCIS, W. N. (1967). *Computational Analysis of Present-Day American English*. Providence, RI: Brown University Press.
KURYŁOWICZ, J. (1972). *Studies in Semitic Grammar and Metrics*. Wroclaw: Polska Academia Nauk.
KYPRIOTAKI, L. (1973). 'Aphaeresis in Rapid Speech', *American Speech*, **45**: 69–77.
LACKNER, J. R., and TULLER, B. H. (1979). 'Role of Efference Monitoring in the Detection of Self-Produced Speech Errors', in W. E. Cooper and E. C. T. Walker (eds.), *Sentence Processing: Psycholinguistic Studies Presented to Merrill Garrett*. Hillsdale, NJ: Lawrence Erlbaum, 281–94.
LA FONTAINE, J. de (1966 edn.). *Fables*. Paris: Garnier-Flammarion.
LAHIRI, A., and HANKAMER, J. (1988). 'The Timing of Geminate Consonants', *Journal of Phonetics*, **16**: 327–38.
Langenscheidts Großwörterbuch Italienisch, vol. i (1978). Berlin: Langenscheidt.
LASHLEY, K. S. (1951). 'The Problem of Serial Order in Behavior', repr. in S. Saporta (ed.), *Psycholinguistics: A Book of Readings*. New York: Holt, Rinehart & Winston, 180–98.
LASS, R. (1976). 'On Generative Taxonomy, and Whether Formalizations "explain" ', *Studia Linguistica*, **30**: 139–54.
—— (1980). *On Explaining Language Change*. Cambridge: Cambridge University Press.
LEECH, G. N. (1969). *A Linguistic Guide to English Poetry*. London: Longman.
LEHNERT, M. (1973). *Altenglisches Elementarbuch*. Berlin: Walter de Gruyter.
LENERZ, J. (1985). 'Phonologische Aspekte der Assimilation im Deutschen', *Zeitschrift für Sprachwissenschaft*, **4**: 5–36.
LESLAU, W. (1969). 'Frequency as Determinant of Linguistic Changes in the Ethiopian Languages', *Word*, **25**: 180–9.
LEVELT, W. J. M., SCHRIEFERS, H., VORBERG, D., MEYER, A. S., PECHMANN, T., and HAVINGA, J. (1991). 'The Time Course of Lexical Access in Speech Production: A Study of Picture Naming', *Psychological Review*, **98**: 122–42.
LEVITT, A. G., and HEALY, A. F. (1985). 'The Roles of Phoneme Frequency, Similarity and Availability in the Experimental Elicitation of Speech Errors', *Journal of Memory and Language*, **24**: 717–33.
LIEBERMAN, P. (1963). 'Some Effects of Semantic and Grammatical Context on the Production and Perception of Speech', *Language and Speech*, **6**: 172–87.
LIGHTFOOT, D. (1981). 'Explaining Syntactic Change', in N. Hornstein and D. Lightfoot (eds.), *Explanation in Linguistics: The Logical Problem of Language Acquisition*. London: Longman, 209–40.

LILJENCRANTS, J., and LINDBLOM, B. (1972). 'Numerical Simulation of Vowel Quality Systems: The Role of Perceptual Contrast', *Language*, **48**: 839–62.

LINDBLOM, B. (1983). 'Economy of Speech Gestures', in P. F. MacNeilage (ed.), *The Production of Speech*. New York: Springer, 217–45.

—— MACNEILAGE, P. F., and STUDDERT-KENNEDY, M. (1984). 'Self-organizing Processes and the Explanation of Phonological Universals', in B. Butterworth, B. Comrie, and Ö. Dahl (eds.), *Explanations for Language Universals*. Berlin: Mouton, 181–203.

LINELL, P. (1976). 'Is Linguistics an Empirical Science?' *Studia Linguistica*, **30**: 77–94.

LISKER, L., and ABRAMSON, A. (1970). 'The Voicing Dimension: Some Experiments in Comparative Phonetics', in *Proceedings of the 6th International Congress of Phonetic Sciences*. Prague: Academia, 563–7.

LIVESCU, J., and SAVIN, E. (1979). *Dicționar român–german*. București: Editura științifică și enciclopedică.

LLOYD, P. M., and SCHNITZER, R. D. (1967). 'A Statistical Study of the Structure of the Spanish Syllable', *Linguistics*, **37**: 58–72.

LOUNSBURY, T. R. (1970). *History of the English Language*. College Park: McGrath.

LUCE, P. A. (1986). 'A Computational Analysis of Uniqueness Points in Auditory Word Recognition', *Perception and Psychophysics*, **39**: 155–8.

LUTZ, A. (1991). *Phonotaktisch gesteuerte Konsonantenveränderungen in der Geschichte des Englischen*. Tübingen: Niemeyer.

MCCARTHY, J. J. (1979). 'On Stress and Syllabification', *Linguistic Inquiry*, **10**: 443–65.

—— (1982). 'Prosodic Templates, Morphemic Templates, and Morphemic Tiers', in H. van der Hulst and N. Smith (eds.), *The Structure of Phonological Representations*, i. Dordrecht: Foris, 191–223.

—— (1985). 'Speech Disguise and Phonological Representation in Amharic', in H. van der Hulst and N. Smith (eds.). *Advances in Nonlinear Phonology*. Dordrecht: Foris, 305–12.

—— (1986). 'OCP Effects: Gemination and Antigemination', *Linguistic Inquiry*, **17**: 207–63.

—— (1989). 'Linear Order in Phonological Representation', *Linguistic Inquiry*, **20**: 71–99.

—— and PRINCE, A. S. (1986). 'Prosodic morphology'. MS, Brandeis University.

MCCLELLAND, J. L., and ELMAN, J. L. (1986). 'The TRACE Model of Speech Perception', *Cognitive Psychology*, **18**: 1–86.

MACKAY, D. G. (1969). 'Forward and Backward Masking in Motor Systems', *Kybernetik*, **6**: 57–64.

—— (1970a). 'Phoneme Repetition in the Structure of Languages'. *Language and Speech*, **13**: 199–213.

—— (1970b). 'Spoonerisms: The Structure of Errors in the Serial Order of Speech', *Neuropsychologia*, **8**: 323–50.

—— (1986). 'Self-inhibition and the Disruptive Effects of Internal and External Feedback in Skilled Behavior', in H. Heuer and C. Fromm (eds.), *Generation and Modulation of Action Patterns*. Berlin: Springer, 174–86.

—— (1987). *The Organization of Perception and Action: A Theory for Language and Other Cognitive Skills*. New York: Springer.

MACNEILAGE, P. F., HUTCHINSON J. A., and LASATER, S. (1981). 'The Production of Speech: Development and Dissolution of Motoric and Premotoric Processes', in J. Long and A. Baddeley (eds.), *Attention and Performance*, ix. Hillsdale, NJ: Lawrence Erlbaum, 503–19.

MACWHINNEY, B., and ANDERSON, J. (1986). 'The Acquisition of Grammar', in I. Gopnik and M. Gopnik (eds.), *From Models to Modules*. Norwood, NJ: Ablex, 3–25.

MADDIESON, I. (1984). *Patterns of Sounds*. Cambridge: Cambridge University Press.
—— (1986). 'Borrowed Sounds', in J. A. Fishman, A. Tabouret-Keller, M. Clyne, B. Krishnamurti, and M. Abdulaziz (eds.), *The Fergusonian Impact*, i: *From Phonology to Society*. Berlin: Mouton de Gruyter, 1–16.
—— and PRECODA, K. (1992). 'Syllable Structure and Phonetic Models', *Phonology*, 9: 45–60.
MAŃCZAK, W. (1980). 'Frequenz und Sprachwandel', in H. Lüdtke (ed.), *Kommunikationstheoretische Grundlagen des Sprachwandels*. Berlin: Walter de Gruyter, 37–79.
MARANTZ, A. (1982). 'Re reduplication', *Linguistic Inquiry*, 13: 435–82.
MARCUS, G. F., PINKER, S., ULLMAN, M., HOLLANDER, M., ROSEN, T. J., and FEI XU (1992). 'Overregularization in Language Acquisition'. *Monographs of the Society for Research in Child Development*, 57 (4).
MARCUS, S. M., and FRAUENFELDER, U. H., (1985). 'Word Recognition: Uniqueness or Deviation? A theoretical note', *Language and Cognitive Processes*, 1: 163–9.
MARSLEN-WILSON, W. D., and TYLER, L. K. (1975). 'Processing Structure of Sentence Perception', *Nature*, 257: 784–6.
—— —— (1980). 'The Temporal Structure of Spoken Language Understanding', *Cognition*, 8: 1–71.
—— and WELSH, A. (1978). 'Processing Interactions and Lexical Access during Word Recognition in Continuous Speech', *Cognitive Psychology*, 10: 29–63.
—— and ZWITSERLOOD, P. (1989). 'Accessing Spoken Words: The Importance of Word Onsets', *Journal of Experimental Psychology: Human Perception and Performance*, 15: 576–85.
MARTINET, A. (1955). *Économie des Changements Phonétiques*. Berne: Francke.
MAYERTHALER, W. (1981). *Morphologische Natürlichkeit*. Wiesbaden: Athenaion.
MEHLER, J., DOMMERGUES, J. Y., FRAUENFELDER, U., and SEGUI, J. (1981). 'The Syllable's Role in Speech Segmentation', *Journal of Verbal Learning and Verbal Behavior*, 20: 298–305.
MENN, L., and MACWHINNEY, B, (1984). 'The Repeated Morph Constraint: Toward an Explanation', *Language*, 60: 519–41.
—— and OBLER, L. K. (1982). 'Exceptional Language Data as Linguistic Evidence: An Introduction', in L. K. Obler and L. Menn (eds.), *Exceptional Language and Linguistics*. New York: Academic Press, 3–14.
MERINGER, R., and MAYER, K. (1895). *Versprechen und Verlesen. Eine psychologisch-linguistische Studie*. Stuttgart: Göschen.
MEYER, A. S. (1990). 'The Time Course of Phonological Encoding in Language Production: The Encoding of Successive Syllables of a Word', *Journal of Memory and Language*, 29: 524–45.
—— (1991). 'The Time Course of Phonological Encoding in Language Production: Phonological Encoding Inside the Syllable', *Journal of Memory and Language*, 30: 69–89.
MOESSNER, L. (1978). *Morphonologie*. Tübingen: Niemeyer.
MOHANAN, K. P. (1982). *Lexical Phonology*. Bloomington: Indiana University Linguistics Club.
MORAVCSIK, E. A. (1977). *On Rules of Infixing*. Bloomington: Indiana University Linguistics Club.
MORGAN, J. (1984). 'Some Problems of Agreement in English and Albanian', *Proceedings of the Annual Meeting of the Berkeley Linguistics Society*, 10: 233–47.
MORGENSTERN, C. (1961). *Palmström. Palma Kunkel*. Munich: DTV.
MOSSÉ, F. (1952). *A Handbook of Middle English*. Baltimore, Md.: Johns Hopkins University Press.

MOTLEY, M. T. (1973). 'An Analysis of Spoonerisms as Psycholinguistic Phenomena', *Speech Monographs*, **40**: 66–71.

MOULTON, W. G. (1962). 'The Vowels of Dutch: Phonetic and Distributional Classes', *Lingua*, **11**: 294–312.

MUGDAN, J. (1977). *Flexionsmorphologie und Psycholinguistik*. Tübingen: Narr.

MYERS, S. (1985). 'The Long and the Short of It: A Metrical Theory of English Vowel Quantity', *Papers from the 21st Regional Meeting of the Chicago Linguistic Society*. Chicago: CLS, 275–88.

—— (1987). 'Vowel Shortening in English', *Natural Language and Linguistic Theory*, **5**: 485–518.

NEWMEYER, F. J. (1991). 'Functional Explanation in Linguistics and the Origins of Language', *Language and Communication*, **11**: 3–28.

—— (1994). 'Competing Motivations and Synchronic Analysis', *Sprachtypologie und Universalienforschung*, **47**: 67–77.

NOOTEBOOM, S. G. (1980). 'Speaking and Unspeaking: Detection and Correction of Phonological and Lexical Errors in Spontaneous Speech', in V A. Fromkin (ed.), *Errors in Linguistic Performance*. New York: Academic Press, 87–95.

—— (1981). 'Lexical Retrieval from Fragments of Spoken Words: Beginnings vs. Endings', *Journal of Phonetics*, **9**: 407–24.

ODDEN, D. (1986). 'On the Role of the Obligatory Contour Principle in Phonological Theory', *Language*, **62**: 353–83.

OHALA, J. J. (1981). 'The listener as a Source of Sound Change', in *Papers from the Parasession on Language and Language Behavior*. Chicago: CLS, 178–203.

—— (1983). 'The Origin of Sound Patterns in Vocal Tract Constraints', in P. F. MacNeilage (ed.), *The Production of Speech*. New York: Springer, 189–216.

—— (1987). 'Explanation in Phonology: Opinions and Examples', in W. U. Dressler, H. C. Luschützky, O. E. Pfeiffer, and J. R. Rennison (eds.), *Phonologica 1984*. Cambridge: Cambridge University Press, 215–25.

—— (1990). 'The Phonetics and Phonology of Aspects of Assimilation', in J. Kingston and M. E. Beckman (eds.), *Papers in Laboratory Phonology*, i: *Between the Grammar and Physics of Speech*. Cambridge: Cambridge University Press, 258–75.

—— (1992). 'What's Cognitive, What's Not, in Sound Change', in G. Kellermann and M. D. Morrissey (eds.), *Diachrony within Synchrony: Language History and Cognition*. Frankfurt a.M.: Peter Lang, 309–35.

OLDFIELD, R. C., and WINGFIELD, A. (1969). 'Response Latencies in Naming Objects', *Quarterly Journal of Experimental Psychology*, **17**: 273–81.

ORTMANN, W. D. (1983). *Materialien zur Didaktisierung der Phonemik des Deutschen*, ii: *Minimalpaare*. Munich: Hueber.

Ó SIADHAIL, M. (1989). *Modern Irish: Grammatical Structure and Dialectal Variation*. Cambridge: Cambridge University Press.

PARKER, S. (1992). 'Geminate Alterability: Another OCP Violation', *Linguistic Analysis*, **22**: 246–50.

PAUL, H. (1880). *Prinzipien der Sprachgeschichte*. Repr. by Niemeyer, Tübingen, 1968.

—— (1916). *Deutsche Grammatik*. 2 vols., Halle: Niemeyer.

PENNY, R. (1991). *A History of the Spanish Language*. Cambridge: Cambridge University Press.

PERLMUTTER, D. M. (1992). 'Sonority and Syllable Structure in American Sign Language', *Linguistic Inquiry*, **23**: 407–42.

PERRY, T. A. (1980). 'Introduction', in T. A. Perry (ed.), *Evidence and Argumentation in Linguistics*. Berlin: Mouton de Gruyter, 1–5.
PHILLIPS, B. S. (1980). 'Old English AN~ON: A New Appraisal', *Journal of English Linguistics*, 14: 20–3.
—— (1981). 'Lexical Diffusion and Southern *Tune, Duke, News*', *American Speech*, 56: 72–8.
—— (1984). 'Word Frequency and the Actuation of Sound Change', *Language*, 60: 320–42.
POLZIN, A. (1903). *Geschlechtswandel der Substantiva im Deutschen (mit Einschluß der Lehn- und Fremdworte)*. Hildesheim: Gerstenberg.
POPPER, K. R. (1959). *The Logic of Scientific Discovery*. London: Hutchinson.
—— (1963). *Conjectures and Refutations: The Growth of Scientific Knowledge*. London: Routledge & Kegan Paul.
POSNER, R. R. (1961). *Consonantal Dissimilation in the Romance Languages*. Oxford: Blackwell.
POSTMA, A., and NOORDANUS, C. (1996). 'Production and Detection of Speech Errors in Silent, Mouthed, Noise-Masked, and Normal Auditory Feedback Speech', *Language and Speech*, 39: 375–92.
POUND, L. (1914). *Blends: Their Relation to English Word Formation*. Heidelberg: Carl Winter.
PRIDEAUX, G. D. (1971). 'On the Notion "Linguistically Significant Generalization" ', *Lingua*, 26: 337–47.
PULLUM, G. K. (1975). 'On Linguistically Insignificant Generalizations', *York Papers in Linguistics*, 5: 97–109.
RAMERS, K. H. (1990). 'Die Hierarchie phonologischer Merkmale. Vortrag gehalten auf der 12'. Jahrestagung der DGfS, Saarbrücken, Germany.
RASTALL, P. (1993). 'On the Attributive Noun in English', *International Review of Applied Linguistics*, 31: 309–13.
RESCHER, N. (1970). *Scientific Explanation*. New York: Free Press.
RIMBAUD, A. (1964). *Œuvres poétiques*. Paris: Garnier-Flammarion.
ROACH, P. (1989). *English Phonetics and Phonology*. Cambridge: Cambridge University Press.
ROBERTS, A. H. (1965). *A Statistical Linguistic Analysis of American English*. The Hague: Mouton.
ROHDENBURG, G. (1996). 'Cognitive Complexity and Increased Grammatical Explicitness in English', *Cognitive Linguistics*, 7: 149–82.
RONNEBERGER-SIBOLD, E. (1980). *Sprachverwendung—Sprachsystem. Ökonomie und Wandel*. Tübingen: Niemeyer.
ROSCH, E. (1978). 'Principles of Categorization', in E. Rosch and B. B. Lloyd (eds.), *Cognition and Categorization*. Hillsdale, NJ: Lawrence Erlbaum, 27–48.
ROSENBERG, B., ZURIF, E., BROWNELL, H., GARRETT, M.F., and BRADLEY, D. (1985). 'Grammatical Class Effects in Relation to Normal and Aphasic Sentence Processing', *Brain and Language*, 26: 287–303.
SAGEY, E. (1988). 'On the Ill-Formedness of Crossing Association Lines', *Linguistic Inquiry*, 19: 109–18.
SALUS, P. H. and SALUS, M. W. (1974). 'Developmental Neurophysiology and Phonological Acquisition Order', *Language*, 50: 151–60.
SAMUELS, M. L. (1972). *Linguistic Evolution: With Special Reference to English*. Cambridge: Cambridge University Press.
SCHRIEFERS, H. (1992). 'Lexical Access in the Production of Noun Phrases', *Cognition*, 45: 33–54.
—— ZWITSERLOOD, P., and ROELOFS, A (1991). 'The Identification of Morphologically Complex Spoken Words: Continuous Processing or Decomposition', *Journal of Memory and Language*, 30: 26–47.

SEIDENBERG, M. S. (1994). 'Language and Connectionism: The Developing Interface', *Cognition*, **50**: 385–401.
SHAPIRO, B. J. (1969). 'The Subjective Estimation of Relative Word Frequency', *Journal of Verbal Learning and Verbal Behavior*, **8**: 248–51.
SHATTUCK-HUFNAGEL, S. (1979). 'Speech Errors as Evidence for a Serial-Ordering Mechanism in Sentence Production', in W. E. Cooper and E. C. T. Walker (eds.), *Sentence Processing: Psycholinguistic Studies Presented to Merrill Garrett*. Hillsdale, NJ: Lawrence Erlbaum, 295–342.
—— (1983). 'Sublexical Units and Suprasegmental Structure in Speech Production Planning', in P. F. MacNeilage (ed.), *The Production of Speech*. New York: Springer, 109–36.
—— (1985). 'Context Similarity Constraints on Segmental Speech Errors: An Experimental Investigation of the Role of Word Position and Lexical Stress', in J. L. Lauter (ed.), *Proceedings of the Conference on the Planning and Production of Speech in Normal and Hearing-Impaired Individuals: A Seminar in Honor of S. Richard Silverman*. ASHA Reports 15, 43–9.
—— (1986). 'The Representation of Phonological Information during Speech Production Planning: Evidence from Vowel Errors in Spontaneous Speech', *Phonology Yearbook*, **3**: 117–49.
—— (1987). 'The Role of Word-Onset Consonants in Speech Production Planning: New Evidence from Speech Error Patterns', in E. Keller and M. Gopnik (eds.), *Motor and Sensory Processes of Language*. Hillsdale, NJ: Lawrence Erlbaum, 17–51.
—— (1994). 'Slips of the Tongue', in R. E. Asher and J. M. Y. Simpson (eds.), *The Encyclopedia of Language and Linguistics*, vii. Oxford: Pergamon, 3966–71.
—— and KLATT, D. H. (1979). 'The Limited Use of Distinctive Features and Markedness in Speech Production: Evidence from Speech Error Data', *Journal of Verbal Learning and Verbal Behavior*, **18**: 41–55.
SHERMAN, D. (1975). 'Noun–Verb Stress Alternation: An Example of the Lexical Diffusion of Sound Change in English', *Linguistics*, **159**: 43–71.
SIEBS, T. (1904). 'Anlautstudien', *Zeitschrift für Vergleichende Sprachforschung*, **37**: 277–324.
SOBKOWIAK, W. (1993). 'Unmarked-Before-Marked as a Freezing Principle', *Language and Speech*, **36**: 393–414.
SPENCER, A. (1991). *Morphological Theory*. Oxford: Basil Blackwell.
SPENCER, N. J. (1973). 'Differences between Linguists and Nonlinguists in Intuitions of Grammaticality–Acceptability', *Journal of Psycholinguistic Research*, **2**: 83–98.
STAMPE, D. (1969). 'The Acquisition of Phonetic Representation', in *Papers from the 5th Regional Meeting of the Chicago Linguistic Society*. Chicago: CLS, 443–54.
STANLEY, E. G. (1952/3). 'The Chronology of R-metathesis in Old English', *English Philological Studies*, **5**: 103–15.
STARK, D. (1982). *The Old English Weak Verbs. A Diachronic and Synchronic Analysis*. Tübingen: Niemeyer.
STEGMÜLLER, W. (1983). *Probleme und Resultate der Wissenschaftstheorie und analytischen Philosophie*, i: *Erklärung, Begründung, Kausalität*. Berlin: Springer.
STEIN, D. (1988). 'Psycholinguistic Issues and Determinants of Syntactic Change', *Papiere zur Linguistik*, **39**: 31–48.
STEINBERG, E. and CASKEY, A. F. (1988). 'The Syntax and Semantics of Gender (Dis)agreement: An Autolexical Approach', in *Papers from the 24th Regional Meeting of the Chicago Linguistic Society*, ii: *Parasession on Agreement in Grammatical Theory*. Chicago: CLS, 291–303.

STEMBERGER, J. P. (1981). 'Morphological Haplology', *Language*, **57**: 791–817.
—— (1982). 'The Nature of Segments in the Lexicon: Evidence from Speech Errors', *Lingua*, **56**: 235–59.
—— (1983). *Speech Errors and Theoretical Phonology: A Review*. Bloomington: Indiana University Linguistics Club.
—— (1984a). 'Length as a Suprasegmental: Evidence from Speech Errors', *Language*, **60**: 895–913.
—— (1984b). 'Structural Errors in Normal and Agrammatic Speech', *Cognitive Neuropsychology*, **1**: 281–313.
—— (1985a). *The Lexicon in a Model of Language Production*. New York: Garland.
—— (1985b). 'An Interactive Activation Model of Language Production', in A. W. Ellis (ed.), *Progress in the Psychology of Language*, i. London: Lawrence Erlbaum, 143–86.
—— (1990). 'Wordshape Errors in Language Production', *Cognition*, **35**: 123–57.
—— (1991). 'Apparent Anti-frequency Effects in Language Production: The Addition Bias and Phonological Underspecification', *Journal of Memory and Language*, **30**: 161–85.
—— (1992a). 'Vocalic Underspecification in English Language Production', *Language*, **68**: 492–524.
—— (1992b). 'The Reliability and Replicability of Naturalistic Speech Error Data', in B. J. Baars (ed.), *Experimental Slips and Human Error: Exploring the Architecture of Volition*. New York: Plenum, 195–215.
—— and LEWIS, M. (1986). 'Reduplication in Ewe: Morphological Accommodation to Phonological Errors', *Phonology Yearbook*, **3**: 151–60.
—— and MACWHINNEY, B. (1986a). 'Frequency and the Lexical Storage of Regularly Inflected Forms', *Memory and Cognition*, **14**: 17–26.
—— —— (1986b). 'Form-oriented Inflectional Errors in Language Processing', *Cognitive Psychology*, **18**: 329–54.
—— and TREIMAN, R. (1986). 'The Internal Structure of Word-Initial Consonant Clusters', *Journal of Memory and Language*, **25**: 163–80.
STEVENS, K. N. (1972). 'The Quantal Nature of Speech: Evidence from Articulatory–Acoustic Data', in E. E. David and P. B. Denes (eds.), *Human Communication: A Unified View*. New York: McGraw-Hill, 51–66.
—— (1989). 'On the Quantal Nature of Speech', *Journal of Phonetics*, **17**: 3–45.
—— and KEYSER, S. J. (1989). 'Primary Features and Their Enhancement in Consonants', *Language*, **65**: 81–106.
STOEL-GAMMON, C. (1985). 'Phonetic Inventories, 15–24 months: A Longitudinal Study', *Journal of Speech and Hearing Research*, **28**: 505–12.
STUDDERT-KENNEDY, M. (1976). 'Speech Perception', in N. J. Lass (ed.), *Contemporary Issues in Experimental Phonetics*. New York: Academic Press, 243–93.
SWEETSER, E. (1990). *From Etymology to Pragmatics*. Cambridge: Cambridge University Press.
SWINNEY, D. A. (1979). 'Lexical Access during Sentence Comprehension: (Re)consideration of Context Effects', *Journal of Verbal Learning and Verbal Behavior*, **18**: 645–60.
SZPYRA, J. (1989). *The Phonology–Morphology Interface. Cycles, Levels and Words*. London: Routledge.
TAFT, M., and FORSTER, K. I. (1975). 'Lexical Storage and Retrieval of Prefixed Words', *Journal of Verbal Learning and Verbal Behavior*, **14**: 638–47.
TENT, J., and CLARK, J. E. (1980). 'An Experimental Investigation into the Perception of Slips of the Tongue', *Journal of Phonetics*, **8**: 317–25.

THAGARD, P. (1989). 'Explanatory Coherence', *Behavioral and Brain Sciences*, **12**: 435–67.
THEOBALD, E. (1992). *Sprachwandel bei deutschen Verben. Flexionsklassenschwankungen starker und schwacher Verben*. Tübingen: Narr.
THORNDIKE, E. L., and LORGE, I. (1944). *The Teacher's Word Book of 30,000 words*. New York: Teachers College.
TIERSMA, P. M. (1982). 'Local and General Markedness', *Language*, **58**: 832–49.
TOON, T. E. (1987). 'Old English Dialects: What's to Explain; What's an Explanation', in W. Koopman, F. van der Leek, O. Fischer, and R. Eaton (eds.), *Explanation and Linguistic Change*. Amsterdam: John Benjamins, 275–93.
TREIMAN, R., GROSS, J., and CWIEKIEL-GAVIN, A. (1992). 'The Syllabification of /s/ Clusters in English'. *Journal of Phonetics*, **20**: 383–402.
—— and ZUKOWSKI, A. (1990). 'Toward an Understanding of English Syllabification', *Journal of Memory and Language*, **29**: 66–85.
TRNKA, B. (1966). *A Phonological Analysis of Present-day Standard English*. Tokyo: Hokuou.
TRUDGILL, P. (1972). 'Sex, Covert Prestige and Linguistic Change in the Urban British English of Norwich', *Language in Society*, **1**: 179–95.
—— (1974). *Sociolinguistics*. Harmondsworth: Penguin.
ULTAN, R. (1978). 'A Typological View of Metathesis', in J. P. Greenberg, C. A. Ferguson, and E. A. Moravcsik (eds.), *Universals of Human Language*, ii: *Phonology*. Stanford, Calif.: Stanford University Press, 367–402.
VACHEK, J. (1961). 'Some Less Familiar Aspects of the Analytical Trend of English', *Brno Studies in English*, **3**: 9–71.
VAN DEN BERG, B. (1958). *Foniek van het Nederlands*. The Hague: van Goor Zonen.
VARGHA-KHADEM, F., and PASSINGHAM, R. E. (1990). 'Speech and Language Deficits', *Nature*, **346**: 226.
VENDRYES, J. (1911). 'L'Assimilation consonantique à distance', *Mémoires de la Société de Linguistique de Paris*, **16**: 53–8.
VENNEMANN, T. (1988). *Preference Laws for Syllable Structure and the Explanation of Sound Change*. Berlin: Mouton de Gruyter.
VIHMAN, M. M. (1980). 'Sound Change and Child Language', in E. C. Traugott, R. Labrun, and S. Shepherd (eds.), *Papers from the 4th International Conference on Historical Linguistics*. Amsterdam: John Benjamins, 303–20.
VON DER GABELENTZ, G. (1891). *Die Sprachwissenschaft: ihre Aufgaben, Methoden und bisherigen Ergebnisse*. Leipzig: Weigel; repr. by Narr, Tübingen, 1972.
WANG, M. D., and BILGER, R. C. (1973). 'Consonant Confusion in Noise: A Study of Perceptual Features', *Journal of the Acoustical Society of America*, **54**: 1248–66.
WANG, W. S.-Y., and CHENG, C.-C. (1977). 'Implementation of Phonological Change: The Shuang-feng Chinese Case', in W. S.-Y. Wang (ed.), *The Lexicon in Phonological Change*. The Hague: Mouton, 148–58.
WANNER, DIETER (1989). 'On Metathesis in Diachrony', in C. Wiltshire, R. Graczyk, and B. Music (eds.), *Papers from the 25th Regional Meeting of the Chicago Linguistic Society*. Chicago: CLS, 434–50.
WARREN, P., and MARSLEN-WILSON, W. D. (1987). 'Continuous Uptake of Acoustic Cues in Spoken Word Recognition', *Perception and Psychophysics*, **41**: 262–75.
WEINBERG, A. (1987). 'Language Processing and Linguistic Explanation', in M. Coltheart (ed.), *Attention and Performance*, xii. Hillsdale, NJ: Lawrence Erlbaum, 673–87.

WHITAKER, H. A. (1971). *On the Representation of Language in the Human Brain.* Edmonton: Linguistic Research.

WIEDEN, W. (1983). 'Synchron–diachrone Grundlagen der Lautmetathese', *Klagenfurter Beiträge zur Sprachwissenschaft,* **9:** 293–312.

WIERZBICKA, A. (1990). 'The Meaning of Colour Terms: Semantics, Culture, and Cognition', *Cognitive Linguistics,* **1:** 99–150.

WIESE, R. (1996). 'Phonological versus Morphological Rules: On German Umlaut and Ablaut', *Journal of Linguistics,* **32:** 113–35.

WILLIAMS, J. M. (1976). 'Synaesthetic Adjectives: A Possible Law of Semantic Change', *Language,* **52:** 461–78.

WINSTON, M. E. (1982). *Explanation in Linguistics: A Critique of Generative Grammar.* Bloomington: Indiana University Linguistics Club.

WURZEL, W. U. (1984). *Flexionsmorphologie und Natürlichkeit.* Berlin: Akademie.

ZABROCKI, T. (1986). 'A Processing Explanation for a Syntactic Difference between English and Polish', in D. Kastovsky and A. Szwedek (eds.), *Linguistics Across Historical and Geographical Boundaries,* ii: *Descriptive, Contrastive and Applied Linguistics.* Berlin: Mouton de Gruyter, 1485–99.

Index

This index does not contain entries such as *English, explanation, language structure*, and *processing*, because they recur so frequently throughout the book.

ablaut 119–20, 128–9, 141–4, 234–5, 238–9, 285
accommodation 121, 205
activation 59, 61, 107, 111–13, 118, 149–50, 158, 162, 217, 229, 242–3, 284–6, 297, 309–10
adaptability 293
addition 140–4, 154–5
addition bias 141, 153–4
address systems 45, 47
adjacent switches 168, 170–2
adult language processing 61
aerodynamic constraints 24
aesthetics 298–9
agglutinative languages 30–1, 38
agreement 160–1
allomorphy 122–3, 131
allophonic variation 120
allophony 229–30
ambisyllabicity 3–4, 82, 265, 273
analytic representation 145, 242, 307–8
antecedent conditions 12, 49
anthropocentrism 151
anticipation 166
anti-egalitarianism 45, 47
aphaeresis 101
aphasia 61
aphesis 101
Arabic 88–98, 274–7, 312–3
/a/-raising 249
archisegment 208–9
articulatory/auditory bottleneck 23, 244
assibilation 197, 216
assimilation 71–2, 113–18, 133, 172–5, 280
autonomy 6–7, 24, 26, 32

between–word errors 107
bipositional errors 159–60
blending 169
body 86–7
borrowing 227–8
Branching Direction Theory 36
bridge effect 155–6
Buhtūri 275–6
Busch 275–6

casual speech 115
categorical perception 201–2
category-changing 31, 182–4

category-preserving 182–4
Celtic 120
centre-embedding 32, 36
child language 62
closed-class items 220–4
cluster simplification 72–3, 119, 231
cluster types 74–5
cluster weight 76–7
coarticulation 171
colour perception 22
colour vocabulary 21
competence grammar 303–5, 313
competition 54, 235–6, 284–5, 287
complementariness 54
complexification 122, 153–5
computational simultaneity 162
conceptual distance 52
conceptualization 283
conflict 11, 48–9
connectio n as explanation 11
connectionism 59
consonanthood 79
consonant loss 228–9
consonant mutation 120, 301
consonant preservation 228
constraint satisfaction 42
contextual synonymy 156
continuity of rhyme 274
continuous perception 202
contrastive psycholinguistics 65
correspondence 282
Croatian 19
cross-level harmony 50
cue reliability 143
cumulative evidence 66

Danish 46
deductive-nomological explanation 12–13
deixis 43
Delectus 275–6
dependency 162–3
deregularization 233–5, 237–40
derivation 7–8
devocalization 187, 190
devoicing 24, 197
diachrony 293
diphthongization 187, 189–90

directionality 161, 166, 172–3, 176–8
discourse 44–5
dissimilarity 83
dissimilation 166, 175–85, 280
distinctiveness 69–72
distribution 108–9
dominance 91
duplication 97
Dutch 46, 129–30, 135–140

ease of articulation 25, 244
ease of fusion 29
ease of perception 35
ease of processing 28, 30–1, 33–6
eclecticism 55
eclipsis 120
e-prothesis 207–8, 251, 253
evidentiary overkill 66
exchange 168–9
explanatory adequacy 4–5
extralinguistic context 43–5

facilitation 297–8
falsifiability 10, 291
Faroese 46
feedback 60, 123
feedforward 60
feminine rhyme 260
feminist linguistics 46
Finite State Grammar 32
flat syllable structure 85, 90
flectional languages 30–1, 38
formalism 1–2, 303–5
form-function/meaning relationship 13–4
fortition 197
frrezes 32–3
French 177, 179–80, 207, 264–73
French Revolution 49
frequency 16, 23, 33, 47, 76–7, 101, 126, 132, 143, 164, 207, 211, 221, 241–54, 285–7
full assimilation 173–4
full-listing model 119
functional explanation 13–4, 40–2
functional load 14–5, 69–70
fusion 131, 133
futurity 50–1

gang effect 251, 254
gemination 92, 97
gender 41–2, 46–7, 254–8
generative linguistics 1–8
genesis of morphology 49
genetic 19
German 30, 83–5, 105, 110–14, 120, 120–30, 135–40, 142–5, 150–1, 204, 211–12, 254–8, 259–63
Germanic 177, 179, 197
glide deletion 249

Grassman's Law 178
Great English Vowel Shift 200, 221–2
Grimm's Law 187–8, 197, 215
grounding 44

haplology 167
Hawaiian 19
head-ordering principle 36
heterosyllabicity 83, 207
hiatus 132
hierarchical syllable structure 85–6, 91
hierarchical word structure 295–6
high-level processing 117, 140, 175, 190–1, 210, 244
holistic representation 145, 242, 307–8
homography 70
homonymy 69–71
homophony 70, 103, 268

Ibu-Zaydūn 275–6
Ibu al Muʕtazz 275–6
Icelandic 46
iconicity 53, 125–34, 292
IC-to-word ratio 35
ideological linguistics 46
individualization 88–9
infinity of causal chain 9
infixing 143
inflectional homonymy 30–1
inhibition 59, 61, 287
integration 130–1, 225–7
interactive activation model 58–60
interactivity 122, 175
interference 79, 89, 94, 119, 153, 235–6
Irish 120
irregulkar verbs 233, 245–6
isloation of linguistic communities 46
Italian 3, 179, 252–3

La Fontaine 266–72
language as fashion 12
language games 96
language use 64, 115, 286–8
Latin 30–1
learning 61
left branching 85–6
left-to-right extension of rhyme 274
lenition 120, 197
lexical access 118–19
lexical accessibility 33
lexicalization 48, 52, 146
Lexical Phonology 305–8
licensing 1
like syntactic category constraint 152–3
linear distance 158–61
linear order 148, 289
linguistically significant generalization 1–2, 9
linguistic complexity 78

linguistic markers 47
linguistics as cognitive psychology 6–7
linkage problem 282
linking 254
linking-/r/ 132
local optimization 42
low-level processing 117, 140, 175, 190–2, 210, 244

masculine rhyme 260
masking 166, 176–80
melodic tier 3, 309–10
merger 72, 203
metathesis 168–9, 170–2
minimal-distance principle 189, 192–3, 197
mobile /s/ 208–10
monophthongization 187, 189–90
monopositional errors 159–60
morphological variation 120, 122–3, 136–40
morphonology 126–8
morphosemantic transparency 37–8
morphotactic transparency 37–8
motor execution 60
Muʕallaqat 275–6
myelination 22

natural development 48
Natural Linguistics 37, 39–40
natural processing order 28
neural excitation 20
no-crossing constraint 3–4, 308–12
node labelling 89–90
no-marking error 235–6, 240, 242
norm 165
North Frisian 46

Obligatory Contour Principle (OCP) 3–4, 308, 311–13
onset dominance 114–15
onset weight 84, 251–3
open-class words 220–1
oral language 62–3
order of processing 28
overmarking 234, 238

palatalization 188, 197, 211–13, 216
parallelness 29, 60, 70, 118–19, 121–5, 162–4, 215, 230, 294, 300–1
parallel syllable structure constraint 159, 180–2
partial assimilation 173–4
partial regularization 234, 238
perception 60, 63
perceptual contrast 23, 25, 57
perceptual rule 34
perceptual strategy 24–5
performance grammar 304–5, 313
perseveration 166
phoneme acquisition 22

phoneme repetition 19–20, 88–98, 313
phoneme theory 15, 69–73
phonological facilitation 124
phonotactics 87–8, 132, 139–40, 146, 204–6, 208, 249
plurality 42, 122, 142
pluricausality 10, 13, 66, 68
polysemy 71
Portuguese 252–3
position-sensitive coding 89
postlexical processing 115
prediction 13, 56–8, 65, 68
prefix stripping 28
prelexical representation 102–3
prepositions 224
prestige 47
primary sign 38–9
principle of least effort 10, 214, 220
principle of rhythmic alternation 26
production 60, 63
productive constraints 23
pronouns 221–4
proper names 102
prosody 104
Proto-Germanich 188–9, 208, 215
prototypicality 33
pseudobiological 5
pseudo-explanation 8
pseudopsychological 8

Received Pronounciation (RP) 47, 75, 82
recognition point 214
reductionism 303–13
reduplication 30, 100
regularization 233–4, 237–40
regular verbs 233
relative clauses 34, 44–5
relevance 52
repeated morph constraint 30, 145–8
repetition loss errors 166–7, 176–9
representational redundancy 145
representational strength 146
resyllabification 131
rhythm 25–6
right branching 85–6, 295–6
Rimbaud 266–72
rime 86–7, 274
rime isochrony 199
Romance 207
Romanian 252–3
root 92–3
rule 2, 7–8, 303

Sapir-Whorf Hypothesis 52
schwa deletion 247–8
secondary sign 38
second-order semantic content 69, 73

Index

segment 70
segment strength 211–12, 216
self-inhibition 20, 311
semiotics 37
seriality 28, 118, 121, 162, 300–1
serialization 60, 79, 88–9, 91–2, 98, 113, 150, 157, 309
signifiant 115–6, 128, 134, 143
signifié 125–6, 128, 134, 143
similarity 79, 89, 110, 125–8, 157, 166, 173, 185–94, 216, 231, 236, 250
single-allomorph system 122
skeleton tier 3, 309–10
Slavic 177
slots and fillers 74
social markers 49
social relationships 45
social stereotypes 47
social values 48–9
sonority 79–80, 191, 208
sonority sequence principle 206
Spanish 83–5, 104–5, 111–13, 179, 183, 203, 216–20, 252–3
speech rate 116
staircase strategy of serialization 158–60
stickiness 149
stress and word class 25
stress shift 133, 246–7
stridency 22–3
strong verb 130
structural asymmetry 80
structural gaps 226–8, 230
structural representation 251
subsegmental analysis 135
substitution 140–4
subtraction 141, 154–5
suffixing preference 27–30, 119, 293–6
suppletion 245–6
suprasegmental analysis 135, 261
surface representation 93–5
syllabic representation 264–5
syllabification 3, 206
syllable omission 99
syllable types 112

synchrony 293
synergetic 18

tautosyllabicity 83
teleological explanation 9, 16–17
template matching 30
terminology 7–8
that-clauses 34
three M's 18
tonic syllable 110
tonic vowel 129–30
trigger 124
trisyllabic laxing 133
trouble-avoidance strategy 98
Turkish 31

umlaut 119, 141–4, 172, 193, 293
underlying representation 93–8
undermarking 234, 238
uniqueness point 213
Universal Grammar 5

variation 16
visual processing 21, 33
voicing 10, 24, 132, 197, 223, 260–1
vocalization 187, 190, 193
vowel harmony 119
vowel length 129–30, 135–140, 200–1, 225–6, 260–1
vowel reduction 219, 248

well-formedness conditions 3, 303, 309
within-word errors 107
word beginning 213–14
word end 213–14
word loss 232
word-onset stability 83
word-onset vulnerability 83
word order 35–6, 50, 163–4
written language 62–3

zero consonant 267
zero derivation 134, 256
Zipf's Law 42, 287

OHIO UNIVERSITY LIBRARY
Please return this book as soon as you have